Here Ther… Elsew…

Dial… Location and Mobility

Edited by
David Blamey

Open Editions

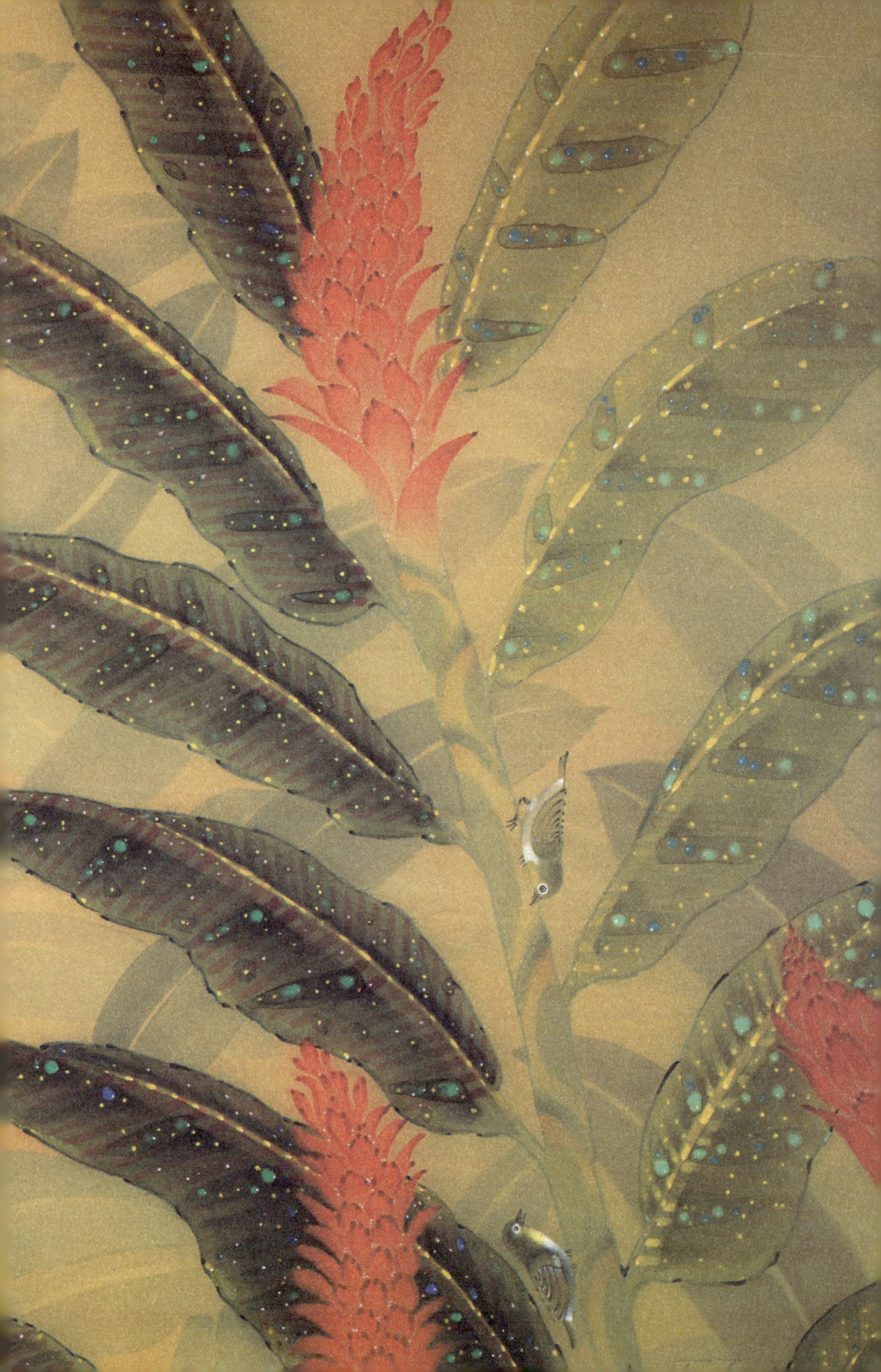

Opposite: Terris Nguyen Temple
Red Ginger and White Eyes, 1998

Barry Curtis & Claire Pajaczkowska
Tim Brennan
Jane Rendell
Layla Curtis
Doina Petrescu
Colectivo Cambalache
Peter Wollen
Johnny Spencer
Roger Begrich & Andrea Mühlebach
Mariele Neudecker
Laura Ruggeri
Terris Nguyen Temple
David Blamey
Fiona Banner
Janice Kerbel
Ian Whittlesea
Lesley Naa Norle Lokko
Markus Vater
Paul O'Neill

First published in London, 2002

Open Editions
45 Handforth Road
London
SW9 0LL

www.openeditions.com

ISBN 0-949004-13-8

A CIP catalogue record for this book is available in the British Library

Printed and bound in Europe
DL: B-2840-2002

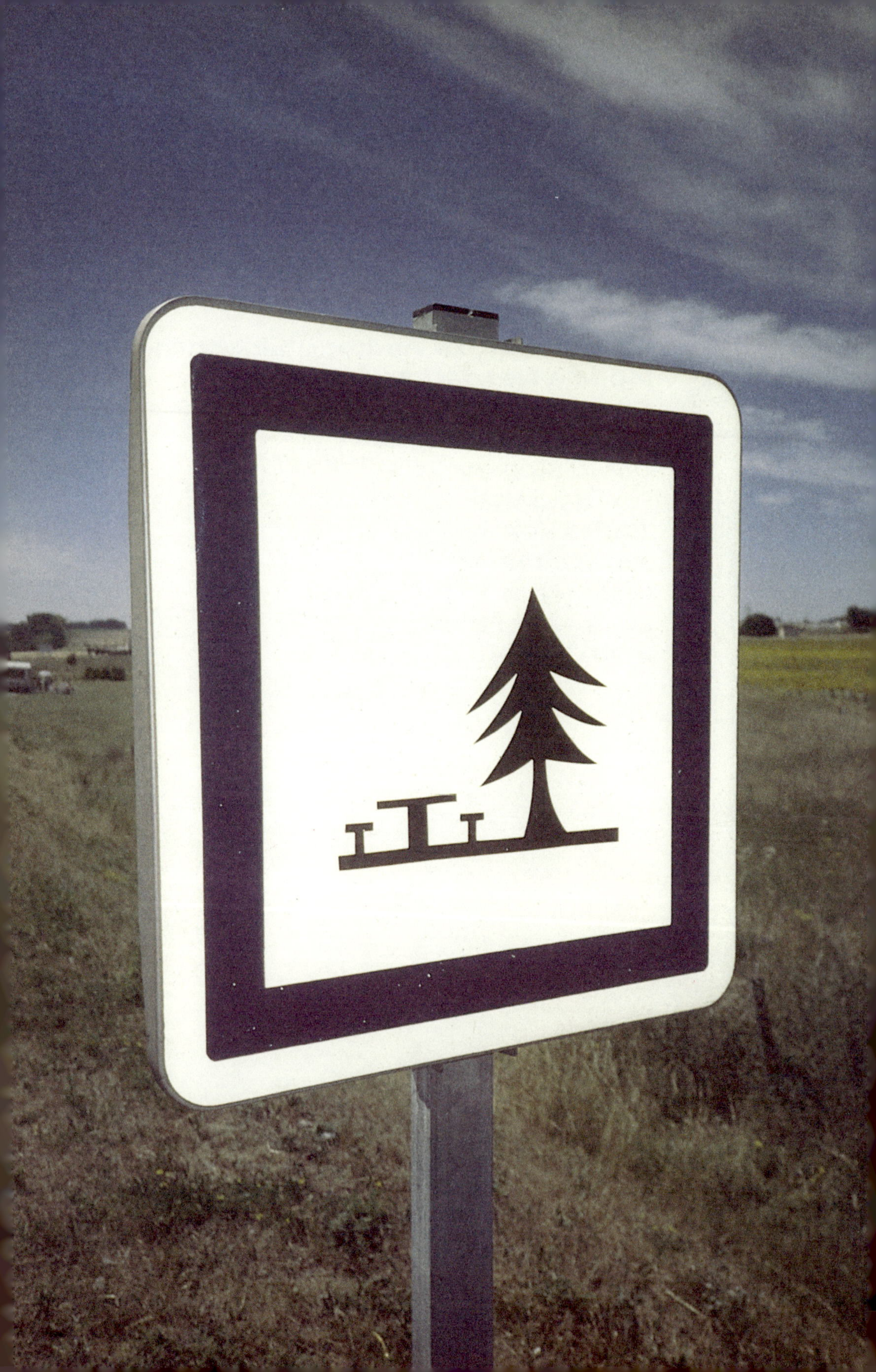

Contents

7 **Introduction: Somewhere Else** David Blamey

23 **Location Envy** Barry Curtis & Claire Pajaczkowska

33 **Blackest Pool** Tim Brennan

43 **Travelling the Distance: Encountering the Other** Jane Rendell

55 **World Political** Layla Curtis

65 **The Tactics of *Faux* Migration** Doina Petrescu

73 **The Street Museum** Colectivo Cambalache

87 **Airports: A Personal Memoir** Peter Wollen

109 **Save a Bread** Johnny Spencer

117 **Travel as Home: An Anthropological Inquiry into the Goa Trance Scene** Roger Begrich & Andrea Mühlebach

129 **Another Day** Mariele Neudecker

155 **Prisoners of the Californian Dream: Panic Suburbs in Hong Kong** Laura Ruggeri

165 **The Other Side of the World** Terris Nguyen Temple

179 **Safe Way** David Blamey

191 **As the Crow Doesn't Fly** Fiona Banner

207 **Bird Island** Janice Kerbel

213 **Flight Times** Ian Whittlesea

225 **Elsewhere, Perhaps** Lesley Naa Norle Lokko

237 **Notes** Markus Vater

245 **Further Reading** Paul O'Neill

259 **Information**

263 **Biographies**

267 **Index**

272 **Acknowledgments**

Come fly with me, let's fly, let's fly away
Frank Sinatra (Cahn/Van Heusen)

If I can speak directly or by electronic mail to a friend in Paris while sitting in California, if I can witness political and cultural events as they occur around the globe without leaving my home, if a database at a remote location contains my profile and informs government agencies which make decisions that effect my life without any knowledge on my part of these events, if I can shop in my home by using my TV or computer, then where am I and who am I?
Mark Poster

Somewhere else better than here
Nowhere else better than here
Felix Torres Garcia

Asking the right questions makes, afterall, all the difference between fate and destination, drifting and travelling.
Cornelius Castoriadis

The flight attendant brought two beers. It was a few minutes after one, too early to start drinking, but he was edgy, and what the hell. It was 5pm somewhere.
John Grisham

Real life is elsewhere
The Situationist International

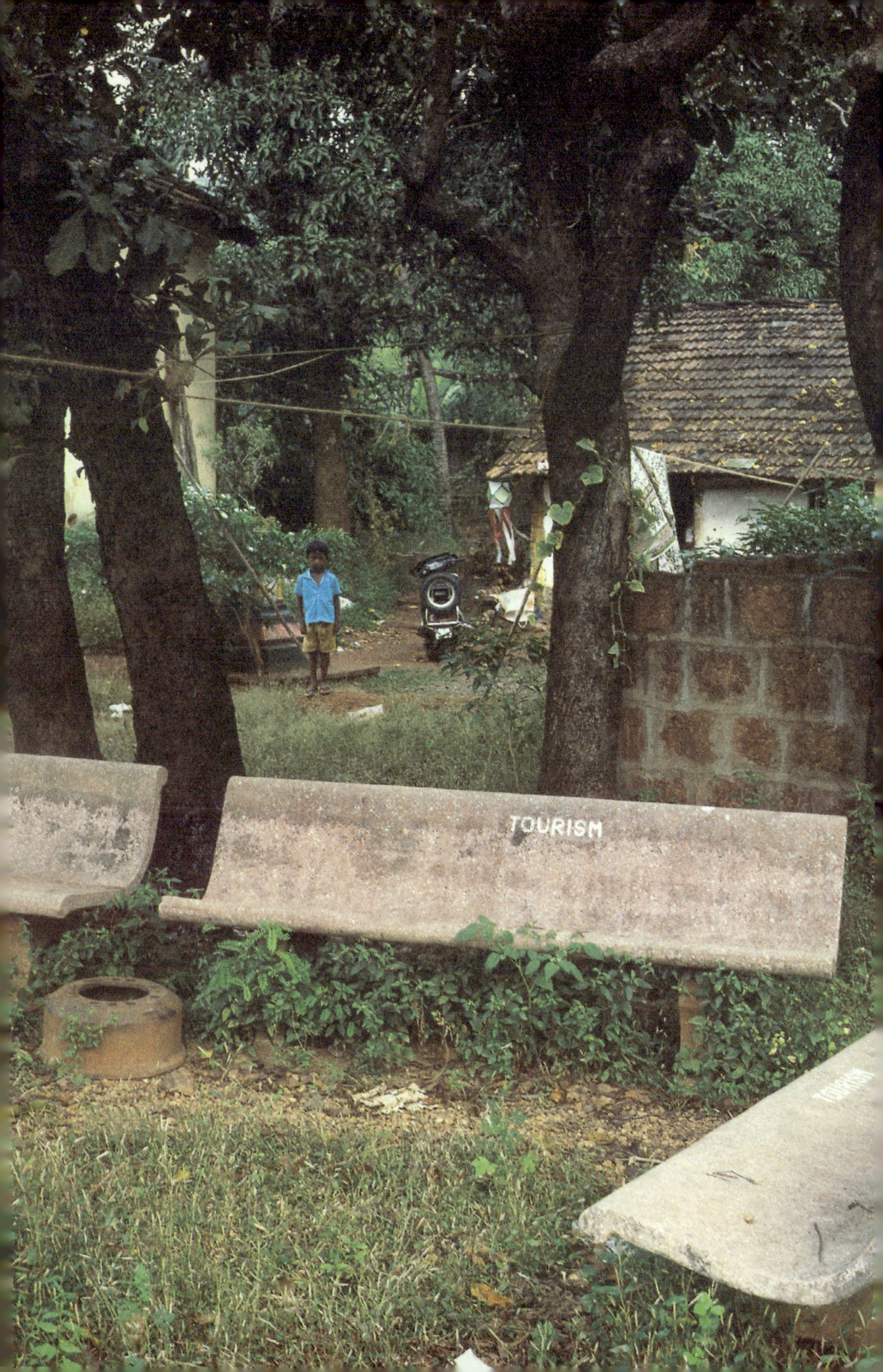
TOURISM
TOURISM

Introduction: Somewhere Else

David Blamey

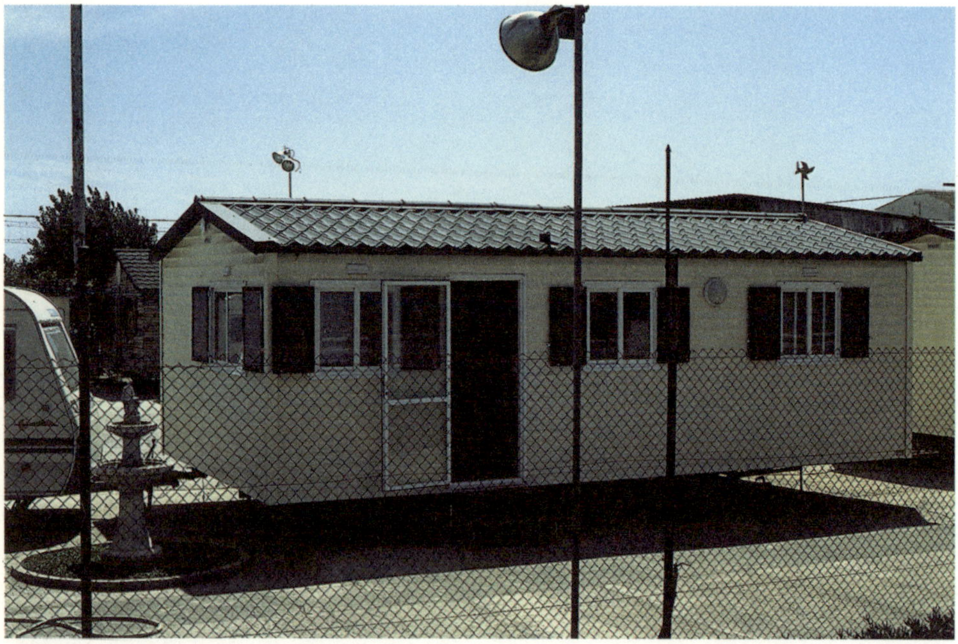

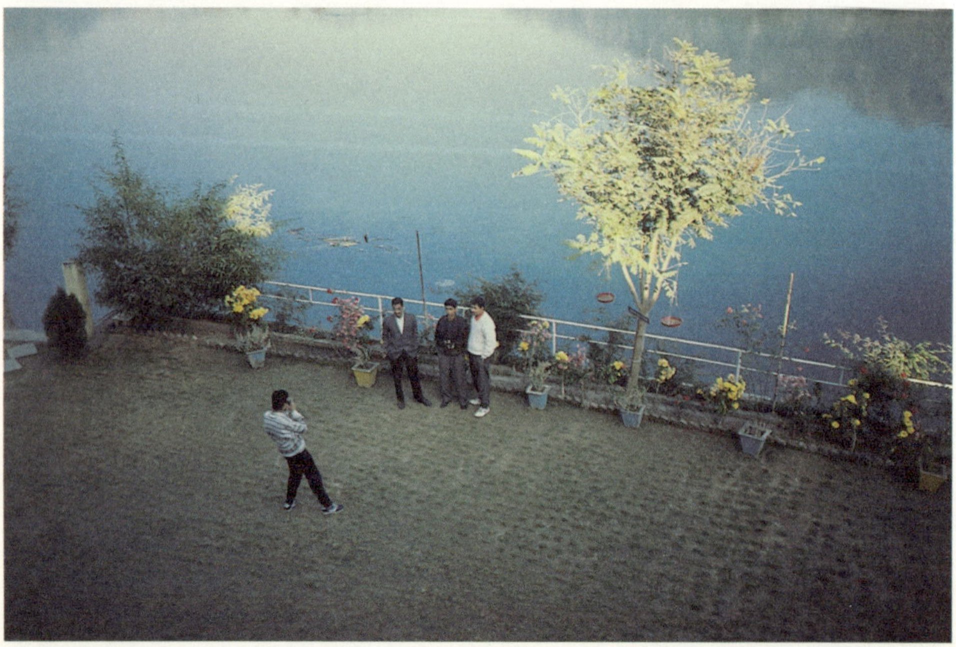

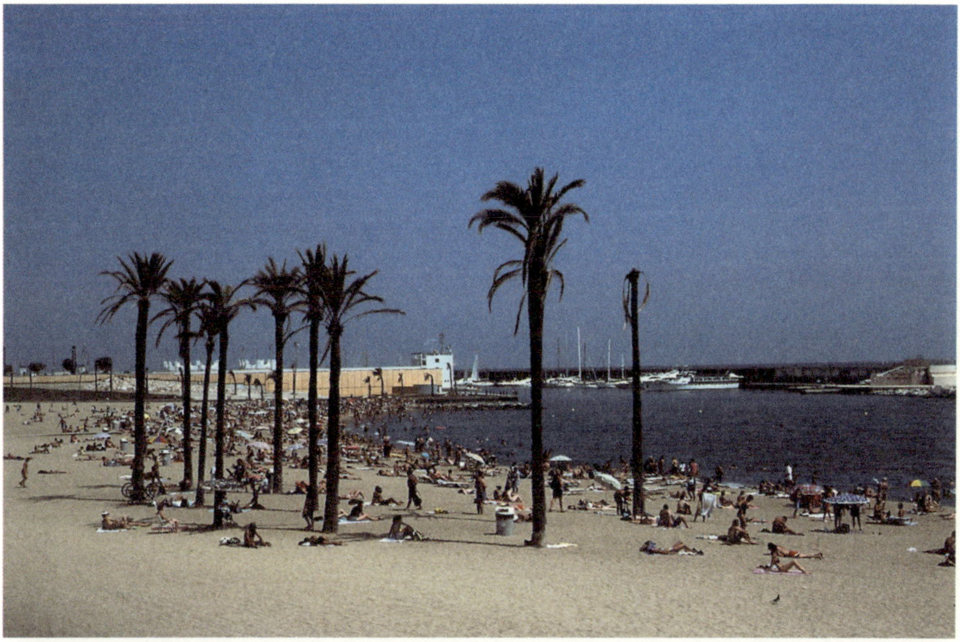

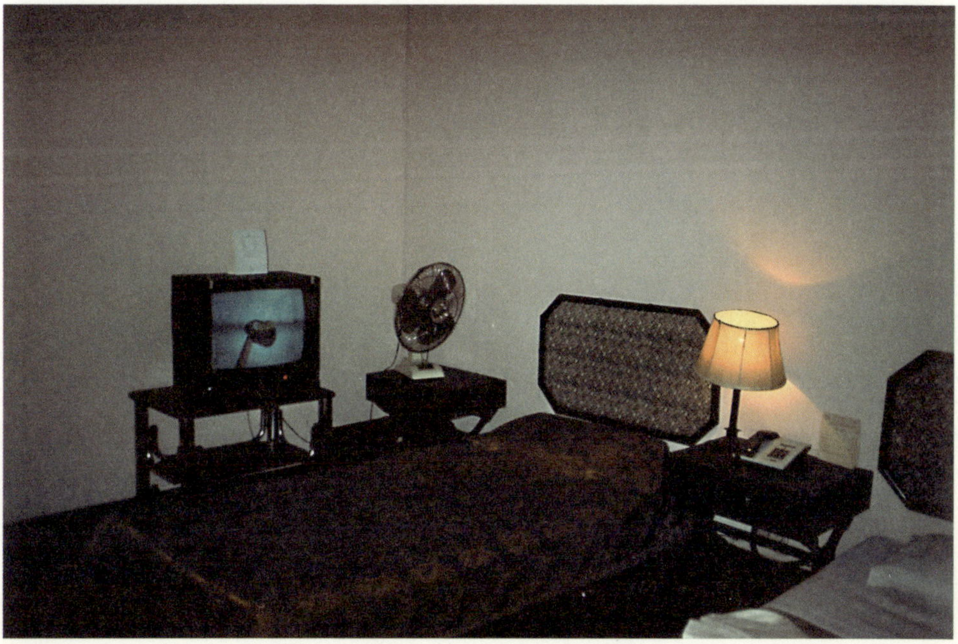

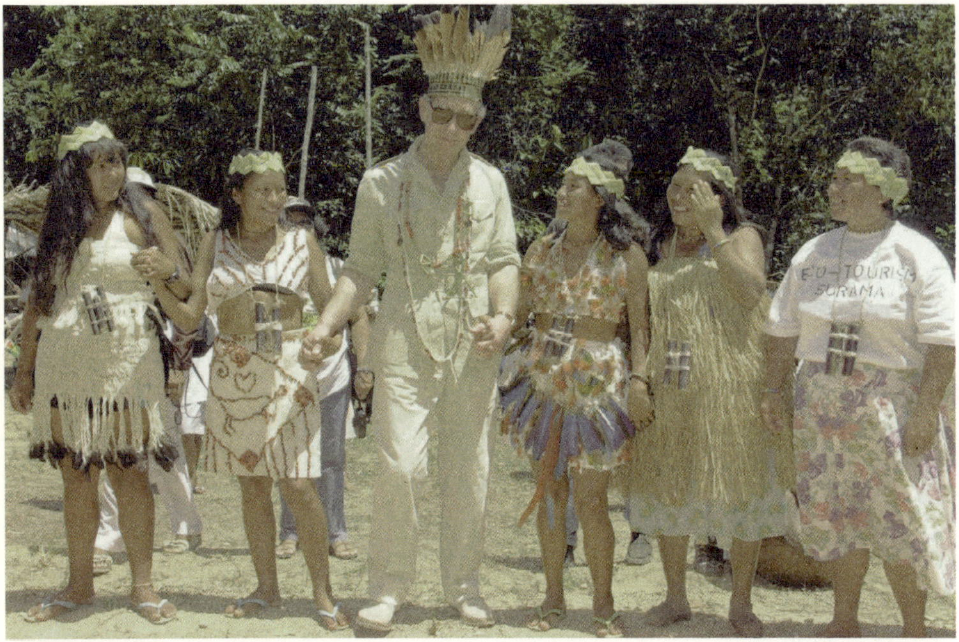
SURAMA

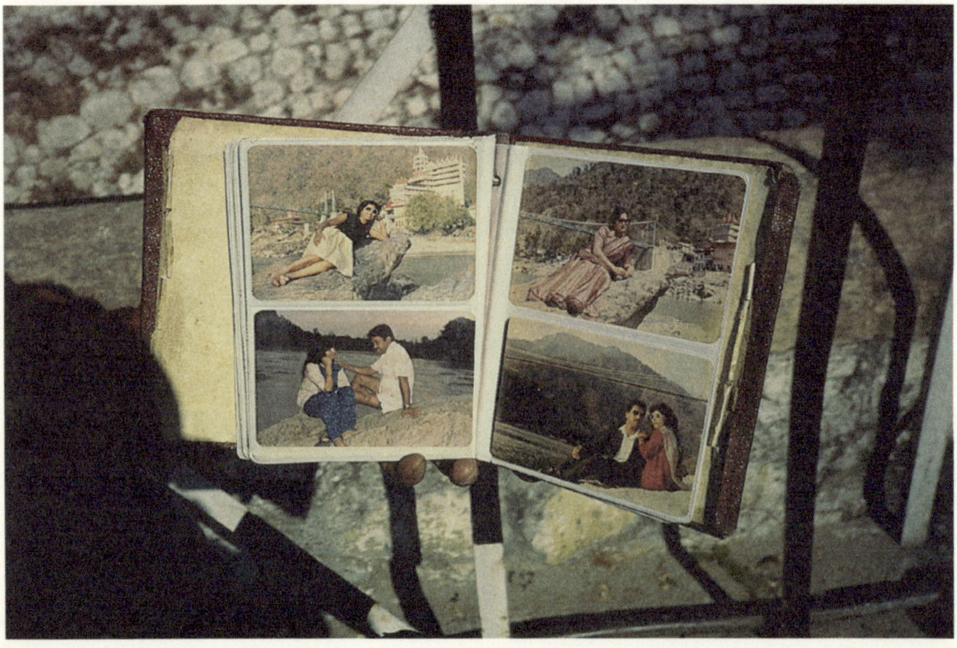

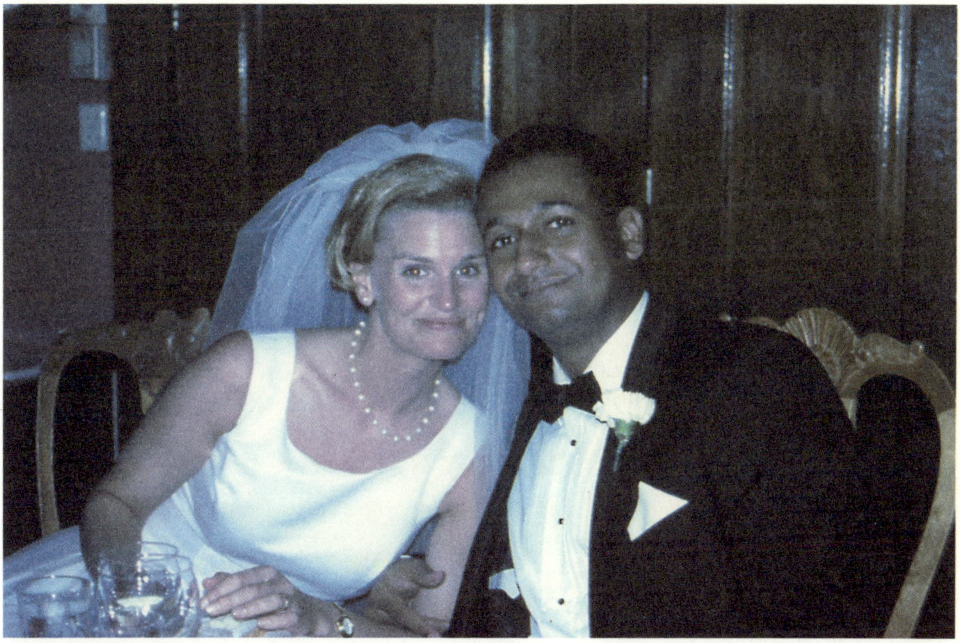

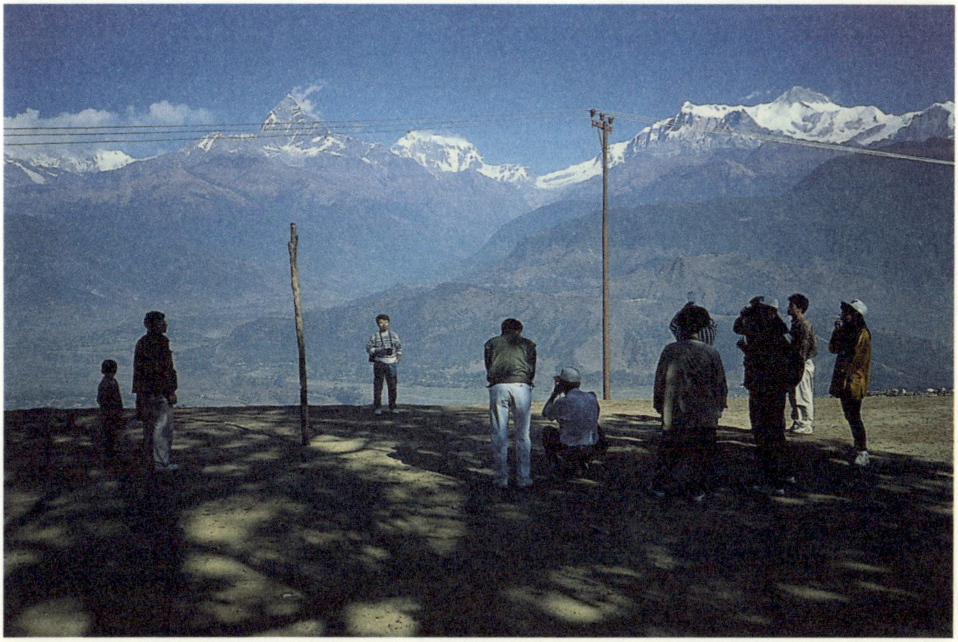

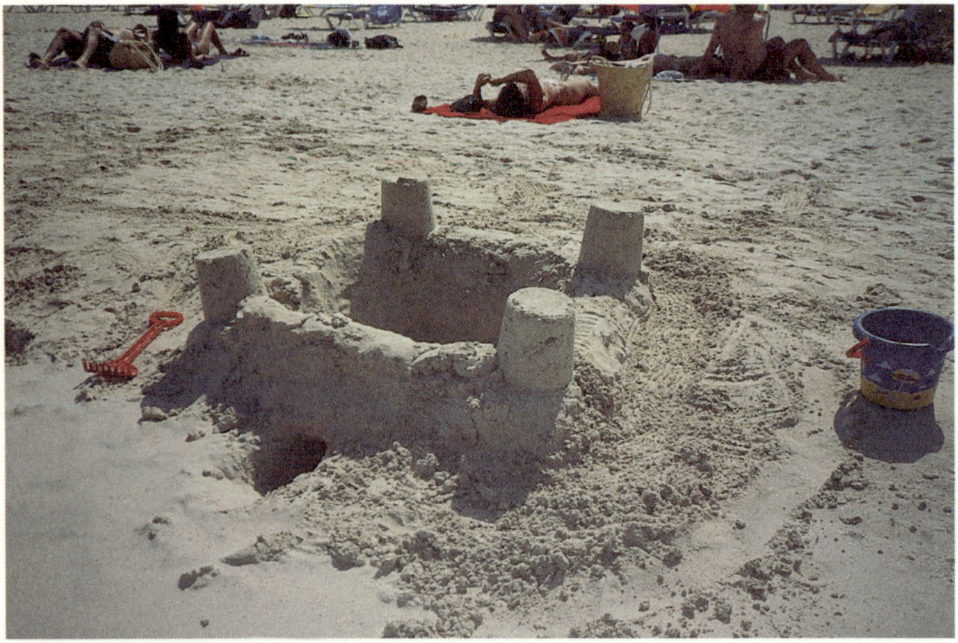

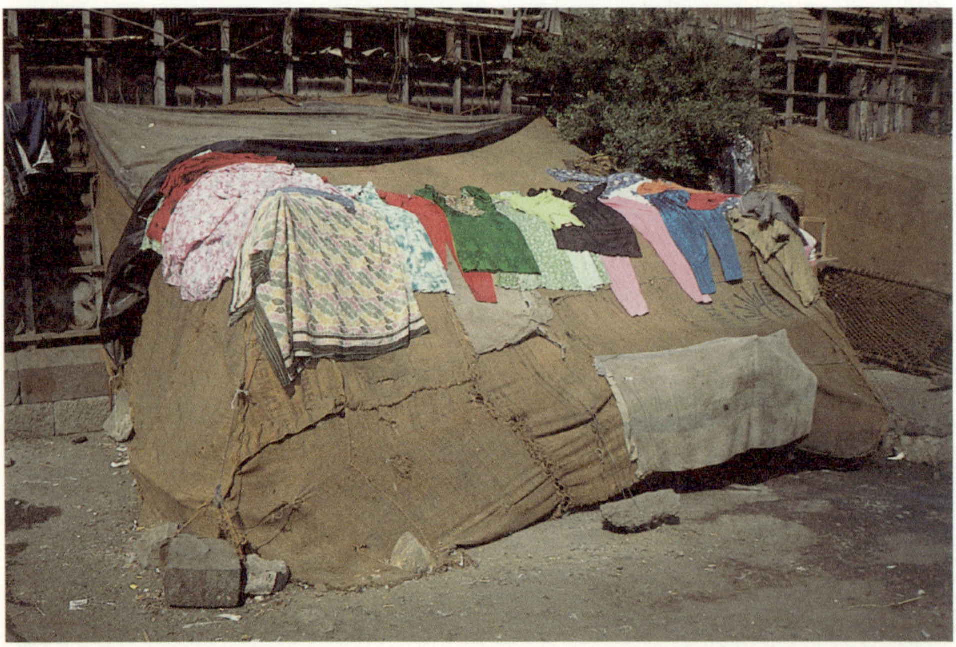

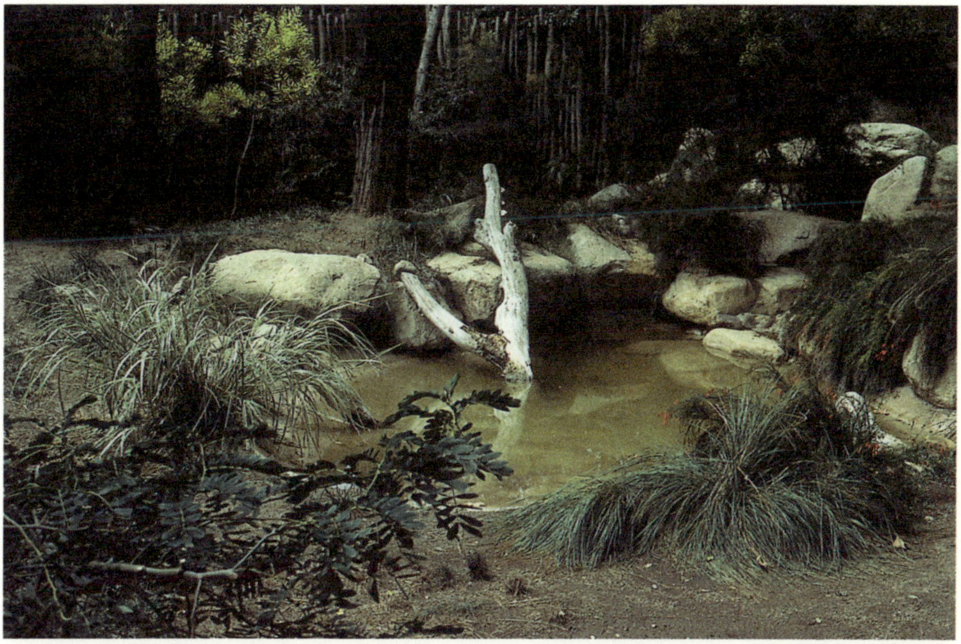

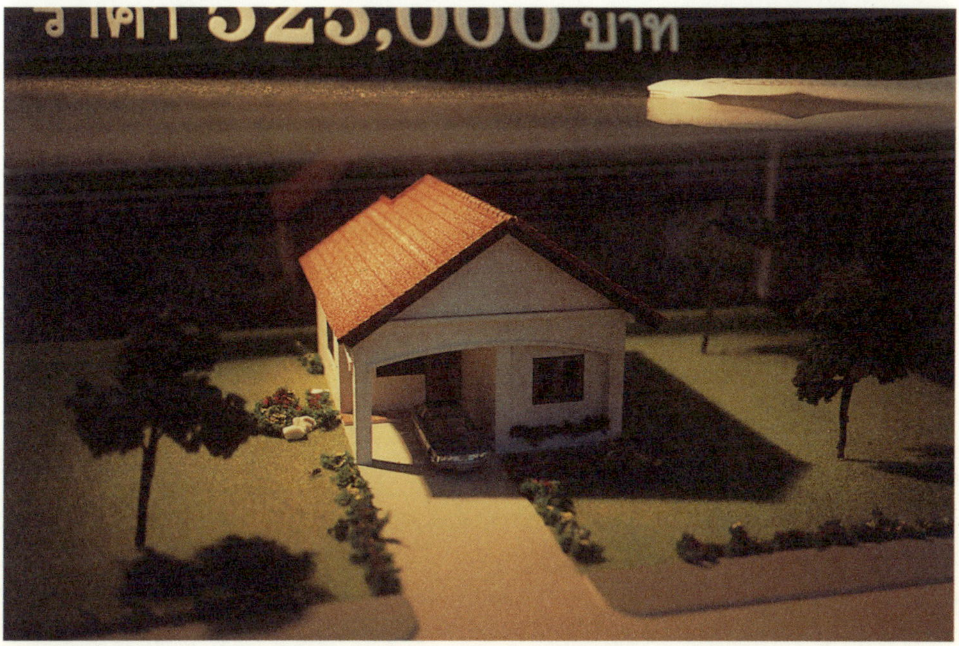
บาท

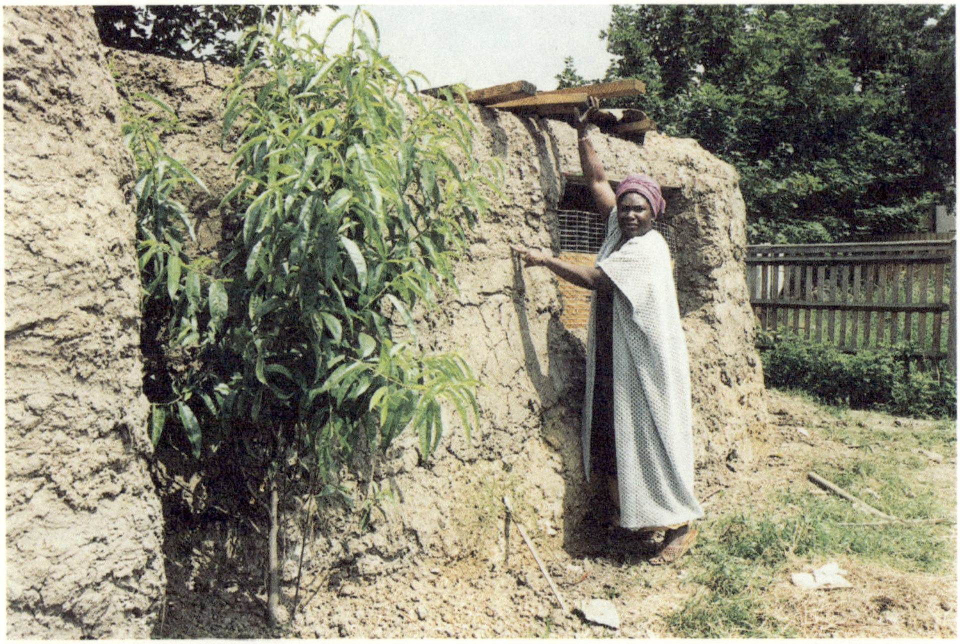

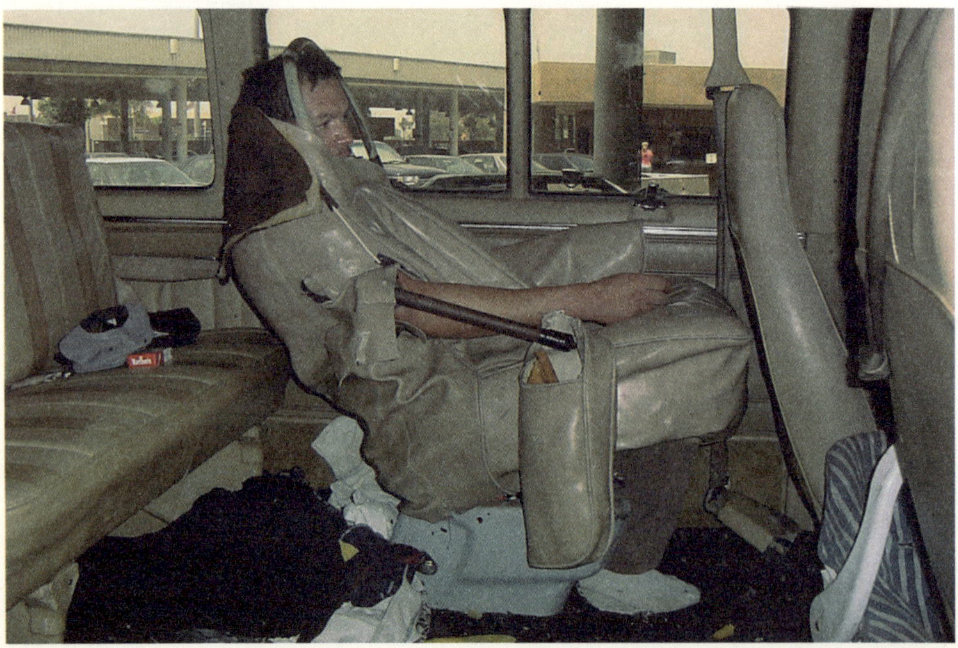

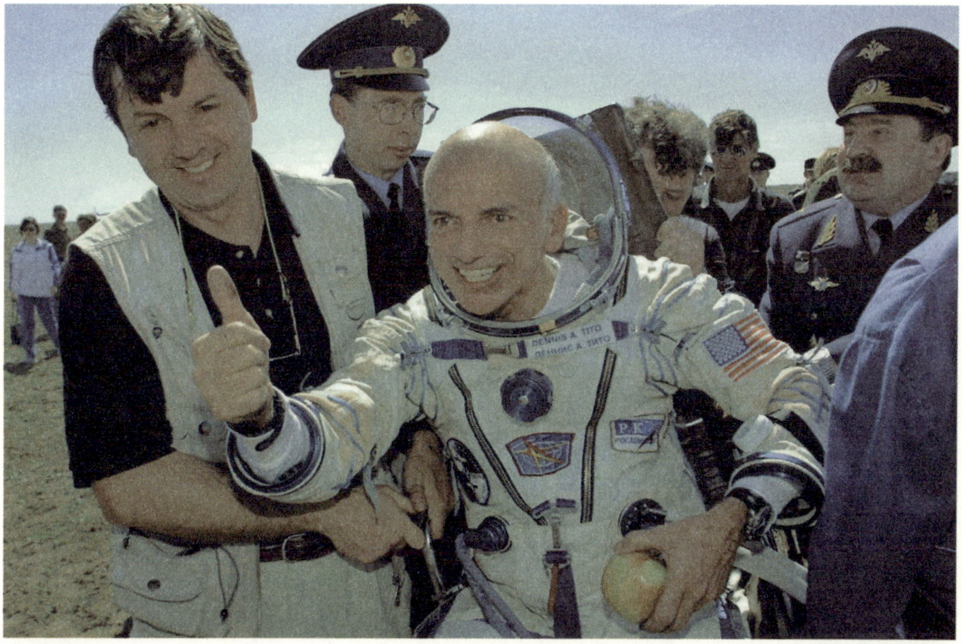
DENNIS A. TITO

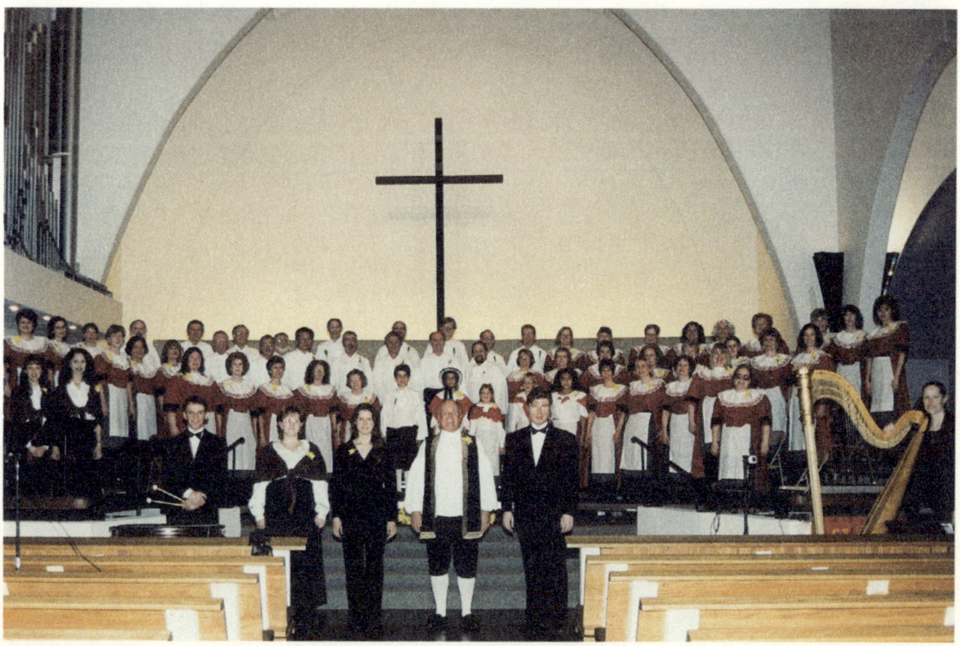

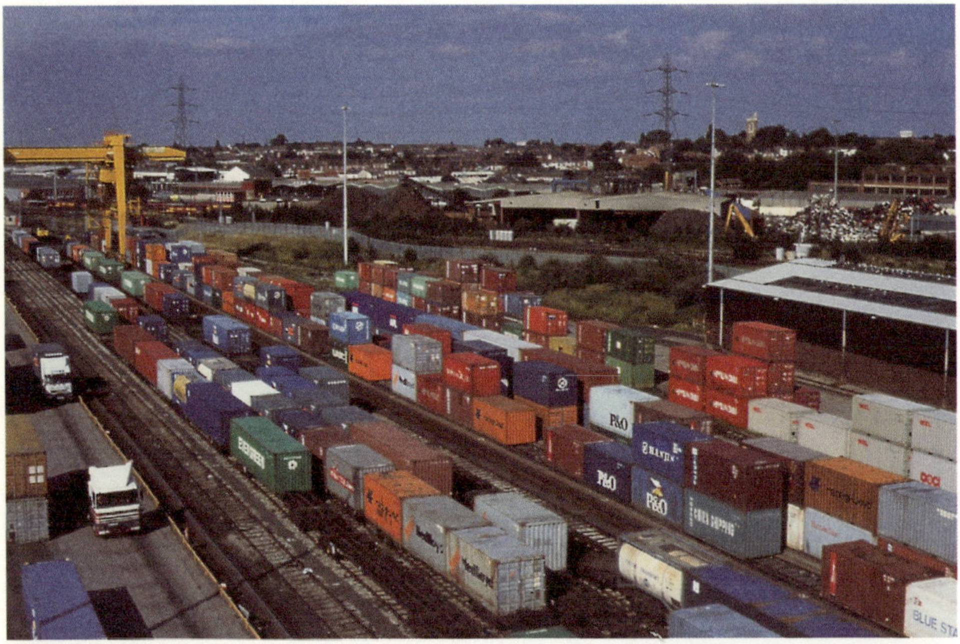
P&O

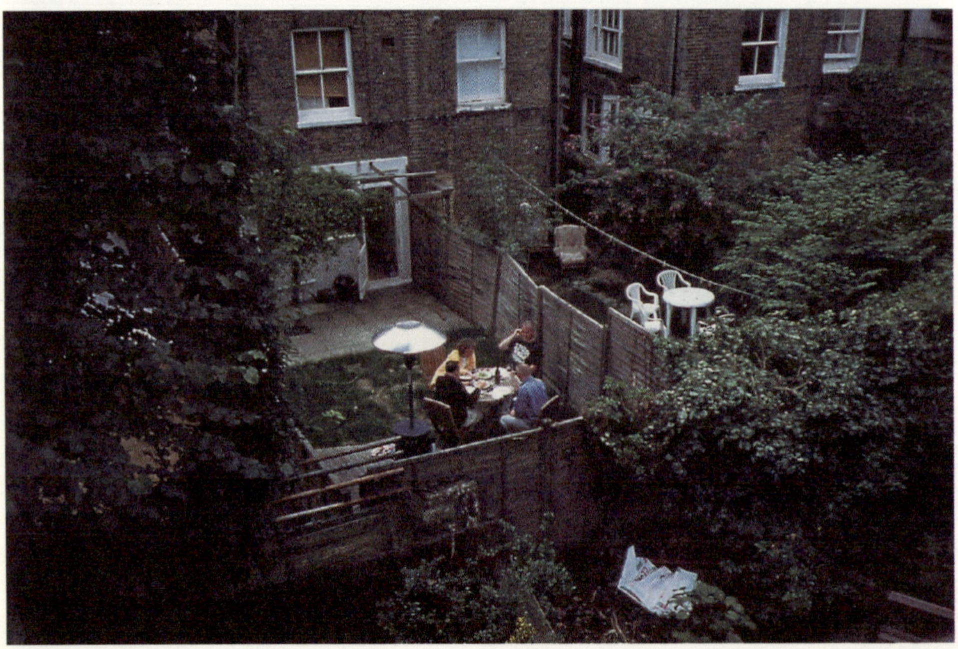

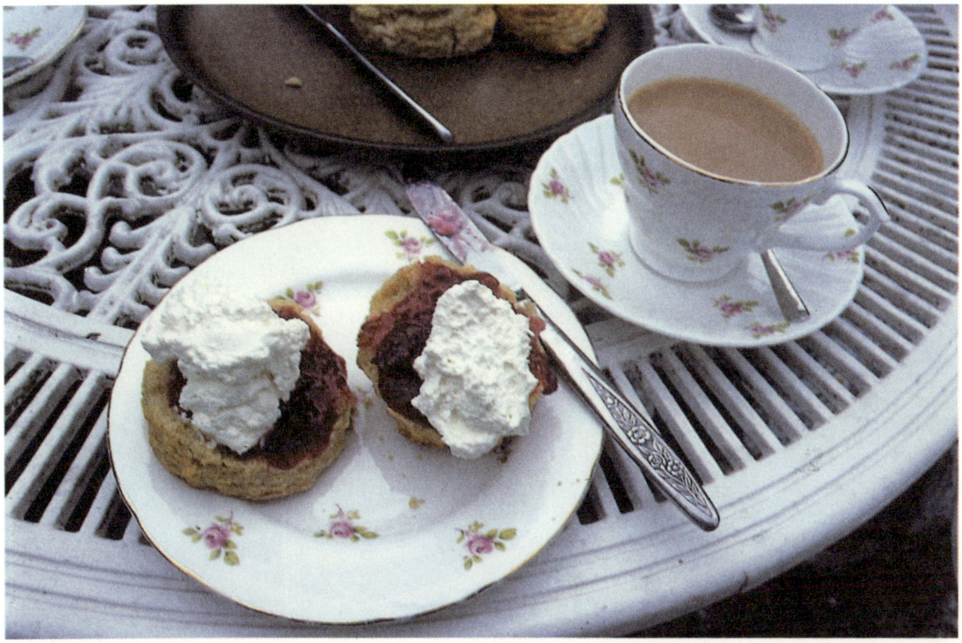

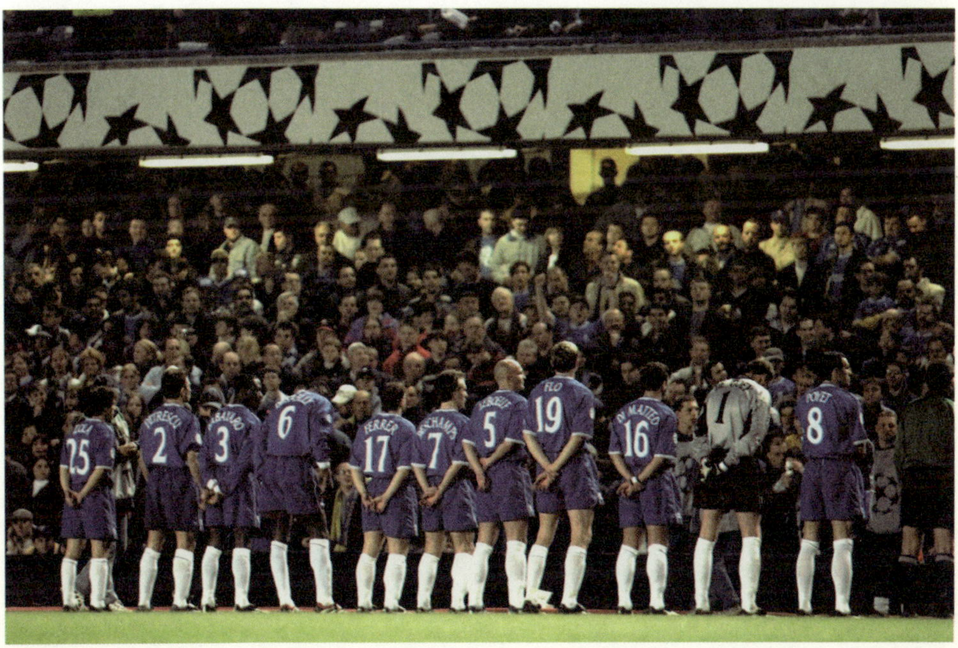
25
2
3
6
FERRER
17
7
5
FLO
19
16
POYET
8

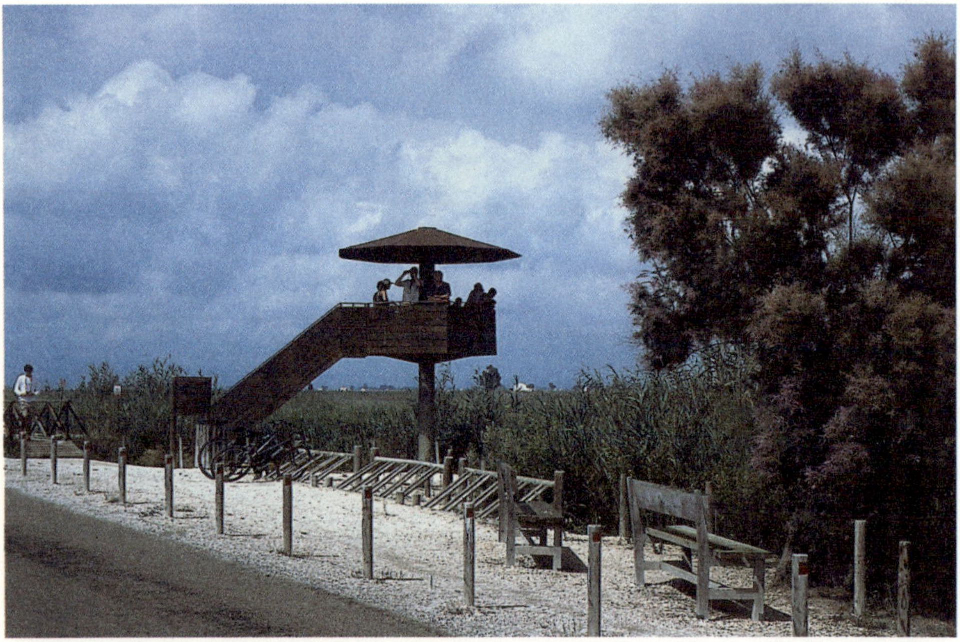

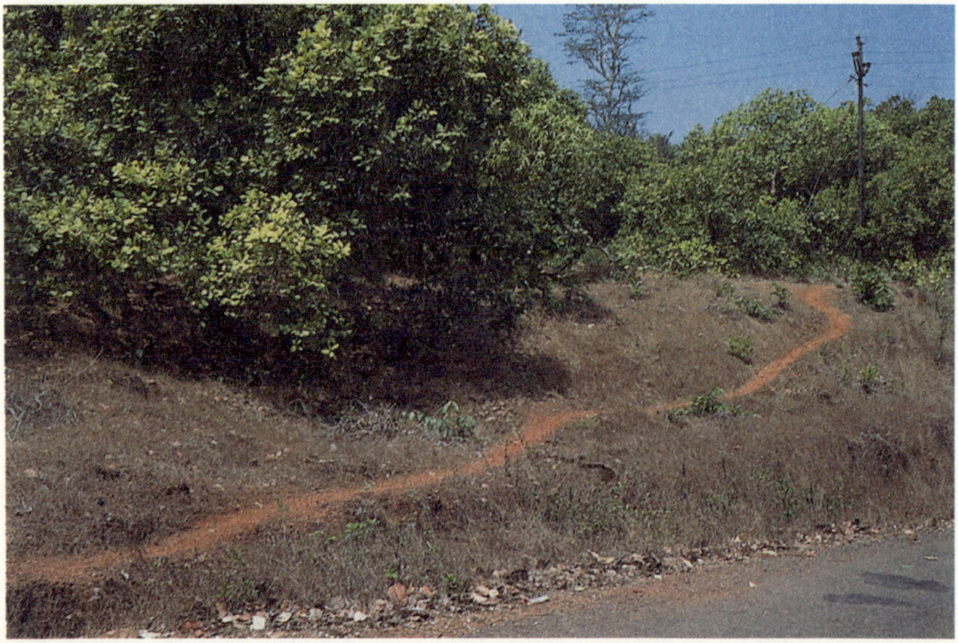

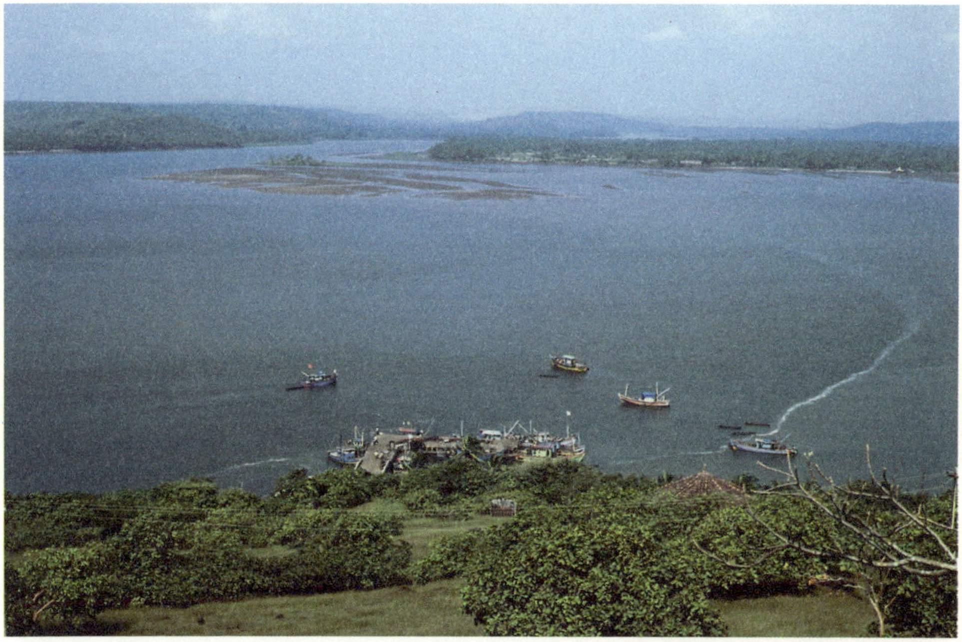

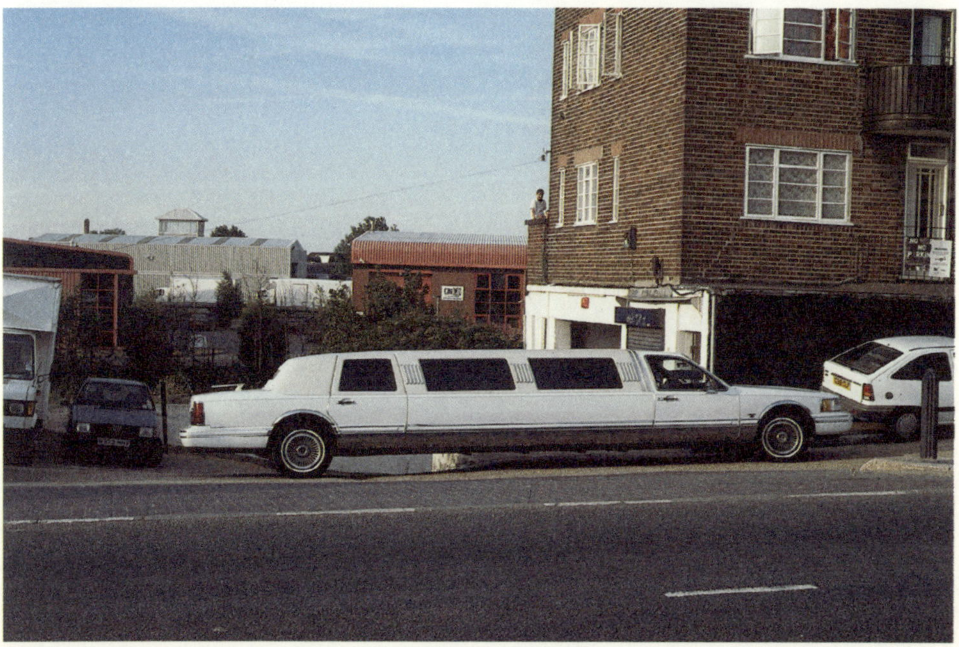

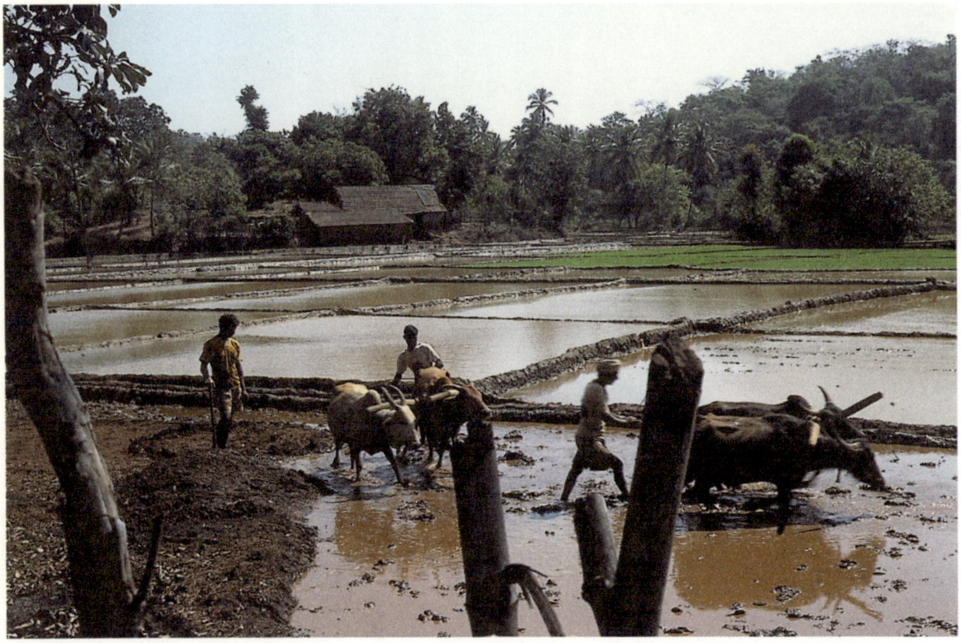

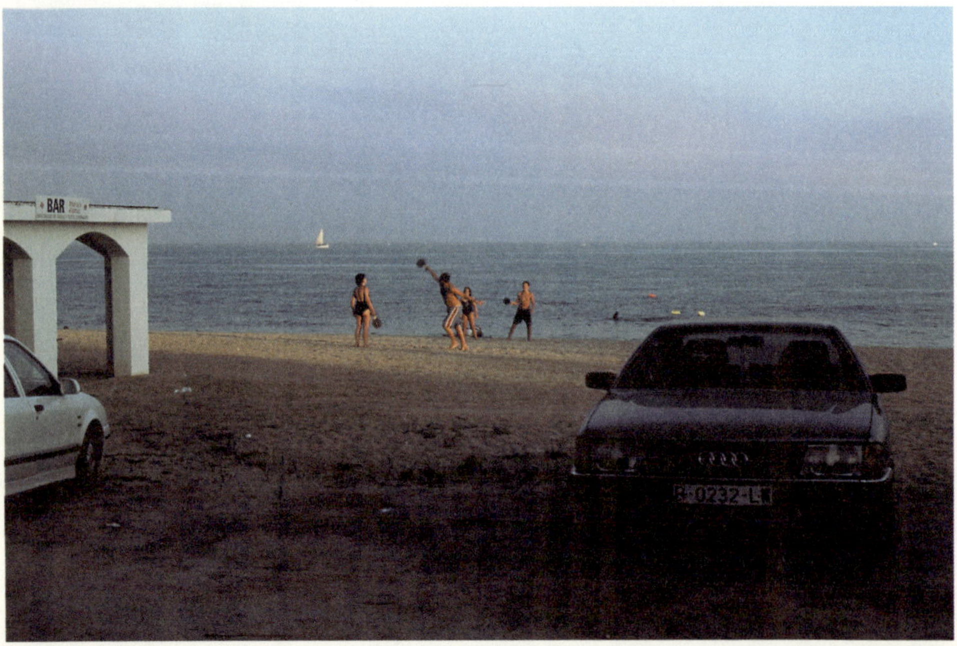
BAR

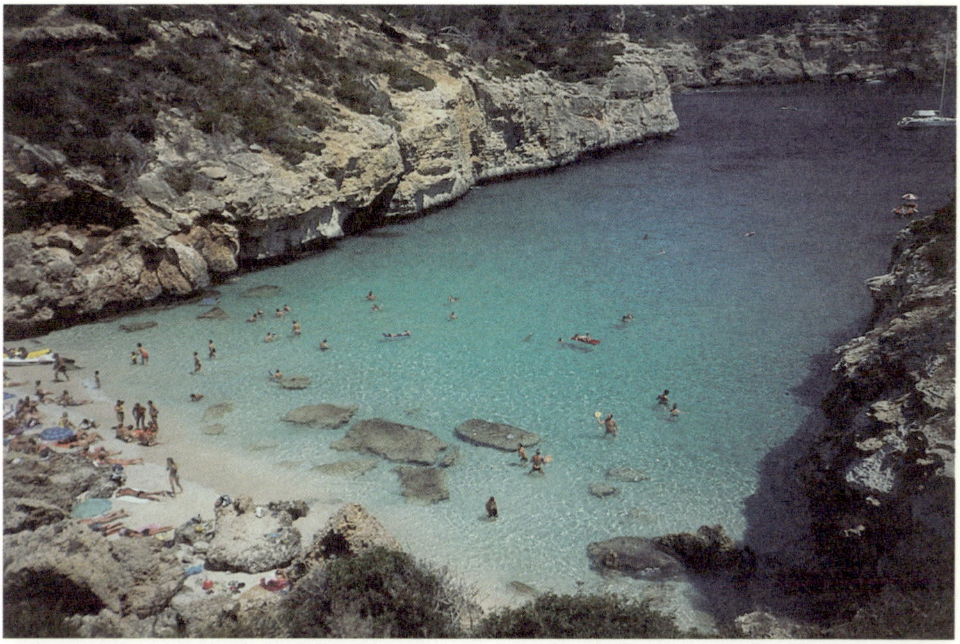

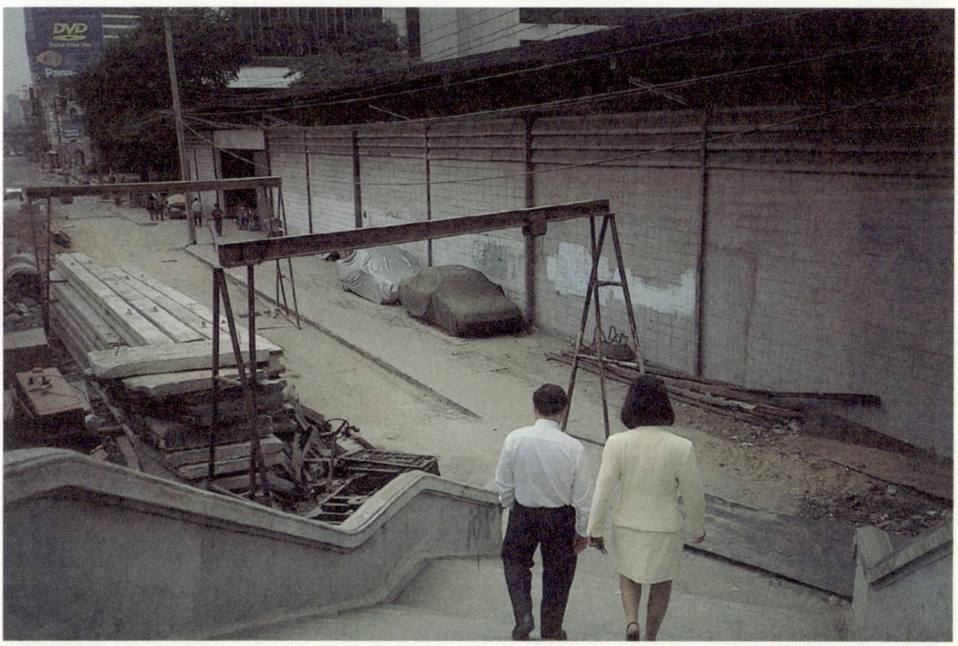
DVD

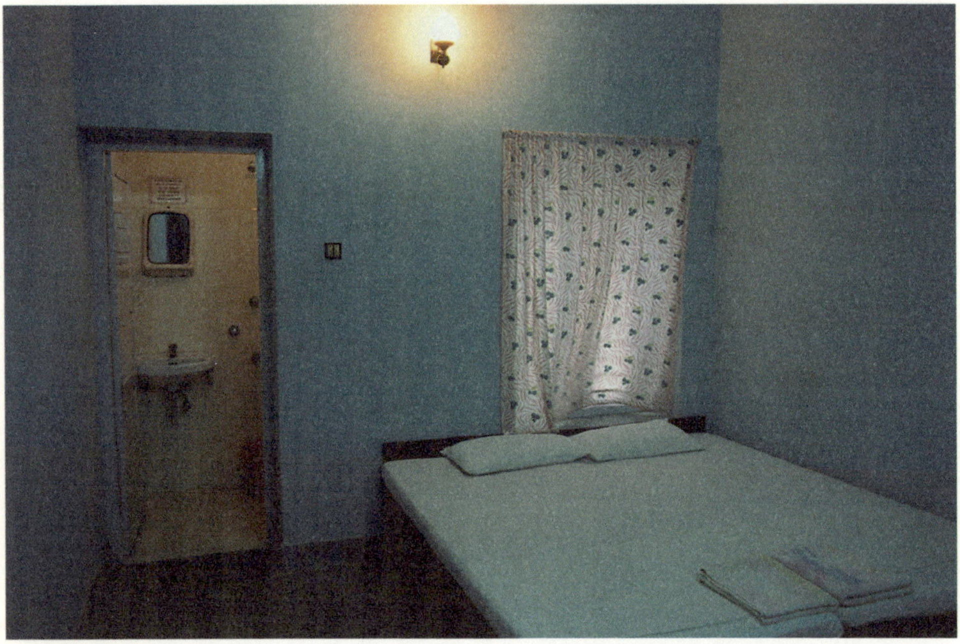

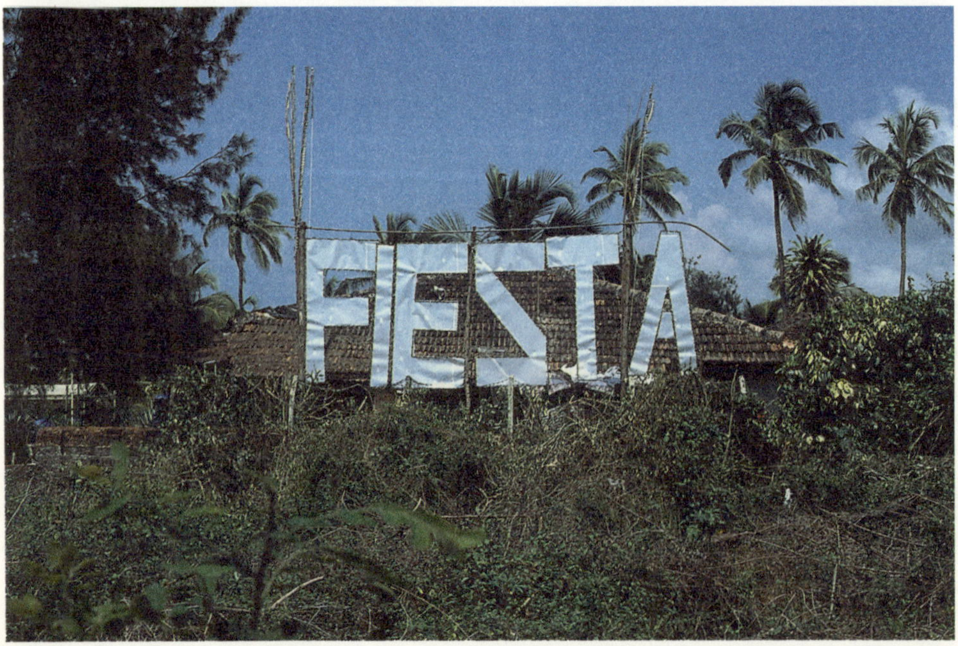
FIESTA

Location Envy

Barry Curtis &
Claire Pajaczkowska

It has become usual, over the past twenty years or so, to think about envy and desire in terms of 'objects'. The envious or desiring gaze is described in relation to what it targets, or looks at. Such analyses have been both instructive and fruitful, but what they obviate is the invisibility of the domain from which we gaze, whether in envy, with desire or with a need to control or possess. Here we think about the non-object, the space and place that is the condition for subjectivity. Conceived as container, envelope, womb or place it is something we have called location. As location is the place from which we are constituted as subjects it usually constitutes the 'blind spot' from which envy and desire issue. The process by which it is transmuted into an external object such as a destination or destiny is part of the enquiry but the central mystery is the staging of presence in relation to a point in space which is both a geographical co-ordinate and a realm of fantasy. When estate agents affirm their holy trinity as 'location, location, location' they are not simply repeating a word, they are expressing the complex, reinforced significance of aspiring, attaining and being which is central to the mystery of locality.

One of the key assumptions of writings about cities and urban experience in the 20th century has been that they are causative of, or constructed by the neurotic tendencies of the subject – that they are super-impositions of planning and projection. In various conceptualisations of what it means to navigate and inhabit the city, the impact of space is posited on shifting sensations and moods – not what is there but what is supplied or projected – markers of past experiences in which the pedestrian becomes an avatar of hopeful or anxious presence. Increasingly the emphasis has shifted from intention to use, as Jonathan Raban noted in his prescient exploration of the 'soft' elements of cityspace – 'the city invites you to remake it'.

The title of this essay refers to the envious dynamic inscribed in moving and looking. The passions aroused by the desire to be located in multiple insides or outsides in order to share in the power, knowledge and privilege of various parallax views or vanishing points. 'Location' is a primary determinant of status, a staging of presence, a desire to visit and enjoy vantages and participate in exercises of othering. In this sense there is no contradiction between travelling and being at home, it is always a dialectic experience – home is an experience imposed on the exotic as well as on exotics of the ordinary.

Cities cannot exist without inhabitation – other than as the clue haunted palimpsest of the archaeological site. They constitute anthropological space with differential geographies relating to ritual as well as pragmatic uses. The relation between inhabitants and locations is one of commitment, it is an existential relation if only a fleeting one, cemented by immaterial aspirations, memories and connections with bodies of knowledge. Like films, cities are 'memorial metatexts' – they are generic yet doubly different – they are unique as agglomerations of places and they are always encountered perspectively, with each turning they are perceived as a complex, provisional reality subject to memory or mood. Marc Augé has made a distinction between places which are constituted by 'individual identities' and non places where shared identity is created but he also acknowledges that 'place and non place are like opposed polarities', place is 'not erasable' and non place 'never totally completed' – in fact both draw kinds of authority from each other.

Locating is an act of aspiration and consolidation. Every step reconfigures the point of view and constitutes an economy of advantage or disadvantage. The creation of areas of safety and interest and withdrawal is one of the ways of making individual claims on urban space, ways of coping with not being able to inhabit the ideal or occupy everywhere.

For over a hundred years cities have been represented as over stimulating and disorienting, denying fixity, intruding on personal distance, disrupting and distracting awareness through throwing stress on looking rather than more holistic perceptions. Cities and their perpetual flux and re-creation were seen as putting human life at risk, either literally or metaphorically. But it is tempting to think of these as anxieties for those who have confirmed status. As Paul Barker has commented in relation to the growth of malls and 'edge cities', people like to stop change at the point which benefits them most. Cities have always offered opportunities for those with unhappy memories of stable structures. They are theatrical spaces within which the tyro can 'fake it until they can make it'. The mythus of city life is permeated with anxieties about false appearances and confusions over depth and surface, the monumental and the meretricious. Policing the fractal city has been a problem in reality and representation because of the need to penetrate interstices with all the verminous metaphors attached to them as gateways to the underworld or sites of breeding. A century ago the same metaphors were used in the exploration of cities like London as were employed in the colonising of 'unknown' parts of the world. The 'street arabs' and 'troglodytes' of the 'darkest city' were testimony to the permeability of the civic and its tendency to rest lightly and provisionally on a more primitive substratum.

Cities have always provided opportunities for mobility, both horizontal and vertical in terms of class and preferment. They offer niches beyond the ecological, a density which increases the chances of affinity groups and the pleasures of anonymity, refuge and identity work. The total visibility of wide open country and village and the comfortable hierarchies of status were supplemented by the rookeries and dense, dark spaces of the 'no go' city where artful dodging took the place of decorum and deference. Cities were a place for new beginnings, particularly for the dispossessed on the run. They offered opportunities for seeing without being seen and losing the conspicuous signs of previous status or reconfiguring whatever signs had provoked persecution.

Cities were also places where the playfulness and identity experiments which motivate survival were fully available and commercially viable. Cities promoted aimlessness in relation to consumption in ways which non urban space never could. The flâneur played a game of withdrawal and closure, stalking the pleasures of the urban scene and occasionally consummating a transaction. Cities supplied a meaningful matrix of consumption and production within which exchange and remodelling could take place with relays from other cities and their hinterlands.

Space perception is fundamentally motivated by anxiety and desire – responses rooted in the primeval mechanisms of survival. Arnheim writes of perception as: 'keyed during the process of evolution to that of occurrences whose observation is vital to us. It is biologically essential that we see people and animals move from one place to another; but we do not need to see the grass grow'.

At the time of writing there was a tendency for the model of humanity to be formatted on hunters rather than builders, cultivators or domesticators and a disinclination to link primitive impulses to issues of shelter, escape and sequestration – as a domesticated space of withdrawal.

Perceptions of movement dependent on parallax vision and positioning are obviously fundamental for establishing the situation of the subject and gauging safety and danger. The agonistic dimension is supplied in countless thrillers and horror movies where the point of view conspires to create positions of safety and threat where visibility becomes a life or death issue and the screen becomes a mask which denies visual access to off-screen space. A point of view which is secured and panoramic is an enviable one. In cinema the spectator's position is usually defended against direct confrontation and the audience are rarely subjects of the gaze. In landscape painting the point of view normally corresponds to a 'safe place' secured by a visible foreground spaced, buttressed by *repoussoir* and *coulisse* compositional elements with vistas laid out for visual exploration. The vista looks back at the place of vantage and confirms its privilege.

Home can be conceived as inside looking out or outside looking in. An enviable space may be one in which this paradox, this geographical impossibility is represented as resolved. Where the tension between being 'at home' with inner and outer moralities can be released in a place that is the 'best of both worlds'. Inside and out, remote, untouched, resolved, bypassed and central. This is the politics of location and the art of the estate agent is to conjure that compound pleasure, both scopophilic and secure – a plausible fantasy of the reconciliation. They are descriptions which are both stereotypical and compelling.

Home is traditionally a place of security and routine. It is a place where the tension between personal tastes and convention is played out through minor adjustments and gambits. Home is both a scenario for personality experiments and a place where the environment becomes instinctual – its a place that produces the need to experience other scenarios both through travel outwards, and by means of perpetual experimentation which integrates those other scenarios in the familiar.

If, as Donald Winnicott suggests, home is 'where we start from' then we are likely to find within the architectural and domestic

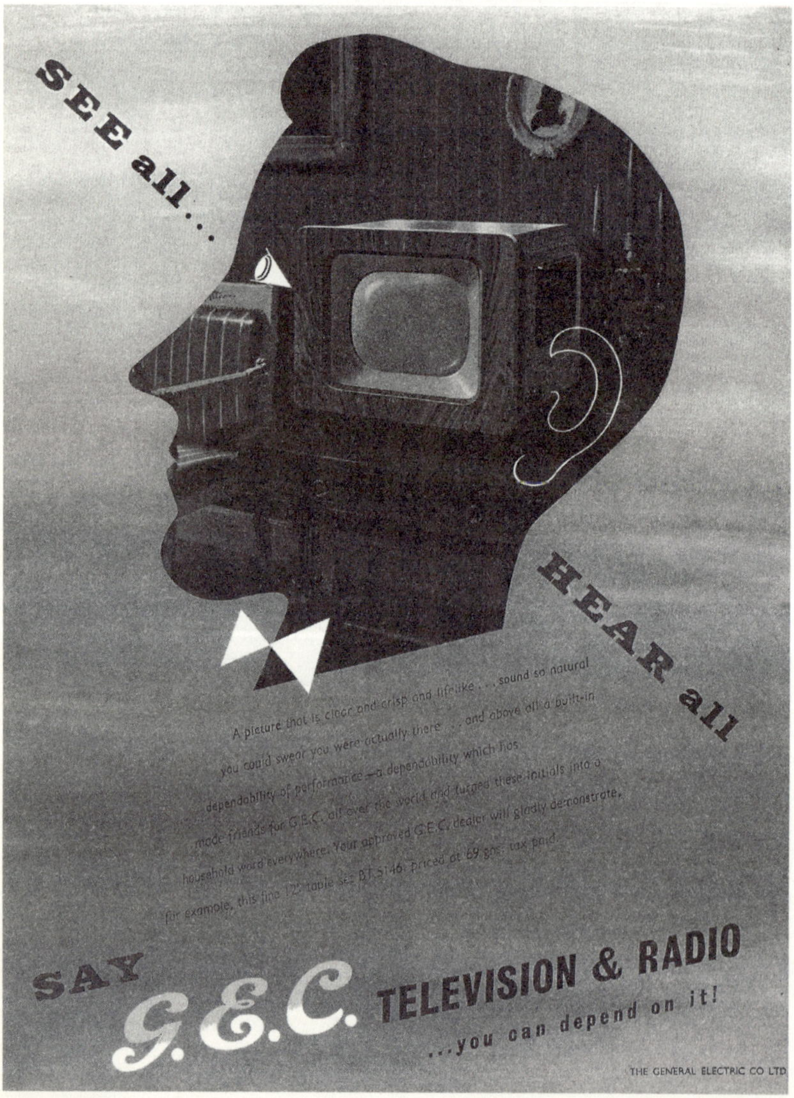

GEC Television and radio advertisement, *Tatler* magazine, 1950

organisation of the home the traces of the memories of the emotional origins that generate our exit velocity from it. Children do not live in a world of objects so much as in a world of states, and it is these states that are revisited and reconstructed through the narratives of adulthood. The intensity of the emotional paradoxes that require containment or housing, if not resolution, through the symbolic organisation of the home is evident in the immense amount of writing and merchandising that targets homemaking. Homemaking, like Proust's madeleine dunked in a tisane, inaugurates the journey back through memory tracing the paradoxes of his containment in, and exclusion from the states that formed the *mises-en-scènes* of his story. Also writing from a psychoanalytic paradigm, Adrian Stokes nominates architecture as the 'mother of the arts' which offers one way of understanding its peculiar status as both material and invisible.

The maternity of the sustaining environment is reprised in the astronaut's relationship to the mother ship, or in the compelling search for a 'matrix', which is simultaneously an electronic web morphed with origins which take on uncanny uterine forms. From home we cross the threshold into the encounter with the alien, either the charming anthropomorphic foetus of Spielberg's *E.T.* or the overpowering, over-fertile proliferation of infectious fear in the matriarchal aspects of the 'monstrous feminine'. The direction in which thresholds are crossed may be reversed to produce symptomatic narratives of safe places under threat of invasion from aliens without.

From Tennyson's dream of dwelling 'in marble halls' to Daphne du Maurier's 'I dreamed I went to Manderly again' the impact of location on the unconscious is clear. As the dream is a disguised fulfilment of a wish, '*une envie*', it is the efflorescence of the green power of envy. Envy, as defined by Melanie Klein, is a primal emotion, an early prototype of admiration, and is the mainspring of personal ontogenetic evolution. First experienced as the psychological aspect of appetite, envy is the partial drive that flows through the circuitry of the unconscious, motivating movement forwards, aggression, and propelling human agency through its narratives. Without the little green monsters of infantile envy, and the invidious glance of the evil eye at the glittering prizes to be won there would be nothing to move us from A to Z.

Envy, defined as a cardinal sin in Christian morality, was mobilised in particular ways in Thatcherite Britain. With the growth of a heritage culture and the conspicuous wealth of entrepreneurs evidenced in real estate, political dissent was dismissed as the 'politics of envy'. The enviable was produced in new ways – particularly in relation to property and interiors. Estate agents began to explore vocabularies of 'original features' and to deploy a vocabulary of conscious Victorian archaism. One image which lingers is of Jeffrey Archer in his surreally privileged penthouse overlooking the Thames. The 'room with a view' was a paradigm of the pleasures of occupying buildings which once had a more public or commercial function. The views themselves were closer to the core of urban life. Corresponding closely to the fantasy montages which accompany the reading of the news.

An iconic image of the time, which has persisted in the iconography of 'imaginary estate', is the reflection of the owner's face in the picture window clinching the proprietorial view with the mirror image. It provides a pictorial resolution of the transparency and the reflectivity which make for the ideal vantage – the resolution to the division between object libido and narcissism.

Such images offer an imaginary resolution to the contradictions of the public persona at home, for even in regressive narcissistic retreat the owner can hover over the landscape. 'Having it all' can mean being at home by virtue of scopic authority or by proliferating homes, *pieds-à-terre* and 'places' in town and country, home and abroad.

The home is a space where traces of the vestigial emotions of envy and appetite are most often found. Children, those brilliant anthropologists and erratic apprentices of the domestic world and its civil society, observe keenly how different spaces are allocated different meanings. The remote control, the telephone and the computer keyboard are enviously meaningful to small children. They soon find that different emotions, states, moods and behaviours are permitted in different spaces, thus the kitchen, the parlour or lounge, the study and the front door are sites for specific rituals and expressions. These spaces are strongly gendered, and carefully demarcated, bearing witness to the power of the envy of the other sex. But perhaps it is the stronger envy of maturity that is most compelling. It provides the motor forces that propel us over the domestic precipice of the Oedipus complex. In its many disguises it is offered to a symptomatic reader as denial, hatred of maturity, craving for power, greed, idealisation and smugness – or the inversion of the aim of envy in order to become 'envied' rather than envious. Children also realise that the interstitial space between TV and sofa is one of the most significant sites of envy, where envy and the gaze are united in an immobile body and where affective energy finds release only in a fired imagination.

Whether 'grown up' citizen of the modern metropolis or street credible of the urban underworld, the journey home from work or from crime is a journey towards an imaginary space in which the subject is allowed to "strip off psychic defences and self-deceptions, built up to hide failure, while the struggle to cope with living despite immaturity is carried on", as the psychoanalyst Harry Guntrip puts it. Metaphorical undressing is an apposite reference to the significance of clothing as container. If location is thought of as a relation of imagination and body, clothing is one of the primary sites of location, and its meanings are signifiers circulating in a vortex of envy. "This season I are mostly wearing nipple clamps" spoken by an unfashionable rural shed dwelling man is the punchline to a *Fast Show* sketch that derives its humour from foregrounding the idealisation in fashion discourse. The psychic exoskeleton of clothing, transforming an active into a passive aim, also overlays object libido with narcissism, offering imaginary protection to the vulnerability that may exist either as a fantasy of fragility (waif) or as the zeal of display (Spice). The location envy of bodily containment gives voice to the envy of the other sex but also to the games that can be played with scale, with appearances of size and age or generation. The origins of envy can be found in the desire to be in 'someone else's shoes', the first 'elsewhere'. Clothing too speaks of the anonymous individualism that is the solace of the urban.

Crossing the threshold that separates home from alien and 'outer' spaces is as much a movement through a temporal as a geographical axis. Leaving home, conceived as an emotional state rather than a geographical one, involves the repetition of losing a lost object, rather than its reinstatement. Fortunately the aim and objects of libidinal drives are mobile and transmutable, otherwise we would be forever recreating Wild Wests and Wendy houses, rather than rediscovering the 'home' within other domains. From this geographical transmutation issues other symbolic transformations. Once lost the original location is rediscovered in forms of envelopment that are as ephemeral as music, as momentary as the taste of the madeleine dipped in tisane, as sublime as the faith in celestial paradise or as solid as a bomb shelter. Space, place, location and domain take on proliferating meanings that span an increasing range of symbols. As the electronic technologies generate more virtual realities that are the product of the rhizomatic network of relationships between subjects described as users, so the uses made of symbolic space become more widespread and simultaneously more immaterial.

'Domain', which is the paradigm of the 'home page' in electronic space, has a complex set of associations. It means property or territory which is 'heritable', that is capable of being transmitted through the family, but it is also a 'sphere of thought and action' – a place of mastery from which one can look or issue forth. Insofar as it may be interactive, or may keep accounts of how many 'hits' or visits it receives it is also intersubjective.

If the paradoxes of resolving need and desire are characteristic of home and domestic space, are they also true of other everyday locations – the office, the airport, the piazza, the hospital? What are the problematics of dwelling in such places, of being 'at home'? Do they represent wildernesses, the 'geometric space' described by Merleau Ponty – space which apparently belongs to no-'body'? Are there different sets of contradictory desires, different ecologies of hope and fear to be negotiated depending on the different states of mind evoked by these places, their functions and uses? There are basic contradictions between needs and desires in relation to space and a drive, particularly in modernism, to satisfy needs as efficiently as possible, either to allow desires to exercise their own logic or to deny that they exist.

The space which satisfies needs is commonplace in the catalogues of interiors by Ikea or Habitat and the world of the colour supplement, where most objects relate specifically to a functionalist fantasy of supporting, storing enabling. The lean trope of functional space is compelling in the way that it figures a life without inheritance, contingency or compromise. The evacuation of clutter from a space interpellates and invites us to enter as air enters a vacuum, just as an empty surface invites us to rest our burdens. The promise of receptivity, however, must contain an exit if it is not to become a prison: conversely the promise of exit without containment is the road, the frontier, the desert – the lonely places of the tracking shot.

Each space contains a sense of what is possible in terms of events that may have happened or may happen in the future. The perceptions which constitute that sense can be highly individuated or, by various strategies, a collective understanding can be constructed. The construction of consensuality is a valuable skill and considerable economic consequences can follow, a process which is recorded in the financial and property pages of newspapers in terms of the mystery of gentrification and renewal.

Every space is a potential, a stage set determining particular generic action or simply a Lacanian 'Other scene' which plays out the drama of fantasy. Moods of anticipation and nostalgia are usually accompanied by some spatial consciousness – all spaces are simultaneously historic in terms of their becoming and available for further development. There is a direct relationship between an increasing quest for the real and the authentic and the morphing of reality which results in constructed simulacra. These consensually imagined and celebrated spaces are a testimony to the desire to recreate what was once 'there' or to experience more keenly the rich orchestration of persistence and innovation which makes historical and desirable locations.

The process of expansion and improvement, combined with discovering the fundamentals of contentment, is often invoked in the activity of making oneself at home. Home is a complex economy of withdrawal and hospitality with different registers of openness and closure in its differentiated spaces. Children again are very close to the ways in which spaces can be multiplied and ad hoc 'homes' can be constructed within officially sanctioned and designated places. There are intense pleasures to be had from inhabiting structures within structures; from cupboards, cardboard boxes, a blanket thrown over two chairs, the underneath of tables and plastic log cabins to the surreal delights of visiting the Ideal Home Exhibition trade fair or the Millennium Dome. Interestingly one of the proposals for countering the loss of popularity of Oxford Street to suburban and exurban malls was to roof it over and thus render it a more coherent and defensible environment.

This reminds us of previous proposals to enclose New York in a dome, to contain London's South Bank Centre in a translucent bubble and the actual roofing over of the British Library's courtyard – all speak of a contemporary desire to make spaces within spaces, to play with the conventional thresholds between inner and outer space, and to resolve the contradiction between the need for protection and the stimulation of the desire for limitlessness.

The anthologising of built structures from disparate geographical locations was an aspect of the imperial pleasures offered by Great Exhibitions. The dialectic between mega and micro structure was at the centre of avant garde and futuristic architecture in the 20th century and one of the evident pleasures of loft living is the potential of developing micro within macro environments – a return to some childhood fantasies combined with a pleasurable delinquency in the subversion of buildings' original functions.

The chief economic justification for malls and large containing structures is their policeability – the individual places which they contain do not appear to have that disturbing interface with outsides which may be undifferentiated, inhospitable or even menacing. They are 'insides' in the sense in which that term is used to connote the safer more intimate spaces within the domestic home. They are mediating structures, partway between the exploratory strategies of the flâneur and the electronic equivalent – the even safer and more comfortable option of interacting with the world on a screen. By the late 20th century the home is sufficiently activated to allow 'cocooning' to be regarded as an optional strategy in discovering the butterfly within.

Houses are connected to the outside by windows, drains, power points, telephones and doorbells – each is a potential source of anxiety

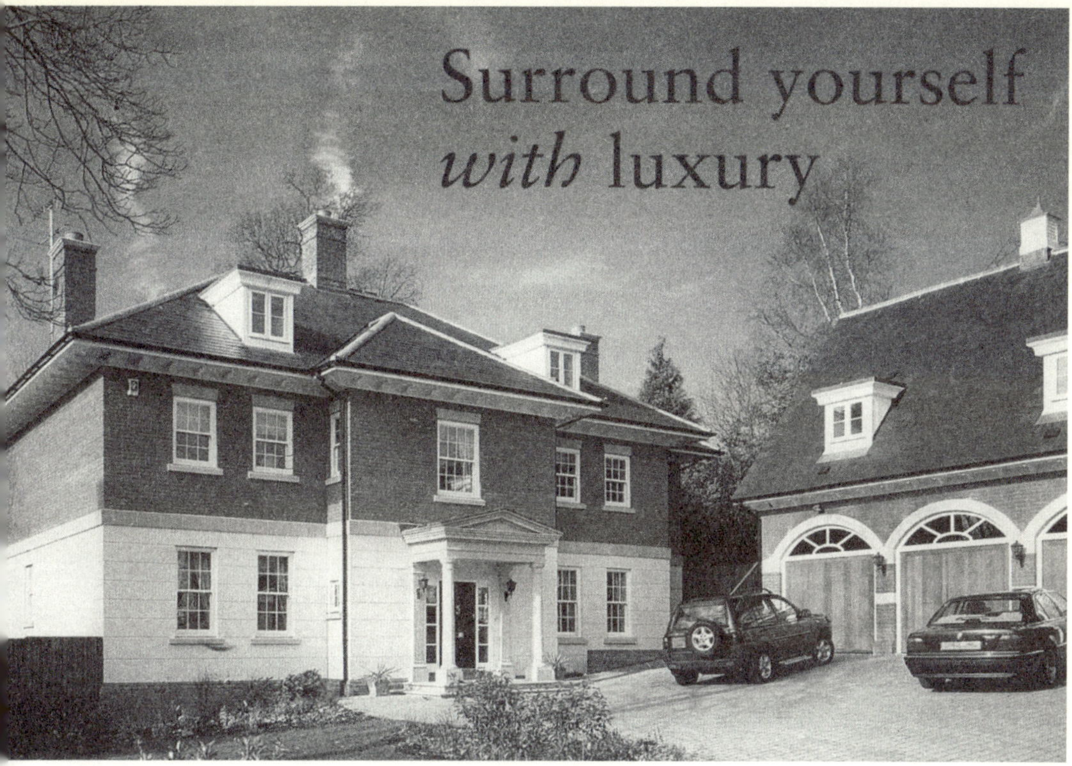

Sunday Times Property section, July 2001

fully exploited in horror films but familiar to anyone who has read a surveyor's report. Houses are particularly disturbing in cases of DIY gone bad – at 10, Rillington Place, the blocked drains of Dennis Nielsen's house in Muswell Hill or the domestic mortuary presided over by the handyman Fred West. This is space perverted – involving concealment, immuring, burying and the sinister use of everyday cooking or household implements for slaughtering, surgery, torture or erasing the signs of crime. Kristin Ross in her excellent 'Clean Bodies and Fast Cars' explores the ways in which household equipment was used for torturing Algerian prisoners in the Civil War.

This is one respect in which modernisation, the expunging of the sinister clutter of the everyday, can also be threateningly inhuman. Modernist space, described at one point in Le Corbusier's work as 'ineffable' – is open, lit, infinitely extendible, cleared of guilty edges and neuroses. Planes meet crisply without mouldings, or 'dust traps'. Modernism's fear of the street as a 'trench' or 'a murky canyon', is one aspect of its anxiety about intersections where matter out of place collects in the fractal edges of brickwork and the piecemeal infectious qualities of the vernacular. In *Vers Un Arch*, Corb celebrates 'boundless space opens up, effaces the walls drives away contingent presences'. In Modernism the edges meet at immaculate angles, there is nothing ingrained or residual.

Walter Benjamin suggested that for the most part architecture is invisible, that it is experienced in a state of distraction, that it resists incorporation into perceptions of the everyday, that it is experienced as a collection of moods and mnemonics. The foci of attention are the places which are designed to break with the flow/narrative aspects of architecture and constitute a spectacle – through the presence of monuments, empty spaces or examples of concentration and excess, such as the crossing and coming together of routes.

This perception relates to what Georges Bataille has referred to as: 'the latent criminality of space' opposing it to the authoritarian nature of architecture, which he sees as a manifestation of society's ideal being 'that which authoritatively orders and prohibits'. Certainly architecture tends to be prescriptive – a model for an articulated and hierarchically ordered way of life. But the rhetoric of architecture is unevenly distributed, usually concentrated more formidably in the façade than in the aspects less viewed. Not only are the rears of houses and public buildings less ordered but they relate more closely to the devices of contrived existence. They are traditionally where the servants and animals lived or the space for hobbies, contact with nature or pursuing the informal aspects of life. The back of buildings speaks of earthly necessity, the front elevation, of desire.

Mapping these different levels of significance on to one another is an ambitious enterprise. It is instructive however to consider the articulation of social, symbolic, imaginary and virtual spaces. From the materiality of town planning through the affective meanings of home to the celestial space of paradise or electronic worlds, the places we create configure the inner divisions by which we are riven and driven. The spatial cultures we inhabit are the streets, shops, cathedrals and garden sheds; the stopping points that punctuate the narrative of the restless quest for departures and possible destinations.

Blackest Pool[1]

Tim Brennan

****

21:35 The Horizon documentary on BBC2 is relaying a kind of detective story about science's interest in Lake Vostok… a body of water the size of Lake Ontario trapped deep below the ice of Antarctica. It has been hidden for three million years… there is no photonic light there… NASA are leading investigations, treating Vostok as a surrogate 'Europa' – an ice-clad moon of Jupiter. What microbic, extraterrestial life lies trapped inside 'Europa' now lies also at the end of their lens midst the Vostok waters… how to pass through the ice without contaminating the liquid beneath is of primary importance.

Vostok is both here and there.

22:51 Miss the on/off button on the remote and arrive at channel 20 – a screen of flickering white noise information left over from the big bang. Switch off… and turn in… to bed.

23:51 Fall asleep thinking of suspension. The liquid seems to creep over the skin, its viscous state inching over… and out.

1 **An Linn is Duibhe**

06:35 Sit bolt upright to the sound of a child... seven months' worth of voice. There are things to be done, the focus being to move the contents of this house to an empty house across the city. [2]

07:30 The living-room is a cold reminder... still furnished, albeit sparsely with the landlord's belongings... carpet (green with minute *fleur-de-lis*); a wall-mounted clock (Victoriana); sideboard (Victoriana); a settee (crimson); two armchairs (green); shelves (stripped pine – Ikea); dining table (deal)... but against one wall: twenty boxes (cardboard)... stacked... blocking out the light from the front window.

****

07:45 Leave the house on foot. Make the penultimate walk along Caledon Road... remember the children playing last night. The road runs a gauntlet of black bin bags. Dustmen are loading the creeping cart... a bag bursts and contents ooze... chicken bones, nappies and paper... a crumpled 'Strongbow'[3] cider can bounces on to the bonnet of a parked car. Turn right on to East Road. The smell of sea air mingles with traffic fumes and dust blown up from the lorries which hurtle, where space permits, towards the nearby port... A queue of juggernauts...[4] over the humpback bridge... over the rail martialling yards. Containers. Dublin mountains come into view. Cloud belt. Rain.

2 Áth Cliath, 'the ford of the hurdles', was nothing more than a crossing-point on the Liffey river until the Northmen chose it as the site for the repair and maintenance of the fleets moored nearby on the haven called Dubh linn, the 'black pool'. John Marsden *The Fury of the Northmen* (New York: St. Martin's Press, 1995) p 102.

3 '*Strongbow*: leader of the Cambro-Normans captured Dublin in 1170, and was buried in... [Christ Church] cathedral in 1176. The original tomb was destroyed when the wall above and roof collapsed in 1562. The business life of Dublin, which centred on the old monument for the payment of rents, meant that a 'new' Strongbow had to be provided. The replacement is from the 14th century and has some fine details of medieval armour, including rowel spurs on the ankles. The small figure beside is believed to be a fragment from the original monument.' John Paterson, *Christ Church Cathedral*, Dublin May 1999, pamphlet.

4 'Juggernaut: Corrupt form of Vishnu's epithet Jaggernath, Lord of the World, when he was enthroned in a temple constructed to resemble a gigantic chariot, wheels and all (Elisofon & Watts, 1979). The temple was planned to represent the moving world, carrying all its freight of gods, heroes, nymphs, creatures, plants, human beings, and all the rest of creation... Each year at the Puri festival, the god rode with his sister and brother on a heavy wagon drawn by hundreds of pilgrims, some of whom were said to court martyrdom and a blessed eternity in heaven by throwing themselves under the wheels of the god's chariot as it progressed...' Barbara G. Walker, *The Woman's Encyclopedia of Myths and Secrets*, (Harper & Row, 1983) p 483–484.

07:50 Over the crossroads... Walter Mosley's Robert Johnson[5] and the sound of Cream[6] flash up (as if unexpected)... Focus on the red light... headlights still on... Cross the road to the pavement. Internal music is punctured by the young woman on the bicycle (a regular fixture around this time). Who smiles... smile back... no one blushes now... it's a daily affair... business as usual...

07:55 Turn right on to the quays... fresh posters on the warehouse walls... pasted at cab height... *Polly Jean Harvey* and *Doctor Faustus*. Thinking of unholy but necessary pacts, of work at home and work at work... decide not to think about it and look into the river... which shade of charcoal cum gun-metal grey is it today? How high is the tide? Blue break in the clouds.

08:02 Docklands Development Authority (DDA)... Red cycle track and *Riverside Walk*... a gentrified pedestrian 'promenade'... step across planking of former transporter swing bridge... remember living in Hull on another eastern sea-board... remember pissing into the Humber and the smell of fishmeal and tanneries... thoughts interrupted by the *Viking* longboat moored to river's edge... The Abbot of Lindisfarne 'blood-eagled' on the shore like Halfden.[7] Rescue archaeology.

****

08:09 Slowing down. The city centre no longer a horizon. Low level. River on the left, close by. Approach the bronze figures with caution. Seven figures... one sack lack and a dog. Title: *Famine*. Facing East. Cartoon like. Life size. Un-life like. Undead. An idea of suffering... In a sense lost. Have stopped here many times. But not to pay respects here... impossibilities here... Look at the lists of company names on the ground... close by the 'feet'... Glance to the right... to the deep green glass of the International Financial Services Centre... Resume walking.

08:11 Dodge the red lights to the other side of the junction. Keep the river on the left-hand side. Keep it close by.

5 Walter Mosley, *RJ's Dream* (Serpent's Tail, 1995).

6 Cream: *Crossroads* (after Robert Johnson), 26 November 1968, *Cream's Final Concert*, a film by Tony Palmer for BBC television.

7 'I know not what I see on Rinansey, sometimes it lifts itself up, but sometimes it lays itself down, that it is either a bird or a man and we will go to it'... There they found Halfden Long-Leg, and Einar made them carve an eagle on his back, and cut the ribs all from the backbone and draw the lungs there out, and gave him to Odin for the victory he had won.'
From the *Orkneyinga Saga*, quoted by John Marsden, *The Fury of the Northmen* (New York: St. Martin's Press, 1995) p 91.

****

08:12 Ten benches look out across the river. On bench three a pair of figures sit huddled… there are more behind them… on the steps of the Customs[8] House…[9] knees up against the rib cage… sodden Aertex blanket. Lion and unicorn perched high above… on bench nine… a red rose placed on a copy of the *Sunday Times*… pick them up… notice how crisp the paper is… as if ironed. It carries a pink raffle ticket stapled to its top left corner. Pause to work this out. Look around. Three sixty degrees. No sign of anyone associated. Pin-hole the flower in a lapel. Walk slowly to the tenth bench whilst thinking of these objects. Decide to sit down briefly. Check the time.

****

08:16 Notice that a section of the front page has been blocked out with a fluorescent yellow highlighter: 'Sci-fi City for centre of Dublin. Project will create 7,000 jobs'. Read on…[10]

08:24 Notice that there are other sections of text highlighted. Check the time. Recognise that there is none to spare. Stand up… facing the Customs House. Peer through the gates to the car park at the rear. There in the bushes… a crown… tucked away from the public… sculpted from Portland stone… at ground level. Recommence walking again. Down river. Another crossroads. Pause. Red Man. Press the button. Wait. Green man. Cross.

08:28 Become aware of the mobile phone ringing, muffled by the leather coat pocket. Pull it out and answer. The meeting has been delayed. Agree to wait for them on arrival. End the call. Glance at the *Laughter Lounge* across the road and decide to go in there. One day.

8 Customs: *[plural noun]* the official department that administers and collects the duties levied by a government on imported goods.
The New Oxford Dictionary of English.

9 House: 7 *[mass noun Brit.]* old-fashioned term for Bingo.
The New Oxford Dictionary of English.

10 "The digital district, the largest urban regeneration project in the history of the state, will require an initial government investment of £100m… Located in the Liberties-Coombe area, it will dwarf Temple Bar and the International Financial Services Centre in terms of size and ambition. The area will be open 24-hours a day, create more than 2,500 new homes and leisure facilities… Over the past decade, companies have scrambled to build phone networks capable of handling large volumes of data and to hook up to the internet. Now the project's emphasis has shifted to the creation of content, such as news or film… Based on New York's Silicon Alley, the district will combine traditional arts such as film, graphic design, music and advertising with new computer based technologies. These will create digital content that can be pumped down phones, televisions and the internet. About twenty-five multinationals are thought to be interested in locating in the area… among the oldest in Dublin…"
Fiona McHugh and Jan Battles, *The Sunday Times*, Nov 5, p 1.

08:34 The pedestrian traffic lights at O'Connell bridge are green. Cross to the central island. Pause... green. Continue to thc other side.

****

08:36 Pass alongside the new riverside promenade being built into the inner wall of the river... like a bailey bridge... hi-tech... suspension cables. Welding sparks.

Catch sight of a little old lady approaching... first impression is that she is Eastern European. Long black scarf. Bent over. Staff in her right hand, inching along. As she passes, notice that there is a white envelope sticker stuck to her jumper.[11] She carries on walking. Lined face, dark. Fifty or sixty years. Blank expression. Scarf covering her hair. White envelope address sticker. Black marker pen. Capital letters. Away from the port. Up river. Black woolly tights. Toes missing from shoes. Open-toed, flat soled. Walking west...

Start thinking of the moves to establish an Orange Order march through Dublin City Centre...

****

08:39 Decide that there is time to stop. Mouth dry. Cross the road weaving between the congested traffic. Enter *The Winding Stair Bookshop* which boasts 'Over 20,000 books.' Proceed to the top floor to a table by the window. Open the newspaper. The waitress approaches. Order a mug of coffee. Flick the pages of the paper to find the next highlighted section of text on page 5...[12]

The coffee arrives. Look out of the window... across the river. Drink.[13] Whilst drinking, notice the newsprint ink on the fingers...[14] Turn the page... Also highlighted...[15]

11 **Sticker: 'FOR P.L.O.' [Palestinian Liberation Organisation.]**

12 **"*Aliens* cult about to clone dead baby girl... A company run by a bizarre cult is to start work this week on creating the world's first human baby. It is intended to be a genetic copy of a 10-month-old girl who died in February... The project is being carried out in a secret laboratory which is believed to be in the American desert state of Nevada. The scientists involved hope their baby will be born towards the end of next year... The company is called Clonaid..."**
L. Rogers *The Sunday Times* Nov 5, p 5.

13 **'The company, registered in the Bahamas, where organisations do not have to reveal their accounts, was founded by the Raelian movement, a religious cult which claims to have more than 50,000 members in 85 countries...' Ibid.**

14 **'Raelians believe humans are all cloned from a group of alien scientists from another planet. This information is said to have been passed on, in a 1973 visitation, to Claude Verilhon. A former sports journalist, he moved from France to Quebec, changed his name to Rael and founded the cult. Apart from cloning, the main preoccupation of Raelians is the creation of an embassy to welcome aliens arriving on earth.' Ibid.**

15 **'Spencer Dock Axe For Roche... An Irish architecture firm has been hired to redraw plans for Spencer Dock, the controversial 50-acre development in Dublin's ►**

****

08:56 Finish the coffee. Fold the paper... Proceed downstairs to the second floor and pay at the till. Continue downstairs and leave. Wait for a break in the traffic and cross to the riverside. Continue past the Ha'ppeny Bridge to the newly constructed Millennium footbridge.

09:01 Halfway across the bridge. Pause. Look downriver. A kind of urban pastoral with the winter sun rising over the Port. Forget this and think of another Millennium bridge across the Thames... closed on health and safety grounds... linking St. Pauls to Tate Modern... London's new cultural cathedral... Peer into the water... London... thinking of Vaughan Williams... *A London Symphony*...[16] smirk at the thought... verging on a free city state... with so much culture and convention that it is impossible to argue effectively... only monologue... cabin fever. Not an ounce of nostalgia... notice that the red rose has slipped from its buttonhole and is floating out to sea...[17] laugh at the pathos of such a bleary-eyed situation. Carry on walking and cross the road on the south bank.

► docklands... The board said that a master-plan would help achieve a better result... Scott Tallon Walker, which designed the Civic Offices at Wood Quay... ['Wood Quay, archaeological site in Dublin city and focus of public controversy in the 1970s. The 4-acre site was redeveloped by the Dublin corporation as its new civic offices. This necessitated the removal of archaeological layers before building work could begin. Controversy arose in 1977 when conservationists, led by Prof. F.X. Martin, OSA, chairman of the Friends of Medieval Dublin, sought more time for excavation than had been allowed. Part of the site was bulldozed by the developer and irretrievably destroyed but much information was recovered by the archaeological excavations which concluded in 1981... Archaeologically the importance of the site rested in its excellent preservation and the deep, stratified deposits ranging in date from c.925 to c.1320. The Viking age levels consisted of fourteen house plots and a stretch of the town defences; thirteen phases of development were recognised in which houses replaced one another in rough succession between the 10th century and the 12th. During the 13th century, land was reclaimed from the river when wooden quaysides were built out into the Liffey.' Ed. S.J. Connolly, *The Oxford Companion to Irish History*, p. 597]... and the first two blocks of the International Services Centre, is regarded as more traditional than Roche and is likely to draw up a more conservative plan.' John Burns *The Sunday Times* Nov 5, p 6.

16 '*A London Symphony* (Vaughan Williams) which is No 2 in a series of nine, has been described as being the first symphony written in the English vernacular: completed in 1913–19, but revised in 1918, 1920 and even as late as 1933, this belongs essentially to the years before World War I... A couple of references to the Westminster chimes (introduction and epilogue), the jingle of hansoms and the cry of 'sweet lavender'... these are suggestive of a particular location and atmosphere... Vaughan Williams always held that the London 'must stand as absolute music, and that therefore a better title might perhaps be Symphony by a Londoner. The Key is G minor." Hugh Ottaway, sleeves notes to *A London Symphony*, Vaughan Williams *Classics For Pleasure* (EMI, 1978).

****

09:16 Straight ahead and into Temple Bar.[18] Turn right at the Norseman pub on to the cobbles of East Essex Street. For an instant there is nobody around... the street seems deserted... like a film set. Pass Wokstation noodle bar where customers are asked by way of a sign to 'Orient' themselves. Then there are people. A gaggle clutching take-away coffees, folded newspapers and briefcases. They pass the entrance to Project, the shutters of Connolly Books and the New Theatre and enter a solicitors' chambers. Black frock coat and gabardines. Meanwhile, opposite, a helicopter lands on the roof of the Clarence Hotel. A familiar face approaches... arrange to meet up later... continue to the end of the street and pause at the pedestrian lights at Parliament Street.[19]

17 'Throughout the hundred days of the 1972 Documenta there was always a fresh red 'Rose for direct democracy' displayed in a glass graduated cylinder of the kind used by chemists: the union of nature and science, mysticism (rosa carnalis, rosa mystica) and revolution. Bud and bloom are in fact green leaves transformed. So in relation to the leaves and the stem the bloom is a revolution, although it grows through organic transformation and evolution'.
Caroline Tisdall, *Joseph Beuys* (London: Thames and Hudson, 1979) p 273.

The UK's Labour Party adopted the red rose as its primary logo in the mid eighties. The introduction of the rose enabled the Party to re-establish itself as New Labour, a political organisation distanced from the primary industrial socialist traditions and re-oriented around a notion of a free market friendly, New Labour mentalité.

18 'In any event, Temple Bar will never be 'finished'; like Paris, it will continue to metamorphose over time as new uses place different demands on the existing framework of buildings. What does merit comment at this stage in the process is the fact that Phase 1 of a time-based, area-based and finance-based intervention towards the achievement of one powerful idea – the realisation of Temple Bar as Dublin's Cultural Quarter. Phase 2... is about to begin.'
Laura Magahy, *Temple Bar–The Power of An Idea* (Temple Bar Properties, 1996) p 9.

19 An area of reclaimed land, formerly the River Poddle, which linked the Liffey to a tidal inland pool located to the rear of Dublin Castle. 'The evidence from 33–34 Parliament Street occurred along with evidence for the clay bank enclosures of the early Viking town on the Poddle estuary shoreline. In this location, the series of banks enclosed what became the strategically important northeastern corner of the viking settlement'.
Margaret Gowen, *Temple Bar – The Power of An Idea*
(Temple Bar Properties, 1996) p 22 Ibid.

09:23 Green man. Cross and continue straight ahead down Essex Street West20 past *The Viking Adventure 1*[21] on the right . Enter the bakery and buy a croissant-to-go. Exit. Bear left at the end of the street. The gradient steepens towards Christ Church Cathedral…[22] consider if there is such a thing as an 'outsider'… slow down. Check the time. Sit on one of the benches behind the church. Consider whether it is possible for there to be a deep England.[23] Return to thoughts of the Orange Order… remember talk of the first Lodge being founded in Dublin's Dawson Street some ten minutes' walk away…

09:33 Continue along the back of the church and pass under the raised buildings of Dublin Corporation. Notice the small amphitheatre to the right… notice the strange inlaid pattern underfoot… like some weird visual ballroom dance score… decide not to step on any of the markings. Turn left at the main road and follow the steep incline to the main junction. Cross the road and continue down St. Patrick's Road.

20 'The large vacant site on the south of Essex Street West now holds the key to the interpretation of the early radio-carbon dates, and could possess further new evidence for the earliest Viking settlement of Dublin.'
Margaret Gowen, *Temple Bar – The Power of An Idea*
(Temple Bar Properties, 1996), p 22.

21 *Viking Adventure*: a post-Jorvic themed Viking heritage experience… 'In the new, more heavily commercial environment… Heritage is a vehicle for economic regeneration through tourism and services in areas of decline of traditional industrles and activities… History and heritage are put up for sale in brochures promoting new developments to prospective buyers – sponsors, purchasers or visiting customers. The brochures root and enrich the project in history and culture with historical photographs in sepia tones; while colour photographs offer bright prospects for present and future development.'
Gaby Porter, *Heritage: Image and History*, Cornerhouse and Impressions, 1990.

22 'Christ Church cathedral, the cathedral church of the archdiocese of Dublin and Glendalough. A cathedral has existed on this site since c.1028 when the Norse king of Dublin, Sitric Silkbeard, co-founded the cathedral of the holy trinity with Bishop Dúnán of Dublin… as the principal church of the Old English colony in Ireland Christ Church played an important role in the civic life of the city…'
S.J. Connolly, *The Oxford Companion to Irish History*, p 87.

23 'In 1500 the descendants of the Anglo-Norman conquerors referred to themselves as 'Englishmen born in Ireland'. Scholars tend to call them Anglo-Irish, the analogy being with the 18th-century elite who allegedly possessed a similar sort of colonial nationalism founded on the local parliament. This term is used up to 1603, especially for magnates inhabiting the borders with the Irish. Scholars use the term 'Old English' for Palesmen and Townsmen after the mid-16th century, though they were actually called 'Anglo-Hyberni' and 'English-Irish' in the literature of the period. Only in the 1620s does the term 'Old English' make its appearance to cover all descendants of the Norman conquerors…'
S.J. Connolly, *The Oxford Companion to Irish History*, p 408.

09:37 Turn first right. *Back Lane*. Pass the Vincent de Paul building on the left. Turn first left… aware that the warren of low red brick houses are always difficult to remember. Turn second left. *Davis Place*. Approach the grey door of number 3. Find the keys next to the mobile in the leather coat pocket. As the keys enter the lock the phone 'bleeps.' Leave the key in the door… it's a text message.

****

09:40 Fumbling… thumb and buttons… read the message.[24]

09:41 Choose not to reply yet. Pause. Notice the mongrel sitting on the corner of the pavement.

09:42 Decide to enter anyway. Unlock the Chubb. Then turn the Yale key the wrong way at first and for a split second believe it is the wrong key. Then turn clockwise and enter the house. Retrieve the post. Notice that it includes a local newsletter.

09:43 The interior has been completely refurbished and bears no relation to the original building. Polished wooden floor. Pine… Smoked glass partition… Open stairs… white, white walls… mock wood burner… dimmer light switches. The amount of daylight is a surprise… the rear of the ground floor being open-plan with a glass extension at the rear. A small indoor tree stands in this 'conservatory'… Weeping fig. Its soil is damp having been watered recently. No other objects can be seen.

09:44 Put the post and the newspaper on to the kitchen work surface. Fill the electric kettle left from the previous visit the day before. Switch it on.

09:45 Check for milk in the fridge. Place two tea bags in a mug from the draining board.

09:46 Gaze out through the steel venetian blinds.

09:47 Listen to the crackle and slow hiss of the kettle as it begins to warm.

09:48 The silence is interrupted by the rumble and click of the boiled water. Pour the contents into the cup.

09:49 Find a teaspoon and press the bags into the side of the mug. Leave the bags in.

09:50 Put the teabags in the green bin bag… pick up the newspaper and post… sit at the glass table.

24 **Text message: "Can't make it today. Sorry. Am dealing with the flood."**

09:51 Flick through the newspaper… Highlighted areas…[25]

09:52 Turn attention to the local newsletter…[26]

09:53 And glance once more at the broadsheet… illuminated…[27]

09:54 Leave the tea to go cold…

25 'Welcome to futureville. A place where computers are so tiny people can wear them in their boots. Where shopping trolleys drive back to their bays... Where business cards are redundant because eyeglasses will display all you need to know about the person in front of you... The government's 'big idea' has been four years in the making... The so-called digital district, a futuristic redevelopment aimed at creating thousands of well-paid technology jobs, will catapult Ireland into the digital world. Stretching from the Guinness brewery on Thomas Street, to the Four Courts and back to St. Patrick's Cathedral, the six-square-mile zone will dwarf Temple Bar in size... outpace the International Financial Services Centre which put the Spring in the Celtic Tiger... outlined the idea over wine and pasta. It was the summer of 1996..." Ahern... "People think these lunches are about food and wine. They are not. Some of the best schemes are cooked up in restaurants"... MIT felt a downtown location would be a better option... MediaLab will come up with ideas which could then be developed by start-up companies or 'incubators'...' Jan Battles, 'The Future is E-Dublin', *The Sunday Times,* Nov 5, p 15.

26 'The excavations also uncovered the foundations of the early Franciscan friary, founded in 1233, extending north as far as the Iveagh Market, and included a church, belfry, dormitory, hall, three chambers, cemetery and 3 gardens on Francis St. Ian Doyle, who directed the Davis Pl. dig, talked about the most interesting aspect of the Franciscan cemetery finds – numerous skeletons. From the partial laboratory analysis so far carried out, the subjects were young adolescents and appear to have died from severe malnutrition and disease.'
Heritage Section, St. Nicholas of Myra,
Francis Street Community Newsletter (Autumn 2000 Vol.6 No.2), p 4.

27 'The Liberties was so named in the 14th century because it lay beyond the city walls. People living there were free from taxes and obligations imposed within the confines of the city.'
Fiona McHugh and Jan Battles, 'Dublin Plans Future World', *The Sunday Times*, Nov 5, p 2.

Travelling the Distance: Encountering the Other

Jane Rendell

[...]
we are voyagers, discoverers
of the not-known,

the unrecorded;
we have no map;

possibly we will reach haven,
heaven.

HD, *Tribute to the Angels* Trilogy
(London: Carcanet Press Ltd., 1997) p 59.

The angel is that which unceasingly *passes through the envelope(s)* or *container(s)*, goes from one side to the other, reworking every deadline, changing every decision, thwarting all repetition.

Luce Irigaray, *An Ethics of Sexual Difference*
(London: The Athlone Press, 1993) p 15.

The distances we travel are physical and psychic, emotional and mental. The others we meet en route take the form of places, objects or people. They may be our teachers, critics, students, lovers, children, parents or friends. Most often the distant other we encounter in our travels is what we thought to be a familiar part of ourselves.

The games we never played

> Home is that place which enables and promotes varied and ever changing perspectives, a place where one discovers new ways of seeing reality, frontiers of difference.
>
> bell hooks, *Yearnings: Race, Gender and Cultural Politics* (London: Turnaround Press, 1989) p 148.
>
> For most of my life, travel has been a certainty rather than a question [...] Travel was unavoidable, indisputable, and always necessary for family, love, and friendship as well as work.
>
> Caren Kaplan, *Questions of Travel: Postmodern Discourses of Displacement*
> (Durham, North Carolina: Duke University Press, 1996) p ix.

PO Box 1606, Riqa, Dubai, Trucial States, Arabian Gulf.
PO Box 387, El Fascher, Darfur Province, Western Sudan.
PO Box 1570, Kabul, Afghanistan.
PO Box 86, Mekele, Ethiopia.
22 Wells Close, Harpenden, Herts, Al5.
15 Mayfield Road, Girton, Cambridge, CB3.
22 Collegiate Crescent, Sheffield.
15 Filey Street, Sheffield.
3 St Quintin's Avenue, London, W10.
12 Mogg Street, Bristol.
22 Barony Street, Edinburgh.
18 Eyre Crescent, Edinburgh, EH3.
60 Lillieshall Road, London, SW4.
2a French Place, London, E1.
48 Enfield Cloisters, Fanshaw Street, London, N1.

I was born in Al Mahktoum hospital, Dubai in the 'middle east'. As a girl I lived in Sudan, Afghanistan and Ethiopia. My movements followed the pattern of my dad's work. Unlike many children in similar situations, I was not put into a boarding school at the age of eleven, but came back to live in England with my mum and sister. I say, 'came back'. The phrase implies that I was coming back to somewhere I had already been. But I had never lived in England before. It was my parents' country of origin, not mine. I have never felt at home back (t)here. But then I have never felt at home anywhere.

Once the women were back at home my dad continued to traverse the drier areas of the globe. He is a hydro-geologist. A man who looks for water and brings it to the surface for people to wash and drink. He does this in lands that are not his own, that he was not raised in, that are strange to him. And with people whose languages and customs are not second nature, not kin, but those that he has to learn anew.

It is only recently that I have come to acknowledge the difficult relationship I have with my dad (the coloniser). Secretly I have always been rather relieved in confessional conversations around the academic dinner table that my relationship with colonisation is through acts of kindness. My dad was in a position to help, to use his knowledge to provide water, and so he did. His knowledge made him powerful, he had skills that allowed him to locate water under a brittle crust. He is a very gentle and unassuming man. He seldom takes the high ground. So why am I uneasy? Because, although generated though a sincere motivation – to help – my dad's particular brand of paternalism was also closely related to acts of colonisation.

I remember nights spent capturing insects on cold stone floors. Our house was not grand. In western terms, it was a shack, but unlike many other houses we had lived in it had a stone floor, running water and a tin roof that did not leak. While my parents were out, a Tigrinian man stood at our gate. He was our watchman. I was uncomfortable around this tall black man with his hardened feet and long white robe and stick. My younger sister played with him, but I felt distanced from him. He never spoke to me. Nor I to him.

At that time all westerners had guards positioned at their threshold. Was it because a western family had recently been ambushed nearby by Tigrinian rebels or was it to suggest that we were important enough to protect? I am still embarrassed by the fact that africans looked after us and our house. 'Why?' I ask my parents now. 'It was the custom then', they say. Westerners provided Africans with paid work. If it is a custom, it's one that shames me. I never played with the watchman. I never travelled that distance. Do the games we never played make me a coloniser too?

Hearing of my interest in angels, messengers and figures of transformation, Commissions East sent me through an interesting project – Quadratura – a collaboration between artist Edward Allington and architects Beevor Mull. Participants were invited to become 'angels' and planning applications were made for access into various spaces through the ceiling. I used to spend a lot of time as kid upsidedown. I would lie on the sofa flinging my head backwards, looking up at the ceiling wishing it was the floor. It was so clean and white. There was no mess. It was unmarked by the past.

Female academics come with baggage

<u>The nomad does not stand for homelessness, or compulsive displacement; it is rather a figuration for the kind of subject who has relinquished all idea, desire, or nostalgia for fixity. [...] I shall take the nomad as the prototype of the 'woman of ideas': in the history of women's struggle the international dimension is implicit from the start. Not only is feminism as such an international movement, like most other major social movements of this century but at the intellectual level also the very conceptual structure of women's studies is the result of intense international networking.</u>

Rosi Braidotti, *Nomadic Subjects*
(New York: Columbia University Press, 1994) p 22 & p 254.

<u>Writing is working; being worked; questioning (in) the between (letting oneself be questioned) of same *and of* other without which nothing lives; undoing death's work by willing the togetherness of one-another, infinitely charged with a ceaseless exchange of one another – not knowing one another and beginning again only from what is most distant, from self,</u>

> from other, from the other within. A course that multiplies transformations by the thousands.
>
> Hélène Cixous, *Sorties* (trans. Betsy Wing)
> from Susan Sellers (ed.) *The Hélène Cixous Reader*
> (London: Routledge, 1994) p 43.

Gloria Anzaldúa
Frances Bartkowski
Rosi Braidotti
Judith Butler
Hélène Cixous
Diane Elam
Elizabeth Grosz
bell hooks
Luce Irigaray
Caren Kaplan
Julia Kristeva
Doreen Massey
Elspeth Probyn
Gillian Rose
Janet Wolff

Moving is not strange to me, both physically and emotionally I am most comfortable in motion. For me, being in motion itself provides a sense of stability – having left but not yet being there. This has a familiar feel to me, and it seems I am not alone. Postmodern feminism is full of stories of travel. Women who have moved out of their place. Much of their written work speaks of their displacement. There is much at stake in constantly moving out of your place. Movements vary in their political dimension. Not all journeying is to be celebrated.

Recent work in feminism, cultural studies and human geography has increasingly focused on issues of identity, difference and subjectivity. The language of these texts is highly spatialised, with words such as 'mapping', 'locating', 'situating', 'positioning' and 'boundaries' appearing frequently. Academics 'explain' this new emphasis on space as typical of postmodern discourse. (Postmodernism in this context refers to a questioning of truth, history and the all knowing modern subject and instead describes a series of discourses exploring new epistemologies and ontologies.) These searches for new ways of knowing and being are being framed in spatial terms. For those concerned with issues of identity – race, gender, sexuality and ethnicity – spatial metaphors constitute powerful political devices which can be employed as critical tools for examining the relationship between the construction of identities and the politics of location. In such on going theoretical disputes as the essentialism/ constructionism debate, positionality provides a way of understanding knowledge and essence as contingent and strategic – where I am makes a difference to what I can know and who I can be. (But I am not going to be (t)here for ever.)

The ability and desire to make connections with new things depends on position. First in one place then in another, I find it is easier to make connections with another when I am out of place. I like to take my baggage across the frontier into a new land – to unpack among strangers only to find all the things I have brought have lost their intended purposes.

This also describes my experience of collaboration and interdisciplinarity. Familiar words but ones which suggest different yet equally complex dynamics about the relationship between two – working between disciplines, working with another. Many female academics I know work between disciplines. They seem to be drawn to the strangeness of new areas of study, to making relationships – connections and distinctions – between things. What travel and interdisciplinary study have in common is their potential for transformation.

To be interdisciplinary you are between two places. But how exactly is the 'between' constituted? Is the interdisciplinary operator one who straddles two places, one who maps the tears and the rifts, the places where things have come apart, and the overlaps and the joins, the places where things come together? Or has s/he come from elsewhere, arrived as a stranger in town? Being someone new in town is a different experience altogether. Here one place has been left and a new unknown terrain entered. What do you do? Match the new to meet up with the standards of the old, or allow yourself to be changed by your new surroundings?

Much of my work involves negotiating a relationship between a particular kind of two: theory and practice. Strictly speaking these are not disciplines but, rather, ways of operating. The conceptual space of critical theory both sustains and inspires me. It allows me a place to reflect on the past and to imagine new futures. It requires that I enter a reflective and rigorous engagement with the world directly around me, but it also provides an emancipatory moment, a glimpse of a world beyond. Feminist critical theory in particular asks me to imagine the world from a different perspective, the perspective of the as-yet-unrealised female subject who questions the very notion of all-knowing and once-and-forever bounded subjectivity.

The relationship critical theory has to practice is not one of exemplification nor of application, but rather of ongoing critical transformative dialogue. Julia Kristeva has expressed her aim of working in an interdisciplinary way, as one of trying to construct a 'diagonal axis' between disciplines and their associative methodological practices. If practice is seen as the making of perfect objects, it is also about 'practising' – trying to get it right but often getting it wrong. Practice intends to answer a set of aims. Critical thinking questions the values of the aims themselves. Thinking is also a practice. It is something we do. We make ideas. Unless we understand thinking as a form of practice, and practice as a thoughtful process, it is impossible to transform the relationship between the two.

Feminism makes it very clear that the relation of theory and practice depends on the particular – on history and geography – there are no universal rules. Historically, it is only by acknowledging the work of earlier feminists that we can operate somewhat 'behind'. Rather than having to work in reaction to dominant male models – either blending in by copying or by overtly attacking – we can adopt different strategies. We are able to be more listening, more empathetic. It is only in this state of mind that we are more able to be ourselves and to open ourselves up to encounters with the other. We travel the distance in order to transform as well as transgress.

A recent project for Artangel by Tim Millar took the form of a performance in Trinity Buoy lighthouse. The artist, dressed as an eighteenth century scientist, performed a number of D.I.Y. versions of famous scientific principles. For his exit, he asked that the audience each rip out two pages from Newton's *Laws of Gravity* and attach one page to each of his shoulders with masking tape. Clad in a pair of paper wings this artist-scientist disappeared up a spiral staircase to the top of the lighthouse. An angel ready to take flight, he was leaving one world to enter another. We, the audience, had an important role in his rituals of preparation. For a brief moment before he took flight, he existed between two worlds.

Caress

> Critical work is made to fare on interstitial ground[...] Instead, critical strategies must be developed within a range of diversely occupied territories where the temptation to grant any single territory transcendent status is continually resisted.
>
> Trinh T Minh-Ha, *When the Moon Waxes Red: Representation, Gender and Cultural Politics* (London: Routledge, 1991) p 229.
>
> The caress is an awakening to intersubjectivity, to a touching between us which is neither passive or active; it is an awakening of gestures, of perceptions which are at the same time acts, intentions, emotions. This does not mean that they are ambiguous, but rather, that they are attentive to the person who touches and the one who is touched, to the two subjects who touch each other.
>
> Luce Irigaray, *To Be Two* (London: Athlone Press, 2000) p 25.

08.05.00
New York earth room
7000 oaks

31.05.00
Touch
A long coastal walk
Between the devil and the deep blue sea

26.06.00
The vertical earth kilometre

26.08.00
Exit: come on in

09.11.00
It's quicker by rail
Holidays afloat
Rounding the cape of good hope

I have recently fallen in love with an artist. In the days and months during which we moved towards each other he sent me a series of postcards. Some were of landscapes, others of land art. All are reference points of our mutual topography – mappings of our merging emotional, creative and intellectual worlds. Before this transformation, I wrote about his work as an independent critic (or so I thought). Recently he told me that he found it hard to recognise his work in my comments. They were so flattering. But this was not the only reason for the lack of recognition. He also believed that as someone in love with him I was not able to be his critic. "Why?" I asked. He was sceptical about my ability to be objective, but in my opinion the critic can never be objective. There is always something about the self at stake...

What is criticism? Who is a critic? What is her/his role? Does the distance between the critic and subject matter or make a difference if the critical viewpoint is meant to be one of 'judgement'? Is this judgement subjective or objective, engaged or disengaged? Being objective seems to imply that I perceive a distinction between myself and the thing I am critiquing – that I am disengaged. Being subjective suggests that I am so engaged in the other that I get lost.

For me, the critic is a travel writer, always going far from home, invited as a guest into someone else's place. To enter another's space necessitates movement out of one's own territory – it involves trust on both parts. To engage with something imagined and made by another is also to journey, from what is already known towards what is as yet unknown. To encounter another requires a willingness to connect, but also to let go, to take risks. Some critics travel like tourists, crossing vast territories but remaining unchanged. Others, like me, are constantly pulled out of the familiar toward the strange, impelled by a desire for transformation. This is nothing if not subjective – a total immersion in the other – in order to return anew to the self.

When writing criticism I am not just negotiating my relationship with an other. I am working between two places, a homeplace or theoretical idea that I have already invested in and the project that has recently come into view. As I start to travel the distance between them, I make loops to stitch them together, loosely. As I move towards one, I glance back at the other, but it has already moved out of view.

Therefore, critical theory has two main roles – it takes me outside myself in two ways. It gives me a place, an elsewhere, from which to reflect upon myself, a place from which to imagine new elsewheres. It gives me an outside reference point, perhaps it is footholding in the world, or perhaps a favourite bag I like to carry. But for who will I journey? Will I travel the distance just because I like to daytrip or are there particular people and places I want to visit?

In Emir Kusturica's *The Underground*, a bride glides the length of a long candle lit table. Smiling, she passes just above her wedding guests feasting on either side. She is apart from the company yet acknowledges her connection as the fringes of her dress, heavy brocade and light lace, caress their finger tips. A moment of encounter and of distance.

Telling it as it is

Perhaps the strange side of my nature can be summed up in a single trait: the need to keep searching, come what may, for new events, and flee inertia and stagnation.

Isabelle Eberhardt, *The Passionate Nomad: The Diary of Isabelle Eberhardt* (Boston: Beacon Press, 1988) p 36.

> They speak like messengers, but gesture seems to be their 'nature'. Movement, posture, the coming-and-going between the two. They move – or stir up? – the paralysis or *apatheia* of the body, or the soul, or the world. They set trances or convulsions to music, or give them harmony.
>
> Luce Irigaray, *An Ethics of Sexual Difference* (London: The Athlone Press, 1993) p 16.

Traveller
Tourist
Migrant
Exile
Refugee
Nomad
Teacher
Critic
Researcher
Storyteller

My early childhood made me into a traveller. For years I travelled physically all the time. My work simply provided money for a trip. And I never went to the same place twice. Recently I have been moving frequently across the planet, but I have not been travelling in the same way. I go on trips with purposes. I give papers at conferences, I teach, I visit buildings, artworks, friends with new babies, but I do not meander off with no purpose other than to lose myself. But none the less I do lose myself. It is just that my body stays still. Through writing, reading, teaching, researching, I lose myself in other people's heads. Sitting in one chair with students coming through the door in an endless stream I am endlessly on the move.

We all like to tell stories but I find that men and women tell them differently. Women like to tell stories about people; about people they know, about themselves and their friends. I used to despise anecdotal teaching, old men taking up valuable time telling boring and irrelevant stories about themselves. How is this any different, I now ask, from the stories women tell? Perhaps it is because the stories women tell in the academy are often about journeys. They describe where they have come from, where they are going and what it is like along the way. These are not stories about places but about travel. These are also stories about lives – about encounters with others and about transformations. The old feminist adage, 'the personal is political' remains strong – just now it seems to favour the form of the travelogue or an autobiographical journey.

At a talk at the ICA a few years back, Susan Rubin Suleiman said something that has remained with me ever since. She described the often painful process of re-reading parts of her older work and the way she would cringe at some of the stories she has told. These were the stories that, with hindsight, she felt did not resonate. They were not a microcosm of a greater whole, not a detail that referenced a larger pattern, did not illustrate in a concrete fashion a complex theoretical idea, they were just personal outpourings. bell hooks has expressed a similar worry – that we are driven by a need to confess. But I am not sure that we tell stories only in order to confess. When I tell stories to my students I usually do so in order to shift the power dynamic between us, to allow a space to be made where they trust me enough to tell me their difficulties and confusions, so that I have a better idea how to guide them. By telling stories I show empathy, I reveal weaknesses, aspects of myself that disempower me. 'I've been there too' – but to travel this distance I put myself at risk. They encounter me stripped bare.

Friends I studied with are often surprised that I teach architecture. They remember me as 'Mystic Meg and her red baggage', oscillating somewhere between Jung and Marx. I never had any answers, only questions. What they don't realise is that I teach 'not knowing'. Teaching for me provides a place to take a risk, it requires a desire and an ability to encounter the other. To admit not knowing and to acknowledge a refusal to provide answers. My students love and hate me for it. They want answers and I will not give them. I do not have them to give. I love the questions.

In Wim Wenders' *Wings of Desire* a tightrope dancer practises for her evening show in a big top dressed in white with tiny feathered wings. Invisible to her but visible to us, an unexceptional man, tired, in a drab overcoat watches her. We know this man to be an angel. Stories are angelic forms. They are messages. Sometimes these messengers are clothed in disguise.

Prepositions: Transformational Messengers

> Far from wanting to possess you in linking myself to you, I preserve a 'to', a safeguard of the in-direction between us – *I Love to You*, and not: I love you. This 'to' safeguards a place of transcendence between us, a place of respect which is both obligated and desired, a place of possible alliance.
>
> Luce Irigaray, *To Be Two* (London: Athlone Press, 2000) p 19.
>
> That's prepositions for you. They don't change in themselves, but they change everything around them: words, things and people [...] Prepositions transform words and syntax, while *pré-posés* transform men.
>
> Michel Serres, *Angels: A Modern Myth*
> (Paris: Flammarion, 1995) p 140 & p 147.

To
At
From
In
Between
With
Among
For
On

Last week I went with a group of women, all feminists – writers, architects and artists – to hear French psychoanalyst and philosopher, Luce Irigaray, talk at The Architectural Association in London. Irigaray spoke of her early research into language with eight year old Italian girls and boys. She discovered that when given a preposition to use, girls made sentences that linked them to people, whereas boys made sentences that linked them to objects.

There were three questions from the floor to Irigaray, all from men, all angry. The first asked her why she believed in matriarchy. The second came from a Lacanian, almost in tears, passionately angry at her stupidity. The final man told her that she had a choice, she could either do empirical research into language or she could speculate and philosophise, but she could not do both, not these two things at the same time. It brought to mind the figure of the angel, described by Irigaray herself, as one who moves between, thwarts all repetition and challenges existing boundaries.

It is not clear whether Irigaray was arguing that gendered identity precedes language, or whether use of language makes us sexed subjects, but this was not the issue here. Architecture was the context for this debate. 'How do men and women live together?' was the question at stake.

Irigaray suggested that women's 'relational' identities provided a good model for living together, for making relationships between two different subjects. She suggested that the architecture of our homes should provide each of the two sexes with separate spaces as well as a place to meet, to invite the other. I am interested in the kind of architecture which occupies this 'place of respect' between two. Described above by Irigaray, this place of 'to' may be the place between theory and practice, men and women, architect and user. For years, although an open feminist in architecture schools, I refused to make any comment on the differences between female and male students and the ways in which they designed, even to myself. But I have been taking it all in, storing it up. There is a difference and it is as Eric Erikson's research showed back in the 1970s – women tend to be more interested in creating indefinable interior spaces, whereas men seem to like making externally located objects that they can look at and define. Women often shy away from drawing the outside of the building, they often do not imagine space as an object viewed in its entirety from the outside, but rather they locate themselves within a place and sometimes refuse to locate the edges. Once a student cried when I forced her to make a model with limit lines.

Design education encourages us to be specific and definitive, to behave as if architecture is an object separate from us, rather than a place we can have a relationship with. I am interested in the kind of architecture that explores the spatial nature of relationships between people, allows us to consider the ways in which people think and make, occupy and imagine space. Place is central to our experience of relating to one another.

In earlier work, Irigaray's contributions to discussions about space and place were concerned with the 'cultural shape' of the female body – the close but not closed metaphor of 'two lips' suggested new ways of living together. Now language structure appears to provide the same utopian impulse. Prepositions in particular possess a strong suggestive role. They are capable of changing 'everything around them' and provide a means of making connections between two, between people and between people and places. Some prepositions emphasise position, the relation of an object or a subject to place, such as on, in, between, through. Others focus on relationships between subjects and objects, for example, among and with, and the directional nature of these connections like for or to. Yet others contain elements of time, as in beyond.

For Irigaray the potential of the insertion of the word 'to' into the phrase 'I love you', making 'I love to you', suggests a new social order of relations between two different sexes. This might involve rethinking the relationships made between people and things, subjects and objects. Considered as prepositions, things have an important role to play in making relationships between people. In processes of making and using, things occupy a place between people. Animate objects tell stories, bridge the private worlds of separate individuals, mediate between real and imaginary. Things suggest a number of different narratives about their histories and their potential future uses. Considered as props they play an important role as mediators, as toys they encourage play and speculation, as gifts they challenge capitalist notions of profit and ownership.

This might also involve a new order to the relationships made between architect and user where interaction and collaboration play important roles and where the qualities of particular end-products are only as important as the processes of making them. The ways in which relationships between makers and users are constructed can constitute a major part of the conceptualisation and realisation of a project, effecting aesthetic and formal decisions. This may tend towards the choreographic, where the work manifests less as an object and more as an event, a series of exchanges people make with one another. Such working methods necessitate engaged and committed contact with others, they present opportunities for questioning one's own ways of thinking and making. In this space of critical dialogue we have no choice but to travel the distance to encounter the other.

In the Kabakov's *Palace of the Projects*, commissioned by Artangel at The Roundhouse, Camden, London the hundreds of embryonic projects housed in a plywood copy of the Tatlin tower are either impossibilities or so simply executed that they seem rather naïve and not very worldly in their intentions. My favourite is a pair of angel wings ready to strap on with instructions for use.

Spinning: a space between

Lucy Irigaray notes in *Je, Tu, Nous: Towards a Culture of Difference,* that when her mother goes away the little girl does not do the same things as the little boy. She does not play with a string and a reel that symbolise her mother. Because she and her mother are of the same sex, her mother cannot have the object status of a reel. Instead the little girl is distressed. She plays with dolls – a different kind of object from the reel – she dances, 'this dance is also a way for the girl to create a territory of her own in relation to her mother'. In her dance she spins around de-stabilising existing connections between herself and her place, making new ones between herself and her (m)other. She creates, 'a vital subjective space open to the cosmic maternal world, to the gods, to the present other' .

Irigaray's notion of the daughter spinning to make room between her and her mother, resonates strongly for me. I imagine being five again spinning round and around in the middle of a room only stopping when the furniture, walls and floor begin to revolve around me, when everything around me slips out of place.

For me, this is the place of prepositions: a space inhabited by angels.

To travel the distance, to think between, I need to be 'spun out of place'. But I also need to be engaged in my encounters with others. Working practices which necessitate both freedom and committed contact present opportunities for questioning my own ways of thinking and making. This creates a real space for critical and transformative dialogue where I discover parts of myself in my encounters with others.

Writing provides me this place.

World Political

Layla Curtis

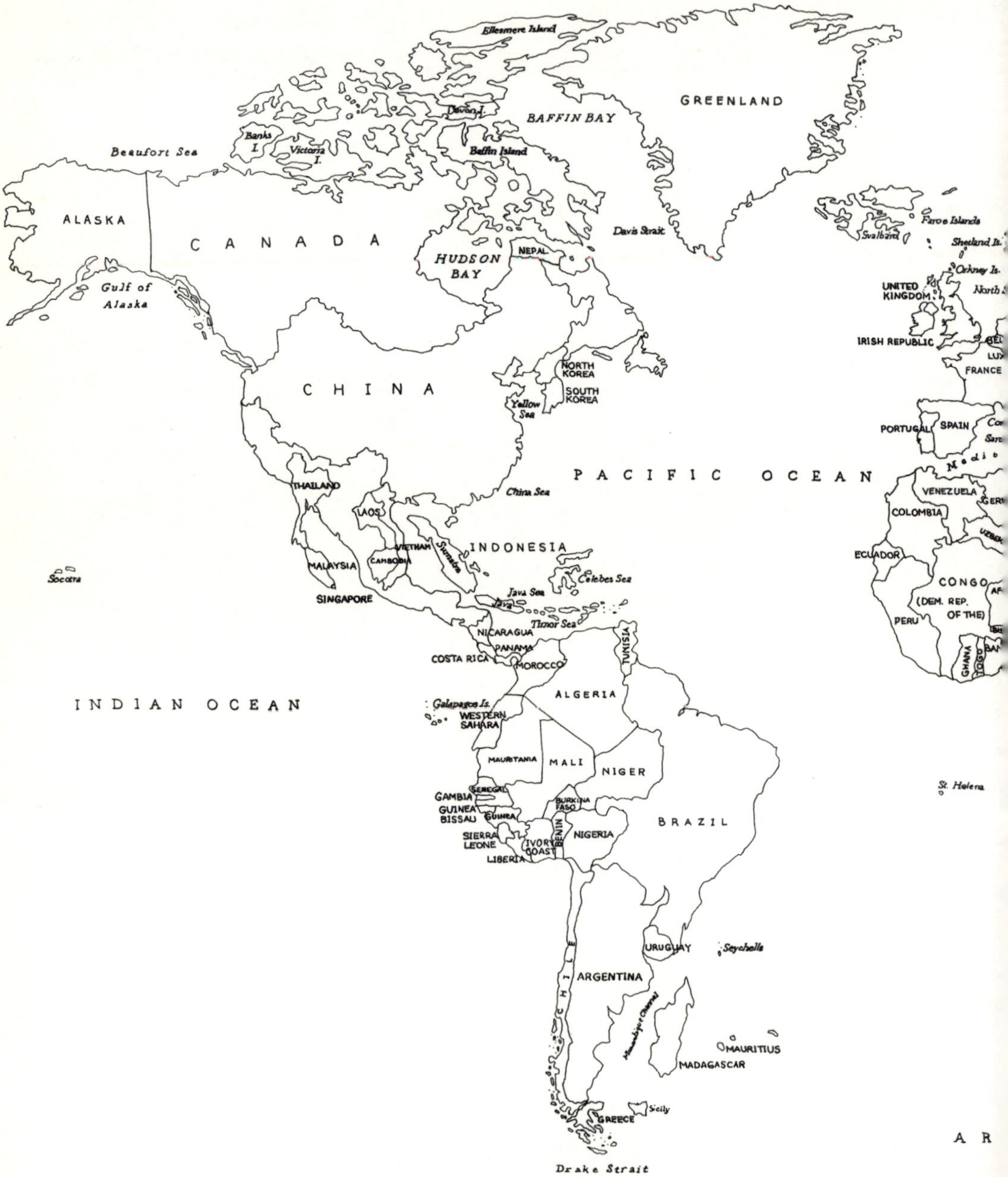
Ellesmere Island
GREENLAND
BAFFIN BAY
Devon I.
Banks I.
Victoria I.
Baffin Island
Beaufort Sea
ALASKA
CANADA
HUDSON BAY
NEPAL
Davis Strait
Svalbard
Faroe Islands
Shetland Is.
Orkney Is.
UNITED KINGDOM
IRISH REPUBLIC
FRANCE
Gulf of Alaska
NORTH KOREA
SOUTH KOREA
Yellow Sea
CHINA
PORTUGAL
SPAIN
PACIFIC OCEAN
THAILAND
China Sea
VENEZUELA
COLOMBIA
LAOS
VIETNAM
Sumatra
INDONESIA
CAMBODIA
MALAYSIA
ECUADOR
Socotra
Celebes Sea
Java Sea
Java
SINGAPORE
CONGO (DEM. REP. OF THE)
PERU
Timor Sea
NICARAGUA
PANAMA
TUNISIA
COSTA RICA
MOROCCO
GHANA
TOGO
ALGERIA
INDIAN OCEAN
Galapagos Is.
WESTERN SAHARA
MAURITANIA
MALI
NIGER
St. Helena
GAMBIA
SENEGAL
BURKINA FASO
GUINEA BISSAU
GUINEA
BRAZIL
SIERRA LEONE
IVORY COAST
BENIN
NIGERIA
LIBERIA
URUGUAY
Seychelles
CHILE
ARGENTINA
Mozambique Channel
MAURITIUS
MADAGASCAR
Sicily
GREECE
Drake Strait

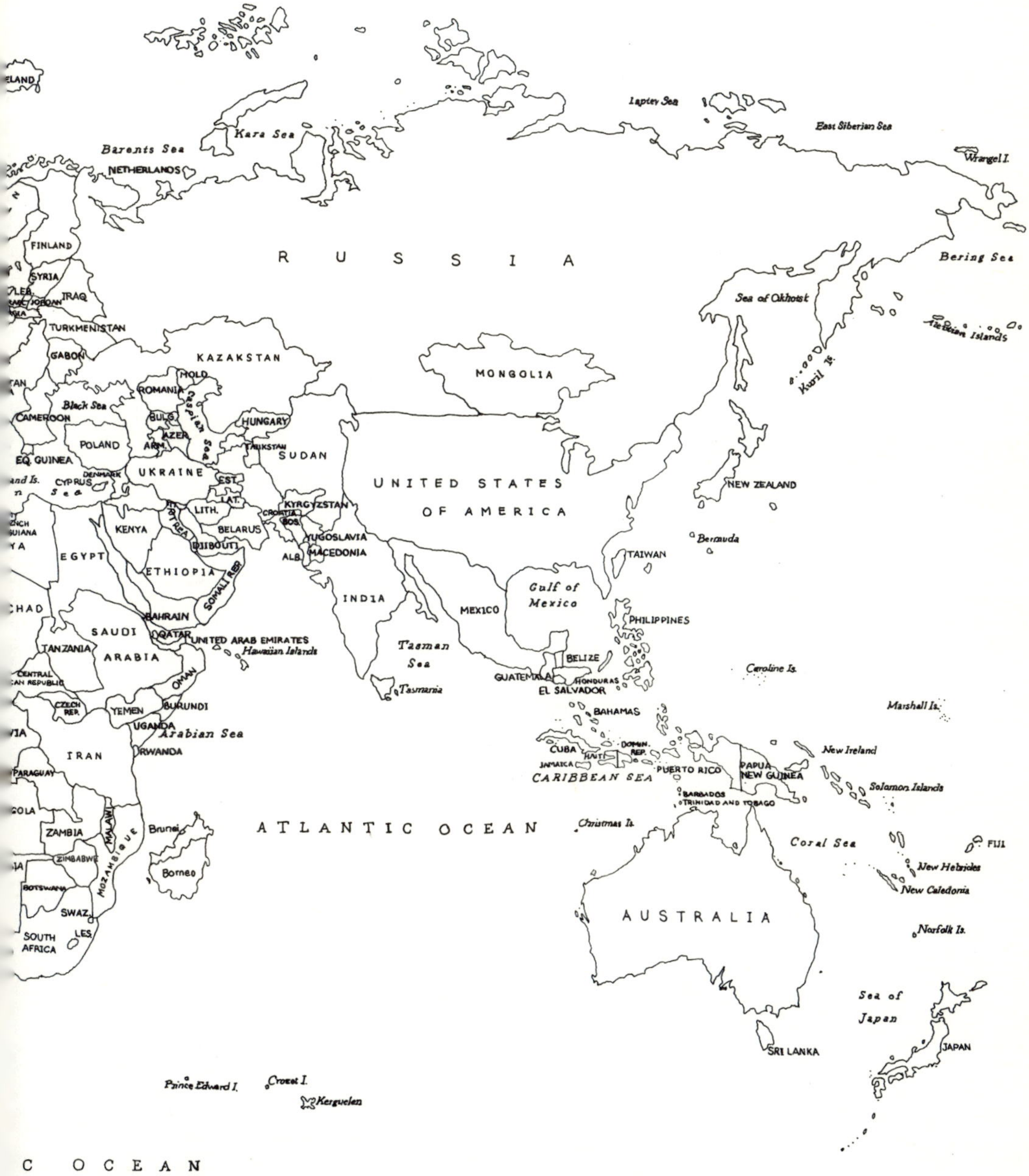
Barents Sea
NETHERLANDS
Kara Sea
Laptev Sea
East Siberian Sea
Wrangel I.
FINLAND
R U S S I A
Bering Sea
SYRIA
IRAQ
Sea of Okhotsk
TURKMENISTAN
Kuril Is.
Aleutian Islands
GABON
KAZAKSTAN
MONGOLIA
MOLD.
ROMANIA
Black Sea
Caspian Sea
CAMEROON
BULG.
HUNGARY
AZER.
POLAND
ARM.
TAJIKSTAN
SUDAN
EQ. GUINEA
UKRAINE
CYPRUS
DENMARK
EST.
UNITED STATES OF AMERICA
NEW ZEALAND
LAT.
LITH.
KYRGYZSTAN
CROATIA
BOS.
KENYA
BELARUS
ERITREA
YUGOSLAVIA
DJIBOUTI
ALB.
MACEDONIA
Bermuda
EGYPT
ETHIOPIA
SOMALI REP.
TAIWAN
INDIA
Gulf of Mexico
CHAD
MEXICO
BAHRAIN
PHILIPPINES
SAUDI ARABIA
QATAR
TANZANIA
UNITED ARAB EMIRATES
Hawaiian Islands
Tasman Sea
BELIZE
CENTRAL AFRICAN REPUBLIC
OMAN
Tasmania
GUATEMALA
HONDURAS
EL SALVADOR
Caroline Is.
CZECH REP.
YEMEN
BURUNDI
BAHAMAS
Marshall Is.
UGANDA
Arabian Sea
IRAN
RWANDA
CUBA
HAITI
DOMIN. REP.
New Ireland
JAMAICA
PUERTO RICO
PAPUA NEW GUINEA
PARAGUAY
CARIBBEAN SEA
Solomon Islands
BARBADOS
TRINIDAD AND TOBAGO
ZAMBIA
MALAWI
Brunei
ATLANTIC OCEAN
Christmas Is.
MOZAMBIQUE
Coral Sea
FIJI
ZIMBABWE
Borneo
New Hebrides
BOTSWANA
New Caledonia
SWAZ.
AUSTRALIA
SOUTH AFRICA
LES.
Norfolk Is.
Sea of Japan
SRI LANKA
JAPAN
Prince Edward I.
Crozet I.
Kerguelen
C OCEAN

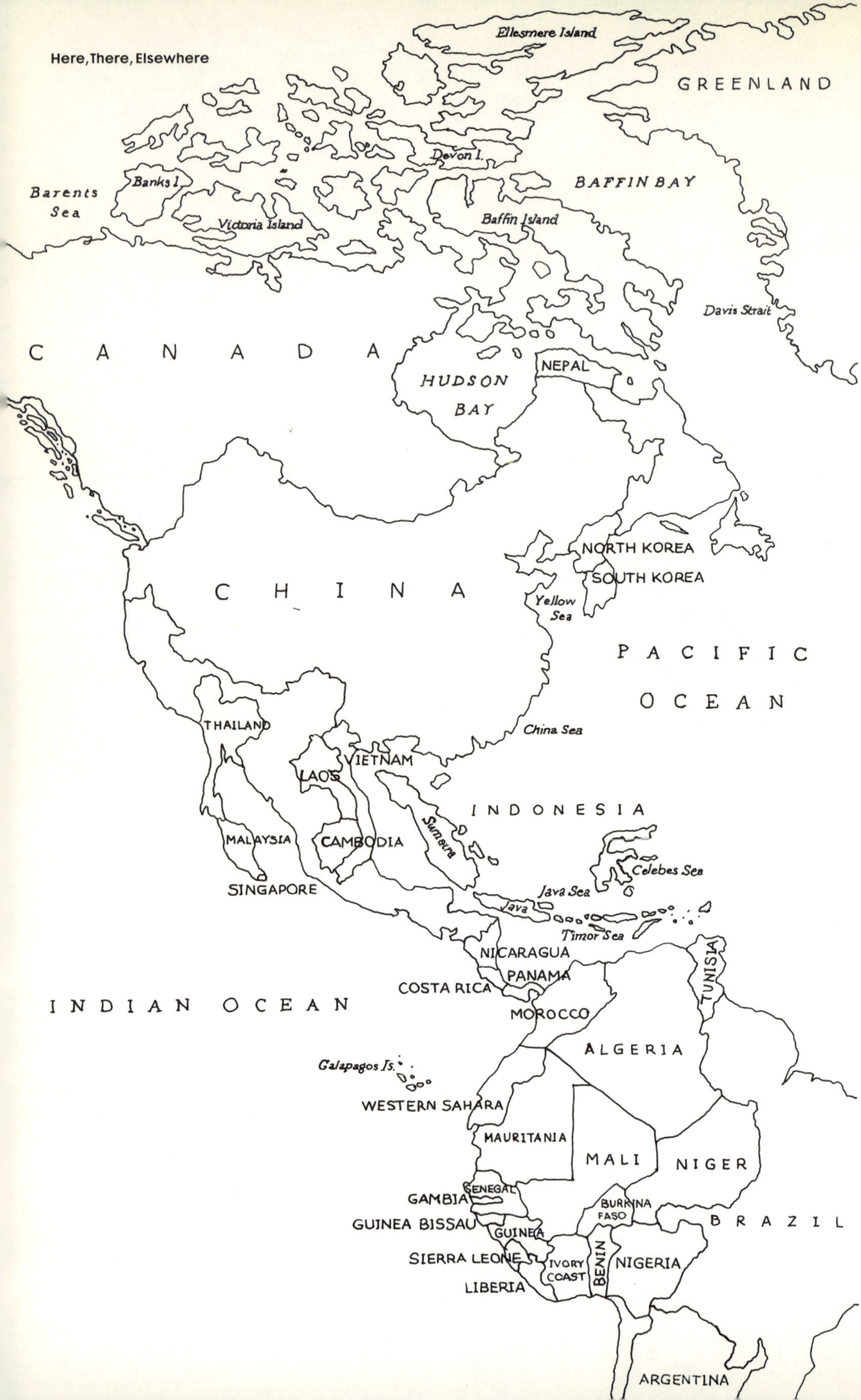
Here, There, Elsewhere
Ellesmere Island
GREENLAND
Devon I.
Banks I.
BAFFIN BAY
Barents Sea
Victoria Island
Baffin Island
Davis Strait
C A N A D A
NEPAL
HUDSON BAY
NORTH KOREA
SOUTH KOREA
C H I N A
Yellow Sea
P A C I F I C
O C E A N
THAILAND
China Sea
VIETNAM
LAOS
INDONESIA
Sumatra
MALAYSIA
CAMBODIA
Celebes Sea
SINGAPORE
Java Sea
Java
Timor Sea
NICARAGUA
TUNISIA
PANAMA
COSTA RICA
INDIAN OCEAN
MOROCCO
ALGERIA
Galapagos Is.
WESTERN SAHARA
MAURITANIA
MALI
NIGER
SENEGAL
GAMBIA
BURKINA FASO
BRAZIL
GUINEA BISSAU
GUINEA
SIERRA LEONE
IVORY COAST
BENIN
NIGERIA
LIBERIA
ARGENTINA

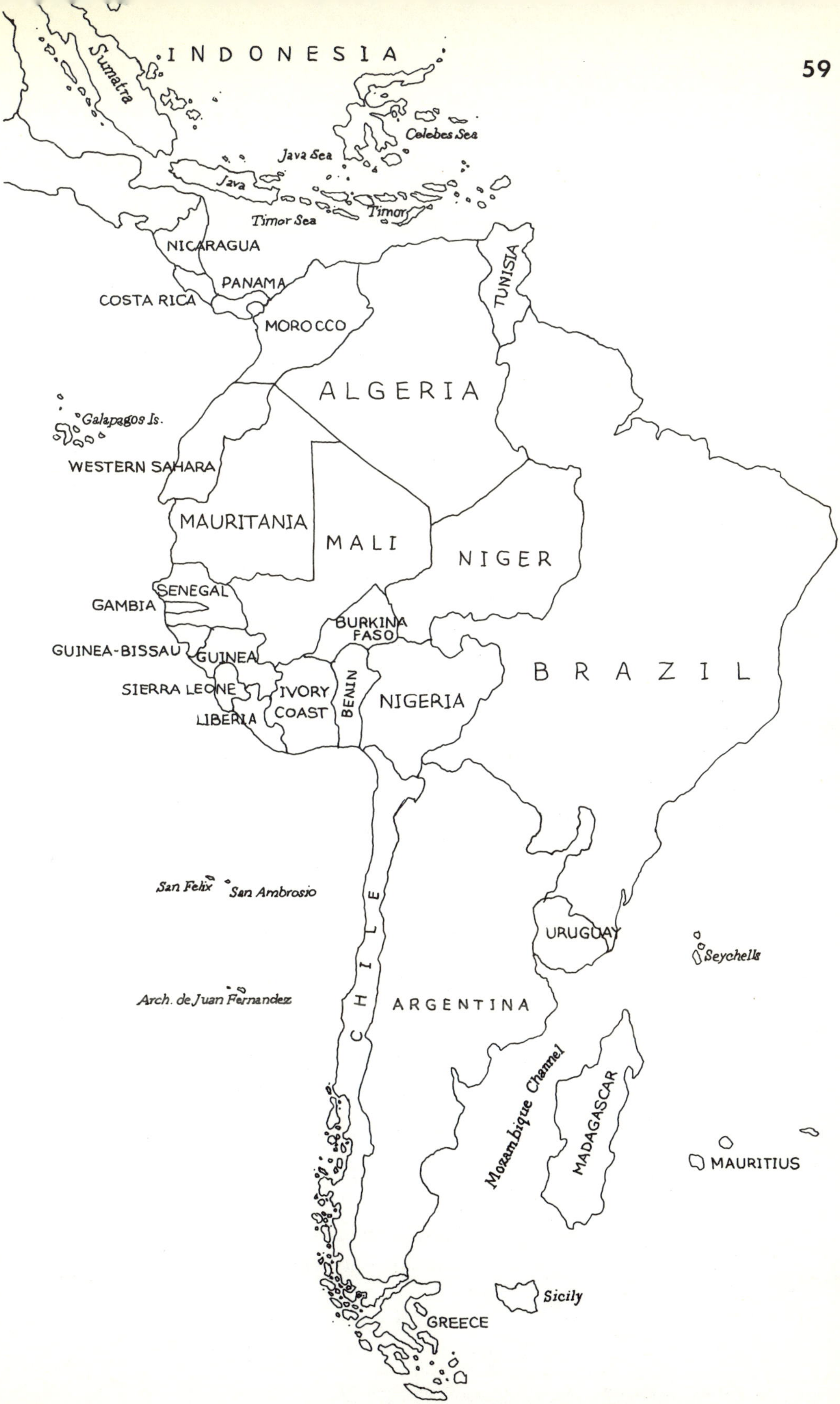
INDONESIA
Sumatra
Celebes Sea
Java Sea
Java
Timor Sea
Timor
NICARAGUA
PANAMA
COSTA RICA
TUNISIA
MOROCCO
ALGERIA
Galapagos Is.
WESTERN SAHARA
MAURITANIA
MALI
NIGER
SENEGAL
GAMBIA
BURKINA FASO
GUINEA-BISSAU
GUINEA
SIERRA LEONE
IVORY COAST
BENIN
NIGERIA
LIBERIA
BRAZIL
San Felix
San Ambrosio
CHILE
URUGUAY
Seychells
Arch. de Juan Fernandez
ARGENTINA
Mozambique Channel
MADAGASCAR
MAURITIUS
Sicily
GREECE

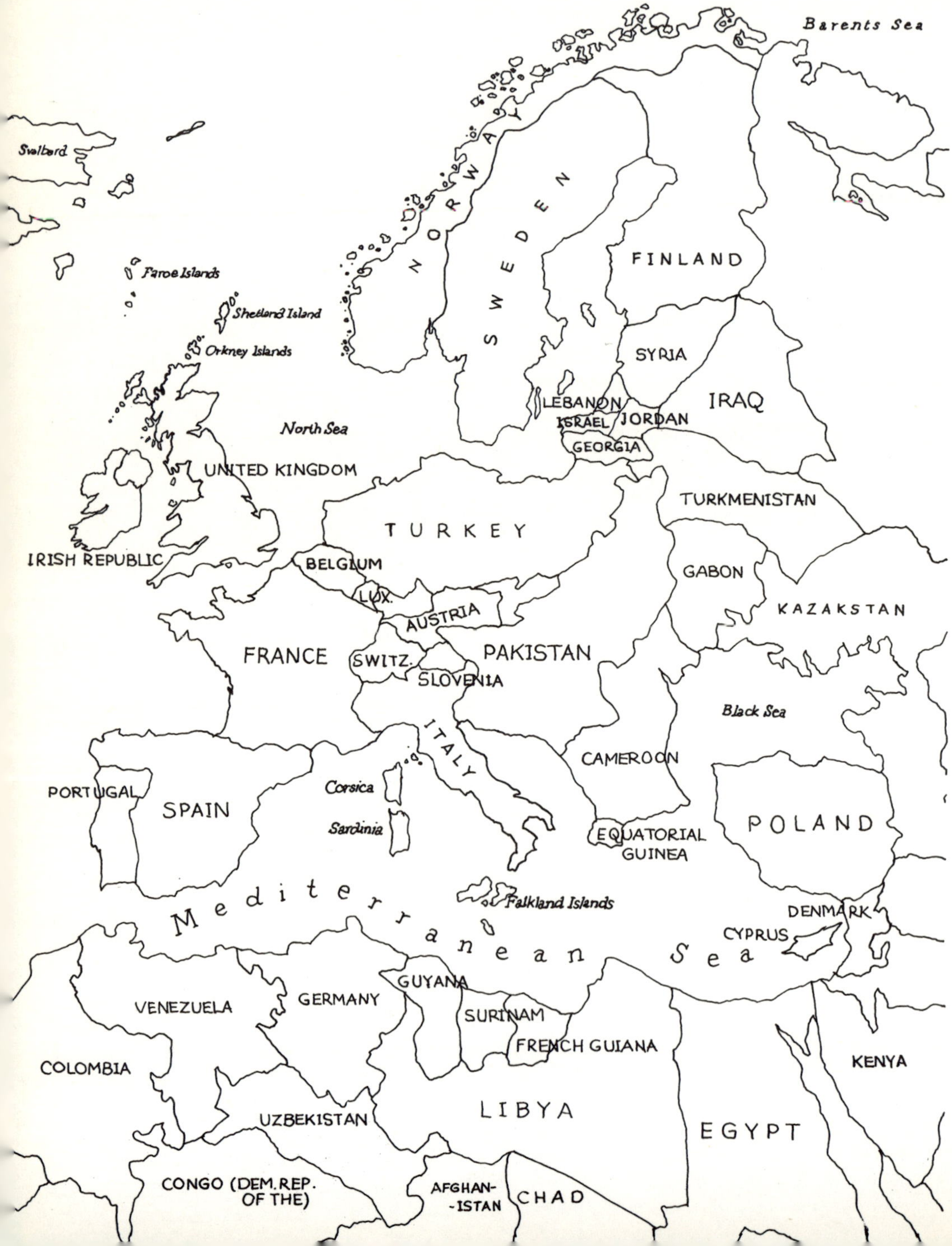
Barents Sea
Svalbard
NORWAY
SWEDEN
FINLAND
Faroe Islands
Shetland Island
Orkney Islands
SYRIA
LEBANON
IRAQ
ISRAEL
JORDAN
GEORGIA
North Sea
UNITED KINGDOM
TURKMENISTAN
TURKEY
IRISH REPUBLIC
BELGIUM
GABON
LUX.
AUSTRIA
KAZAKSTAN
FRANCE
SWITZ.
PAKISTAN
SLOVENIA
Black Sea
ITALY
CAMEROON
PORTUGAL
SPAIN
Corsica
Sardinia
POLAND
EQUATORIAL
GUINEA
Falkland Islands
DENMARK
Mediterranean Sea
CYPRUS
GUYANA
VENEZUELA
GERMANY
SURINAM
FRENCH GUIANA
KENYA
COLOMBIA
UZBEKISTAN
LIBYA
EGYPT
CONGO (DEM. REP.
OF THE)
AFGHAN-
-ISTAN
CHAD

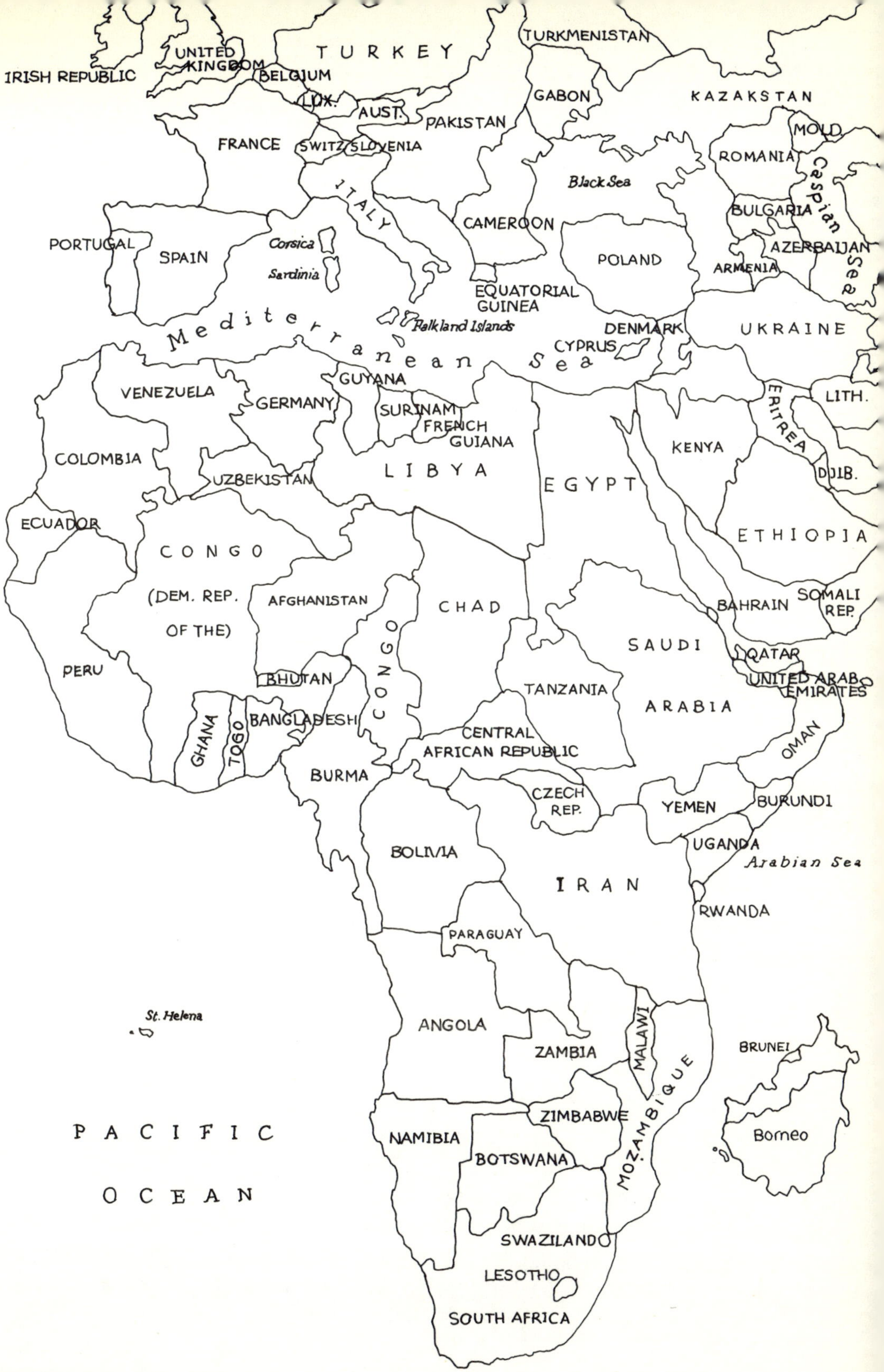
IRISH REPUBLIC
UNITED KINGDOM
BELGIUM
LUX.
TURKEY
TURKMENISTAN
GABON
KAZAKSTAN
AUST.
PAKISTAN
FRANCE
SWITZ.
SLOVENIA
MOLD.
ROMANIA
Caspian Sea
Black Sea
ITALY
CAMEROON
BULGARIA
PORTUGAL
SPAIN
Corsica
Sardinia
POLAND
AZERBAIJAN
ARMENIA
EQUATORIAL GUINEA
Mediterranean Sea
Falkland Islands
DENMARK
UKRAINE
CYPRUS
GUYANA
VENEZUELA
GERMANY
SURINAM
FRENCH GUIANA
LITH.
ERITREA
KENYA
COLOMBIA
LIBYA
EGYPT
DJIB.
UZBEKISTAN
ECUADOR
ETHIOPIA
CONGO (DEM. REP. OF THE)
AFGHANISTAN
CHAD
BAHRAIN
SOMALI REP.
CONGO
SAUDI ARABIA
PERU
QATAR
BHUTAN
UNITED ARAB EMIRATES
TANZANIA
GHANA
TOGO
BANGLADESH
CENTRAL AFRICAN REPUBLIC
OMAN
BURMA
CZECH REP.
YEMEN
BURUNDI
UGANDA
BOLIVIA
Arabian Sea
IRAN
RWANDA
PARAGUAY
St. Helena
ANGOLA
MALAWI
ZAMBIA
BRUNEI
MOZAMBIQUE
PACIFIC OCEAN
ZIMBABWE
NAMIBIA
Borneo
BOTSWANA
SWAZILAND
LESOTHO
SOUTH AFRICA

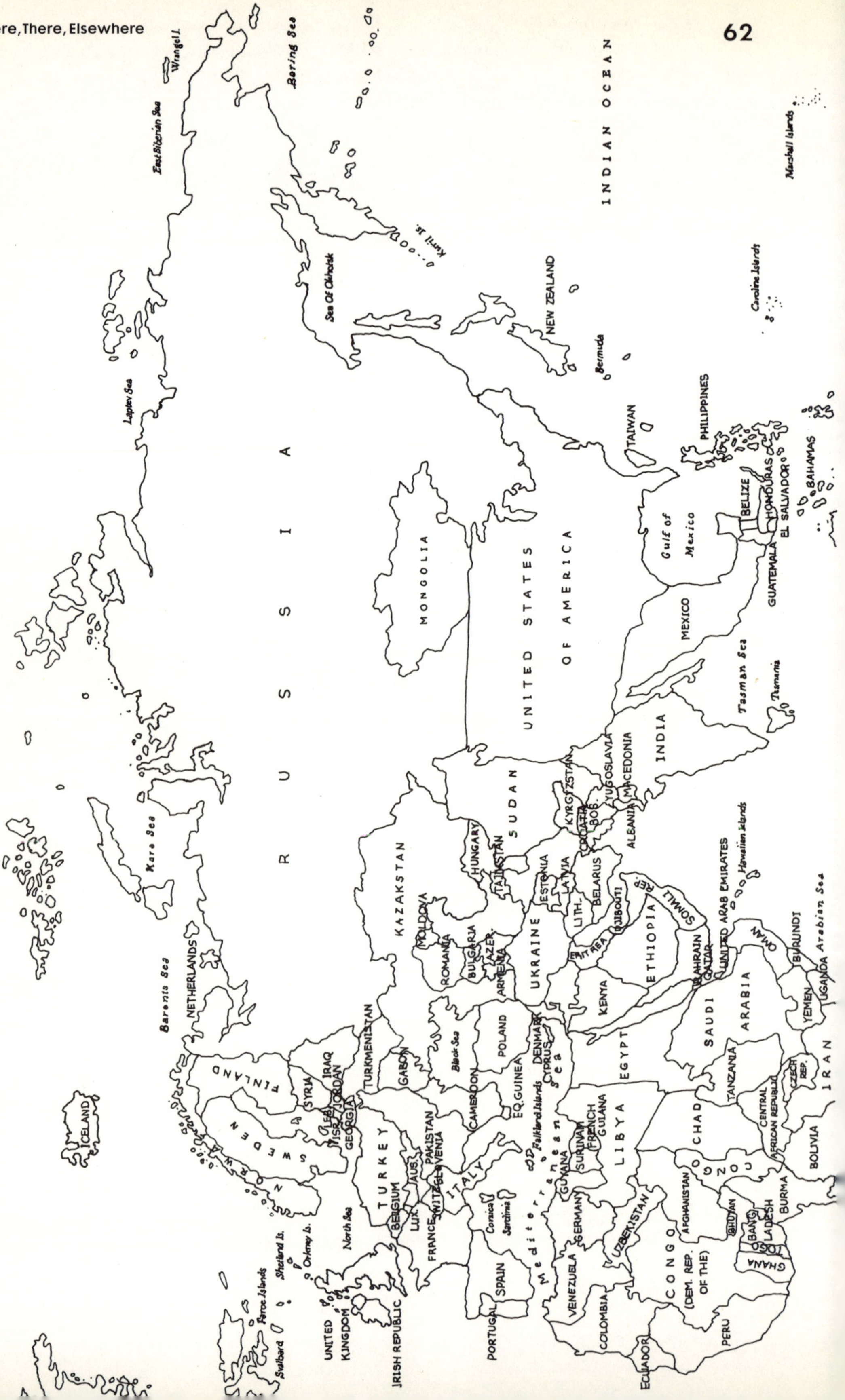
Wrangel I.
Bering Sea
East Siberian Sea
Laptev Sea
Kara Sea
Barents Sea
Sea Of Okhotsk
Kuril Is.
INDIAN OCEAN
Marshall Islands
Caroline Islands
NEW ZEALAND
Bermuda
TAIWAN
PHILIPPINES
BAHAMAS
BELIZE
HONDURAS
EL SALVADOR
GUATEMALA
Gulf of Mexico
MEXICO
Tasman Sea
Tasmania
R U S S I A
MONGOLIA
UNITED STATES OF AMERICA
INDIA
SUDAN
KYRGYZSTAN
YUGOSLAVIA
MACEDONIA
CROATIA
BOS.
ALBANIA
Hawaiian Islands
KAZAKSTAN
HUNGARY
TAJIKISTAN
ESTONIA
LATVIA
LITH.
BELARUS
DJIBOUTI
SOMALI REP.
ETHIOPIA
UNITED ARAB EMIRATES
OMAN
BURUNDI
Arabian Sea
UGANDA
YEMEN
MOLDOVA
ROMANIA
BULGARIA
AZER.
ARMENIA
UKRAINE
ERITREA
KENYA
BAHRAIN
QATAR
SAUDI ARABIA
NETHERLANDS
TURKMENISTAN
GABON
Black Sea
POLAND
DENMARK
CYPRUS
EGYPT
TANZANIA
CZECH REP.
IRAN
FINLAND
SYRIA
IRAQ
JORDAN
LEB.
ISR.
GEORGIA
CAMEROON
EQ. GUINEA
Falkland Islands
Mediterranean Sea
LIBYA
CHAD
CENTRAL AFRICAN REPUBLIC
BOLIVIA
ICELAND
SWEDEN
NORWAY
TURKEY
PAKISTAN
SLOVENIA
AUS.
SWITZ.
ITALY
SURINAM
FRENCH GUIANA
GUYANA
NIGER
AFGHANISTAN
BHUTAN
BURMA
BANGLADESH
TOGO
GHANA
North Sea
Shetland Is.
Orkney Is.
Faroe Islands
BELGIUM
LUX.
FRANCE
Corsica
Sardinia
GERMANY
UZBEKISTAN
CONGO
CONGO (DEM. REP. OF THE)
SPAIN
VENEZUELA
Svalbard
UNITED KINGDOM
IRISH REPUBLIC
PORTUGAL
COLOMBIA
PERU
ECUADOR

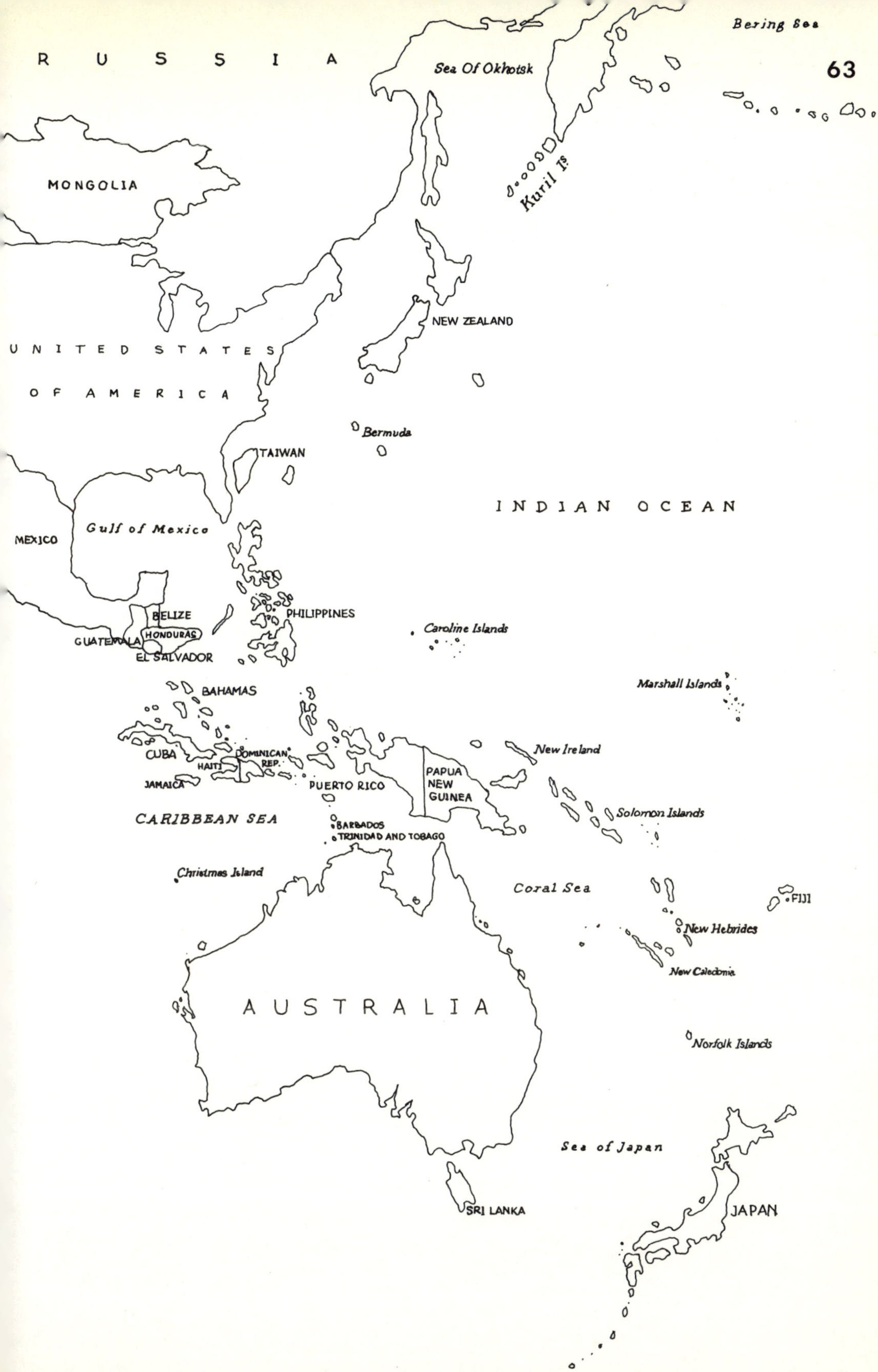
Bering Sea
R U S S I A
Sea Of Okhotsk
MONGOLIA
Kuril Is.
NEW ZEALAND
U N I T E D S T A T E S
O F A M E R I C A
Bermuda
TAIWAN
INDIAN OCEAN
MEXICO
Gulf of Mexico
BELIZE
PHILIPPINES
HONDURAS
GUATEMALA
EL SALVADOR
Caroline Islands
Marshall Islands
BAHAMAS
New Ireland
CUBA
DOMINICAN REP.
HAITI
JAMAICA
PUERTO RICO
PAPUA NEW GUINEA
Solomon Islands
CARIBBEAN SEA
BARBADOS
TRINIDAD AND TOBAGO
Christmas Island
Coral Sea
FIJI
New Hebrides
New Caledonia
AUSTRALIA
Norfolk Islands
Sea of Japan
SRI LANKA
JAPAN

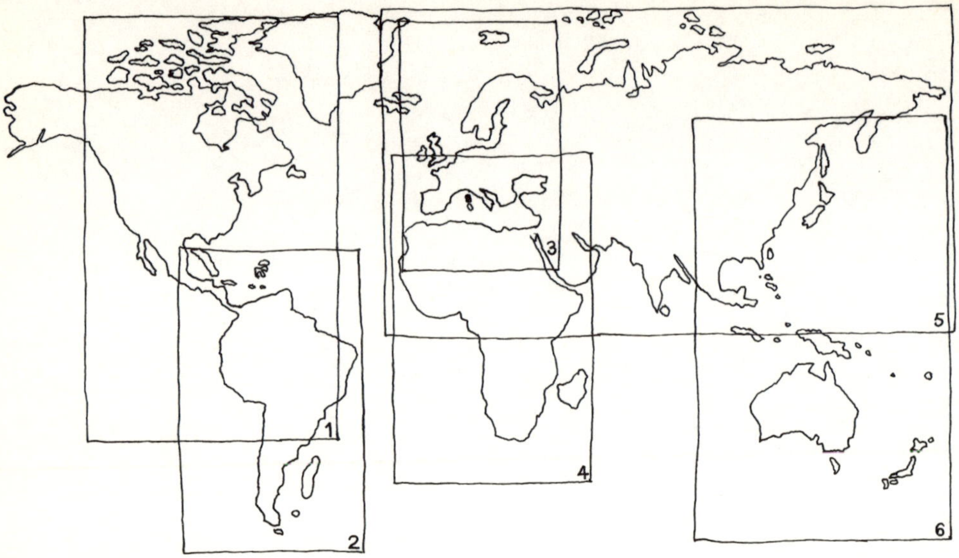

1 North America
2 South America
3 Europe
4 Africa
5 Asia
6 East Asia & Australasia

The Tactics of *Faux* Migration

Doina Petrescu

'Each culture proliferates on its margins'

Mapping marginal phenomena is no longer a marginal undertaking. What remains marginal are the methodologies, paths and rhythms one can adopt with this undertaking. Marginality and migration, their politics and poetics, are a matter of both 'playing' and 'plying'.

The Oas is a region of Northern Romania, close to the frontier between Romania, Ukraine and Hungary. The peasants of Oas represent a new sociological category of *faux* migrant that functions with a double social identity and a double economy. Through migrating initially in search of work the peasants have discovered that they can make a profit by temporarily changing countries and entering a different legal system.

While maintaining their homes in Romania, the Oas migrants periodically leave for the west to obtain the status of 'political asylum seeker'. This enables them to reap the financial and social benefits available to asylum seekers, whilst keeping their domestic economy going at home. In the case of a French asylum application, social assistance consists of 1200F per month, which is double the average Romanian monthly income. Moreover, asylum seekers are entitled to sell the homeless peoples' newspaper, *L'Itinerant* in public places, and earn a supplementary income based on the number of issues sold. Their applications for political asylum are rejected as soon as they are officially processed, but the procedure takes several months. This gives the migrants long enough to make a profitable 'season' out of their trip. Another family member will come back for the next season and continue subsidising the family income in this way.

Compared to the classic model of migration, the new Eastern European migrant no longer seeks settlement in western cities; instead, they look for temporary opportunities and benefits that can be transferred to and recycled within their local economies. These migrants are both attracted by the western model and resistant to it. They subvert the rules and laws of western European societies by interpreting and exploiting them for their own profit. Through their subversive practices, they invent new spatial patterns and forms of mobility. They introduce new dynamics by negotiating boundaries and openings between the new economies, policies, institutions and the social remains of the ancient bipolar division of Europe. This new social phenomenon belongs to both an archaic and a new socio-economic order that succeeds and exceeds the simple communist-capitalist division. It is a mutating structure which corresponds to the everyday realities of an expanding European Union. At the same time, their spatial practices produce alternative ways of living and holds a critical position within the conditions of social and economic mobility in Europe.

The *faux* migrant double economy functions within a phenomenological rule which alternates between stability and instability, legality and illegality, visibility and invisibility. The logic of making oneself invisible during a western season is doubled by the secondary logic of exposure and representation during the eastern part of the cycle. In their home villages, the migrants display their social prestige and economic success through a progressive accumulation of buildings and objects.

Passage Lines

Deleuze opens his article, *Politics* with the following: 'As individuals and groups we are made of lines which are very diverse in nature.' In fact, in order to discuss politics, Deleuze talks about lines as an abstract and complex enough metaphor to map the entire social field, to trace its shapes, its borders and its becomings. They can map the way life proceeds at several rhythms and at several speeds. They map individual cracks and collective breaks within the segmentation and heterogeneity of power. Lines are always attached to geopolitics. Countries are also made out of lines. The lines of frontiers belong to conventions, codes and rules, and not to relations.

Migrants are the products of frontiers. They cross them, forcing their porosity, mocking their political seriousness, but at the same time, they need them, attracted as always by what is on the other side. Codes and rules demand subversion and frontiers similarly demand crossings, deviations and detours, which in turn create other kinds of lines. "The detour seems to come out of a certain idea that 'the straight kind' exists. When one says 'line', one implicitly thinks of it as straight and true." (François Deligny.) Migrants are always asking for 'rights of detour'. A mapping of their existence would comprise of detours and deviations. From frontier to frontier, from periphery to periphery, from squat to squat, the line of migration is always tangled with detours. Deligny has proposed a particular way of mapping the daily lives of autistic children. His cartography traces customary lines and supple lines; where the child makes a curl, finds something, slaps his hands, hums a tune, retraces his steps, and then makes meandering lines, '*lignes d'erre*'.

> ...a *chevêtre* [an entangled curl] is similar to a detour as long as the need for, the cause of this detour escapes our knowledge. The term '*chevêtre*' indicates that there is something there that attracts a profusion of *lignes d'erre*.

If a map of European mobility were to be made, it would be criss-crossed with meandering lines which make detours and deviations from one country to the next, looking for that 'something that attracts'. This map would include lines of migration: entangled customary lines, supple lines and curls indicating other kinds of social behaviour, other economic and political opportunities than the 'straight'. The 'lines of flight' would be an important feature of such a map. Deleuze defines the 'line of flight' not only as a simple line, but as the force that maintains a tangle of lines:

> ...there is a third type of line, stranger still, as though something were carrying us away, through our segments but also across our thresholds, towards an unknown destination, neither pre-existent nor foreseeable.

"I came here by flight" says a migrant, referring to the illegal way he crossed over the frontiers of several countries on his way to France, "and I will return by the sending-off" which in French immigration legislation means a plane ticket with financial assistance of about 1000F for reinstatement in the country of origin. A new kind of logic recalculates this 'sending-off', this 'going back home', as the real purpose of initial departure. Nothing happens other than a detour, a curl, a delay, and a subsidy. This 'curling' logic transforms impedimenta into pathways, obstacles into objectives, conflicts into alliances, policies of rejection into politics of welcoming. It transforms a 'bad end' into 'happy end'.

The migrant's main objective is to make profit from a line of flight. They have invented a new market product that is the migration itself, the double crossing of a frontier, the transversion, a movement by detour, the pure displacement of a person from one country to another and back again.

Analogies and Diagrams of Life

The politics which negotiate so many entangled 'lines' must stick to a diagram. For the destiny of an individual or a group, the diagram is the profitable 'passage through catastrophe'. Deleuze talks about diagram in the context of Francis Bacon's painting and notices that, 'the diagram is chaotic, a catastrophe, but also a germ of order or rhythm'. For migrants, 'losing everything', 'leaving it all behind' is not a tragedy but a trick. Playing as if all is lost is to put oneself in a state of diagram, in a 'state of factual possibility', as Deleuze says. It transforms the impossible into a state of possibility. "How did you get here?" The migrant replies mockingly, "I walked across the garden." In this logic, the garden of the migrant's family house extends topologically as far as Paris, just as the mouth in some of Bacon's portraits goes from one edge of the face to the other. According to Deleuze:

> The diagram is therefore the operative totality of insignificant and non-representative, lines and zones, traits and spots.

A community is not made up exclusively of 'individual lines' but integrates equally 'insignificant and non-representative' zones, lines and spots of places and things with which individuals co-habit and operate diagrammatically in their practice of migration. Deleuze has observed that the language of the diagram is analogical:

> It is the notion of modulation (and not that of sameness) that is generally apt to make us understand the nature of the analogical language or the diagram. Modulation, which functions in the analogical synthesisers as an addition of 'intensive subtractions'.

Notions of 'subtraction' and 'intensity' can be associated with migration. Migration functions as a modulator for the social field. The migrants respect codes and conventions so long as they can be modulated. They make their own intensive subtractions and transport them to make an addition somewhere else. They are practising a 'relational' way of doing things within the conventional thought structure. But, for the migrant the analogy is not simply a way of doing but a policy which is enacted from thing to thing, person to person, situation to situation. A policy based on analogy is more precise, clearer, and more adequate to the practice of migration than a policy ruled by codes and norms. Know-how, tricks and lucky finds are linked by proximity. Analogical thought works by correspondence, not by comparison. As imaginative insight it recognises something familiar in the alien and unfamiliar. The migrant reading of the alien cityscape keeps the familiar at hand. The Romanian migrants that squat abandoned houses near *La Defense* (the main business district in Paris) call the *Grande Arche*, 'the great granary'. The biggest square in the district is called 'the vague field' – the place where they cross paths with tourists and financial officials during the week, and play football on Sundays. This particular way of naming places shows how the hostile environment of a financial metropolis can be compressed and reduced to the size of a village.

The home environment is kept in everyday language in the same way that personal belongings are kept in plastic bags in the squat. Living out of plastic bags is a way of living in the metropolis whilst resisting it. The configuration of the native village, the order of streets and houses are topologically compressed within the squat. Neighbourhoods and familial relations regulate the occupation of rooms. Boundaries transported from home with their existing customs modulate the intimate conditions within the promiscuity of the squat. The intimate, the private and the collective are kept separate and allowed to cross each other through discrete boundaries. As a dwelling place for several families, the room becomes an intense and complicated space. Under these conditions, the borders of intimacy are continually subject to negotiation. "And making love? We manage. We acknowledge it by posters on the door."

The whole creative, poetical power of analogy resides in finding possible correspondences and connections between mutually exclusive modes of otherness. The inner logic of the squat comprises of subtractions, additions, mixtures and compressions of displaced elements.

'Squat' is itself a migrant word. It came originally from the Old French *esquatir* – 'to flatten', and acquired new meanings in English and then re-entered modern French. *Esquatir* comes originally from the Latin *decogo, cogere* – to compel, to bring about by force, to condense, to contract.

In the same way, elements of metropolitan life are brought back to the village and flattened together to create a capitalist appearance within an ex-socialist lifestyle. Western materials, shapes, objects, habits and words are all displaced and reinterpreted locally. Western expenditure and

Opposite: Squat near La Defense, Paris, January, 1998. One single room acts as bedroom, wardrobe and kitchen for 2-3 families. Time spent in such a space could vary between several days and several months, according to the time schedule for the evacuation of the squatters and the demolition of the building. Photograph: D Petrescu.

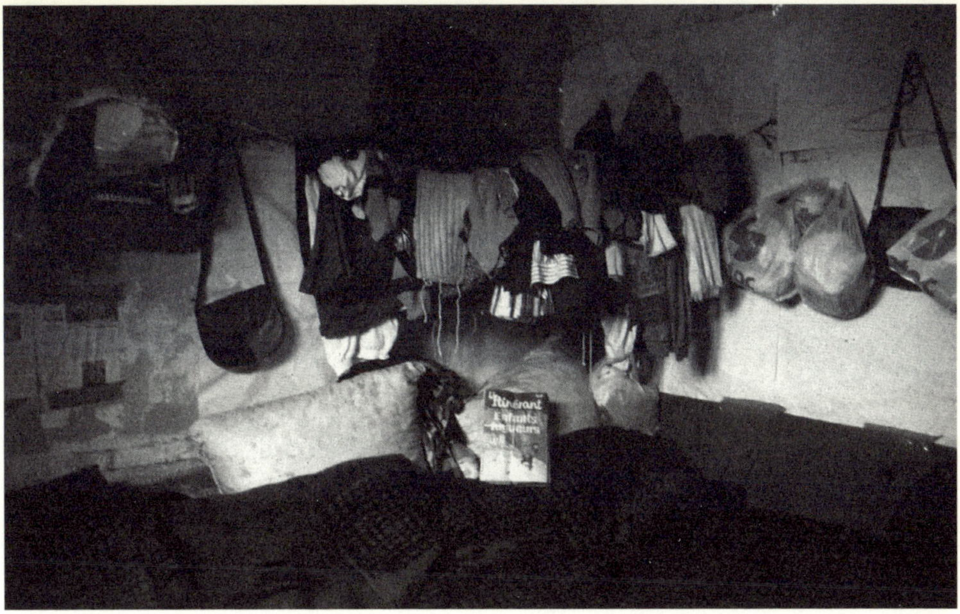

consumption are simulated without contradicting the existing mentalities of saving and spending. The excess can be read in the façade: "Let's put in an extra window – people will think I have an extra bedroom". The rules of metropolitan living are displaced and parodied. With their emphasis on appearance and display, the peasants' home villas are extremely impractical and uncomfortable in spite of their generous proportions.

Tactics

A culture of simulation is a culture of opportunism and profit. The tactic of copying a pattern, reproducing it and selling it, is always more profitable over time that the pattern itself. All tactics are time-based procedures. According to de Certeau:

> Tactics are procedures which gain validity in relation to the pertinence they lend to time, to the circumstances which the precise instant of an intervention transforms into a favourable situation, to the rapidity of the movements that change the organisation of space, to the relations among successive moments in an action, to the possible intersections of duration and heterogeneous rhythms.

The migrant's economic profit is based on management of the time between the completion of an application for political asylum and the 'sending-off' which returns them home. Their asylum applications are automatically rejected, but that was the idea behind them. The application refusal is calculated from the outset. The Oas migrants have no desire to stay permanently and the applications are merely part of a strategy to obtain time. During this acquired time the migrants receive financial assistance from the French government, social assistance from the Red Cross and are allowed to sell *L'Itinerant*. The tactic consists of creating a delay and then profiting from it. They work on time, with time, against time, rendering time capable of performing economically, and associating the self-timing of bureaucratic administrative systems with the speed of the savage financial performance.

Enjoying time

'We have nothing that is ours except time, which even those without a roof can enjoy', observed Guy Debord in quoting Baltasar Gracian in the motto of, *Society of the Spectacle*. Debord talks about time-merchandise, time as an exchangeable value, devalued or pseudo-valued time. Situationists by definition, the migrants reconsider the value of time – enjoy its liquid qualities, its economic and spectacular aspects.

> By virtue of the resulting space of play, and by virtue of freely chosen variations in the rules of the game, the independence of places will be rediscovered without any new exclusive tie to the soil, and thus too the authentic journey will be restored to us, along with authentic life understood as a journey containing its whole meaning within itself.

The migrants know how to take advantage of time, how to reside and profit from their mobility, how to invent economic games and put into play both their spaces, places and their lives. The migratory practice implies a 'drift' stage, which extends from the scale of a locality to the scale of several countries. Variations in speed are regulated by both unexpected decisions and long term elaborated desires. The trajectories are always different, depending on the opportunities of movement and passage. The journey to the west, the 'flight', is generally a journey by foot which takes several months and involves continual negotiations with the existing conditions for clandestine travel. The way back, the 'sending-off', is usually the result of an official decision to expel the applicant and the journey takes only an hour or two.

Putting space into ply. Plying travels. Plying for money. Plying with residence. Plying between places. Playing with plies of time. Playing with pleasure.

Jokes

Migration is perhaps to the social field what 'pleasure' is to the 'text'. According to Barthes:

> Pleasure is not an element of the text, it is not a naive residue; it does not depend on a logic of understanding, and on sensation; it is a drift, something both revolutionary and asocial, and it cannot be taken over by any collectivity, any mentality, any idiolect. Something neuter? It is obvious that the pleasure of the text is scandalous: not because it is immoral but because it is atopic.

Atopical by definition, the migrants' practices make them scandalous. They are revolutionary in the same way as the Situationists because, dissatisfied with being consumers of products, they have become consumers of 'social and civic opportunities'. For the same reason they are also asocial because they divert and skirt the rules of democratic society. Revolutionary, they reverse and recycle the legislation according to social reality and are able to convert the illegal into legal. Asocial, they take advantage of social rifts, defects and slowness. While profiting from the remains of outdated laws and administrative procedures, they make economic use of the urban environment by reusing leftover, unoccupied spaces. Despite their ignorance of the language and rules of the place they travel to, the peasants are successful in establishing their own markers, both individual and collective. They develop human networks that involve border passing intermediators, visa providers, employees, lawyers and policemen. They take advantage of both the interstices of cities and of rules and laws. They pitch this human network against the institutional network and tackle administrative automatism with radical subjectivity. The migrants' methods are comparable to what Freud calls, 'the technique of Witz' (the technique of jokes) and the disruptions caused by 'the return of the repressed': verbal economy and condensation, double meaning and misinterpretations, displacements and alliterations, multiple uses of the same material.

The Oas peasants misuse laws and rules, cross and displace habits and expectations. In Paris they live in squats, but in their villages they live in huge villas. Similarly, the Witz brings together diverse things and thoughts, condenses, combines or marries them in a misalliance that makes the listener laugh, and can even surprise the joke-teller. The *faux* migrant's tactics don't exactly make the administrative authorities laugh; instead they leave them open-mouthed at their own bureaucratic inefficiency.

The Witz – the comic and the humorous – are, according to Freud, means of libidinal saving. Saving money is the migrant's declared purpose. If 'dream work' is an individual product, the Witz is a social product. It can only exist through a community, by an 'economic necessity of a third', by hawking, by migration. The technique of Witz consists of juxtaposing disparate elements to produce a sudden flash which sheds a different light on the customary meaning of language. De Certeau speaks about the art of 'pulling tricks' and 'taking an order by surprise'. 'Cross-cuts, fragments, cracks and lucky hits in the framework of a system' – these are the migrants' equivalents of Witz, but instead of language and linguistic constructs, they are attacking laws and policies.

In *The Pleasure of the Text*, Barthes speaks about 'a subtle subversion':

> By subtle subversion I mean, on the contrary, what is not directly concerned with destruction evades the paradigm and seeks some other term: a third term, which is not, however, a synthesising term but an eccentric, extraordinary term. An example? Perhaps Bataille, who eludes the idealist term by an unexpected materialism in which we find voice, devotion, play, impossible eroticism; thus Bataille does not counter modesty with sexual freedom but...with laughter.

To the serious 'idealism' and 'modesty' of western democracy, the Romanian migrants oppose what Barthes calls, 'an unexpected materialism', the materialism of a Bataillan burst of laughter which shakes the good manners of the established system of welcome and exchange. The 'unexpected materialism', as well as the 'laughter', does not belong to the dialectical materialism of the Marxist-Leninist ideology that the peasants have experienced in Romania but rather to a Batallian 'base-materialism' that was already operating during the communist period, inside and within this ideology. The same 'base-materialism' proves to be good enough to undermine also the 'ideal materialism' of western capitalism.

Networking with Thresholds

Within their practice, the *faux* migrants identify thresholds between logics, politics, laws and economies. For the Oas peasants, the threshold is their working space. By selling newspapers in front of the city's most profitable market places, they are developing a whole new economy on the threshold. According to one recent sociological study, 'within a year, the Romanian peasants established the most successful network for selling the newspaper *L'Itinerant*. By making an inventory of thresholds and places of passage in the city while considering their profit value, the peasants have completely re-mapped the urban space and located a network of invisible economic values which correspond to their own market system. This threshold infrastructure derives from specific kinds of movement in the city. The thresholds of supermarkets are places where capitalist flows take place and are, as such, strategic places to catch these flows and to drain and divert them.

The migrants' temporary occupation of thresholds is based on the *detournement* of both private and public space. With their spatial and economic investment in the thresholds, they intensify and complicate the traditional uses of space in the city. As with drifting, random encounters take place at the thresholds where successful trading depends on emotional relationships. Rather than the newspaper, the migrants are selling their own condition. This threshold selling is in itself a critique of the conventional urban culture, which operates in the zone of subjective experience. It is a spatial and economic experience, powered by the body. At the threshold, instead of bartering their merchandise, the migrants display themselves. As marginals, the *faux* migrants combine neo-liberal practices and post-communist ideologies through tactics, analogies, diagrams and jokes. They map without moralising the thresholds of an expanding European Union and its lines of flight.

The Street Museum

Colectivo Cambalache

Top:
The 'Swift'
Plaza Che Guevara,
Universidad Nacional
Bogotá

Bottom:
Impromptu installation
Facultad de Artes Plásticas
Universidad Nacional
Bogotá

Opposite:
Carrera 30
Street Bench Installation,
Bogotá. Objects include:
Hair band, pencil case with
Columbian Cherry Cola logo,
purses, personal organisers,
beauty products, 'Olleta'
chocolate drink vessel etc.

More information p 261.

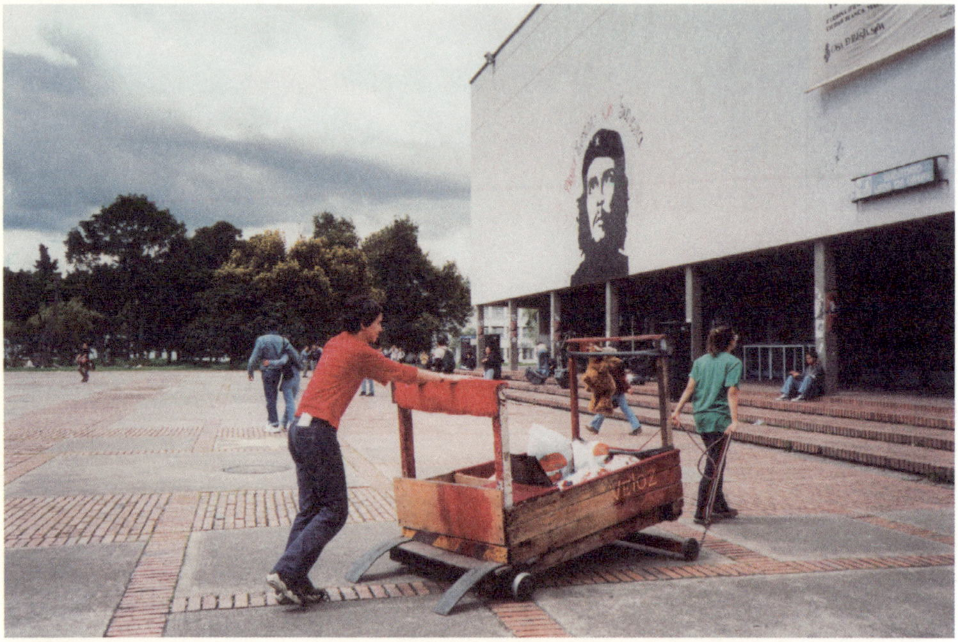

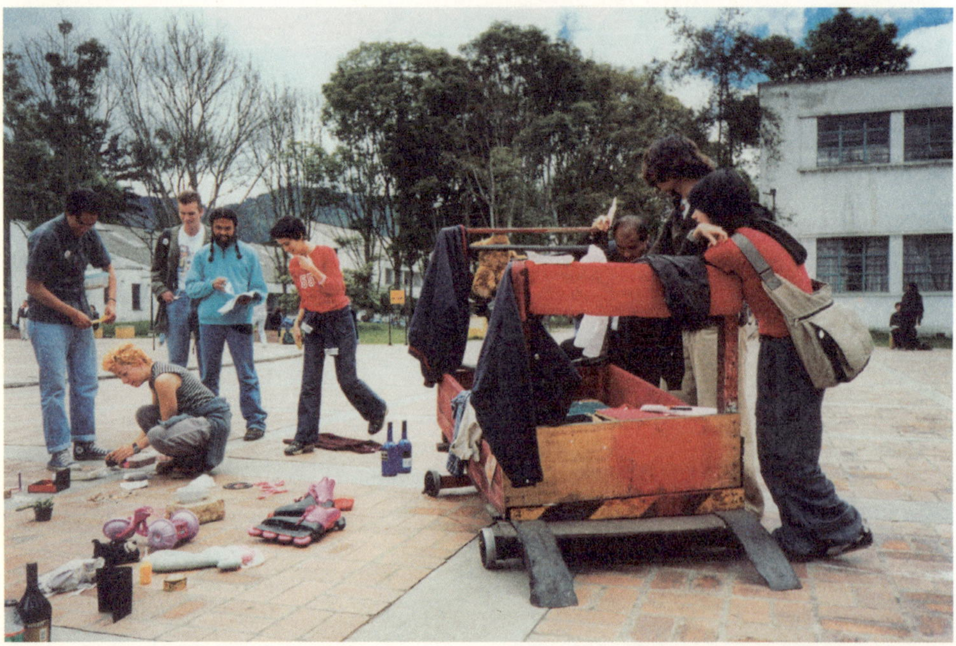

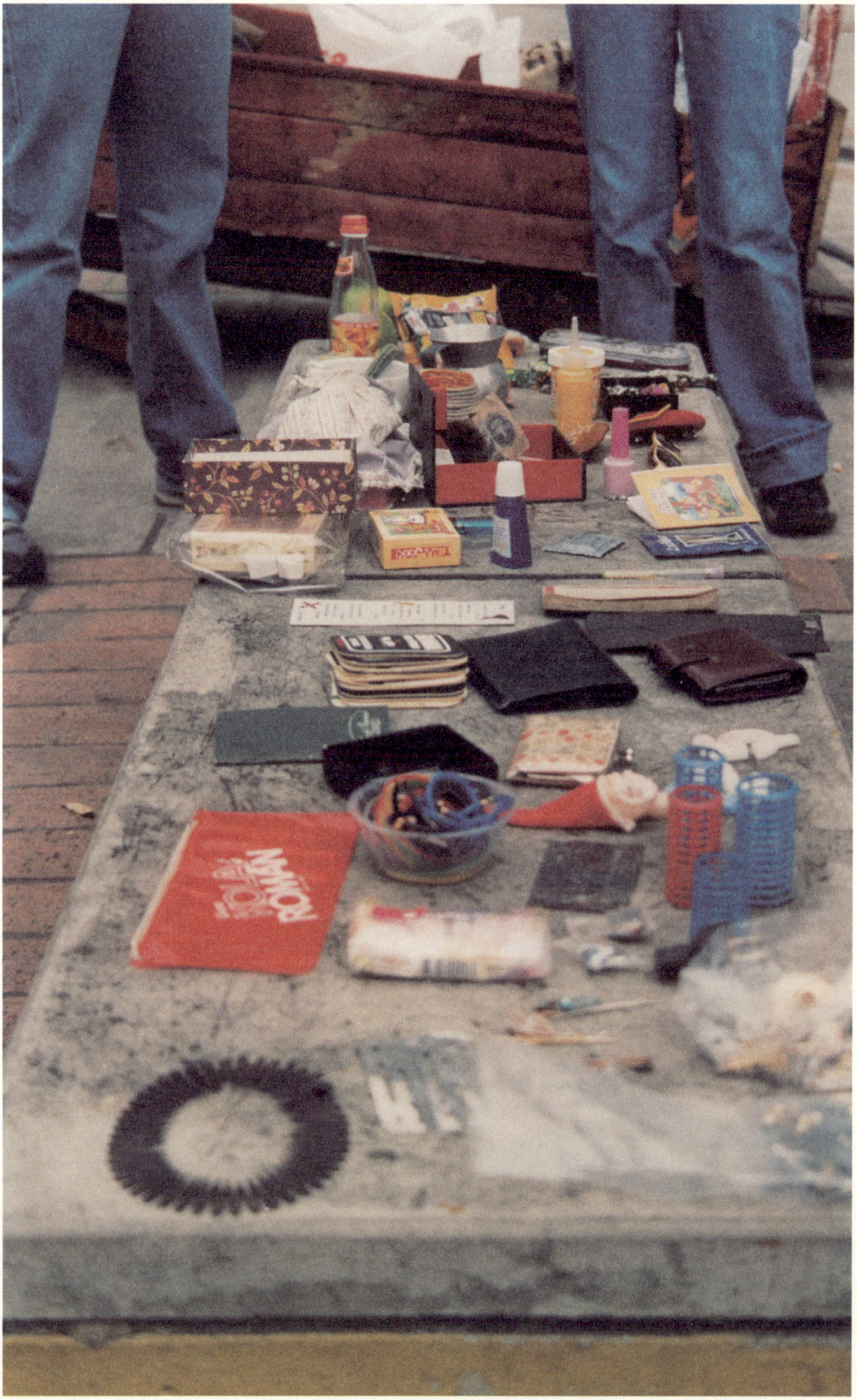

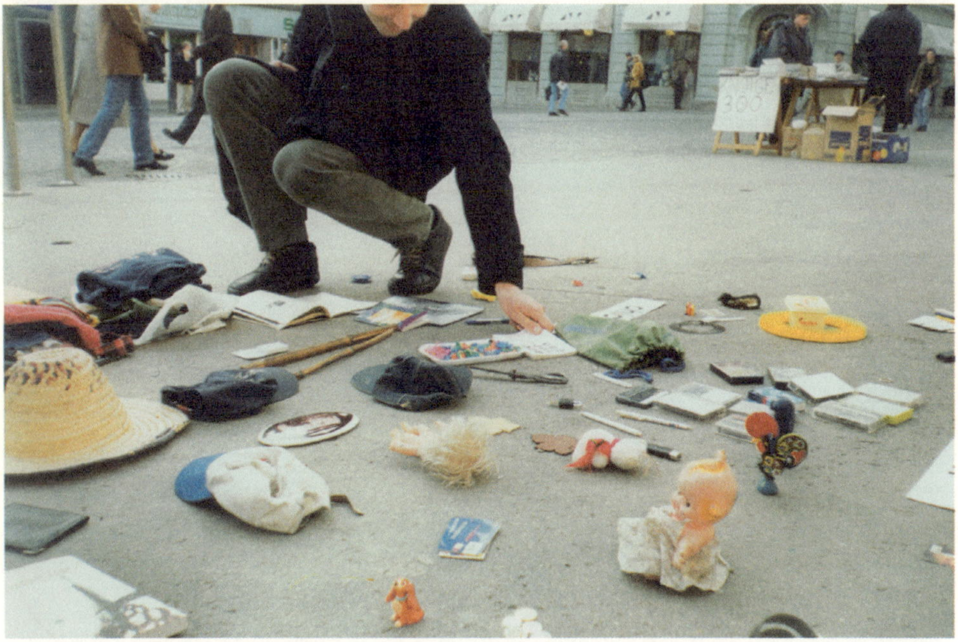

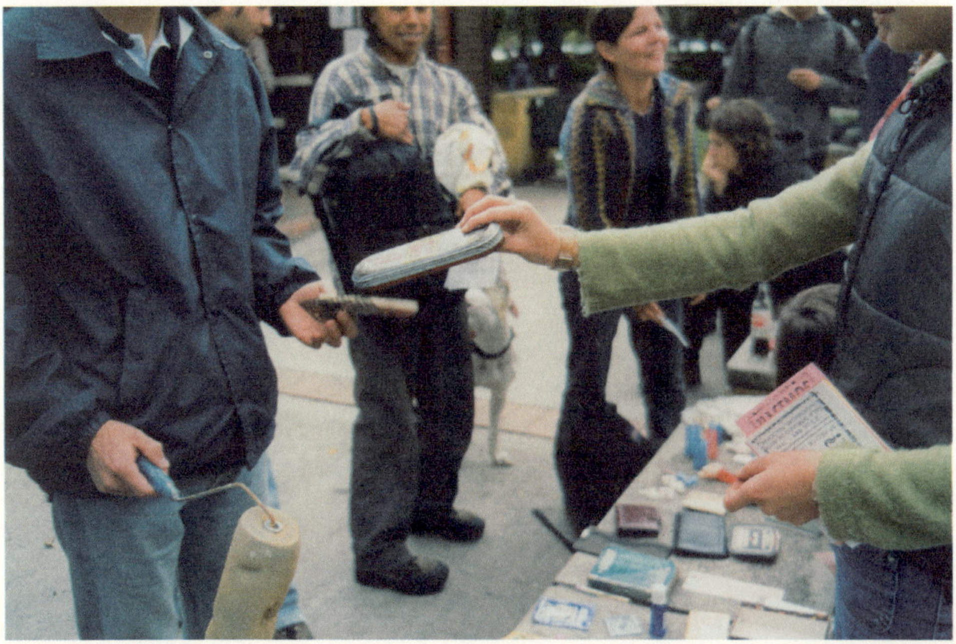

Top:
Display of Street Museum objects from Columbia and Slovenia. Impromptu street installation, Copova Ulica, Ljubljana

Bottom:
Exchange of objects
Carrera 30
Street Bench Installation
Bogotá

Top:
Impromptu street installation showing detail of display sections: Hair products and Pens.
Viejo San Juan, Puerto Rico

Bottom:
Street Museum
Impromptu street installation
Viejo San Juan, Puerto Rico

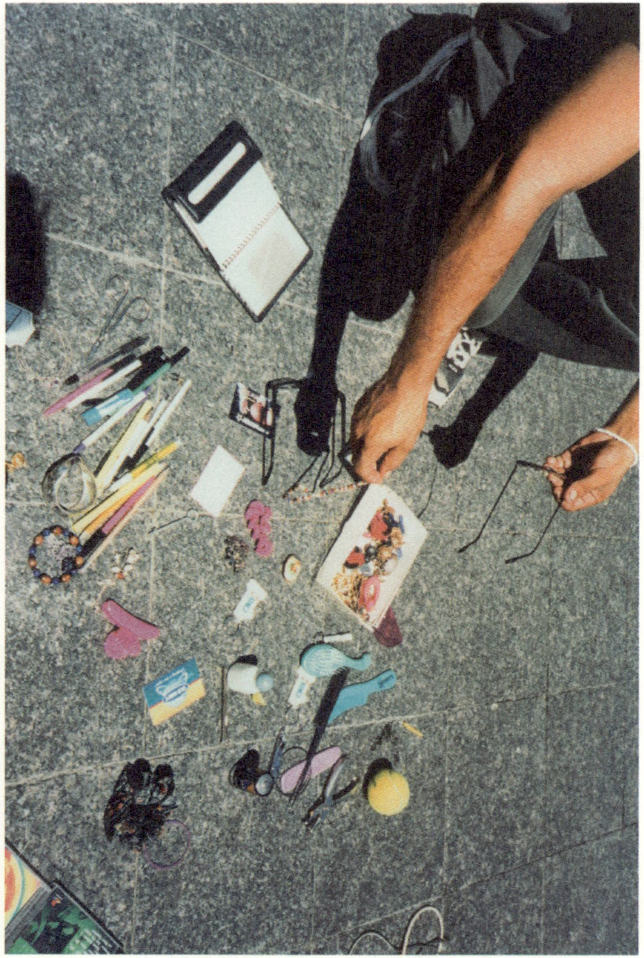

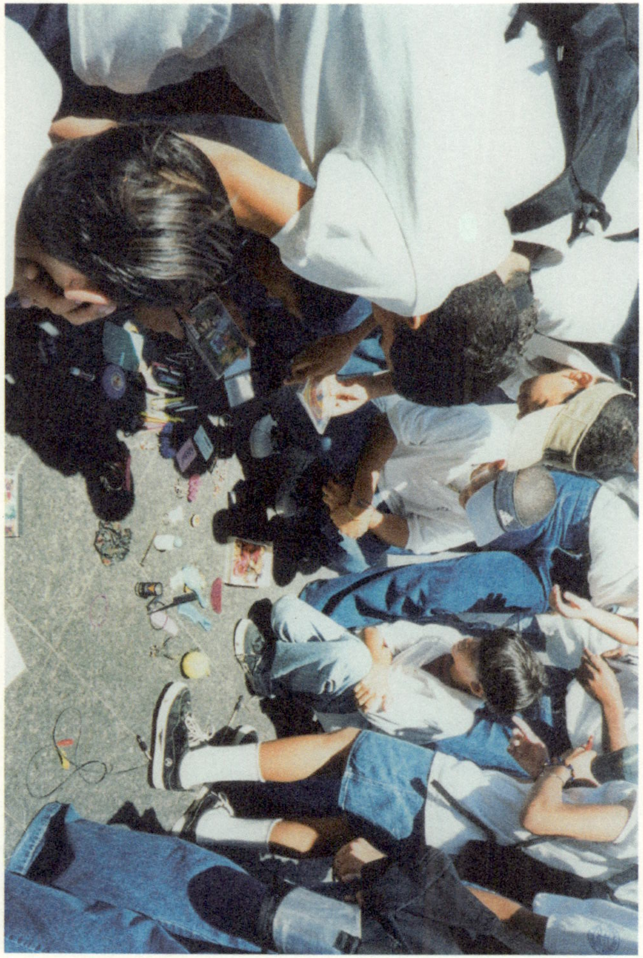

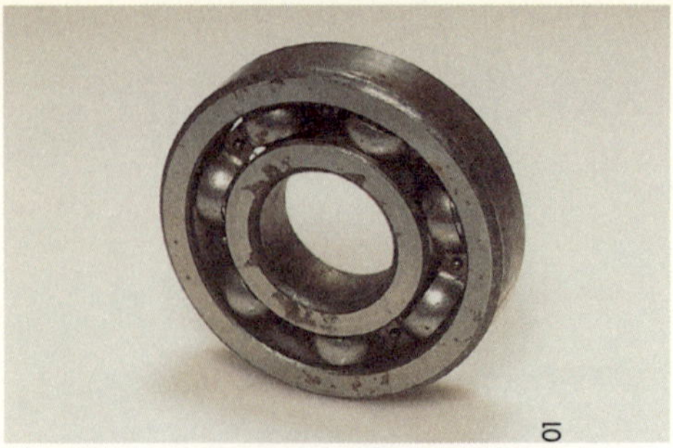

01

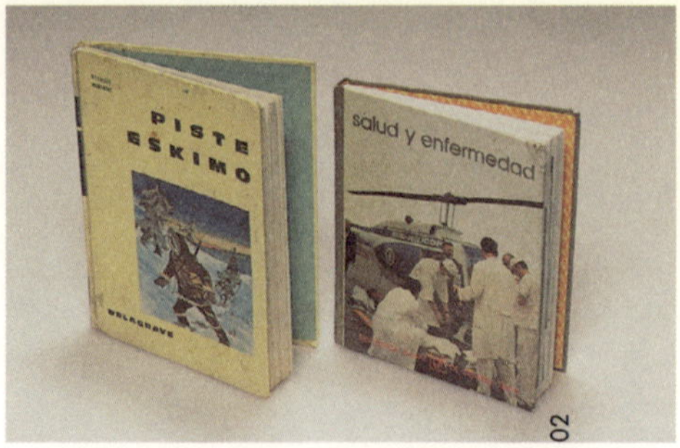

02

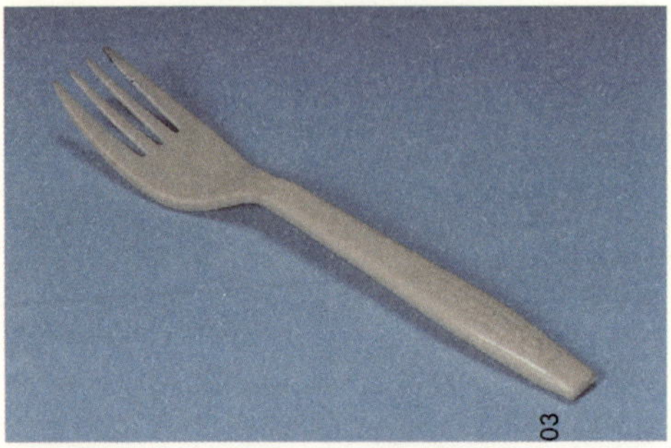

03

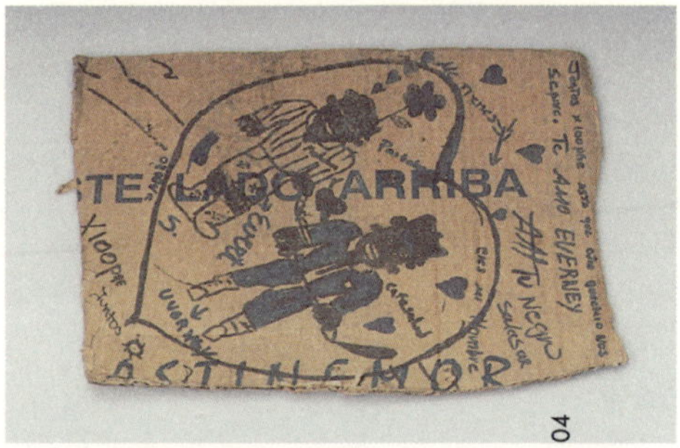

04

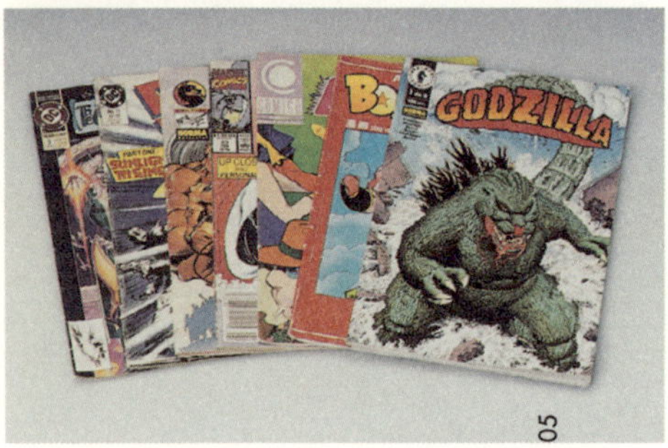

05

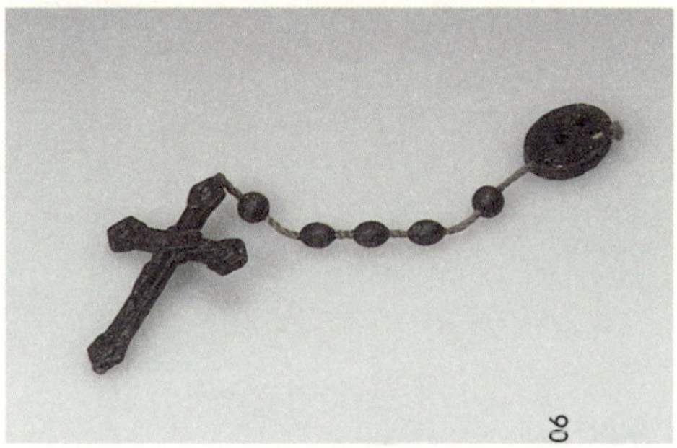

06

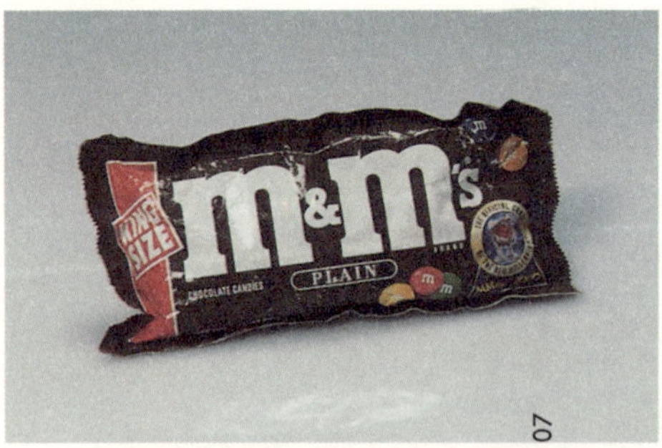

07

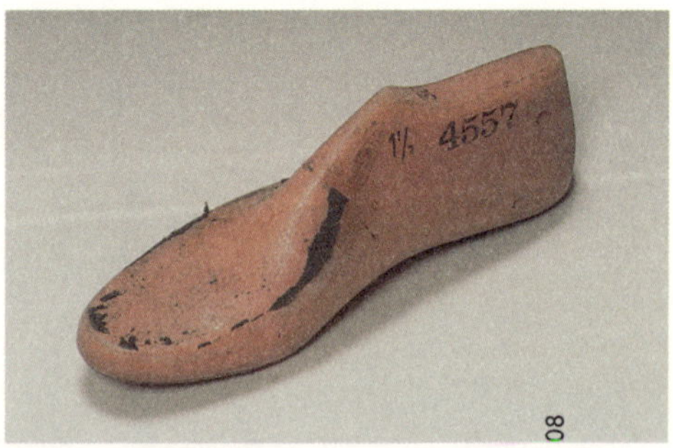

08

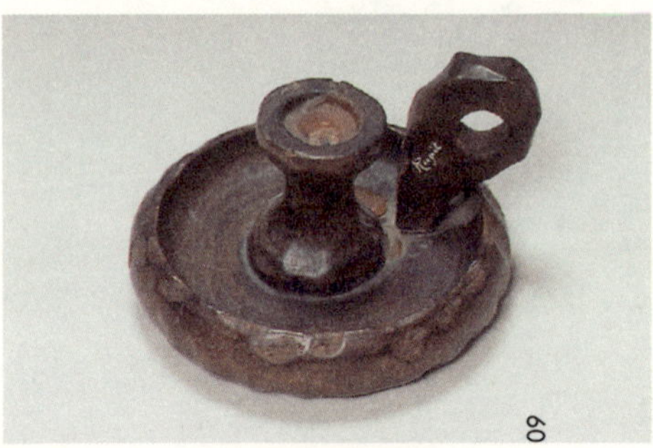

09

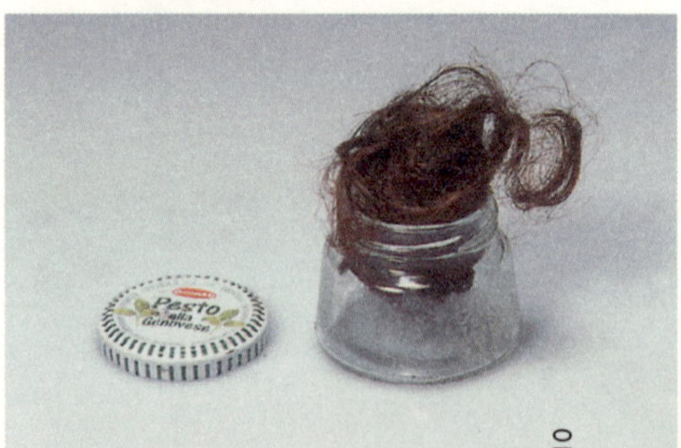

10

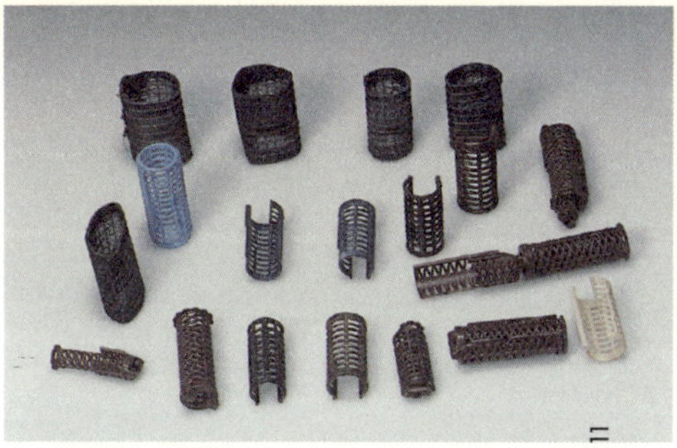
11

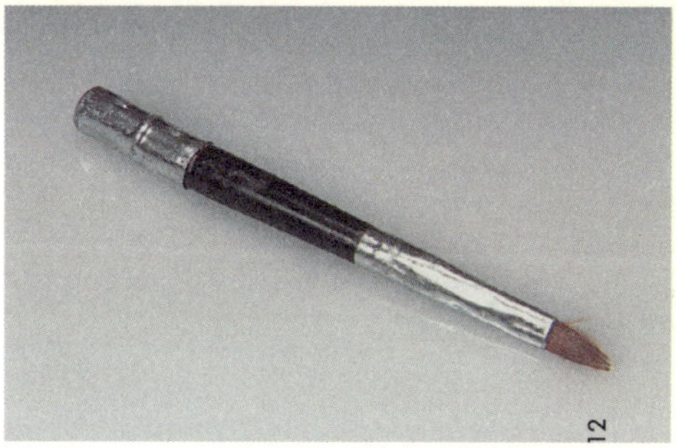
12

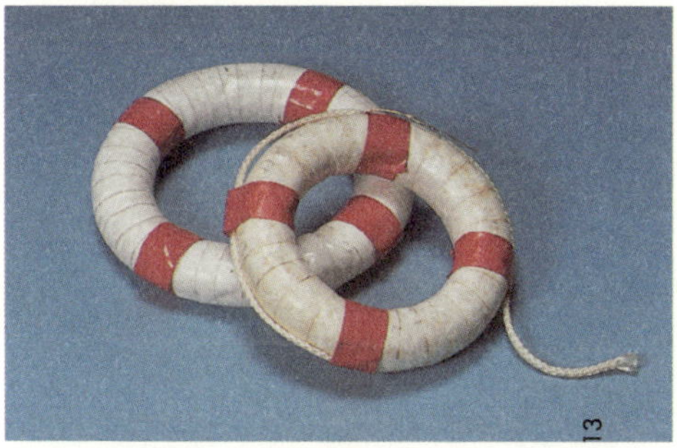
13

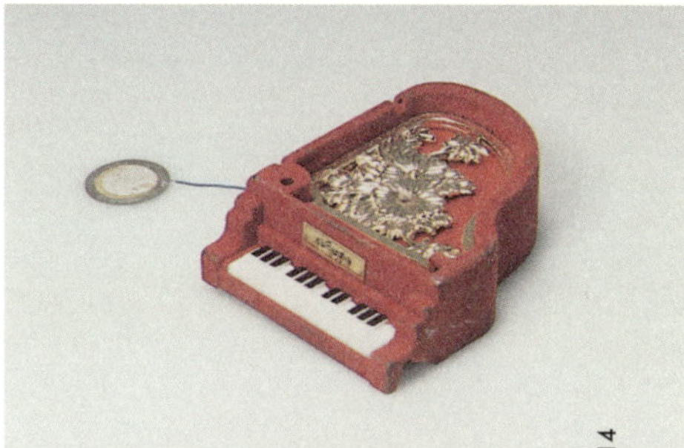
14

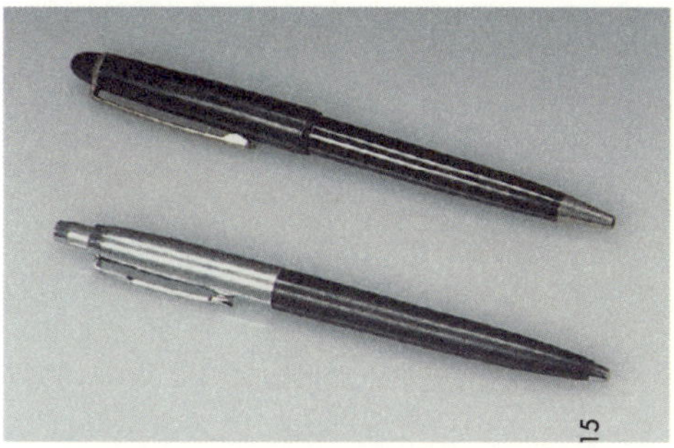
15

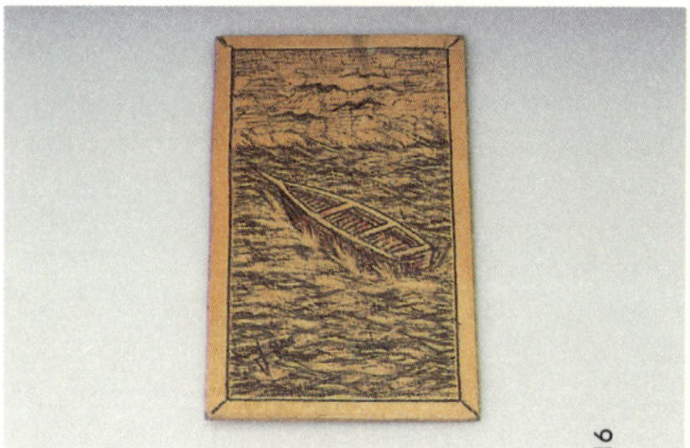
16

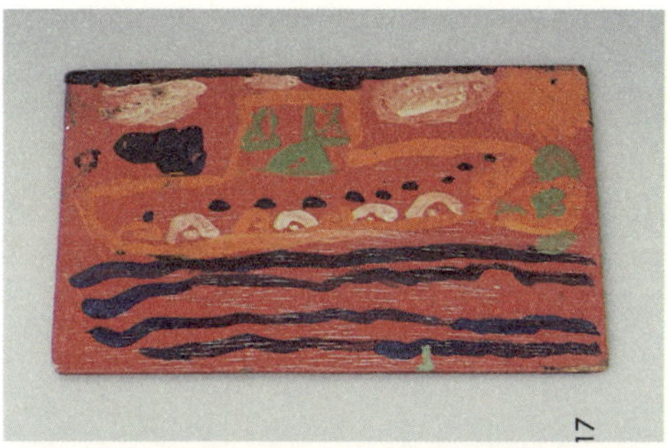
17

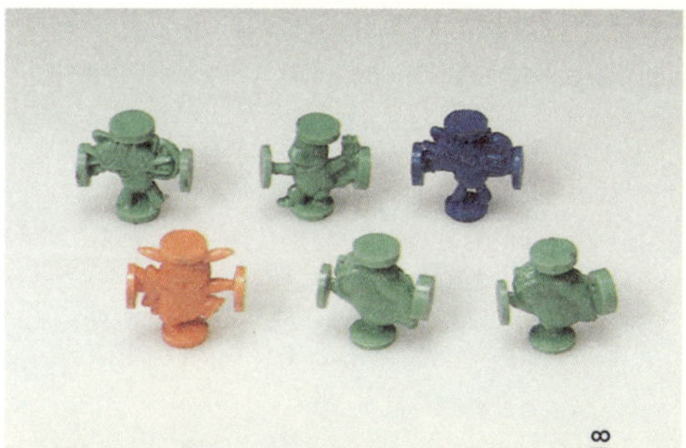
18

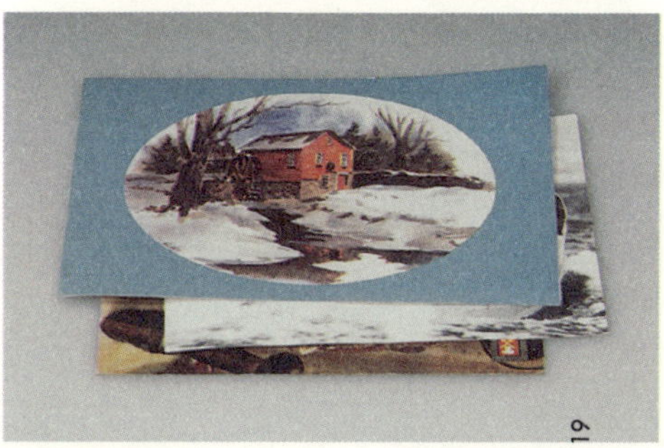
19

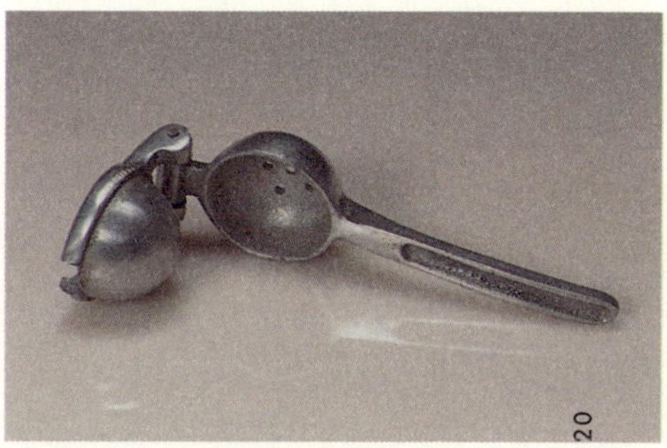
20

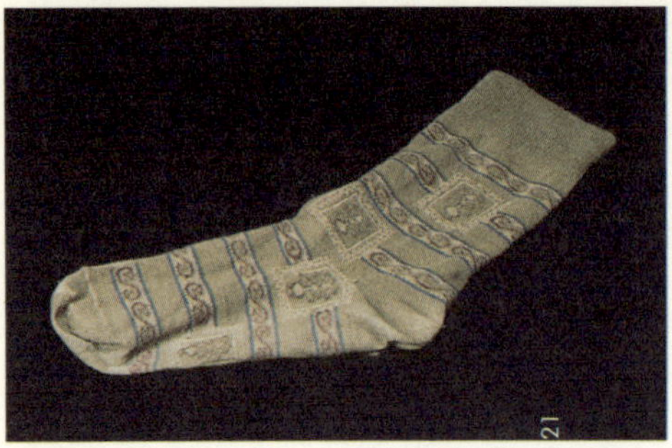
21

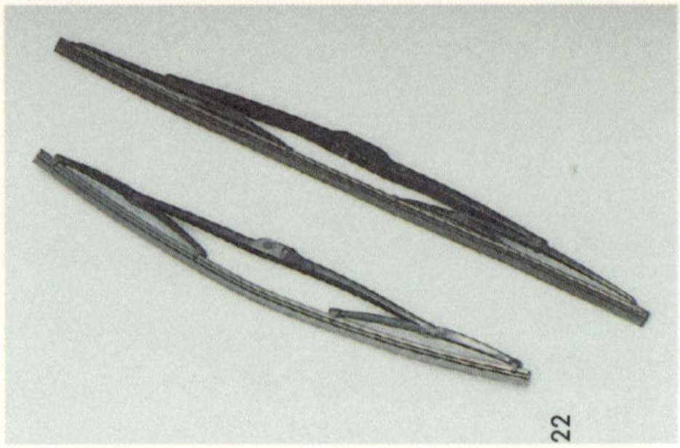
22

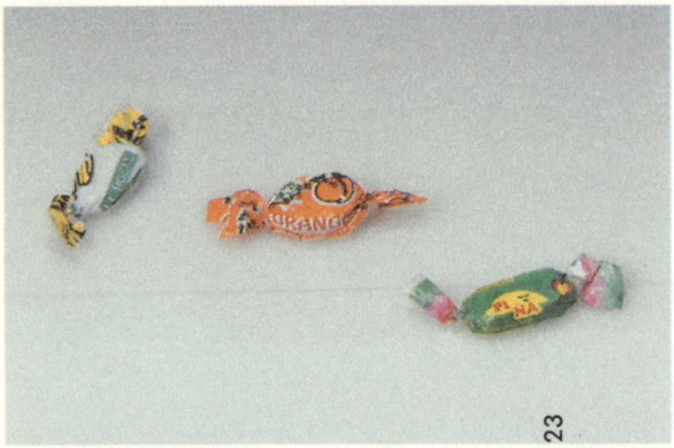

23

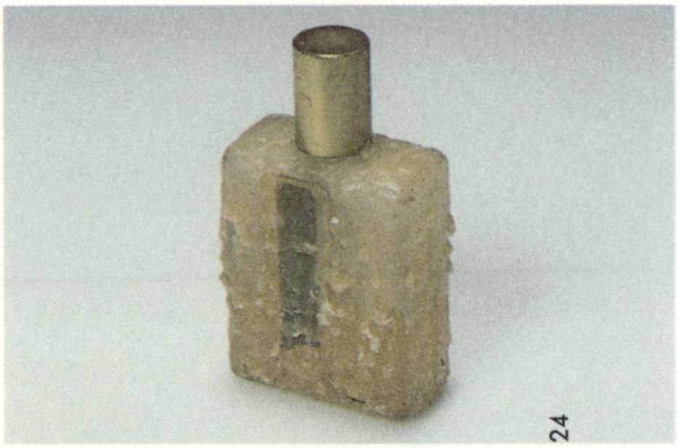
24

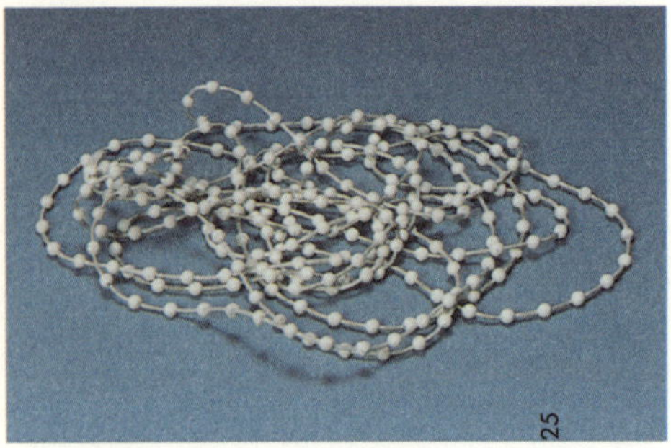
25

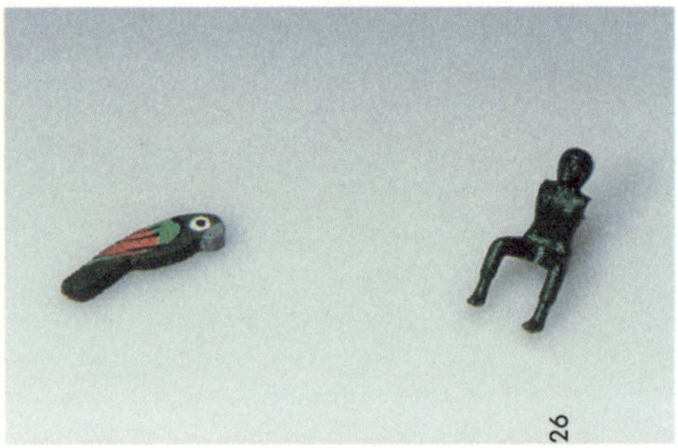
26

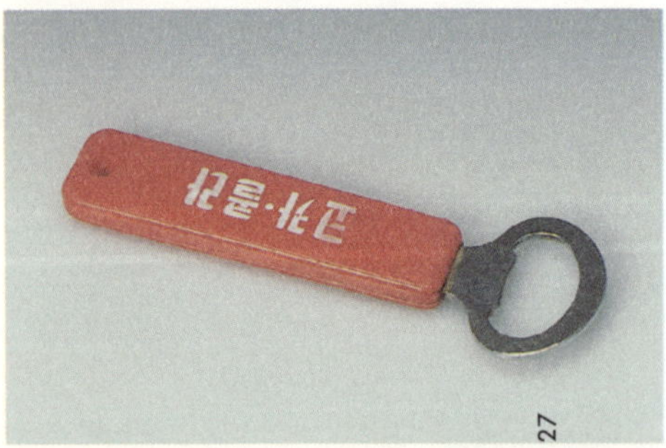
27

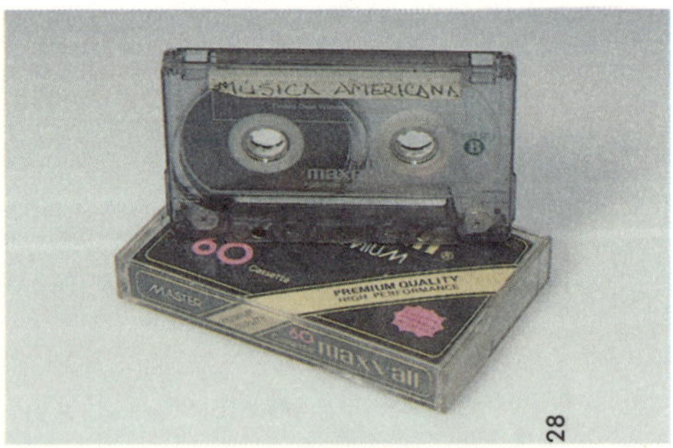

28

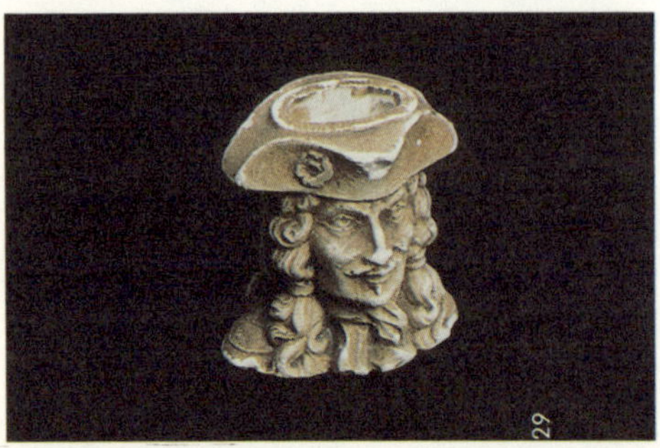
29

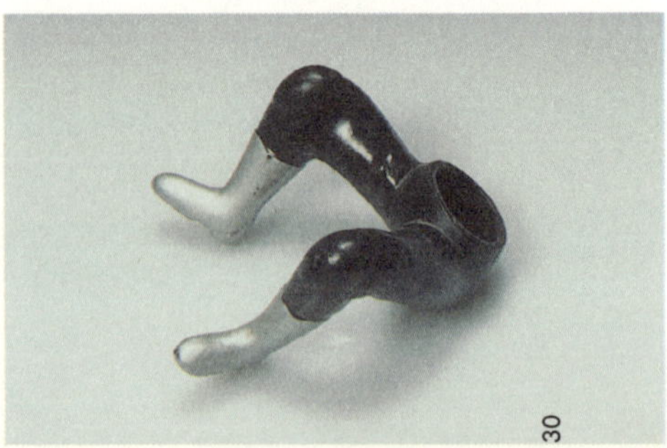
30

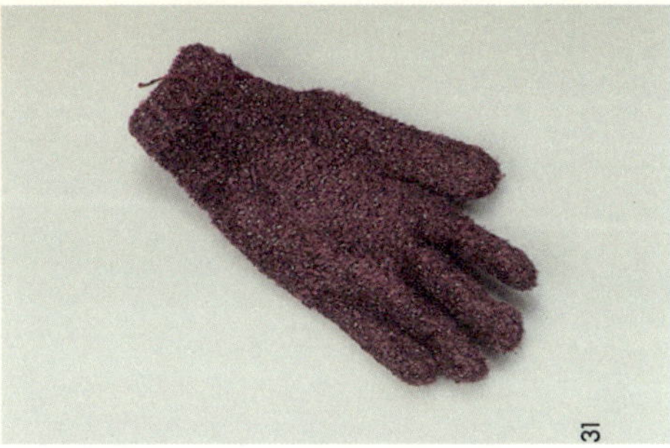
31

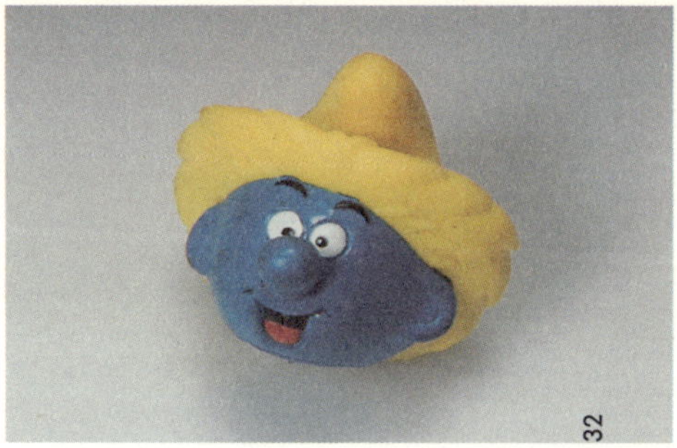
32

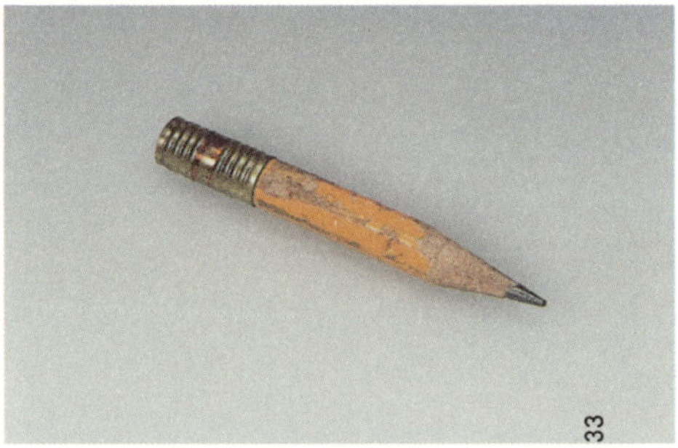
33

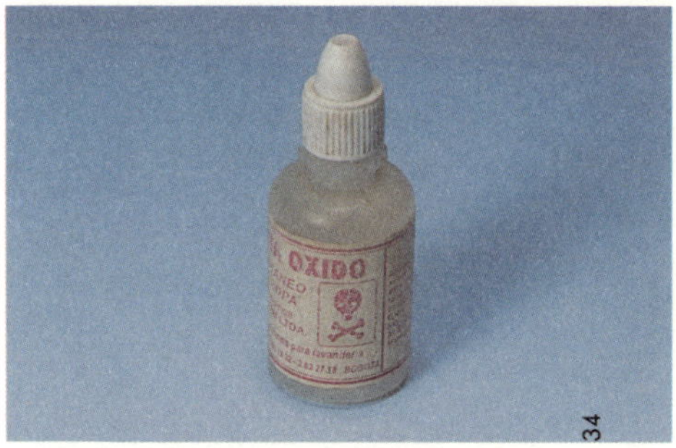

34

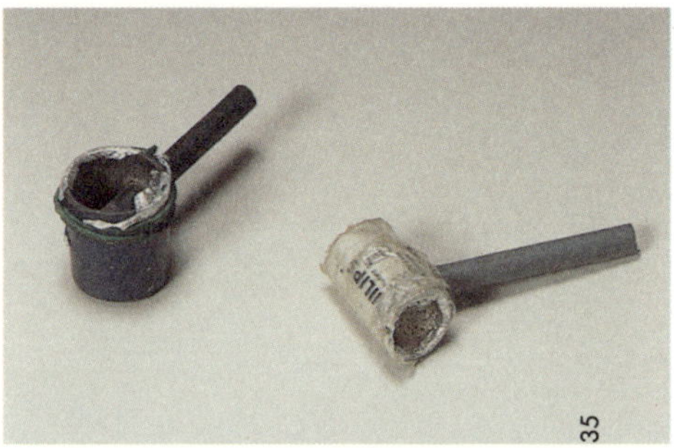
35

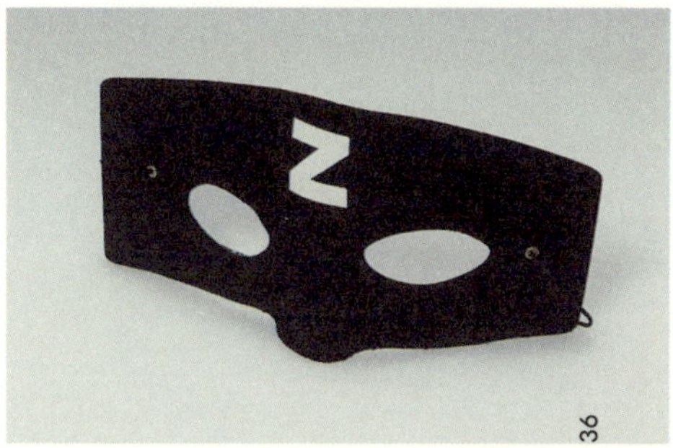

36

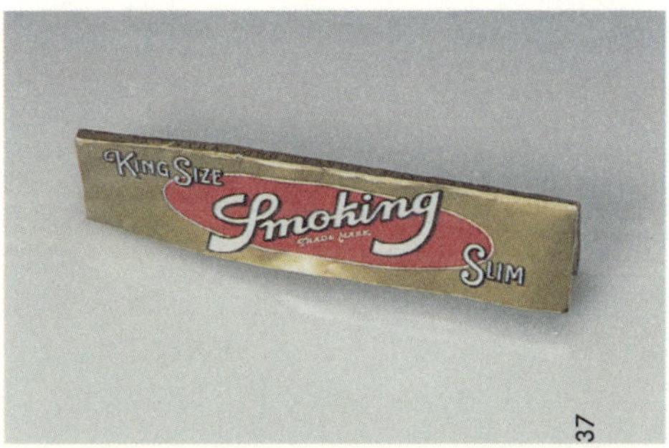

37

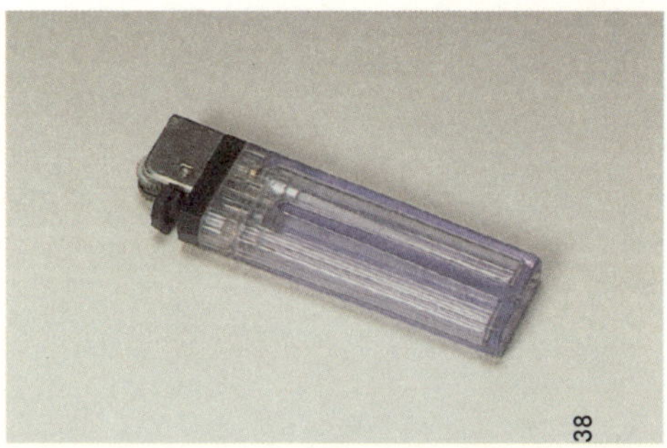
38

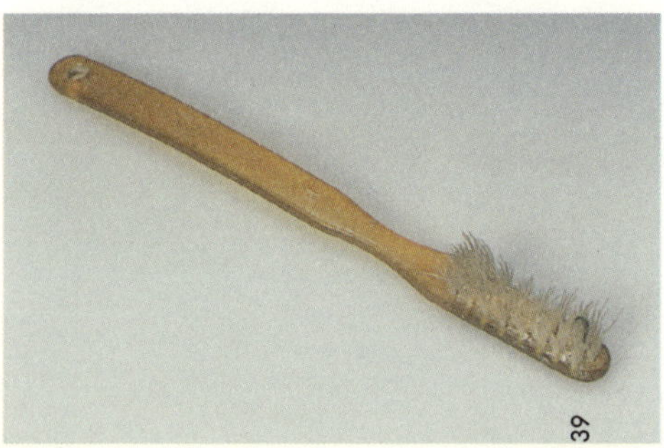
39

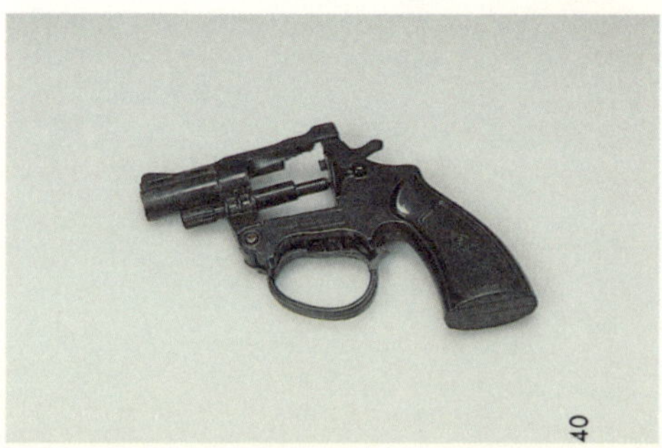
40

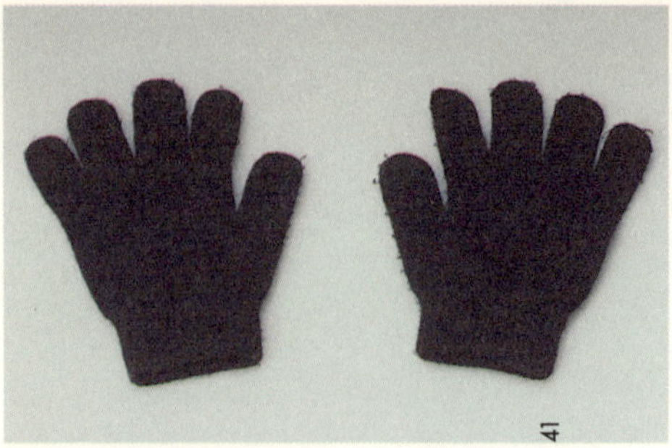

41

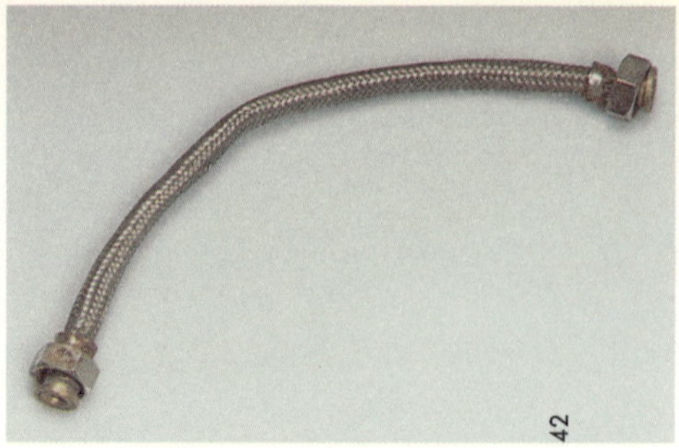

42

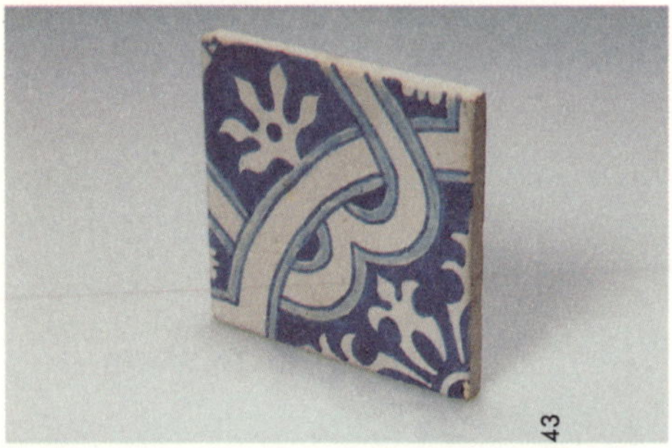

43

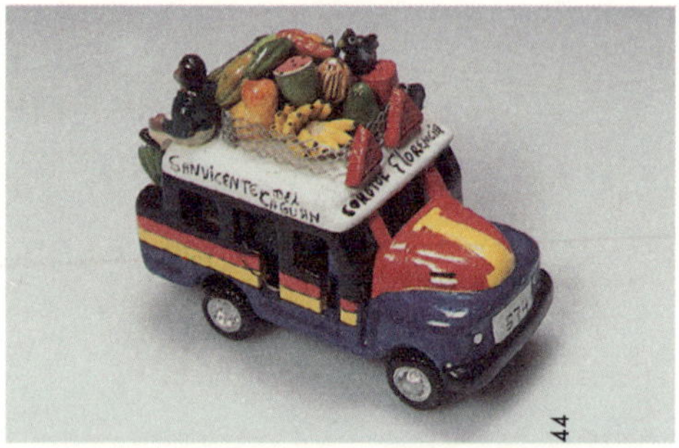

44

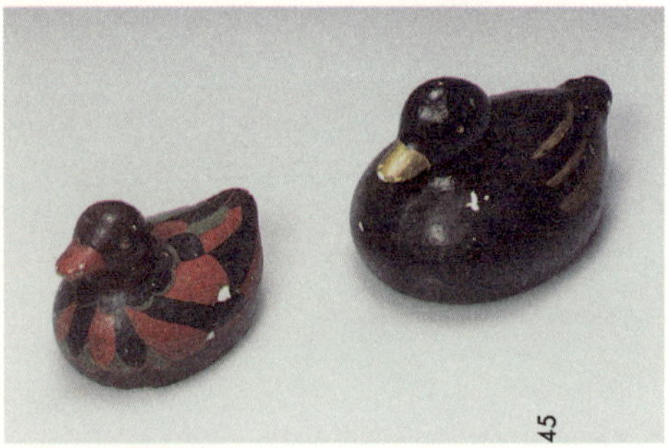

45

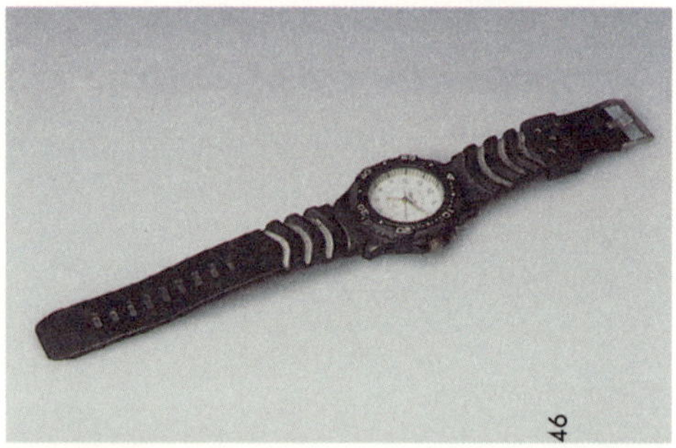

46

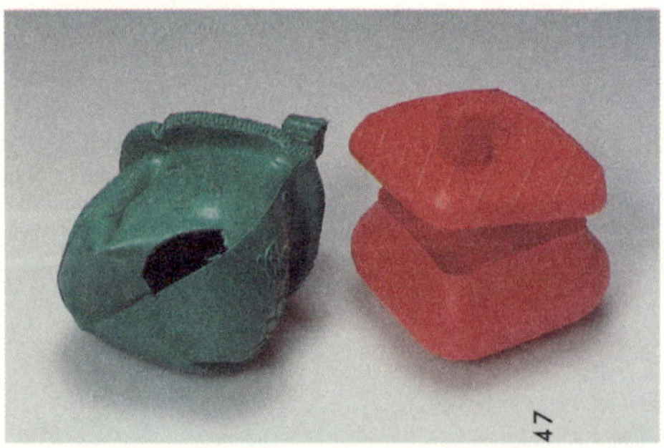

47

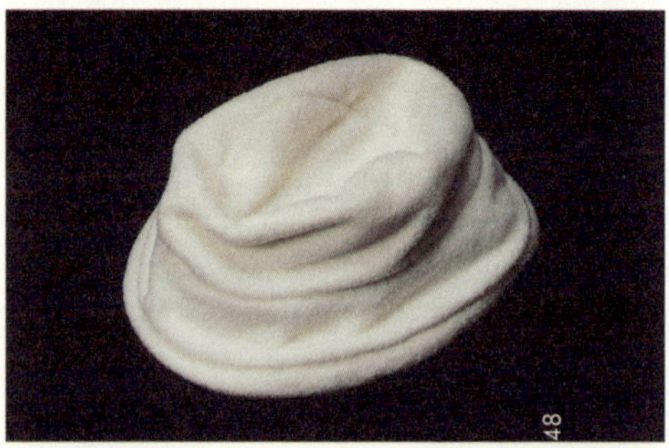

48

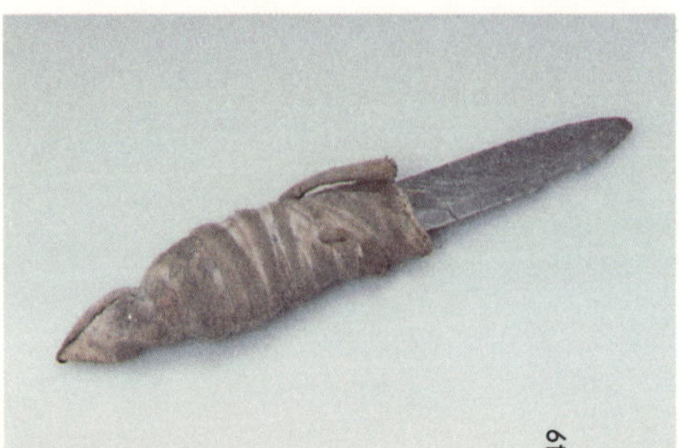

49

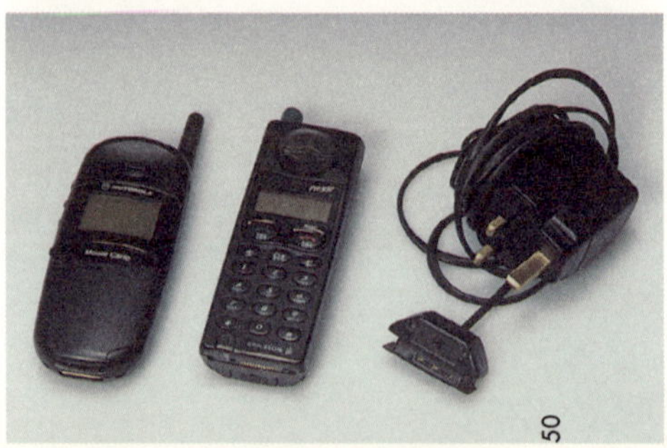

50

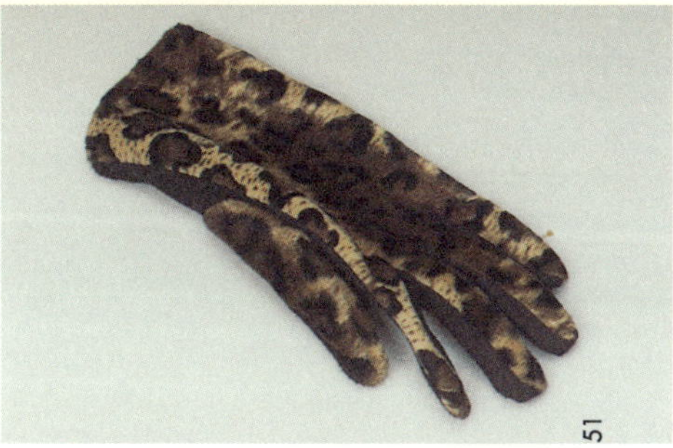
51

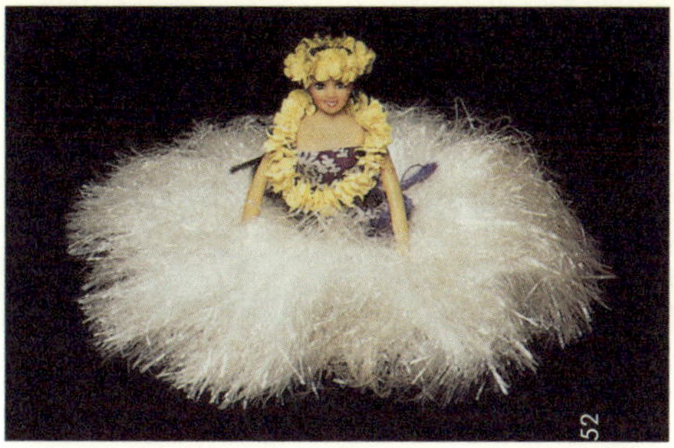
52

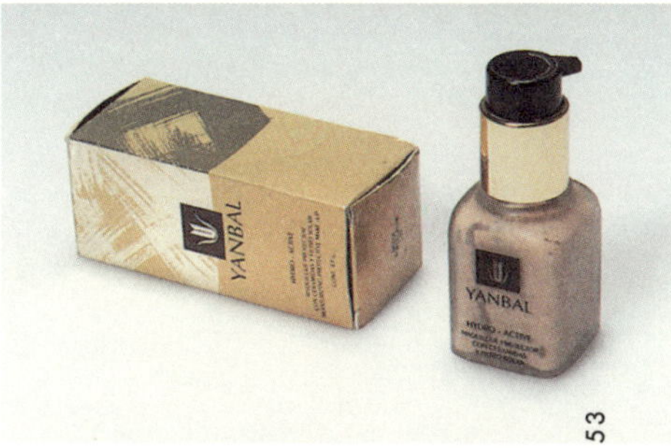

53

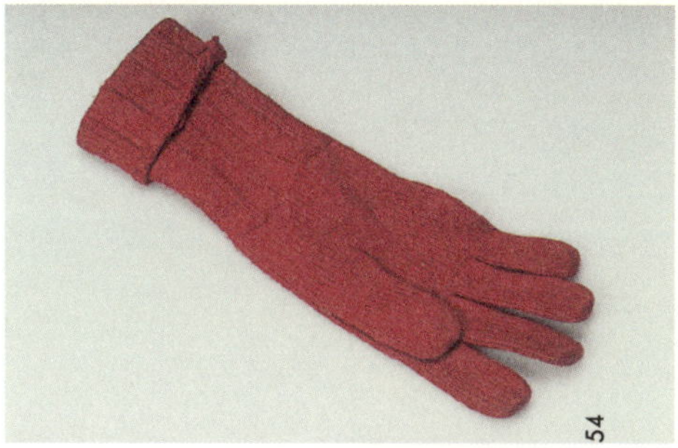
54

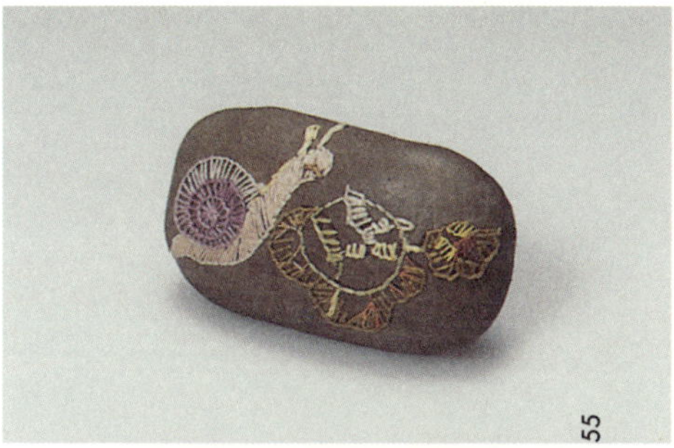
55

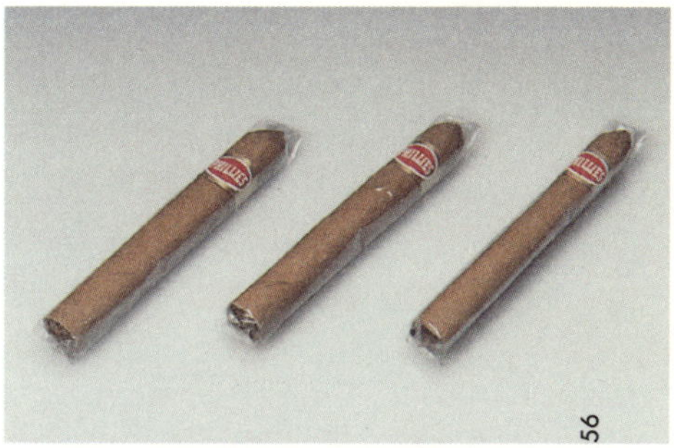
56

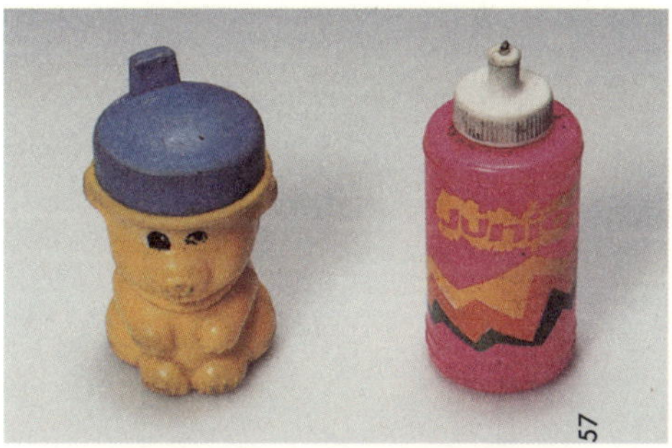
57

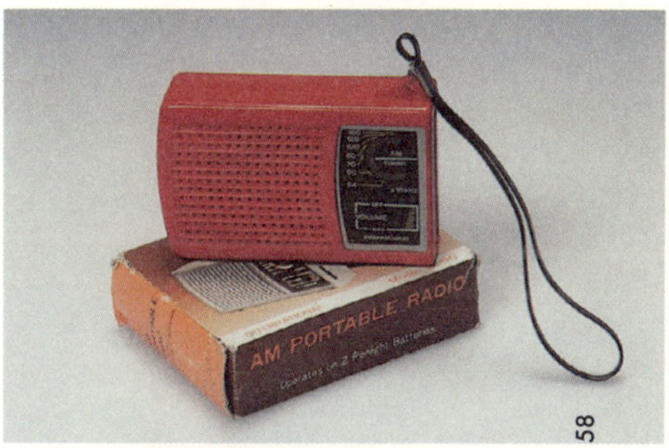

58

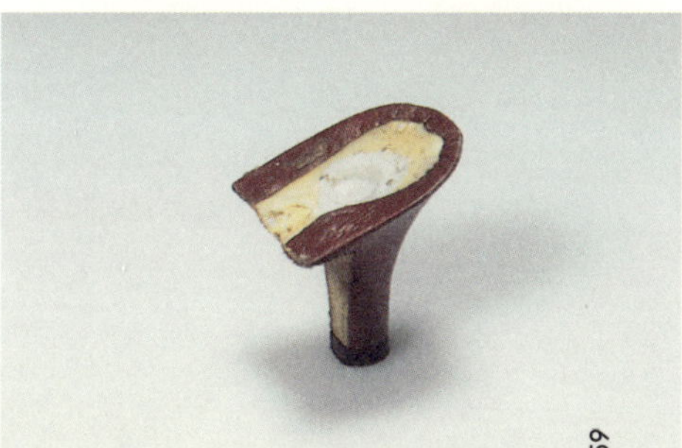
59

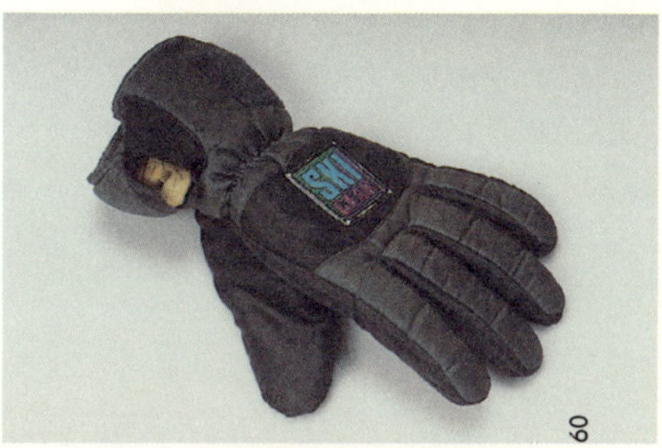

60

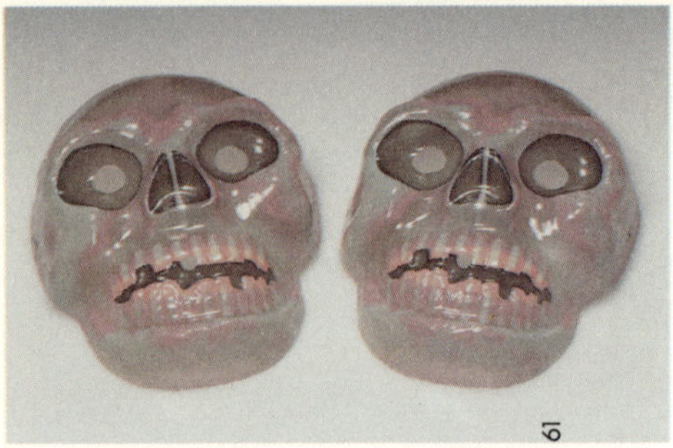

61

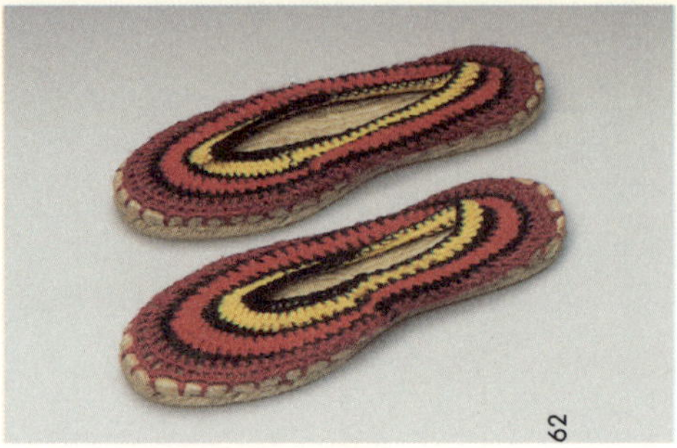

62

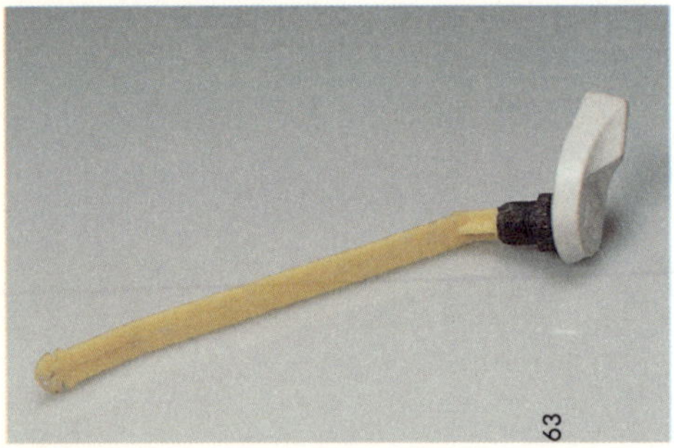

63

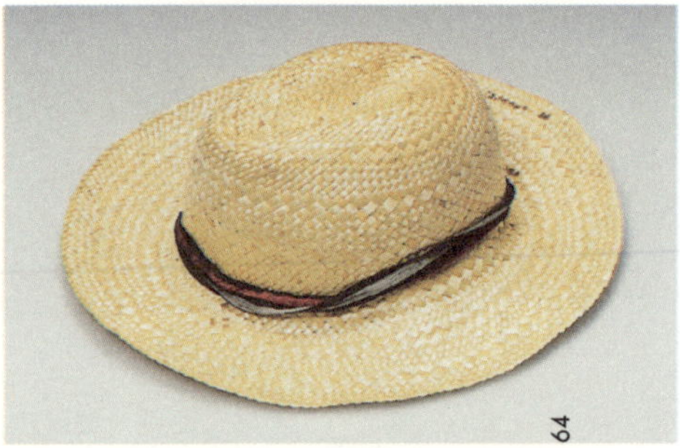

64

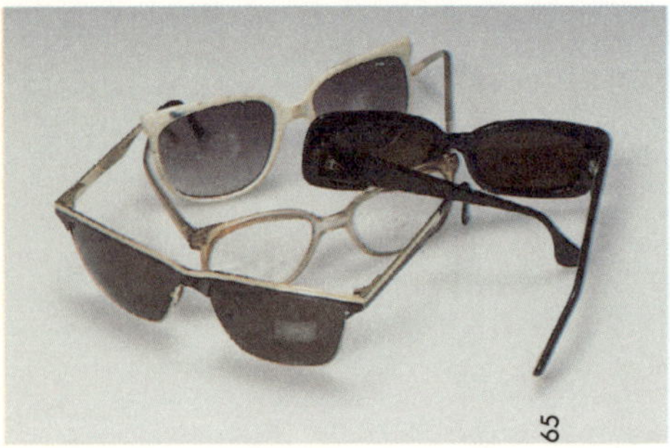

65

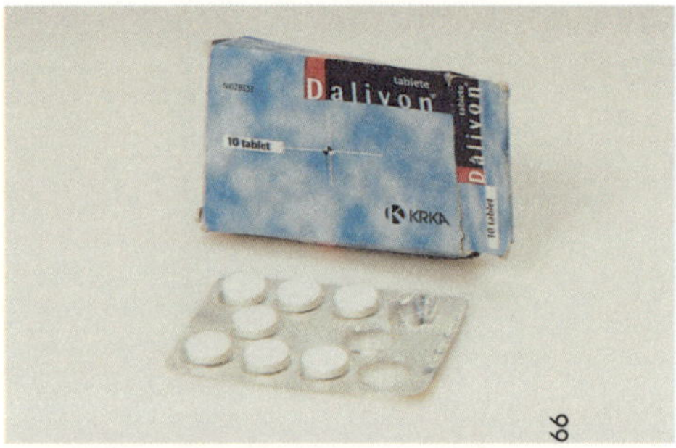

66

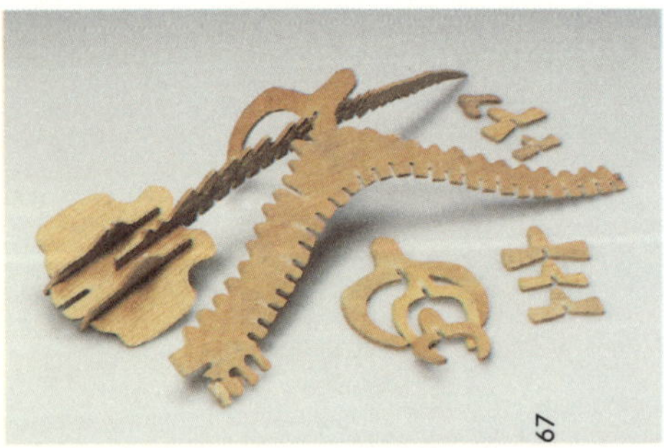

67

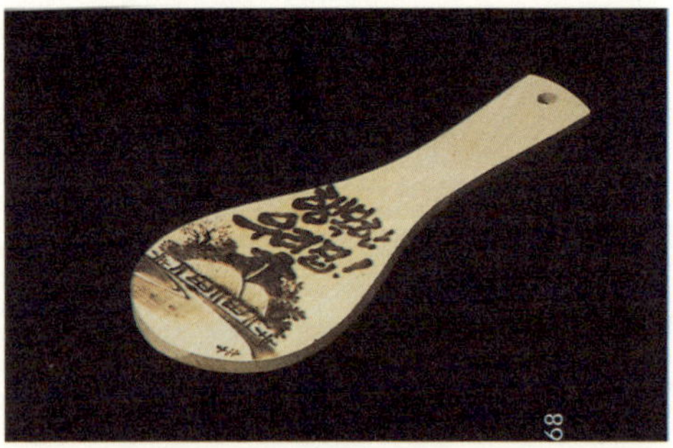

68

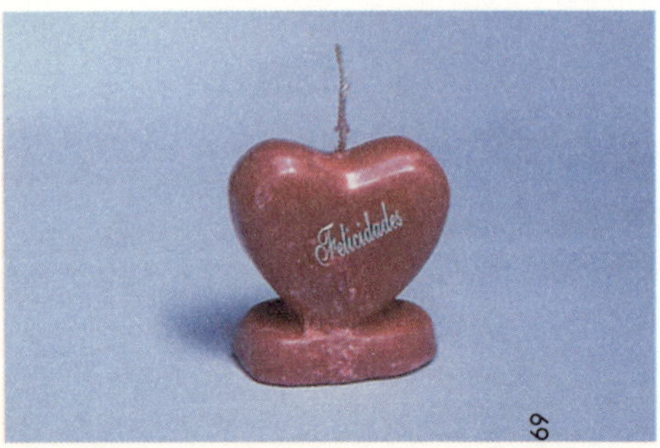

69

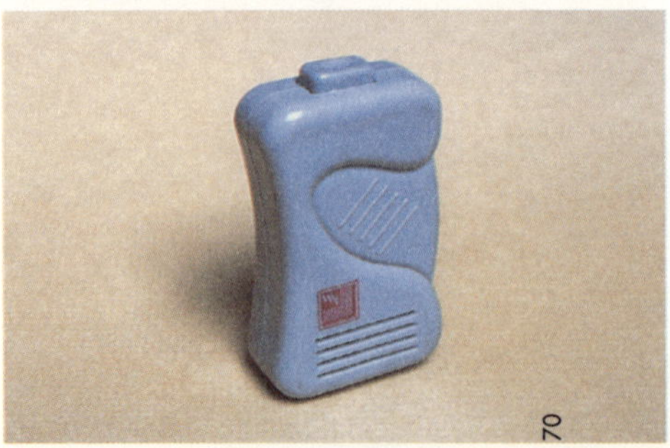

70

01 Ball bearing: probably used as a wheel on a wooden porter's cart Bogotá

02 Story and education books, Bogotá

03 Plastic fork

04 Drawing of two black lovers on cardboard with a love declaration, Bogotá

05 Comic magazines in English and Spanish

06 Plastic crucifix. Probably part of a rosary bead amulet

07 "King size" M&M-brand chocolates, London

08 Shoemaker's mould

09 'Rustic' style plastic candle stick

10 Pesto jar containing human hair Bogotá

11 Selection of hair curlers, Bogotá

12 Discarded make-up brush

13 Toy life preservers, Puerto Rico

14 Music box, Bogotá

15 Ball point pens

16 Drawing of an empty canoe by a Colombian street artist. Ballpoint pen on wood, Bogotá

17 Seascape painting, acrylic on wood, Bogotá

18 Pokemon figures. Plastic toys

19 Various postcards depicting 'exotic' scenes, Bogotá

20 Lemon squeezer, Bogotá

21 Sock, nylon

22 Windshield wipers: obtained on Bogotá black market

23 Boiled sweets

24 Perfume

25 Curtain or blind cord adapted as a string of fake pearls

26 Parts of children's toys

27 Bottle opener with printed inscription, Korea

28 'Musica Americana' cassette tape

29 Rococo plaster head

30 Lower part of 'Super Hero' plastic toy, Bogotá

31 Glove. Iford, Essex

32 Children's toy part. Smurf wearing straw peasant hat

33 Pencil used until it can no longer be held

34 Stain remover, Bogotá

35 Crack pipes made with an empty pen barrels and bottle tops, Bogotá

36 Canvas 'Zorro' mask, Seville

37 King size cigarette papers, Barcelona

38 Disposable lighter

39 Used toothbrush

40 Toy gun

41 Pair of gloves, London

42 Plumbing pipe, Bogotá

43 Ceramic tile, Seville

44 Typical 'Chiva' Colombian rural bus, Bogotá

45 Painted plaster duck figures, Bogotá

46 Plastic watch, electric

47 Empty plastic money boxes, broken open, Bogotá

48 White soft hat, London

49 Handmade knife, Bogotá

50 Mobile phones plus re-charger, London

51 Leopard skin ladies glove, acrylic, London

52 Hawaiian doll: La Alameda, Seville

53 Empty make-up bottle

54 Woollen glove, London

55 Embroidered hair broach depicting a snail, Bogotá

56 Three 'Philly Blunt' cigars, Puerto Rico

57 Childrens' drinking bottles, Bogotá

58 Portable radio

59 Stiletto heel, Bogotá

60 Ski glove, London

61 Halloween 'scull' masks

62 Espadrilles, Seville

63 Plumbing part, Bogotá

64 Straw hat

65 Various sun glasses

66 Painkillers, Bogotá

67 Wooden dinosaur figure dissembled, Bogotá

68 Wooden rice spoon

69 Heart-shaped candle with 'congratulations' inscription, London

70 Personal alarm, London

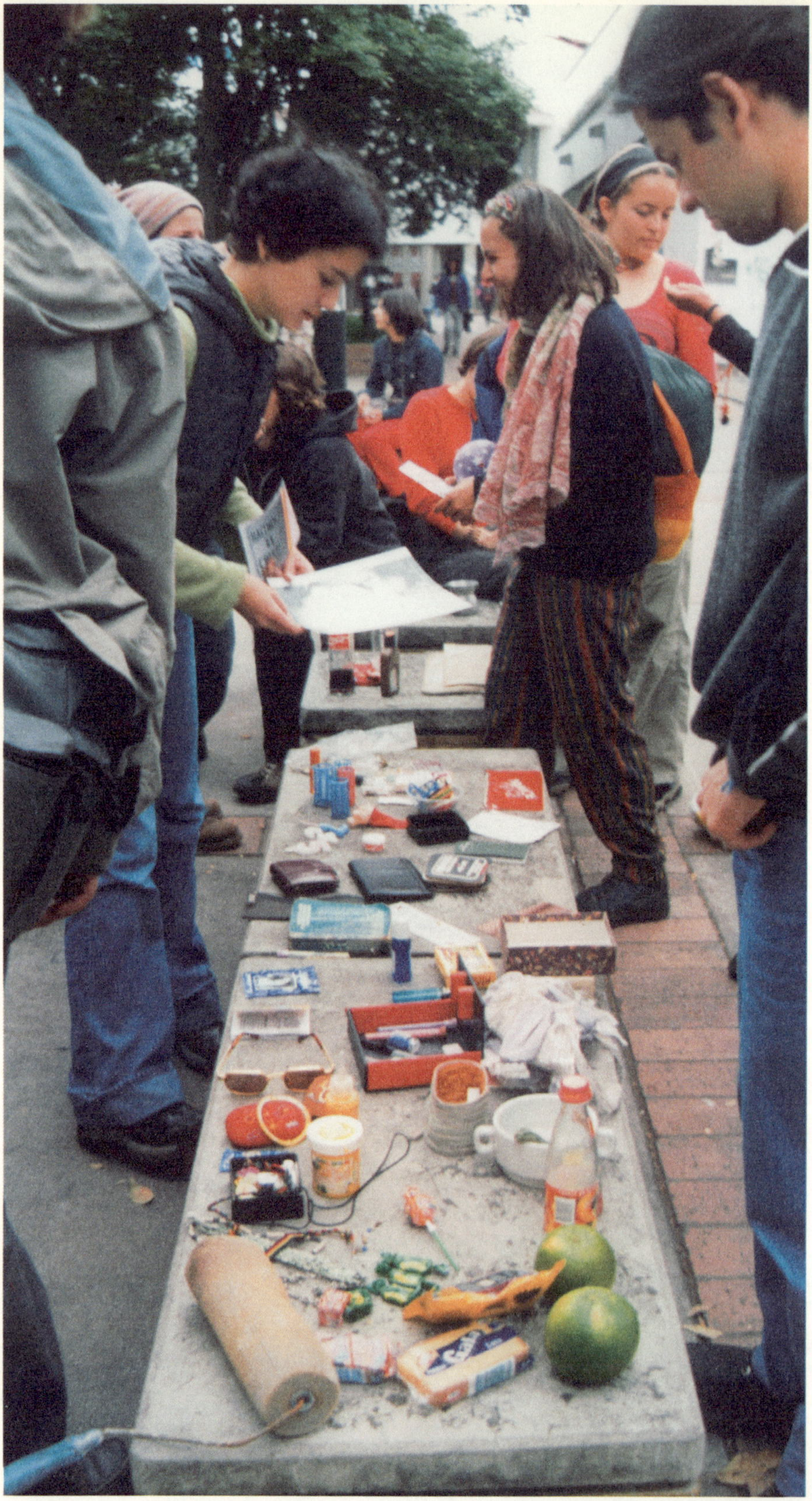

Exchange of objects, Carrera 30
Street Bench Installation, Bogotá

Airports: A Personal Memoir

Peter Wollen

I once found myself at Charles de Gaulle in Paris waiting for a plane to Gatwick, so I whiled away the time trying to count all the airports that I had ever visited in the course of my life. Chronologically the list began in 1951, when I had just become a teenager and going to Heathrow was part of my birthday celebrations. By the time I started counting airports – somewhat like Don Juan, I must admit – I had become over-accustomed to them. I had begun to see them as obstacles to be overcome if I was to enjoy the benefits of travel. They had become part of everyday life for me – I found that I had averaged more than two new airports a year since that very first flight and, of course, I had visited many of them numerous times. Airports have become sites for a set of routines which I could perform almost in my sleep, with their overtones of penance as I stand in line, the moments of paranoia as I go through security with a computer, or the moments of panic as I sprint to reach a gate in time. So, here is my list, in the form of an eastward circumnavigation of the globe, beginning as it should with my very first airport:

London, Heathrow 00.36 W

My very first flight, back in 1951, when I was just thirteen. At that time, you could take off in a very small plane, circle round admiring the view and then descend to earth again.

Luton 00.24 W

I have nothing whatever to say about Luton airport.

London, Gatwick 00.10 W

I hate this airport. I have nothing good to say about it.

London, Croydon Airport 00.05 W

This airport is deserted now, but I have a real fondness for Croydon because it is the site from which Amy Johnson took off on her epic solo flight to Australia in a Gypsy Moth.

London, City Airport 00.00

Built almost on the Greenwich Meridian, you can see the Millennium Dome as you fly in, looking like the soap bubble splashing out in Harold Edgerton's famous photograph.

Lympne 00.10 E

I associate this airport with Salvador Dalí, but I can't remember why. It is the first airport from which I flew to France when I was still a teenager and flying was an adventure.

Stansted 00.16 E

This is a new airport, designed by Norman Foster, like the airport in Hong Kong. I arrived back at Stansted once from Maastricht after the trains to Liverpool Street had stopped running and I was forced to take a taxi to Epping, from where I could get an Underground train back home. I had never been to Epping before, although my parents, who came from the East End of London, used to reminisce happily about hiking through the forest.

Southend 00.44 E

Southend is a sea-side resort with flights across the Channel and that very English institution, a pier, which you could saunter down eating your whelks and cockles on your way to enjoy the pier-head show, with its minstrels and comedians. Or so I like to think!

Barcelona 02.10 E

The great Catalan architect, Gaudí, was a kind of outsider architect – self-taught and gifted with a visionary imagination. One of the most memorable experiences of my life was to be on the roof of *La Pedrera* while Antonioni was filming there, with its strange tiled chimneys, and to look down on the sinuous walls and balconies below.

Beauvais 02.08 E

I flew to Beauvais on my way to Paris, where I was due to stay for a few weeks on an exchange with the French boy who had stayed with my family in Exeter, where we made him an apple-pie bed one night. I remember being very surprised to see people eating cheese with sugar. My French exchange later became a senior official at the World Bank and then left to become Chairman of a huge cement company. However, I haven't seen him since the year of my Beauvais-Paris trip, although we once talked on the telephone.

Paris, Charles de Gaulle 02.20 E

At one time I visited Paris as the co-curator of an exhibition celebrating the Situationist International, held – paradoxically – at the Centre Pompdou, a building detested by the S.I.'s co-founder and principal theorist, Guy Debord. Pompidou was responsible for the suppression of the May 1968 uprising and the museum named after him was built on a site created by the kind of massive urban clearances that Debord had always denounced so eloquently. Nonetheless, though he necessarily refused to attend the exhibition, he communicated with the curators through an intermediary. At the opening another S.I. veteran, JV Martin, pulled out a gun and adopted a rather threatening attitude. He was disarmed by Jørgen Nash, the principal figure in the dissident Second Situationist International and a fellow Dane, who got him into a taxi which took him back to his hotel.

Paris, Orly 02.20 E

Anybody with any deep interest in the cinema will immediately associate Orly airport with Chris Marker's great film, *La Jetée*, which was largely shot there. *La Jetée* was subsequently re-made by Terry Gilliam as *Twelve Monkeys*.

Perpignan 02.53 E

Perpignan is the city where Cabestan's heart is buried under a stone at the entrance to the Cathedral – a heart which was offered up to be eaten on a dish and written about by Ezra Pound, a poet fascinated by the jongleurs of Catalunya, both French and Spanish.

Ostend 02.54 E

I flew to Ostend in order to see a retrospective of work by Piet Mondrian, the first major exhibition of its kind. What I remember most is that they played boogie-woogie piano through the sound system, in keeping with Mondrian's own taste in music.

Montpellier 03.52 E

This city is the site of an extraordinary architectural complex designed by Ricardo Bofill, the architect whose work was featured to great effect in Terry Gilliam's film, *Brazil*.

Brussels 04.21 E

I had my return air tickets and my passport stolen at Brussels airport. They were retrieved soon afterwards by the police and handed back to me at the last minute, just as the plane was due to leave. I had to race to catch the plane, ending my final sprint with a leap into the plane just as they were closing the door.

Schiphol 04.42 E

Although near Amsterdam, this is the airport that I use for Rotterdam, another city which has a Film Festival. It also has a fine art museum which, among many other things, has a collection of clothes designed by Martin Margiela. It is the site where he first exhibited his clothes on which mould was formed due to the application to them of cultures of bacteria and fungi from blotting paper wrapped around the tailor's dummies and the application of agar to the fabric, causing discolouration through red bacteria, pink yeast, green mould and yellow bacteria. The utensils required for this procedure included atomizers, pipettes, pipette points, thermometer, rubber gloves, wooden spoon, test-tubes, an 'enting needle', a candle, hypodermic syringes, a siphon, test-tubes and a test-tube stand, a beaker measure for pouring, a cylinder measure for spraying and paper milk-cartons.

Maastricht 05.40 E

I went to Maastricht to celebrate the centenary of René Magritte and read a paper on *Magritte and the Bowler Hat*. I was very tempted to buy a bowler hat from Lobb's and wear it during my talk, but my courage failed me. Appropriately to the occasion, I saw a procession of camels pass by down the narrow street in which I was enjoying some refreshment on a kerbside table outside a small café. They were just a few feet away.

Luxemburg 06.09 E

I went to Luxemburg in order to discuss film theory, a strange occupation in a country with no film industry at all. I had just published a book on the semiotics of film.

Zürich 08.32 E

The birthplace of Dada. I was there filming a model of Tatlin's tower, a huge spiral structure designed soon after the Russian Revolution but never built. The camera went up and round the tower in an ascending spiral movement, a series of 360 degree circles combined with an ever-ascending crane shot. After a number of takes, it seemed time to put a stop to the process, but the cinematographer insisted on doing one last take. When asked why, he replied: "Swiss tradition of quality". He got his way.

Locarno 08.47 E

Another film festival site, close to Ascona, point of origin of modern dance, sun-bathing, pacifism, anarchism, dada-ism – many of the progressive movements which blossomed during the first decades of the twentieth century and whose origins are chronicled in Martin Green's book, Children of the Sun. While I was in Locarno, tribute was paid to a centenarian film-maker who was still able to reminisce about his early years.

Genoa 08.57 E

This is where I first met Valie Export, who had her own entourage with her. Now she makes avant-garde DVDs and I imagine she has her own network of fervent Internet fans.

Hanover 09.46 E

This is where you can visit Kurt Schwitters's *Merz* room, painstakingly recreated in the city art museum. I am not sure whether it was really a good decision to paint it all white, although it does give the room something of the appearance of an ice-grotto.

Pisa 10.23 E

I always liked the Leaning Tower of Pisa, but I never lingered in the city. It was the best airport to use in order to get to the home of a friend who I visited every summer for a number of years, a farmhouse with a granary full of bats and a view across the Val d'Arno.

Florence 11.15 E

I first went to Florence with the principal purpose of seeing a particular painting by Pinturicchio in the Uffizi. As time went by, I began to prefer the Pontormo paintings in the Certosa. After my daughter was born, I also made it a habit to visit the *Città de Sole* toyshop whenever I was in Florence, founded by my former colleague, Carlo Basso, because he was dissatisfied with the range of toys available in Italy at the time his wife gave birth to twins. His wife, incidentally, was the language scholar, Lydia Lonzi, a student of Roman Jakobson and the sister of Carla Lonzi, author of *Sputiamo Sul Hegel* (*We Spit On Hegel*), a powerful feminist political and philosophical tract.

Rome, Leonardo da Vinci 12.20 E

I could never quite understand why an airport with this name was in Rome and not in Milan. The airport in Rome should have been called Michelangelo. Perhaps it was because Leonardo could be associated with the birth of aviation through one of his fantasy engineering drawings, as if he had indeed designed the first flying machine.

Rome, Fiumicino 12.20 E

The first time I visited Rome I was eager to see the classical sites, the relics of the Roman Republic and the Empire. The next time I wanted to see the Sistine Chapel and the great collections of paintings. When I ended up living and working in Rome, as a journalist, I became more interested in the baroque, especially the work of Borromini – I became especially fond of Sant'Ivo and the tromp l'oeil colonnade in the Palazzo Spada. For me, Rome is a baroque city rather than a classical or a medieval or even a Renaissance city.

Venice 12.21 E

I first visited Venice in the snow. I was mainly interested in Tintoretto, as a result of reading Sartre's essay on his paintings. Years later I found myself on a vaporetto with my luggage going to the Lido, a journey which gives you a view of the Island of the Dead, made famous by Bocklin. There is a perpetual anxiety that Venice will one day sink and vanish away. I can think of worse fates. I worry about the flood of tourists much more.

Copenhagen 12.34 E

I went to Copenhagen en route to visit Jørgen Nash, the brother of the CoBrA artist, Asger Jorn, co-founder and financier of the Paris-based

Situationist International, from which Nash had split to found the secessionist second International. Nash was a poet rather than a painter and he gave me a long poem to take to a Danish film-maker, named Thorsen, based in Silkeborg, where the Situationist archive is held. Thorsen was best-known for making an erotic film about the life of Jesus. Nash referred to him as the 'Vitamin Bomb'. A second reason for going to Copenhagen was that I wanted to see the Grundtvig Church, one of the great works of the Arts and Crafts period of architecture.

Berlin, Tempelhof 13.25 E

I flew to Berlin especially to see the wrapping of the Reichstag by Christo and Jeanne-Claude. I was picked up at the airport by the friend of a friend and driven to a bar, where we managed to get something to eat, and then, soon after midnight, we drove to the Reichstag, where an enormous crowd was camped out on the grass, playing musical instruments and performing shadow-plays on the reflective silver material in which the building had been wrapped, moving and gesturing in front of the powerful spotlights that illuminated the building. I still have a little square of woven silver fabric as a memento.

Zagreb 16.00 E

At the art school in Zagreb I remember my Croatian hosts expressing some surprise when I said that I thought the most intelligent question came from a student from Kosovo, going on to explain that this was because the Serbs refused to offer the Albanians any proper education and consequently they were not expected to show any intelligence.

Vienna 16.22 E

For me Vienna is the city of Freud and Hundertwasser. Hundertwasser is one of those fortunate artists who was able to design the museum in which much of his work is exhibited. His architecture is more interesting to me than his painting or even his conceptualist *Endless Line*. Hundertwasser designs buildings with grass on the roof and trees growing on them, decorated with bright colours and strange mosaics. He could make even a garbage incinerator into a thing of beauty. He is to Vienna what Gaudí is to Barcelona or Mackintosh to Glasgow or Plecnik to Ljubljana.

Stockholm 18.03 E

I can't remember the exact reason why I visited Stockholm, although I know it was something to do with the University, because I do recall quite clearly being shown the office of an elderly professor who had been openly pro-German during the war, as apparently many were. I also visited the extraordinary Munch collection in the Thielska Galleriet, a private collection kept in a private house that was now open to the public.

Budapest 19.05 E

My main memories of Budapest are of the elephant house at the zoo and of visiting a fashionable restaurant in which a number of the customers were none too discreetly accompanied by body-guards, who scanned everyone who entered while they also enjoyed a delicious dinner. At the modern art museum there was an exhibition of video work by Victor Burgin, concerning the Hungarian psychoanalyst, Sandor Ferenczi and his complex relationship with Freud, a reminder of the old Austro-Hungarian days and the close cultural interconnection that existed between the two capital cities. The Hungarian school of psychoanalysis has had an influence on my own work through Michael Balint's writing on 'thrills' – specifically his essay on 'philobatism' and thrill-seeking through flying, an essay which was crucial to the thought behind *AMY!*, the short film Laura Mulvey and I made for the anniversary of Amy Johnson's flight from England to Australia.

Belgrade 20.37 E

I flew to Belgrade to be on the jury at a Film Festival, in which awards were made to films selected from each of the Yugoslav republics, except Kosovo, where, I presumed, nobody had enough money to make even an amateur film. The Slovenian film was a standard European experimental film, which could have been made in London or Berlin or Vienna; the film from the Voivodina was a punk film; the Macedonian film was full of folk-dancing; the Croatian film was pseudo-professional and quite conventional, but, to my surprise, there was no film at all from Serbia. I commented on this to the Festival organisers, remarking that I had been told that Belgrade was a centre for Super-8 film making. It turned out that Super-8 wasn't eligible but, to my amazement, one of the festival organisers showed up the next morning saying he had brought a film. It turned out he had created it himself overnight. He had screened *Psycho*, filmed one scene directly off the screen and somehow managed to get it printed as a rush job overnight. It was titled *Breakfast* and consisted of the episode in the motel office during which Tony Perkins offers breakfast to Janet Leigh. It was silent, of course, but, as a film scholar, I already knew what they were talking about. I am glad to say that our jury awarded it a prize.

Helsinki 25.03 E

Here I visited the bar designed in 1920s Soviet style by the Kaurismäki Brothers.

Sodankylä 25.50 E

This airport is north of the Arctic Circle in Finland, in the land of the Midnight Sun. The proper thing to do is to visit a sauna and then run into the snow, but I spent my time watching movies and talking to people. It was in Sodankylä that Monte Hellman told me how much he had been influenced by *Waiting for Godot*. I had asked him about Beckett, because I had been struck by the pointless wandering and futile interpersonal relationships which seemed so typical of his own strange and inconclusive low-budget Westerns.

Johannesburg 28.02 E

A cab driver in Johannesburg was very much surprised when I told him that I couldn't drive and usually travelled by bus or train. You never saw white folks on buses or trains in Johannesburg, he told me. They all drive cars.

Cairo 31.14 E

I was in Cairo for a Film Festival, where I got into many animated discussions about the Israeli occupation of Palestinian territory, which was one of the subjects of my film, *Friendship's Death*. My own personal interest in Cairo was focussed more on another film, *Riddles of the Sphinx*, that I had made with Laura Mulvey and which contained footage of the Sphinx at Giza, just outside the city. I was also able to see paintings made by the Egyptian surrealists, a fascinating branch of the global surrealist movement.

Beirut 35.31 E

After rockets were fired at the plane I was travelling in, it had turned around and flown back to Beirut. So I inadvertently visited Beirut airport twice on the same day.

Amman 35.62 E

On my first flight to Amman, the plane had turned back because of the rocket fire. The second flight, however, was successful. Since a civil war was in progress at the time, my visit was a somewhat hair-raising experience. I was in a hotel filled with journalists, who would fling themselves flat on the floor when shelling came too close. Some time after my visit to Jordan I wrote and directed a movie set in Amman, called *Friendship's Death*.

Al Mafraq 36.14 E

'Revolution Airport'. While I was in Jordan in 1970 I asked if I could be taken to visit the Roman ruins at Jerash where, to my great surprise, there were Syrian troops bivouacking amid the marble columns. Without any consultation, the driver veered wildly off-course on the way back to Amman, heading into the desert in the direction of Al Mafraq. He had decided to take us to what was known as 'Revolution Airport', the site where two hijacked airliners had landed. The planes were still there, encircled by two separate rings of tanks – one, I believe, Jordanian and the other, I presumed, Syrian. A few days later, the hostages were released and the planes were blown up.

Moscow (Civil) 37.35 E

I visited Moscow to shoot film for a documentary on the lives and works of the Russian artists Komar & Melamid. When I left for the airport to return to England my Muscovite partners put me in a taxi, paid the driver in advance and told him I was deaf and dumb, worried that if he knew I was a foreigner he would double the price of the journey. So I sat there mute and, when we arrived, I just looked blank and failed to thank him. Probably it was a wise course of action. Earlier, filming on the site of a famous demonstration against the suppression of an experimental art show, local youths had tried to shake us down for a large sum of money and been fought off by our cameraman. The other moment that sticks in my mind is our visit to the morgue where Komar and Melamid had first met as art students, a scene they instantly recognised when they first saw the film.

Moscow (Military) 37.35 E

On another trip to Moscow, as part of a small delegation of British film-makers, including Derek Jarman and Sally Potter, I was driven through a gate, across the runway and right up to the plane, without entering the airport buildings at all – a taste of life as lived by the nomenklatura. During this trip Derek Jarman filmed me reading Eisenstein's copy of

John Reed's famous history of the October revolution, *Ten Days That Shook The World*, a book in which every mention of Trotsky had been blanked out and made illegible. My other memory is of watching the world chess championship, Kasparov against Karpov. I only managed to get in because I was a foreigner and I'd brought my travel chess set with me.

Baku 49.56 E

While I was in Baku, I went to inspect the monument erected to honour the nineteen Bolshevik Commissars executed by the British during the Civil War which followed the October Revolution. When I expressed some enthusiasm about it to the Azerbaijani friend who had taken me there, he told me that if I liked strange monuments, I should try to visit one which I would find on the beach some distance north of the city. He suggested that I ask to be taken to see the Zoroastrian fire-temple, where there is a perpetual flame lit by burning oil. On the way there, I should explain I wanted to see the strange monument on the beach and persuade the driver to veer off course and take me there. The monument proved to be one of the great masterpieces of outsider art, comparable with the Watts Towers in Los Angeles. It was built by a retired mason to commemorate his daughter after she had been drowned while swimming in the Caspian Sea.

Bahrain 50.35 E

Another place where I changed planes. Basically I associate Bahrain with racehorses. The ruler, I believe, has an excellent collection of galloping horses. Unfortunately there was not quite enough time to leave the airport before another plane took me on to Singapore.

Teheran 51.30 E

I lived for one year in Teheran, at Piche Shemiran. While I was there, I visited Isfahan and Persepolis and Shiraz and wondered at the mosque of Sheikh Lotfollah and the winged bulls and the Qashqai House. I think of Iran as a country of poets – Hafez, of course, and Firdausi and Jalal-ud-Din Rumi and so many others. In Teheran avenues were named after poets. I wonder what they are called today. I also remember vividly how a friend – a sculptor who boasted members of the royal family among his clients – once told me that Princess Ashraf, the Shah's twin sister, had ordered a poet to be murdered. I visited the poet's grave with my friend in order to pay my respects. Now the Shah is dead and Princess Ashraf is head of the family. She lives in the big mansion just up the hill from where I sit now – a house big enough to be seen from the plane as it descends to land at LAX. At least, that is what I was told by an Iranian cab-driver as we drove past it, reminiscing about Iran as I brought my daughter back home from school.

Singapore 104.0 E

Singapore is the site of the Tiger Balm Gardens – a park containing a series of sculpted tableaux illustrating episodes from Chinese novels or providing moral lessons through scenes of criminal or immoral behaviour which inevitably lead those involved into disaster. I stayed in the Raffles Hotel, fortunately before it was modernised, where I enjoyed my Singapore Sling, as I pondered the civic prominence of the Singapore Cricket Club and the Church of England Cathedral. I also visited the site of The Great World, a famous – or should I say notorious – amusement park, now fallen into decay, with creeping plants twined around the antique roller coaster.

Hong Kong 114.14 E

There is an excellent museum of teapots in Hong Kong. The most incredible feature of the city, however, is the gathering of Filipina maids in the financial district every weekend, on their day-off. As you cross from the mainland to the island on the ferry you hear a strange noise which turns out to be the sound of conversation as the maids show each other family photographs or discuss working conditions, seated on the pavement outside some bank.

Taipei 121.30 E

I have vivid memories of the paper funeral paraphernalia which was displayed in shops and I brought back with me a passport to Hades and even a cheque-book full of cheques to be drawn on the Bank of Hades, so that I would not be indigent in the after-life. I also visited the old British fort which still existed at the northern tip of the island, offering yet another opportunity to muse on the smudgy finger-marks left across the world by generations of British sailors, soldiers, governors, administrators, missionaries and so on.

Seoul 126.58 E

I associate Seoul with traffic jams, slowing down my journey to Chonju even on what appeared to be a twelve-lane highway – trucks, cars and buses desperately swerving and accelerating to gain lane advantage whenever the opportunity offered and then being forced back into a snail-like progression foot by foot and yard by yard. The traffic was like a gigantic river of mechanical sludge in contrast to the fast-flowing river of water that runs through the city, spanned by a series of bridges and walled in by forests of tower-blocks.

Osaka 135.30 E

The airport at which I first landed in Japan, on a visit which took me to a garden in Kyoto in which the winter snow had been carefully raked as if it was the summer sand and a bar in Fukuoka where I was introduced to the Great Camel Battleship, who gave me his card, reminisced about his theatrical appearance at the Roundhouse in London and finally exchanged a series of haikus with me.

Tokyo Narita 139.45 E

Landing, I couldn't help remembering that the airport had once been the site of an immense popular struggle, an effort to save homes and a way of life. In Tokyo, I paid my respects at the graves of two great film-makers – Mizoguchi Kenji and Ozu Yasujiro. Ozu's grave is actually outside Tokyo, near the sea. Mizoguchi's is in the city, in the grounds of a Nichiren Buddhist temple. Ozu's grave has many bottles of alcohol on its plinth, available for pouring libations. He was a great drinker and I also visited the tavern where he had his own bottles reserved on the shelf and insisted on silence as he drank. Mizoguchi has another grave in Kyoto, which I have also visited. It seems that there was a dispute over the proper whereabouts of his grave – essentially between the family, based in Tokyo, and the film industry, based in Kyoto. The dispute was settled by an agreement to divide the bones, left after cremation, and bury one half in Tokyo and the other in Kyoto.

Melbourne 145.00 E

Here I was awarded a Silver Boomerang. Peter Greenaway got the Gold. What I remember most, however, are the wrought-iron balconies and the excellent red wine.

Sydney 151.10 E

On this trip I saw a duck-billed platypus as well as wallabies and emus and koala bears. It was strange to be in a country which was defined somehow in terms of the uniqueness of its flora and fauna – there was a strange mismatch between the platypus or the koala bear and the Sydney Opera House or Australian rules football, between nature and culture, as symbols of what Roland Barthes would have called Australian-ness. (Incidentally, the first and only time I met Roland Barthes, after climbing up a flight of rickety stairs to his office, I was struck mainly by the fact that he had a weighing machine right next to his desk.)

Honolulu 157.52 W

I had hoped to hear Hawaiian creole spoken here, a language which developed out of the mix of languages spoken by the plantation labourers on the big sugar estates.

Hilo, Hawaii 155.05 W

I went to Hawaii specifically in order to visit the volcano on Big Island. The cab-driver who took me up to the crater of Kilauea told me that he regretted Queen Victoria's refusal to annex Hawaii for the British Empire. If she had agreed to accept Hawaii as a colony, he pointed out, it would now be an independent nation like Fiji or Tonga. He was surprised that I wanted to visit the volcano – I actually walked on the lava crust within the crater – because, for him, it was simply a destructive and much-feared force of nature.

Whitehorse 135.03 W

Travelling to Whitehorse, in the Yukon Territory, I was reminded of Charlie Chaplin and his classic film of The Gold Rush. Chaplin, I recollected, escaped financial ruin at the time of the great Stock Exchange crash, because he kept all his wealth in gold, buried in the garden, I believe.

Inuvik 133.40 W

Inuvik is in the far north of Canada, on the Arctic coast. There is an Inuktituk language radio station and everybody in the hotel bar seemed to have a story to tell, prefaced by the question, "I expect you're wondering how I ended up here?" The most surprising answer was, "I lost a bet." Through the window you could see snow flying sideways in the wind.

Vancouver 123.10 W

Vancouver is one of my favourite cities. I visited it again recently and as the plane descended into the airport I could see the ski-lift at Grouse Mountain, standing out against the snow, and remembered travelling up on it. I also like Stanley Park, with its totem-poles and its view of the huge yellow mound of sulphur on the other side of the water. Vancouver also boasts my favourite second-hand bookshop, which has kept its character even though its site has changed a few blocks, with great stacks of books piled up all over the floor as well as serried ranks of books on shelves and in cabinets.

San Francisco 122.23 W

Like so many others, the first time I visited San Francisco I went on the Vertigo tour, going to see the various sites shown in Hitchcock's film, ending up at the mission church at San Juan Bautista, where the horse was still in the stable but the chapel had no tower. My other must-sees were the Diego Rivera murals, of which there are a number, including one in the Stock Exchange club, and the local murals – a tribute to Rivera in their own way – to be found in the Coit Tower (which can be clearly seen from the street outside the house in which Jimmy Stewart lives in Hitchcock's film, at 900 Lombard Street).

Oakland 122.13 W

In Oakland I saw *The Wizard of Oz* in a wonderful art déco cinema, the Paramount, worthy of the film. It had a theatre organ, of course, and elaborately decorated washrooms.

Santa Barbara 119.42 W

In Santa Barbara I saw a performance of Brecht's *The Measures Taken* which left a deep impression on me, a mixture of astonishment and dismay. It is also where, driving on the main highway into town, I looked out of the car window, only to be confronted by the traumatic scene I remembered so well from my childhood viewing of *Bambi*, the scene in which the fire rages through the forest, destroying everything. To me, it was linked to the idea of the blitz, the war and the bombs and my own memories of being carried down and put safely in the space under the stairs when the sirens sounded at night. Of course it turned out to be, not a hallucination but an image projected on the huge screen of a drive-in cinema, as I found out later on returning to the scene of my re-lived trauma. It is obvious to me now that *Bambi* was really a war film, with a father who is away at the front, a mother whose home is destroyed and a child who is left an orphan and a refugee. P.S. The airport at Santa Barbara provides a charming example of Spanish Days pastiche.

Burbank 118.18 W

This is the airport I often find myself using when I fly to another city in California, such as San Francisco. It always reminds me of the catch-phrase 'Beautiful Downtown Burbank' which was used in *The Rowan and Martin Laugh-In*, an American comedy show aired on British television. I still think of myself on arrival back at Burbank as if I was checking in to the *Laugh-In*. I somehow expect a gale of hilarity to greet me as I land.

Los Angeles 118.25 W

The original name of Los Angeles was 'El pueblo de la Reina de Los Angeles sobre el rio de la Porciúnculá'. This is often forgotten nowadays. The city is usually just called L.A. and the airport is known as LAX. Still, even in its truncated form, the name of the city reminds us that it was once Spanish and then Mexican, before the American conquest.

John Wayne Airport, Orange County 117.55 W

This airport boasts a life-like statue of John Wayne with his characteristic turn of the shoulders and swaggering stride, an icon of the American conquistador.

San Diego 117.09 W

I first visited San Diego to appear as one of a panel at the annual conference of the Modern Language Association. This particular panel was devoted to the work of Christian Metz, the creator of contemporary film theory, who had recently died. I remember the first time I met Metz, which was actually in Milwaukee. I was surprised to learn that, before becoming a film scholar, he had been both a simultaneous translator for the United Nations and a jazz musician. In fact, I always felt his commitment to jazz was more deeply rooted even than his commitment to film. Hence his liking for improvisation in films and his suspicion of conventional narrative.

Yellowknife 114.29 W

I don't remember much about Yellowknife except that people downed drinks with several layers of differently coloured liqueurs and expressed great pride in their town, claiming there would be a fine future there for a film-maker. At least that was my cab-driver's view.

Missoula 114.01 W

The main feature of this small Montana town was a beautifully carved merry-go-round, made by the citizens themselves as a contribution to civic life. In the University Library, I whiled away the time before I gave my lecture reading a novel by Percy Lubbock.

Edmonton 113.30 W

I had planned a visit to the Arctic Ocean on a journey which would involve as many means of transportation as possible – pedestrian, automobile, bus, train, boat, etc. The shopping mall in Edmonton, supposedly the world's largest, has a submarine in which visitors to the mall can descend and I wanted to fit this experience in between the train station and the airport. However my taxi driver told me that, because of traffic, I would miss my flight if I stopped to take the submarine, so I had to miss out on that particular vehicular mode.

Salt Lake City 111. 53 W

I was fortunate enough to be chair of the Jury at the Sundance Festival, which is held at a ski resort in the mountains overlooking the city. That was the year in which all the awards, as it turned out, went to African-American directors. The most scandalous choice was the award that went to *Chameleon Street*, a great film directed by Wendell B Harris Jr. It was neither blaxploitation nor emotional realism, but the strange story of a confidence trickster whose life has been altered by watching Jean Cocteau's *La Belle et la Bête*.

Denver 104.59 W

This is an enormous airport at which I once made the mistake of changing planes, without having realised quite how long it would take me to get from one gate to the other. I was sorry to miss visiting the city and especially the Governor's mansion, where the experimental film-maker Stan Brakhage had been employed by former Governor Love as an artist-in-residence. The Governor would hold his gubernatorial meetings while Brakhage concerned himself with filming the light reflected and refracted by the Governor's ash-tray, dancing around the corner of the gigantic desk with his hand-held camera as he strove to capture every nuance of each glint and dazzle. Meanwhile the Governor would talk with a series of visitors, advising them not to be distracted by the strange vision before their eyes, but to carry on with their conversation with the Governor as normally as possible.

Guadalajara 103.20 W

It was in Guadalajara that I got into an argument with Raquel Tibol about Dr Atl. I mentioned Dr Atl was one of my favourite artists, an idiosyncratic choice since Dr. Atl did little else but paint erupting volcanoes. Legend has it that when the volcano Paricutin erupted Dr. Atl rushed to buy land on the volcano's slopes from fleeing farmers, so that he would have an unobstructed viewpoint from which to paint. Raquel Tibol dislikes Dr. Atl, since he supported the fascists in the 1930s. Earlier in his life, however, he had been an anarcho-syndicalist and it was at this time that he rallied key sections of the working class to support Obregon and the Revolution, a fact which Raquel Tibol angrily disputed.

Aguascalientes 102.12 W

I visited Aguascalientes because it was the birthplace of José Guadalupe Posada, the great Mexican cartoonist and popular illustrator. I have a Posada print on my wall, which was given to me by the photographer Manuel Alvarez Bravo after a discussion in which he observed that photography – his own chosen medium – was simply a variant of the print, which was Posada's chosen medium as well as that of Dürer, an artist whom Alvarez Bravo greatly revered. My own Posada – two lovers embracing – was printed by Alvarez Bravo himself.

Mexico D.F. 99.10 W

I spent a lot of time in Mexico City on account of co-curating an exhibition of paintings by Frida Kahlo and photographs by Tina Modotti. My most memorable experience was my visit to see a lady whom I believed had the largest single collection of Kahlo paintings. I had heard many amazing stories about her before we met, which may or may not have been true – for instance, I was told that she had been the mistress of a former Mexican president who gave her the land on which Mexico City's railway station was built. When the railway company failed to pay the rent, so it was said, she ordered her people to put a fence round the property, running across the tracks. When I first met her, after waiting a long time outside although accompanied by a quite high functionary from the Mexican Foreign Office, I was ushered into an enormous room where the first thing I saw, hanging over the fireplace, was a famous portrait from the 1930s, showing her in an elaborate Mexican dress. Now, forty years later she was standing there wearing a version of the very same dress, still looking exactly the same as the portrait over her mantelpiece.

Dallas, Fort Worth 96.49—97.18 W

I visited Fort Worth in order to look at a collection of prints made by the Mexican illustrator and artist, José Guadelupe Posada. It was organising this exhibition that led me to the Mexico City home of Arsacio Vanegas, the grandson of Posada's printer and the man who trained Fidel Castro and Che Guevara in wrestling skills before they embarked for Cuba on the *Granma*. Arsacio kindly gave me a retablo with a ballad of his own composition, describing their departure. I thought about his grandfather and about Posada.

Minneapolis, St. Paul 93.16—93.06 W

In Minneapolis I talked at some length to Peter Greenaway. We had each made our first feature films for the British Film Institute at the same time – *Riddles of the Sphinx* and *The Draughtsman's Contract* – but had never met, although I believe we had been in the same room together one time in Athens, Ohio. Now we talked about our childhood memories of Rupert Bear annuals, a long narrative cartoon with captions under each drawing in rhyming couplets. I was surprised he did not recall the Chinese Magician.

Palenque 91.90 W

This is the site of another famous Mayan pyramid, the mural paintings from which are now in the great Archaeological Museum in Mexico, D.F. Miguel Covarrubias, the Mexican artist, caricaturist and author, was a friend of Nelson Rockefeller, who had an interest in Mexico. Covarrubias told Rockefeller that if you just jabbed a pencil down at random on the map of Mexico you would come up with a spot where you would find ancient pre-Columbian artefacts. Nelson Rockefeller's pencil point landed on Palenque.

Yaqchilan 90.32 W

This is not really an airport. It is a grass clearing, just long enough for a small plane to land, somewhere in the jungle on the Mexican side of the border with Guatemala, with a hut and a hammock in which the pilot reclined while I and my friends inspected the ancient ruins, still overgrown by jungle plants. Eventually the pilot got up and found us, telling us it was time for us to leave before a storm broke. He was very like the pilots in a Howard Hawks film, equally weathered, curt and professional.

Merida 89.37 W

I visited Merida en route to the same Mayan pyramids that had inspired Eisenstein, who was fascinated by the way the facial profiles of the local people matched those depicted on ancient Mayan works of art and began to understand how the recurrent theme of death had dominated Mexican culture since the pre-Columbian epoch, in Maya ritual as in the processions of penitentes that he filmed. I read in the paper earlier today that, not for the first time, the state of Yucatan (of which the Merida is the capital) is threatening to secede from the Republic of Mexico. The first time, however, the secessionists were on the left. Now they are on the right, hard-core remnants of the PRI, a once revolutionary party which gradually succumbed to the lure of unchallenged power and pervasive corruption.

Oshkosh 88.33 W

I think it was Oshkosh. It could have been Sheboygan or Milwaukee or even Racine, where I visited the Johnson's Wax building, designed by Frank Lloyd Wright? Or Kenosha, where Orson Welles was born? In any case, it was the most convenient airport for Appleton, Wisconsin, where Harry Houdini was born and where there was an excellent museum dedicated to the great illusionist. If memory serves, the airport from which I flew out was the only one I know which could boast of having an excellent second-hand bookstore.

Champaign-Urbana 88.15—88.12 W

They have, or used to have, a fine collection of Eisenstein's drawings and other memorabilia at Champaign-Urbana, brought there by a former pupil of Eisenstein, back in the years when he was in disgrace and teaching at the State film school in Moscow.

Chicago, O'Hare 87.56 W

This is the Windy City's huge and extremely uninteresting international airport.

Chicago, Midway 87.45 W

This is the Chicago airport most convenient for visiting downtown, where there are three things not to be missed – first, there is the small version of Picasso's monumental civic sculpture, specially created for Chicago and scaled down so that it can be touched by blind visitors unable to see the original; second there is the collection of Cornell boxes exhibited at the Art Institute, miniature works of three-dimensional collage; third, there is the journalist's pub on South Wacker Drive, a street which runs under the downtown area like a tunnel, originally built to give trucks access to the basement floors of Chicago's downtown department stores. Last time I landed at Midway I took a taxi into town driven by a Moroccan who complained bitterly about the lack of culture exhibited by Americans in comparison with the French, specifically including their drinking habits in his indictment.

Chicago, Migg's Field 87.36 W

This is not really a commercial airport. It is worth flying into precisely because it is so small and right on the lake-front, so that it is rather like landing on an aircraft carrier.

Indianapolis 86.09 W

At the airport for Indianapolis I got a shoeshine and a shave, which I very much needed because I had forgotten to bring my electric razor with me. The first time I went to Indianapolis was to attend a conference on

'Popular Culture', taking place in a hotel with a banner that read WELCOME POPULAR CULTURE, but my main interest was in seeing the fine houses celebrated by Booth Tarkington and Orson Welles in the novel and film of *The Magnificent Ambersons*. The famous crop-duster attack in Hitchcock's *North by Northwest* takes place some miles outside Indianapolis, on the highway from Chicago.

Atlanta 84.23 W

I have only been to the airport at Atlanta because I was en route to somewhere else and I had to change planes. I would very much have liked to see the city, but instead I passed my time in the airport remembering its destruction by fire in *Gone With the Wind*.

Tallahassee 84.17 W

Here I was accommodated in a hexagonal or octagonal Holiday Inn, a tower-block which had wedge-shaped rooms. I was staying on the top floor, which appeared to be allocated for the elite. As well as bedrooms there was a breakfast area where top floor guests all sat around a large table. Every one of my companions at breakfast turned out to be a bishop. They had assembled in the Holiday Inn to attend some kind of episcopal get-together.

Tampa 82.27 W

Like Tallahassee, Tampa is located in Florida, but instead of encountering bishops, I encountered alligators, who took their breakfast in a swamp rather than a Holiday Inn.

Athens 82.06 W

I am referring now to Athens, Ohio, which has nothing resembling a Parthenon.

Havana 82.22 W

In Havana they have a museum dedicated to relics of Napoleon Bonaparte, a lot of it porcelain. It is much more interesting than the Hemingway house. There is also a bar located in an American airplane which had been shot down. Also I was fortunate enough to visit the fashion centre, selling mainly to Canada, and a music studio, where I learnt to recognise guaganco and filin (a kind of blues) and other genres of Cuban music, beyond the better known world of son.

Gainesville 82.20 W

Here I saw a number of alligators and discussed Derrida a great deal.

Detroit 82.03 W

I really like Detroit. I have especially happy memories of the Mo-Town Museum, dedicated to Berry Gordy and his musicians and record label. The next best thing is the Diego Rivera mural in the art museum. In sharp contrast, there is Henry Ford village, a model community created by the nostalgic magnate to celebrate the rural and lily-white culture which he revered so much. Ford was a brilliant engineer but, politically, a monster who both sympathised with Hitler and collaborated with Stalin.

Key West 81.48 W

A pleasant place, unfortunately dominated by the cult of Ernest Hemingway. My visit was partially redeemed by the presence of some extraordinary outsider art.

Orlando 81.23 W

This is the airport for Disney World, but I was there to change planes. Sadly it has been Disney the maestro of kitsch that has survived, rather than the artist Eisenstein admired.

Palm Beach 80.20

A resort town with many rich people and a fine museum. Their exhibition of video art was well worth visiting. I was particularly struck by a video piece made by John Baldessari, titled *Four Minutes of Trying to Tune Four Glasses*, for the Phil Glass Sextet.

Pittsburgh 80.10 W

The home-town of Andy Warhol, where he worked on his paper dolls and attended mass with genuine devotion, a frail and sickly child who became the Courbet of his century.

Toronto 79.20 W

I have an architect friend who was asked to submit plans for re-designing the centre of the city. Among his ideas was that the buildings should be tall so that they generated swirls of wind strong enough to blow your hat off, which he regarded as an essential element of the urban experience. I also associate Toronto with the work of Michael Snow – jazz musician, conceptual artist, hologram designer, avant-garde film-maker – whose installation of flying geese is one of the city's most memorable features. I have a soft spot for Toronto because I designed an Electromedia billboard in the centre of the city as part of a project for commissioning public art. It featured space-creatures warning the inhabitants of Toronto against the threat to life on the planet potentially brought about by man-made destruction – it looked comic but it was fundamentally tragic.

Buffalo 78.53 W

I went to Buffalo in order to make a television film about the photographer, Milton Rogovin. It was a fascinating experience. I went to visit the people, mostly African American or Latino, whom he had photographed during his career – often at regular intervals over a long period of years – and talked to them, in their own homes, about their experience, which most of them remembered very clearly and talked about eloquently.

Rochester 77.37 W

Rochester, the home of Eastman Kodak, was also, for many years, the home of Louise Brooks, the star of Pabst's *Lulu*, before she was lured to Paris by Henri Langlois to preside over the Cinemathèque, along with Marie Meerson.

Washington 77.20 W

A horrible city, with all the trappings of empire and corruption. I suppose

I might make an exception for Maya Lin's Vietnam Monument, but even then I prefer her water sculpture at Yale, which documents the historical disparity between the numbers of male and female students admitted over the years.

Ithaca 76.30 W

Everybody I met in Ithaca seemed to be a follower of Jacques Derrida. It seemed a long way, culturally as well as geographically, from Derrida's native Algeria, written about so movingly in his book on linguistic hybridity, or even from Paris, his adopted home. There was something uncanny about this delightful little university town, set in pleasant hill country, covered with heavy falls of snow in winter, having now become a principal outpost of Derrida's very Parisian theories of deconstruction.

Syracuse 76.09 W

This is Syracuse in New York State, not the Syracuse in Sicily which, sadly, I have never visited. Syracuse makes me feel guilty because I was asked to write an article on silence and noise for a magazine based there and I am already falling behind schedule. As soon as I have finished writing this, I must read John Cage's *Silence* and try to understand Jacques Attali's strange career as both a banker and a public intellectual, the author of *Noise*.

Philadelphia 75.10 W

I went to Philadelphia to deliver a paper on Heidegger and Junger, two vastly over-rated German writers, deeply compromised by their collaboration with fascism, both of whom nonetheless became cult figures in recent years in France, where leading figures in the intelligentsia convinced themselves that there was nothing in particular to forgive. There is something about the latest wave of French intellectuals that has always puzzled me – why is it that they go to such lengths to overlook the trahison of their favoured clercs?

Newark 74.10 W

Another site which I visited because of Komar & Melamid who were carrying out a project in the nearby New Jersey city of Bayonne, a waterfront town with a vast oil terminal, an Olmsted park and an art-world roll-call which included early work by Robert Smithson, who was brought up in the area and used it for site-specific pieces.

Newburgh 74.01 W

In the taxi from the airport to Bard College, where I was to attend a planning meeting for an exhibition on 'Global Conceptualism', I talked to the cab-driver who turned out to be a former U.S. Navy 'Seal' who had been dispatched on shore on a secret mission during the war against Iraq, travelling underwater clinging to a torpedo. At least, that's what he told me. When he got there he had to lie low and send back information about bomb targets.

New York, La Guardia 73.70 W

This airport used to have extraordinary murals, painted by Stuart Davis, Arshile Gorky and others, celebrating the achievements of aviation. They were taken down long ago and are now lost to view.

New York, Kennedy 73.45 W

This airport used to be called Idlewild and was famous for Eero Saarinen's architecture. His building is still there, but it no longer dominates. It is just another airport terminal.

Boston 71.04 W

The Paris exhibition on the Situationist International subsequently travelled to Boston, where I was introduced to Tony Oursler, the artist, who had been employed by the ICA to create a video installation showing events in Paris during May 1968. I was against its inclusion in the exhibition because I thought it contributed to the very 'spectacularisation' of politics to which the situationists themselves were so virulently opposed. It was effective as an installation though and I don't hold it against him in any way.

Halifax 63.35 W

My main memory of Halifax is of a visit to a deserted motel, located so that travellers and sightseers could observe the high tide or 'bore' which sweeps down the Bay of Fundy. There was a huge clock with hands designed to be pointed to the hour and minute when the high tide would sweep by, but nobody had touched the clock for many months.

Gander 54.35 W

I had to change planes at Gander in order to get to Havana. Gander is on the island of Newfoundland which is part of Canada, a country which has normal diplomatic relations with Cuba. You have to fly down the East Coast of the United States and then round the tip of Florida, taking care not to enter U.S. airspace.

São Paulo 46.37 W

This is a strange city, whose most charming feature, I thought, was its Librairie Française, a really excellent bookshop with a fantastic stock of books. I went to São Paulo to give a lecture at the University, where, to my surprise, the students mostly wanted to hear my views on Quentin Tarantino, then bathing in the cult success of his film, *Pulp Fiction*. I said that it was too early to say anything much about Tarantino – I was a long-time auteurist, but my understanding of auteurism in the Hollywood context meant, not that you had made one successful film, but that you had made a series of films which, viewed as a unit, illuminated each other and formed a single coherent body of work,

Rio de Janeiro 43.12 W

If you are lucky enough to end up in Rio like the bank-robber played by Alec Guinness in *The Lavender Hill Mob*, you should make a special effort to visit the Carmen Miranda museum, with its wonderful collection of extravagant shoes and other such memorabilia. While there I met the artist Artur Omar who drove me through all the stop lights, explaining that it was Sunday. He also takes the credit for formulating the idea that there was a particular film genre called the 'Festival genre', consisting of films especially made for success in film festivals. The films of Kiarostami might be good examples of this genre. Like other successful films in the genre they frequently feature children.

Reykjavík 21.57 W

I have never been outside the airport in Iceland – a stopover breaking the flight from Luxemburg to New York or from Madrid to Gander. I always wanted to leave the airport and go into town, perhaps even travel to the volcanos in which Iceland abounds. But there was never enough time. A brief look round the airport shop and then the boarding call.

Lisbon 09.10 W

I was on my way to the Film Festival at Troia, where a Syrian film director publicly denounced my film, *Friendship's Death*, because of its line on the Palestinians, only to come up to me afterwards and tell me that personally he had liked the film very much, and he hoped I understood that he had to follow the official line in public. I did.

Santiago de Compostela 08.37 W

Visiting the Cathedral in Santiago, we were suddenly told to stop whatever we were doing as tourists and sit down. Several nuns appeared to fill the first few rows of chairs. It turned out that the very ancient Generalissimo Franco was visiting the shrine under the high altar. After he emerged from the crypt he fell, while descending the steps, and had to be caught by his aides, who then carried him out of the cathedral, followed by a bevy of bishops and gendarmes. His feet hardly touched the ground as they rushed him out. It was a scene straight out of a Buñuel film. Soon afterwards he died and Spain was free at last.

Cork 08.29 W

My maternal grandmother came from Cork and I have many happy memories of the city. Cork was the first city in Ireland to hold a Film Festival, back in 1956, originally specialising in short films but gradually evolving into an international event. I particularly remember discovering a really excellent bookshop when I visited the city most recently as a guest of the Festival.

Glasgow 04.15 W

The most interesting site in Glasgow is the re-created Mackintosh house, an outstanding example of his early modern architecture. The Glasgow School of Art was also designed by Mackintosh as well as the Willow Tea-Rooms. Glasgow, like Barcelona, is fortunate to have had an architect who stayed in his home-town and built such great buildings there.

Inverness 04.13 W

On the way to the airport, I asked the taxi driver what his longest journey had been. He told me he had once taken a group of tinkers from Inverness to Brighton. They were tinker royalty, he explained, and they paid in advance with a great wad of banknotes. They were going to a funeral of great significance to tinkers and, somewhere near to Wolverhampton, they made a detour to buy suitably respectful suits from a draper's shop.

Madrid 03.45 W

It seems obvious, even trivial, to say that in the Prado you can see see Velasquez's *Las Meniñas* and Goya's portraits and Picasso's *Guernica*, not to mention the work of El Greco and Zurbaran, but it's salutary to be reminded how important Spanish painting has been in the history of art, a history which often seems to look through a distorting mirror.

Edinburgh 03.13 W

My proudest achievement in Edinburgh was importing the artist Nan Goldin to recreate the slide-show I had first seen in a tacky bar on the old 42nd Street, where I was one of an audience of friends and hangers-on. Edinburgh is also where I met Samuel Fuller for the first time. I remember him re-enacting everything he talked about as though he were directing a film, taking up camera positions and running from one point to another.

Manchester 02.12 W

I like to think of Manchester as the city it used to be in the nineteenth century, the city of the Hallé Orchestra and the Rylands Library and the home of Friedrich Engels.

London, Heathrow 00.36 W

My first flight, my first step towards cosmopolitanism. I am happy to use the term, with its echoes of Anarcharsis Cloots and the cosmopolitan deputation he led before the assembly in Paris, the cosmopolitanism celebrated by Herman Melville and CLR James.

Johnny Spencer

Save a Bread

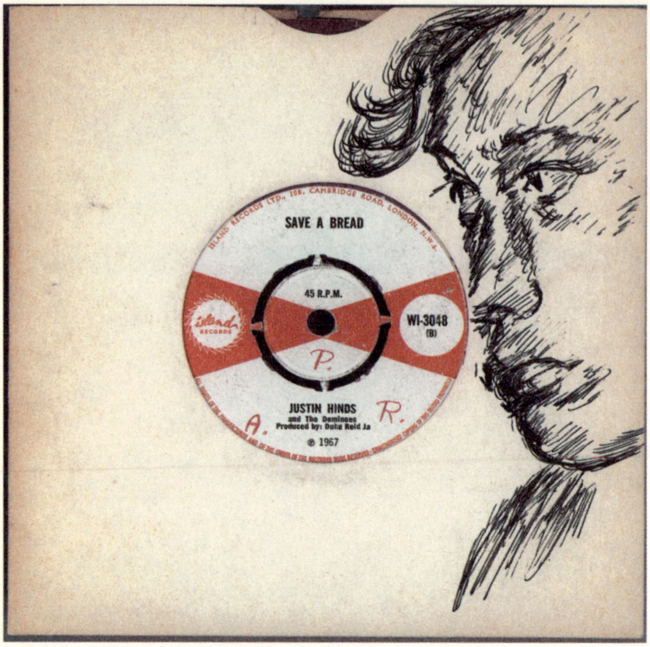

SAVE A BREAD

Justin Hinds, singing, "What you know you know, what you don't know you don't know", on the record 'Save a Bread', which he cut for Duke Reid's Treasure Isle label in 1967. Special request for the West London Succession boys, a big shout going out to the Mute posse and the RFH massive, big it up Rasta. Lets start with the facts. It's no small thing that bread has been a staple part of our diet for over 3,245 years, Isaiah, whoever he was, said "wherefore do ye spend money for that which is not bread". Now, as I sit and eat my sandwich made from sweet tasting fresh bread I have to report that sadly the ordinary Southern England white loaf, one amongst many national varieties baked by the local baker, is about to disappear. This benign institution, the local baker, after so many years of providing not only the staple diet of many folk but also meaningful employment and a vital constituent part of communities, has become another victim of the relentless craving for profit, power and control by the supermarkets. Worse still, it's bad enough that our daily bread is being monopolised and governed by fewer and fewer of these corporations, but that the elected councillors and politicians are aiding and abetting those corporations is a scandal. The question needs to be asked, "Whats Going On?" And that one goes out to NN and all the eco warriors.

DRESS REHEARSAL FOR AN EVEN DARKER FUTURE

Take transport, just to touch on one or two aspects of the whole outrage: all but the most woolly-headed know that the majority of shoppers now have to use their cars when doing their shopping. This situation has been brought about in part because local and national governments have for years pursued a policy of penalising shoppers who chose to travel by car to shop anywhere but supermarkets or shopping malls. The authorities build and alter existing roads in favour of the supermarkets creating unobstructed artificial desire lines for easy access and a safe zone for the persecuted motorists stationary vehicle. With what can only be described as criminal acts, an ever growing raft of laws are aimed specifically at the motorist and the motor car, laws primarily designed to increase tax revenue for the authorities, but which amongst other things have had the additional effect of forcing shoppers away from the secondary shopping locales into the relatively more convenient and cheaper supermarket car park. And don't be fooled for one minute thinking that it is ironic or somehow paradoxical that the motorist should be persecuted so when it is the car that is one of the biggest sources of internal revenue and employment for the government. Of course laws like yellow lines and their attendant parking meters (brought in by Baroness Castle when she was Transport Minister for the Labour Party in the 1960s, and who is now mysteriously trumped up as a darling of the people) are introduced without any regard to whether the people who will suffer most from them agree or not. They are just put

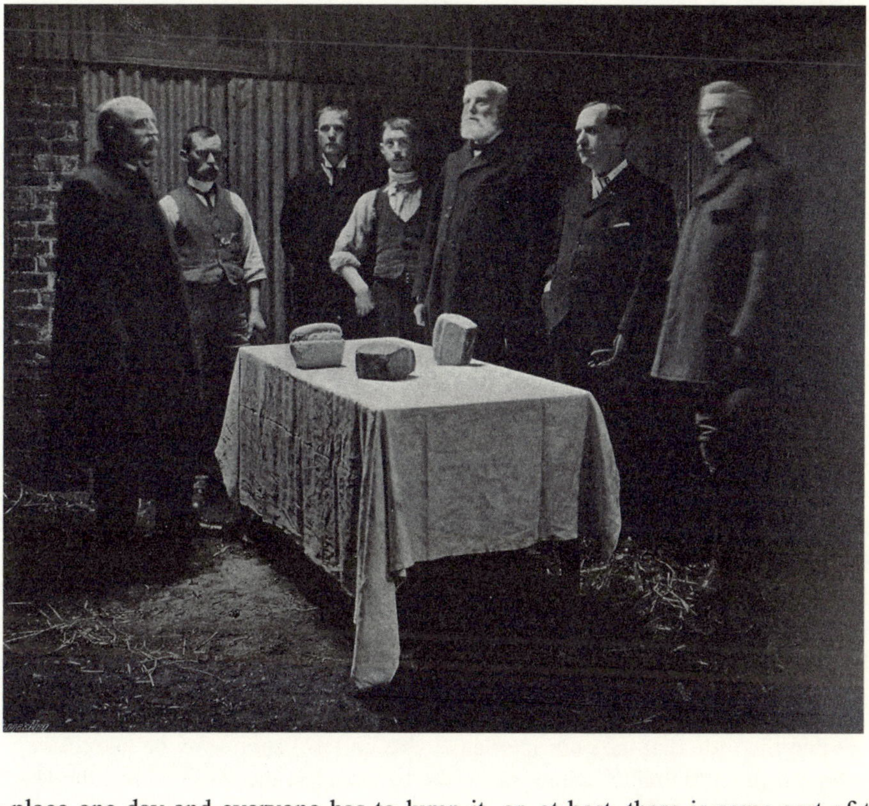

into place one day and everyone has to lump it, or, at best, there is some sort of trial program which we are told is limited, and then once all dissent has blown over, those initial laws are exaggerated and bloated to the point of oppression, by which time the majority have 'grown used to it' and anyway they are now trying to adjust and come to terms with a more recent government scam. Local governments treat local shops and motorists with contempt, with their one way streets, blocked or obstructed roads, red lines, yellow lines, bus lanes that have metamorphosed from being only operating rush hour restrictions into twenty-four hour ones, people employed to take money from a motorist if they stop, to CCTV cameras that watch the citizens' every move. (When was the law passed allowing for that, and was the man in the street told about it?) It's hard to know if these would be/soon to be politicians are just following the Neo Liberal dogma of car hating or are carefully putting into place, piece by piece, the mechanisms that are part of what is making our neighbourhoods into 'societies of control'. Neighbourhoods that were once vibrant and active because of local small scale commerce have become empty and threatening. With little or no human interaction on the streets its no wonder that CCTV cameras are seen by some as not a threat to civil liberties and a stimulus for paranoia but a means of providing an otherwise non-existent presence. Punitive transport laws are only one of the points of attack that the small shopper/retailer has had to contend with, there are many others designed to favour the big conglomerate over the small individual. Take for instance the endless stream of laws issuing from Brussels aimed at the food industry that favour the giant food manufactures, producers and retailers, many of which are now subsidiaries of the supermarkets. Laws on everything to do with farming, production and marketing, even how the goods should be sold. Just who does it favour if beans are sold by the litre or pound if that's what folk want, if not the global producers and retailers so that they can homogenise and reduce cost in areas like packaging, pricing, vending, etc. in their relentless pursuit of economic growth. Again we now have a situation where yet another member of the aristocracy, Baroness Symmons, the New Labour European Minister, is supposed to be speaking on behalf of the people within those power structures that are hell-bent on bringing this and other nightmares into fruition. Listen to those educated and privileged tones issuing from her when she deals with bodies like the WTO as a representative of a party that in its early days men and women gave their precious time and hard earned money to, so as to be able to have *their* voice heard. I am sure that many of those early pioneers would weep to see that the privileged power elites they fought so long and hard to break from the yoke of have usurped the very movement that they struggled to bring into being. Interesting, in this context, is the recent employment of Baroness Morgan of Huyton as a special assistant to the Prime Minister, a very important role in the party's decision-making mechanism. Also worthy of note is where the departing occupant of the job, Tony Blair's much valued friend and advisor Anji Hunter, who's friendship with the PM goes back some thirty odd years, is off to with all her valuable inside knowledge - she has left to join BP, who are one of the foremost players in the new social landscape; the takeover by corporate interests of our public institutions, policy and culture. Witness BP's current (Summer 2001) very real and scary [because they mean it] bullshit message of being the protectors of society's values and ethics in their ongoing advertising/culture shaping media campaign, but that's another story. It's a day in the tale of two cities, no matter how the commoner is studied by the privileged when receiving their education, they never seem to care that the little that the poor man's got (his culture) shall soon be taken away. Far more honest that the Public School boys, the baronesses, the millionaires, the lawyers, the sons and daughters of multinational corporations and political dynasties, historically the peoples oppressors, were to have dropped the word 'labour' from the title of their new party. William Morris's quote from his News From Nowhere would then be as true now as it was when he wrote it one hundred years ago:

> Men fight and lose the battle, and the thing they fought for comes about in spite of their defeat, and then it turns out to be not what they meant, and other men have to fight for what they meant under another name.

How many of these individuals from the ranks of the privileged does it take for the 'thin veneer' of egalitarianism to become transparent and reveal the same shape of bodies in power on this island as in the 16th, 17th, 18th and 19th centuries.

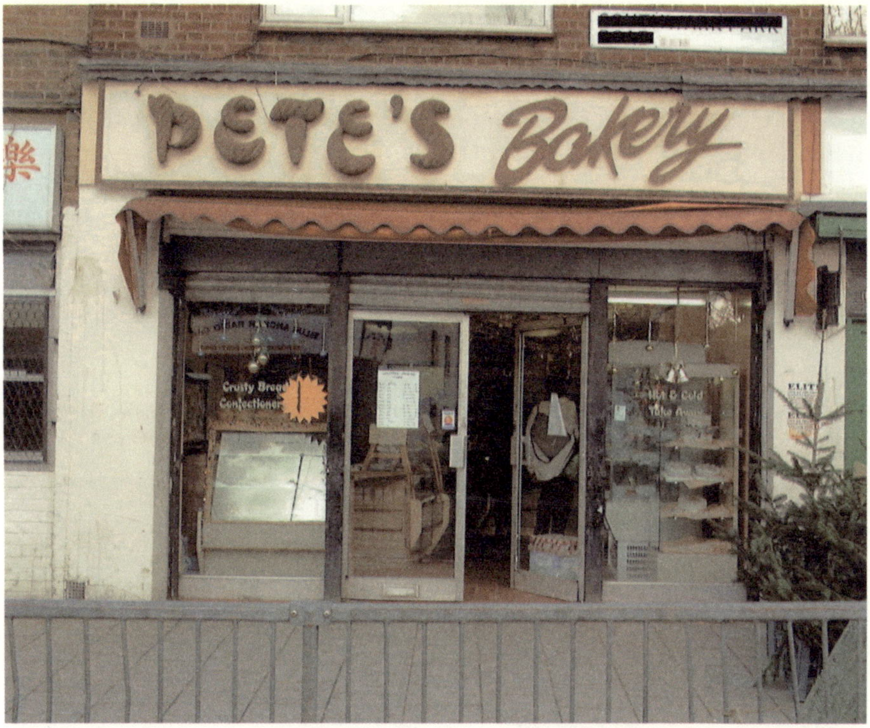

THE HARDNESS OF THE BUTTER IS PROPORTIONAL TO THE SOFTNESS OF THE BREAD

Over the last twenty years my search to buy the bread I prefer has become more desperate. Bakers once considered by me, good or OK, have either disappeared altogether or become 'boulangeries', selling simulacra of breads from around the world, breads that are probably only a faint echo of the fine bread they represent (taste the difference between something as simple as an English French Stick and a French French Stick). Some bakers have turned into small retail chains, others into sandwich bars, but however they adjust in order to fight against the insidious EU, supermarkets and the councils, the net result is the same; the ordinary loaf and the bread roll suffer. The simple pleasure of walking to the bakers and returning home with a fresh, warm, loaf of bread, bread that not only tastes good on its own but will be edible for a couple of days, is becoming a thing of the past. While this claim can be dismissed as nostalgia, in reality it is the food manufactures who are simulating and re-presenting food at the level of a cultural style, who often sell their product by using a period theme, a cynical and hollow use of the past which has in part given the term nostalgia it's negative connotations. Yet nostalgia, or the loss of a sense of authentic history, can help us measure the distance we have come, and appreciate the reality of change. Sadly, bread, once a simple foodstuff that didn't require a lot of knowledge for its use, has now become part of the information economy. Aspects of the humble loaf are the matter of symbolically manipulated information, resulting in our understanding and judgment subject to and dependant on such information. Once our judgment is reliant on information and not on our own 'genuine knowledge' then the situation arrives where - *what we are told we get is what we believe we get.*

GLOBALISATION, I FART IN YOUR GENERAL DIRECTION

The move by our ruling and power elites towards ever-larger organisations in political/corporate power structures, EU, WTO, G8, BP, Bloomberg etc, has brought about a corresponding erosion of the individual's power and an undermining of democratic processes, choice and freedom. The policing (constricting) and reconfiguring of thought, custom and culture is part of the drive to bring about a one world global culture with equivalent mass markets where the three basic demands of pan capitalism; control, order and production are universally fixed in place. These markets, which at present still stubbornly correspond to national and local boundaries, are being eroded by the homogenisation of product and the destruction of identities, whereas the trend should be in the opposite direction, to domestic markets and local initiatives. Since the economy in Great Britain changed from industrialisation to a post-industrial 'knowledge economy' our diet and eating habits have changed dramatically.

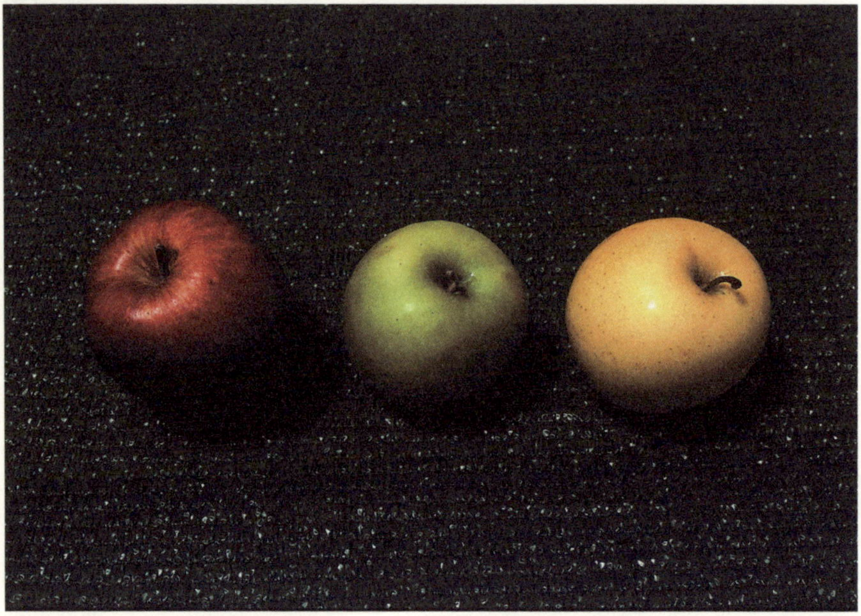

Not so long ago there were dozens of various types of apples on sale in our shops. Now the supermarket has limited the choice to three: red, green, and yellow.

Concordant with globalisation the diet of the commoner has been ever more inclusive of 'world foods', foodstuff that for the most part is fed to a much poorer population. While quality fresh 'local' produce [dairy products, fish, meat and vegetables] have increasingly become a pleasure of those rich enough to afford them, the vast majority of people are sold manufactured or dried, imported food. That the worth of fresh food is in its substance and not its brand, packaging or certified nutritional value, can be experienced by a visit to one of the monthly 'local farm' markets that appeared during the 1990s in the wealthier parts of London, where food is sold by retailers who are growing or producing their own food on a small scale usually just enough to sell on the day. Food at these markets is sold without packaging, and judgements are made through the senses and personal contact with the producer.

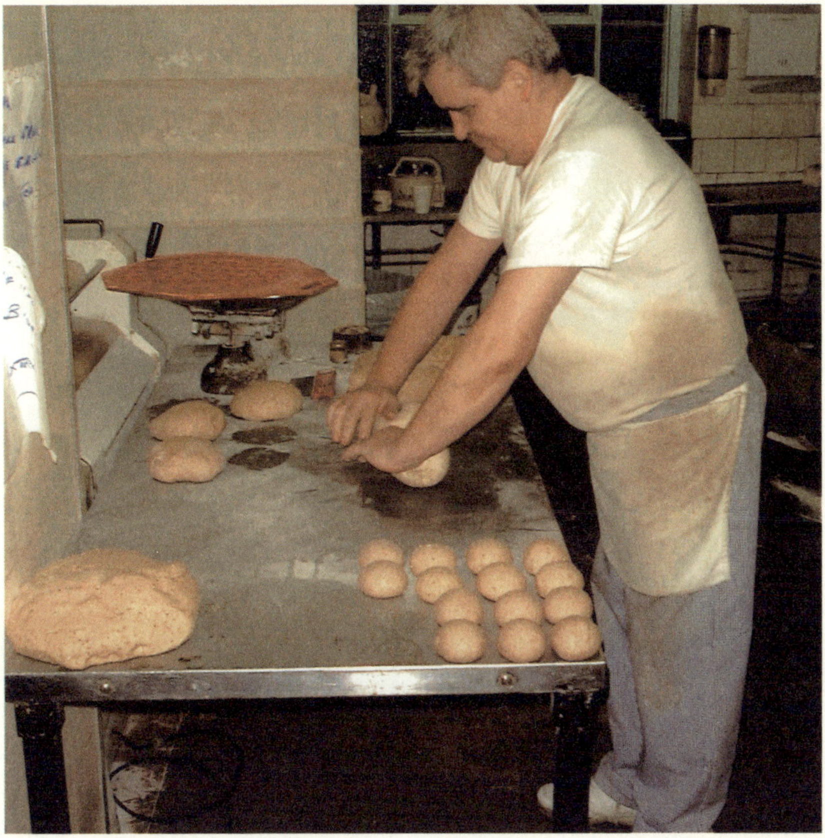

ALL ACCOUNTS OF THE WORLD ARE EQUALLY FICTIONAL.

Really and truthfully speaking there is nothing new in bad bread deals. For the past 250 years or more complaints about the poor quality of our bread have been frequent and forcibly expressed. Elizabeth David, the food specialist, pointed out in 1977 that over 80% of the bread then sold in Britain was produced in factories, and all but about 5% of the rest was made with the same characterless flour supplied by the milling monopolies which control our bread industry. It's just that within that 20% there was a type of bread that was tasty, nourishing and stable, which has all but disappeared. I now have to make a journey of eighteen miles (round trip) to 'Pete's, in the Blue', to buy a half-decent loaf. According to baker Peter Morley, as well as the experience of the baker making judgments on factors like the weather, the missing ingredient in today's bread is time. And time is the one thing that is thought of as is inviolable, but think on this, "As the information economy demands an end to seasonal, biological and clock time, to annihilate time as it seeks a rhythm of even more rapid turnover and obsolescence, the result is timeless time governed by the space of flows. We buy images and services, or consumer durables that no longer represent anything but the continually deferred promise of enjoyment... rather than for any inherent value it may have." Thank you, and our next record is 'Sleep Now in the Fire', by Rage Against the Machine.

Postscript: Since the time of writing, Steve the baker has downgraded the flour and this has inevitably brought about a change in the taste and consistency of the bread. Although the bakers' say they, "have had no complaints", the bread is now, sadly, no longer the bread written about above.

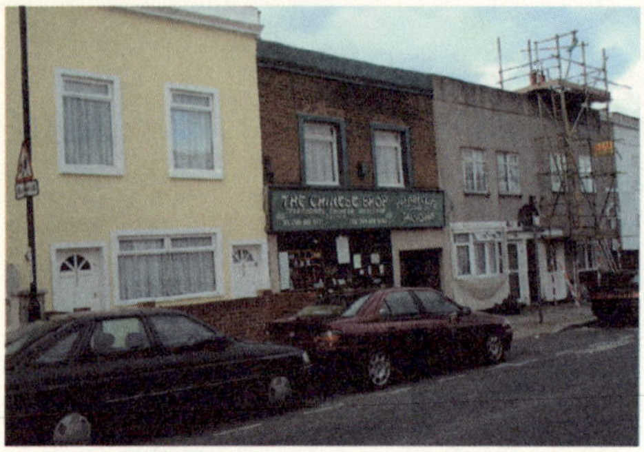

I drive an eighteen mile round trip to buy a decent loaf, yet a five minute walk in one direction from my house not so long ago would have seen all sorts of small shops producing and selling fresh food. All four buildings in this picture were once shops, the yellow one the most recent conversion.

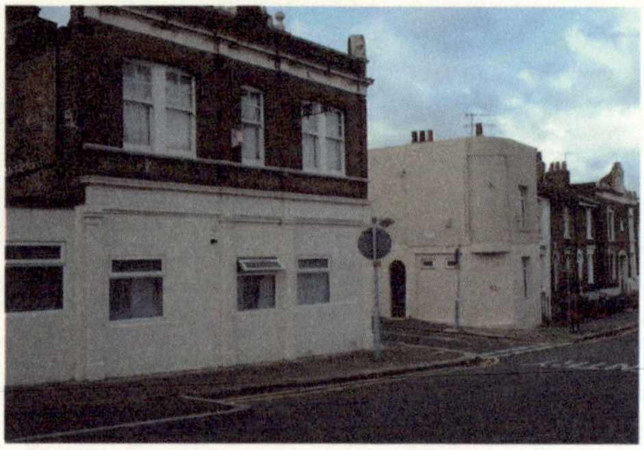

10 yards along from the Chinese shop there was once another corner shop. The pub opposite has in the last month been turned into flats. It's only the poor man's culture - how could those in Downing Street and Brussels be expected to know or care about that when global issues are at stake for them.

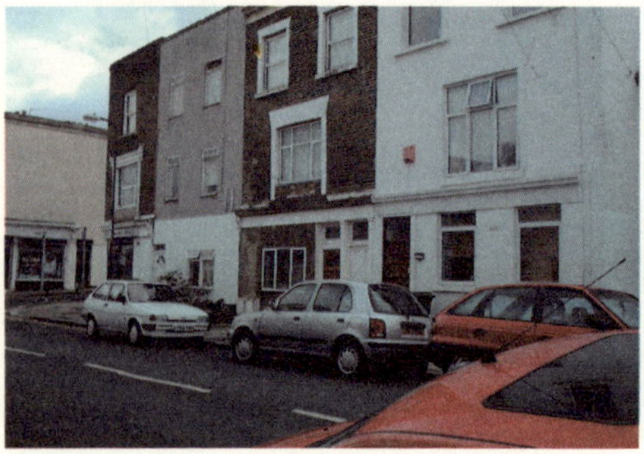

Turn right and 20 yards along the next street there is another four shops, three of which have been converted. The corner onc gave up the ghost last Summer. On the opposite corner an Asian chemist is still open, perhaps it will survive if drugs take over from liquor as the sedative that eases pain.

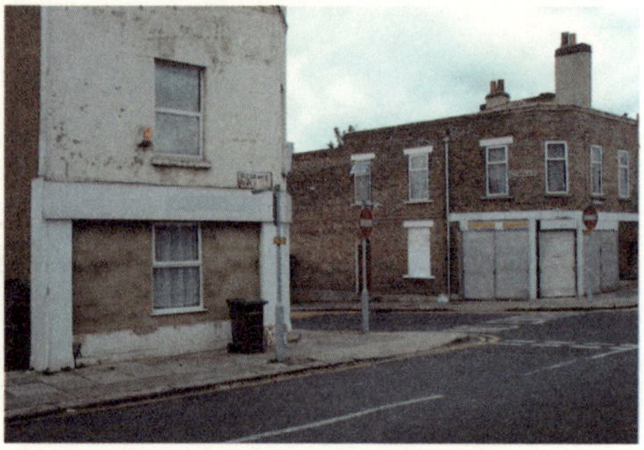

The other side of the road from the chemist; the render is still drying on the conversion on the left. Talking of the left, what rules and regulations will the council come up with next, preventing traders trading in ways they disapprove of; complicated road schemes is a good one.

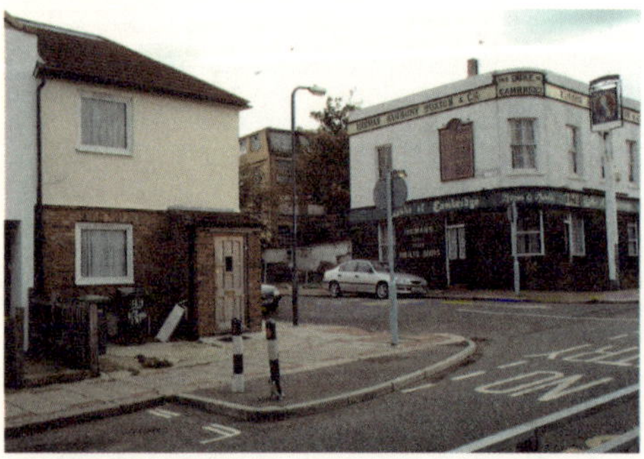

Turn right again and another corner shop bites the dust. The pub opposite is now a private residence. All these shops, pubs and other retail outlets, including milkmen and paper boys, have received a mortal blow from Brussels but were once a vital part of the community that is now hollow.

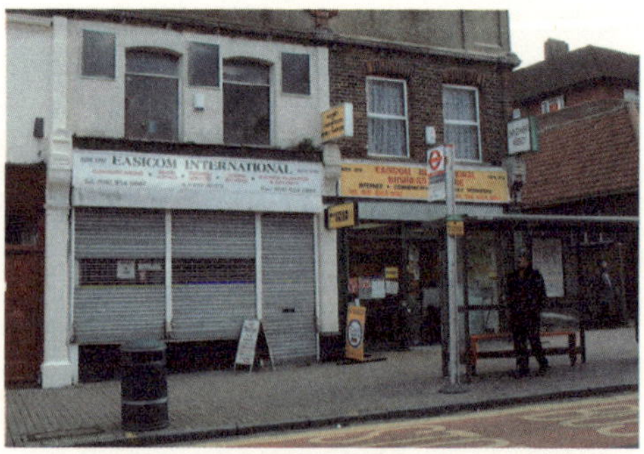

These are just some of the changes in one small block near my home. I can no longer walk around the corner and buy a decent loaf or some fresh fish but I can go and call a country in Africa... Oh what wonderful benefits information services and globalisation gives to the common man.

Travel as Home: An Anthropological Inquiry into the Goa Trance Scene

Roger Begrich & Andrea Mühlebach

We are on our way to a weekend Goa party. The flier I am holding in my hand contains the obligatory signs, notably the *Om* symbol,[1] that for insiders mark the event as a Goa trance party. The parties we have attended over the past few weeks and months had the most diverse of names – *Psychedelic Rituals*, *Om Namaha Shivaya: Truth, Simplicity, Love*, *Cosmica*, *Chaos in Paradise*, *Chakra*, *Prophetic DJs from Outer Space*, *Spirit Dreams*, and *Somewhere in Nowhere*.

We have travelled more than a hundred kilometres so far, and are now slowly approaching our destination in the middle of the Swiss Alps. Travel is part and parcel of how the scene works, as parties are organised nearly every weekend in places that are often far away from the larger city centres.

The destination itself is secret. Many of the parties are on the verge of illegality, and places need to be kept secret for that reason. But there is more to it than that. An aura of adventure, exploration, and discovery saturates the night surrounding us. We 'follow the signs', as is stated on the flier, and orient ourselves via fluorescent *Om* and peace symbols, and other markers that are attached to trees and fences, guiding us along the way. Finally, we approach the party site and park our car under the trees. Walking in the dark of the night, we begin to hear the familiar rhythmical thudding of Goa trance music, see candles flickering on the ground, make out the dim fires and lights emanating from teepees and tents, and the fluorescent decorations hanging from trees and painted on rocks. The crisp alpine air is thick with the smell of incense.

1 ॐ Sanskrit: mantra consisting of the sound \'om\ and used in contemplation of ultimate reality (Webster 1993:810). As Arthur Macdonnel writes, it is 'the subject of many speculations', ranging from something akin to the Christian 'Amen' to its usage in 'invocations, at the commencement of prayers, at the beginning and end of Vedic recitation, and as a respectful salutation' (1929: p 59–60).

The Scene

Since the late 1960s Goa, located on the western coast of Southern India, has been a hippie and so-called "freak"[2] paradise, and a mecca on the Asian "hippie trail". In the 1980s and especially the 1990s, Goa became a site of mass tourism, a large part of which is still hippie tourism concentrated mostly on the Northern Goan village of Anjuna. Here, people from all over the world, particularly from Western Europe, the USA, Israel, and Japan, come together to form a transient community of travelling people, parties, drugs, rituals, objects, and images. Today, the term Goa is used not only to refer to this geographical location, but also to a specific type of electronic (techno) music – Goa, or psychedelic trance – that emerged around the early 1990s at parties in Goa, replacing the live drumming and rock music of earlier times. With the increase of mass tourism, as well as changing means and frequencies of communication, the Goa scene has been carried from Goa out into the world, forming a transnational party culture. In many parts of Western Europe, as well as in places like Israel, Japan, New Zealand, Portugal, Australia, South Africa, Argentina, and Brazil, people are coming together to party outdoors and to, as the Goa freak Nirava put it, "have a little bit of India here... a little bit of homeliness". The transnational Goa scene emphasises its links to India materially via fluorescent decorations which often depict Hindu or Buddhist religious mythology, "chai" (tea) shops, specific types of drugs,[3] drink, and food, and immaterially via certain types of stories, music and dance. The freaks we spoke to regarded the Goa scene as an alternative to the mainstream techno scene, and insisted that an entire philosophy underpinned the parties. In line with this view, our reading of the scene critically focuses on some of the meaningful processes that characterise it. This essay thus aims at representing an alternative to approaches that treat the world of techno and the scenes it is made up of as nothing more than 'a culture of abandonment, disengagement, and disappearance' (Hutson 2000:37).

The Goa scene, as a transnational music and party phenomenon, is a symbol of our times. Enabled by the mass travel and mobility characterising much of the world today, the scene has become a global network of moving people, parties, and images that come together at specific moments and places to form particular kinds of communities of familiarity and belonging. The Goa scene in Switzerland is one particular nodal point within this global network. Our thoughts about it build on a point that has often been made in cultural anthropological debates on the effects of transnationalism and globalisation: movement and travel, roaming and rootlessness, are always concomitantly linked to forms of stability people generate for themselves. In the face of the global, people identify with reference points that often have to be painstakingly created, reinforced, and maintained (Appadurai 1990, 1991; Basso and Hart 1996; Clifford 1997; Gupta and Ferguson 1992; Hannerz 1996; Hastrup and Fog Olwig 1997; Malkki 1992). In a sense, then, this is a paradox: people, despite or because they move both physically and imaginarily, create senses of homeliness,[4] identification, and rootedness in a world of flux and flow.

In the Goa scene, not surprisingly, it is Goa in India that is the reference point recreated and reimagined with great verve and care. But the Goa scene provides us with an interesting twist to this narrative of flux and stability once we consider what exactly this sense of home consists of. On the one hand, there is Goa, a far away place that freaks in Switzerland recreate in an effort to "feel at home". On the other hand, however, Goa freaks feel just as much at home in moving between places – Goa and Switzerland. It is not only the reference point Goa that they celebrate, but their cosmopolitan selves, not only roots, but 'routes' (Clifford 1997). Home, then, is travel, and travel is home. A similar point has been made by Anthony D'Andrea:

> While all displaced peoples have very 'localized minds' (immigrants orienting their identities and melancholies to their homelands), subjects related to this 'freak ethnoscape' pose a quite different picture. [These] subjects tend to constitute a universe of displaced peoples with displaced minds [...] Sublimating and celebrating rootlessness, these subjects seem to elaborate a cosmopolitan project that reconsiders the local, perhaps embracing the 'global' as a new locality (2000:7).

What enables these processes of identification? Primarily, we think, the act of imagination, which as a social force has 'acquired a singular new power in social life' today (Appadurai 1996:53). Imagination is a social practice that is inescapably tied to and enabled by 'images, ideas, and opportunities that come from elsewhere' (Appadurai 1996:54). But this knowledge of the 'elsewhere' and the attempt to reproduce it in Switzerland also fuels a nostalgia fundamental to the Goa scene. It is a nostalgia for an 'authentic' Goa not only imagined and sometimes missed by those who had been there ("All we would need is a beach and palm trees, and it would almost be Goa").[5] Even those who had never set a foot into India often spoke of Goa as a world vanishing in the face of encroachment, commercialisation, and decline.

It is not only the imagined Goa – both in Switzerland and in India – that makes up the scene, but also imagined selves. For, as Feld and Basso have pointed out, we must be aware of the fact that 'as people fashion places, so too, do they fashion themselves' (1996:11). It will be important here to talk about experiments in self-making today, which in the Goa scene are often linked to the distinction made between travellers and tourists. Indeed, freaks we spoke to often evoked ideas of travel rather than tours,

2 The term 'freak' has become a vernacular expression in German, and denotes a person who lives according to beatnik/hippie ideals, and tends to dress accordingly. For more details, see D'Andrea 2000.

3 So-called psychedelic drugs such as LSD, cannabis, and magic mushrooms, rather than the substances more commonly associated with the rave/techno scene, such as Ecstasy, MDMA, and speed.

4 We define 'home' and 'homeliness' in a very broad sense of the term, namely as an identificatory reference point providing some sort of sense of familiarity and comfort. It can, but need not be linked to a particular geographical location.

5 A statement by Jean-Pierre, a party-organiser who had never been in Goa.

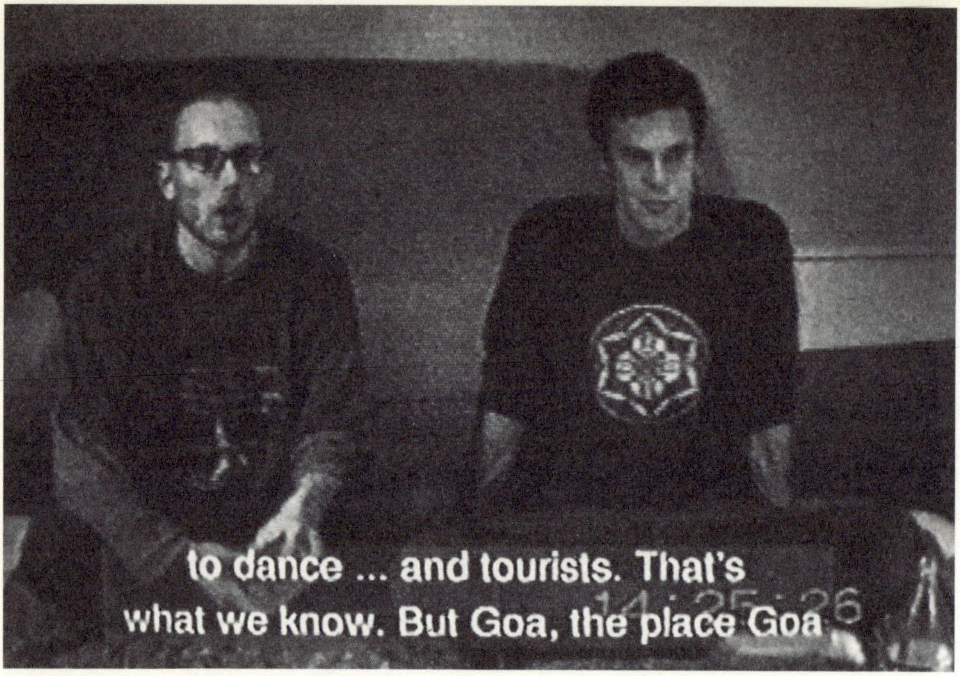

of cosmopolitanism rather than localism, and conceptualised themselves as moving subjects – both physically and imaginarily – in a moving world.

This paper emerged from an ethnographic video project of ours that tried to represent the Goa scene in Switzerland in all of its hybridity, ironies, and contradictions.[6] Most of our research, and all our recordings, were done in 1997. A number of points made in this article, however, are based on conversations with a number of "freaks" since 1997, and especially in the year 2000. The freaks we encountered were a heterogeneous group of people from all walks of life – from artists, students, and teachers, to people doing all sorts of odd-jobs. Some had, all in all, spent years in India, while others were still dreaming of going. Yet others were not concerned about Goa at all, nor with the idea of travelling there. Some avidly reproduced rituals of drug taking as they had learned them in India, and evoked Hindu Gods such as Shiva and Ganesh in conversations. Still others, including a well-known Goa DJ, were never really impressed by this re-imagining of India. Some organised their lives around going to India, or going to Goa parties while not in India, while for others the Goa scene was only one scene among many techno scenes they frequented. All of them, however, had things to say about Goa, Goa in Switzerland, and their own positions within this transnational scene. It is these imaginaries that we wish to capture.

Making Goa

It is perhaps not surprising that every single person we spoke to about the nature of the Goa scene, regardless of whether they had ever been to Goa or not, spoke of the importance of "the right people". A certain kind of people, and the experiences shared, were regarded as essential both for the 'here' and 'there' of the scene, for the Goa of Switzerland and the Goa of India. If they had ever been to Goa, the Swiss freaks always spoke of friends and acquaintances who had first taken them to Goa in India, and who had provided them with an informal travel and information network there. Once in Goa, it was these and other people one shared one's experiences with, and who "had seen those sunsets, and danced in the same sand".[7] It would be common to meet these same people back in Switzerland. They were one of the reasons why Goa freaks travelled so far to parties every weekend. The Goa-scene in Switzerland, we were told, was a "piece of India"[8] to many freaks because of the presence of people with whom they felt that they shared a common realm of experience and imagination. These commonalties were born not only in Goa but in the network of people which spans the globe and connects places and parties to each other. Familiarity and homeliness were thus located both in a place and a global space of travellers and partygoers who embodied Goa. It was as if Goa moved through time and space, and had indeed become what can be called, leaning on Appadurai (1996:6), a diaspora of fun.

Still from video *Trancenational Goa: Travelling People, Parties, Images* (1998).

This community of familiarity and interconnection acquired its cohesion through a particular philosophy and the crucial importance of certain collective (or what were often called "tribal") experiences such as the organisation of parties, the tripping on drugs, the long hours and days of dancing to repetitive music together and a shared – if relatively vague – concept of ecologism.[9] Goa "philosophy" also contained, for some of the freaks, the fact that having been to Goa was a prerequisite for organising a good Swiss Goa party. Nirava, who had acquired an Indian name ("Quiet Friend")[10] and had spent, all in all, nearly three years in Goa and other parts of India, put it in these words:

> "It's a certain feeling that you need to have experienced in Goa, to be able to bring it across here. At the parties here, I immediately feel who's been in Goa. I can feel who's been in Goa not as a tourist, but who's really invested himself there, who's been there as a person […]."

6 All research was conducted with a video camera. The end product was the video *Trancenational Goa: Travelling People, Parties, Images* (1998), which can be obtained from Andrea Mühlebach at: akmuehle@midway.uchicago.edu

7 Statement by Cynthia, who had been in Goa twice, and who at the time of the interview was preparing for a two-year trip around the world with her Japanese boyfriend, also a Goa freak.

8 Quotation from an interview with Nirava.

9 We cannot delve into this debate here in detail. It will have to suffice to say that the Goa freaks we interviewed often stressed that their "philosophy" entailed the love and respect for nature – an attitude made manifest on party-fliers frequently sporting the words 'Protect Mother Earth'. Goa freaks also argued that Goa parties, which ideally took place outdoors, brought many young urban people out into nature where they would otherwise not go. Experiencing the natural surroundings under the influence of psychedelic drugs was also represented as an innovative ecological approach. Finally, great emphasis was placed on not leaving trash behind, and on selling drinks in recyclable cups or glasses.

10 As a Sannyasin, a follower of the popular guru Baghwan Shree Rajneesh, a.k.a. Osho, she was given that name by a spiritual master.

Here, Nirava distinguishes between the "mere tourist" and the "real traveller"; the superficial person and those who had "really invested" themselves in India. The celebrated cosmopolitanism that makes up the scene then, is for Nirava of a particular kind: It must entail having "been there as a person" and not as a "tourist", and as having gone beyond the surface of travel as mere consumption, to travel as reciprocal interaction and investment that resulted in a particular type of knowledge about Goa.

This internationalism, we were told by the party-organiser Jürg (who had never been to Goa) was a "virus" that had emerged there and that the Goa freaks tried to recreate at parties in Switzerland. But the cosmopolitan freak did not have to have been in India. All Swiss Goa freaks felt cosmopolitan to some degree, regardless of whether they had ever travelled or not, and they stressed their links to India both through physical and/or imaginary travel. Tini, for example, was a "hippie of the 1990s"[11] who had never been to India, but who stressed the importance of what we call "mind expanding stories," or what has been referred to as "traveller talk".[12] This genre played a crucial role for both the scene and the people who moved in it:

> "It's nice that people come [from] and go [to India], and tell me stories – they're always new stories for me. You hear stories about the beautiful sunset, the good people and parties, drug stories [...]. [Y]ou hear the same things from different people and from different perspectives, again and again."

Tini, in a way, saw himself as an imaginary traveller who had learned about Indian spirituality via stories and the images they repeatedly evoked. "I've never been there", Tini said, "but I know him [Ganesh, the elephant-headed Hindu god] well now, just like Shiva, and all his followers [...]. I learned from people who've been to Goa".

The reproduction of values specific to Goa freaks thus relied on a number of collective experiences – parties, drugs, traveller talk. It relied also on ritual enactment. Ritual actions punctuated every Goa party, and were carried out explicitly by a hard core of insiders, most of whom had been to Goa numerous times. The smoking of the chillum[13] is a prime example: As a well-regulated procedure of hashish consumption, it includes the occasional utterance of mantras such as "Bom Shiva", "Bom Shankar", or "Bom Bolai", accompanied by a touching of the forehead with the pipe. Many people took this ritual quite seriously, carefully following the rules of conduct. The making of chai is another practice endowed with ritual aura. The chai shops, central to Goa parties, are places where party-goers sit on mats on the floor and "chill out", smoke marijuana, engage in traveller talk, eat, and drink Indian tea. The preparation of the tea is itself ritualesque as freaks sit over large pots of boiling tea, adding specific amount of milk and spices, endlessly stirring and tasting while people wait until it is finally ready. When approaching freaks for a cup of chai, we were frequently sent away again because it was "not ready" yet. Clearly, the freaks seemed to want to convey to us the feeling that this procedure required a certain knowledge and above all patience.

Rituals, then, were enacted with great care and seriousness, although we did encounter some cynicism about them. Lauri and Dani, who at the time of the interview had both never been to India, spoke of rituals as "stereotypical acts" giving the participants "the feeling that you belong to a higher, special caste. But they're rituals that you like to stick to because they're like tradition, something that reminds you of beautiful moments in the past... and you like repeating them".

While moving within the Goa scene, we again and again got the impression that it was not only a very hybrid phenomenon, but also one that was shot through with incongruities. It was not only that we were regularly confronted with Swiss people dancing to Goa trance in the middle of the Alps, and evoking Shiva while sitting in their apartments in Zürich or Basel. There was more to it than that. The music called Goa, for example, was in the early and mid-nineties not produced in India itself, but sampled and mixed in living rooms and studios in Europe. The sounds were then taken to Goa where they were "tested" and, in the form of DAT tapes, exchanged among DJs coming from all over the world. The most successful pieces were selected and eventually, back in Europe, pressed on vinyl and marketed. From there, they were taken back to India and other places within the global Goa diaspora, and played as "Goa sound". The music, then, was just as much a product of the global Goa network as it was a product of the place Goa. Today, however, the geographical location has ceased to be the crucial yard-stick for musical success. The music played at Swiss Goa parties is still largely of European and Israeli origin, but the significance of Goa as a testing ground has now been replaced by international Goa mega-parties spanning the globe.

Then there is the *Om* symbol which is so fundamental to the scene and yet, so devoid of fixed meaning. Or perhaps it is fairer to say that it is a hybrid, completely overdetermined sign which contains as many meanings as people across the globe have given to it.[14] For Nirava, who first saw the symbol painted on a rock in Goa, *Om* was something like a revelation that "just hit" her. Without knowing what it signified, she from that day on always returned to the painted rock when she went back to Goa, knowing only then that she "had come home". Only later, at Goa parties in Switzerland (not in India!), did she learn what the symbol was all about. For the party-organiser Etienne, a celebrity among Swiss Goa freaks at the time, it was as much a marketable sign used on party fliers as it was a symbol of his own "playful" spirituality. For Jürg, who had never been in India at all, the *Om* took on deep significance in his everyday life: When driving his car, he told us, he always looked at the *Om* sticker he had stuck on his car horn, and refrained from honking by thinking "Hey, shanti [peace], we're all human". Ironically, DJ Cosmix, who was very popular at the time in the Swiss scene, had nothing at all to say about the *Om*, apart from the fact that it was a useful symbol that in the beginning

11 Some Goa freaks referred to themselves as such.

12 Laurenz Bolliger used this term during an interview at a Goa party.

13 The chillum is a conical, ceramic pipe traditionally used in India to smoke hemp. It is smoked mainly, though not exclusively, by Sadhus, and more by men than by women.

14 See Edward Said (1983) on the movement of ideas, concepts and theories through time and space.

had helped mark parties as extraordinary events later known as Goa parties.

In all of their hybridity and incongruity, the Goa parties were sites where meaningful attempts to imaginatively evoke a distinct, distant place were made. Collectively and communally, rituals were enacted, stories told, parties organised and realms of experience shared. In all of this, the geographical location Goa was of eminent importance to many people we spoke to. Yet at the same time, it was clear that what was happening in Switzerland had taken on a life and meanings of its own. Lauri and Dani went so far as to say that the place Goa did not matter at all, and that it could "be covered by a volcanic eruption while the scene here [in Switzerland] would still exist".

Thus, very different types of significance were attributed to Goa as a reference for identification. If Goa in India was a home for some in the Goa scene, Goa in Switzerland was just as much a home for others. Feeling at home somewhere, it seemed to us, was as much about places as it was the way of life these places stood for. And the way of life that was held high amongst Goa freaks was the traveller's way. Indeed, travel was home for many of the freaks we interviewed. They felt that they experienced and passed through worlds either through physical travel or imaginary travel. The latter was enabled by traveller talk and/or through the psychedelic trips one embarked on with the help of drugs. But with all this travel and movement, what happened to the supposedly real, authentic Goa of India?

Everyone knew that the act of transportation and travel between Goa and Switzerland was always also an act of translation and, thus, of slippage. That is to say that certain meanings were lost and others gained as symbols were transported across the globe. Time and again people said that a party "had nearly made them feel as if they were in Goa". It was this "as if" that characterised much of the traveller talk going on at parties. In other words, much talk about Goa was nostalgic talk – about what one missed about India, about what one missed at Swiss Goa parties (such as the Goan beaches, skies, and sunrises), about what one's travels were like, and about when one would go again. The place that was evoked via the Goa parties, then, was a place that was never quite what it could or should be. There was a sense of lack, and a sense that the authentic Goa was never properly reproducible. For many Goa freaks we spoke to, even Goa in India was not what it used to be. Authenticity was lacking both 'here' and 'there'. This feeling of lack, as we will show below, was part and parcel of the scene.[15]

Travellers and Tourists

Many partygoers who had been to Goa, and even those who had not, felt that they were (potential) travellers, rather than tourists. The distinction is one that is frequently associated with hippie culture in general, and its 'idealisation of mobility' (Saldanha 1999b) in particular. Travellers, Saldanha has argued, 'do take interest in the Other, travellers don't add to the destruction of nature and local economies, travellers hate home, travellers are creative' (Saldanha 1999b). Paul Bowles made a related point by stating that 'another important difference between tourist and traveller is that the former accepts his own civilisation without any question; not so the traveller, who compares it with the others and rejects those elements he finds not to his liking' (1993[1949]:13).

The importance of such an attitude was echoed by DJ Cosmix who, referring to the days before and during the early Goa trance scene, talked about how "people went to Goa looking for something." They left the "industrialised, commercialised world" for a place where they wanted to find themselves. Etienne confirmed this from his own perspective, stating that his link to Goa in India was mainly a spiritual one. Many of the freaks from all over the world, he said, went there to "trance" and to "find their spirit". In Cosmix' eyes, the entire Goa scene represented a search for an alternative to a society where the "god of capital" reigned. Once again, as Nirava showed us above, travelling is about a search for inner depth and person-hood. This remains one of the interesting facets of the scene as a whole – that the search for one's "inner spirit" leads one into the world at large.[16]

Nevertheless, the scene was not only about searching, but also about finding. Both Nirava and Cynthia spoke vividly of what they had brought with them from India: "Humour, bargaining skills, the no-stress attitude", a "caring" mentality, and a "love for ritual". Nirava also spoke of the objects – the mats, cushions, cutlery, ashtrays, and so on – that she had kept in India, leaving traces of homeliness and belonging behind, as well as the promise of return. And back in Switzerland, most of these travellers flaunted their Indian connections – Nirava by wearing bindis and saris to the kindergarten she worked at, and Etienne by "sticking *Om* symbols all over the place", and thus "playfully bringing [his] spirituality across".

Those Goa freaks who had spent considerable time in India never mentioned feeling displaced. They spoke about simultaneously belonging to two places. A sense of cosmopolitanism was frequently evoked not only in the traveller talk which abounded, but in the statements made by people like Nirava who said that she felt as much at home in Switzerland as she did in India. Similarly, Etienne spoke of the fact that there were two families in Goa to whom he could go back and stay with "any time". They felt that they had roots in two places.

This type of cosmopolitanism was not something one simply had, but something one actively pursued. For "the more you travel", Lauri said with a touch of cynicism, "the cooler you become". Most people we interviewed voiced their willingness and yearning to travel as soon as they had the time and the money to do so. What they all had were roots and routes that they wanted to expand and an imagination that had made these thoughts and goals possible.

But when people spoke about "homeliness", they often also spoke about the loss of it. The Goa scene in Switzerland, many Goa freaks agreed, was not what it used to be. Just like the Swiss Goa scene, which in its

15 Though never articulated explicitly in our presence, some freaks might have been aware of the irony that it was freaks like them who were very much implicated in the decline of the 'authentic' Goa by regularly travelling and spending time there. We thank David Blamey for pointing this out to us.

16 The fact that travel is not only an act of consumption but also a (varyingly) conscious engagement with the world is of course not particular to the Goa scene of the late 1990s. Travel has always played an important role for many sub or countercultural movements (e.g., modern, beat, hippie, new age) that aimed at questioning one's place of origin (c.f. Holland and Huggan 1998, Chambers 2000, Rojek and Urry 1997).

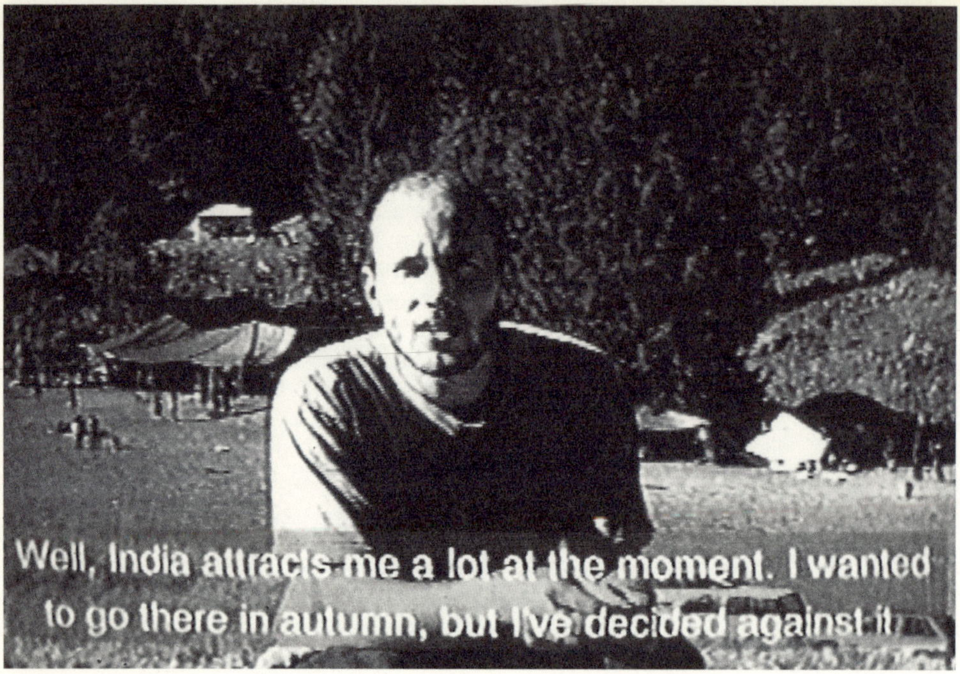

Still from video *Trancenational Goa: Travelling People, Parties, Images* (1998).

beginnings had been small, intimate, and less commercialised, the Goa scene in India was regarded – even by those who had never been there – as having been hijacked by mass tourism, motor traffic, drug addicts, and corruption. There lies an irony in this: The Swiss Goa scene was all about recreating a far-away place which, however, was always already never what it used to be, even for those who had never been there. Appadurai describes such nostalgic practices as "creating experiences of loss that never took place, [...] creat[ing] what might be called "imagined nostalgia", nostalgia for things that never were" (1996:77). Similarly, thc place Goa freaks aimed at recreating was a place that had ceased to exist – or perhaps never existed – both 'here' and 'there', both in Switzerland and in Goa.

And yet, nostalgia here is more than a gesture towards emptiness. It is a meaningful act that creates points of reference in changing, unstable times. The positing of a 'once was' in relation to a 'now' creates frames of meaning and temporal stability in a world of increasing flux (Steward 1988:227). Despite the fact that the Swiss and the Indian Goa were regarded as vanishing worlds, it was precisely these worlds that provided a meaningful temporal framework to the freaks. They also lent a type of authority to those who claimed that they had known both the 'once was' – the authentic Goa – and the 'now' – the inauthentic. Leadership was thus performed and attained by those who had "been there" and had in-depth knowledge about far away places and former times.

This nostalgic search for the "authentic" Goa is not only a Swiss Goa phenomenon. Nostalgia also characterises critiques of the local Goa trance scene by Goan Indians. As Saldanha has argued, middle class Catholic Goan activism has for years tried "hard to imagine a Goa outside or before tourism" (Saldanha 1999b), and has nostalgically evoked a Goa before the 'imperialism' of hippie culture. Interestingly, as Saldanha goes on to state, it is not the lucrative tourism that local Goan activism targets, but the dirt-cheap mass traveller culture which is often regarded as degenerated, drug-ridden, and morally reprehensible. The Swiss Goa freaks and the local Goan activists thus connect the current ills characterising Goa to (seemingly) different outside forces – mass tourism and hippie traveller culture respectively. These are two competing visions of encroachment that differentiate between kinds of tourism in very specific ways.

Cosmopolitanism

A look at the Indian Goa scene will help us think about differences between Swiss celebrations of cosmopolitanism and visions of cosmopolitanism in Goa, India. For Goa freak cosmopolitanism, in the eyes of an anthropologist colleague of ours, is "sectarian: it exists only for those who share the same experiences, codes, values, and practices".[17] The comparison will lead us to the question of whether one can sustain the distinction between tourists and travellers at all. Should the entire Goan industry be seen as purely touristic? Some commentators from the growing field of tourism/travel studies have suggested that this distinction, usually based on differing travel experiences, is hardly useful (Chambers 2000; Rojek and Urry 1997). In the case of the Swiss Goa scene, it does seem to us that travel and tourism have merged to some degree. Indeed, it seems as if yesterday's travellers are preparing the ground for today's tourists. In the last few years, for example, a Swiss Goa party organisation has regularly organised week-long package tours to Ibiza, advertising their trips with the slogan "Sea, sun, good feeling, tribe, and spirit".

At the same time in Goa, India, it seems that the freak industry has begun to move very close to tourism, as so-called travellers – in contrast to prevailing myths – often do not necessarily delve into local cultures, genuinely investing themselves. Saldanha has said that "exploitation, indifference, international crime, racism, institutionalized corruption, and noise pollution… is the flip side of the coin which is rarely mentioned – or dare I say noticed – by people in the Goa trance subculture" (Saldanha 1999a).

It seems as if the celebrated image of traveller culture that engages with places and local populations must be revised. Also, the question of who is included in this celebration of the cosmopolitan needs to be posed. Though Saldanha has argued that Goan trance parties in Goa "are not at all an enclosed enclave of white drug taking travellers" (Saldanha 1999b), he points to the limited entrance Indian locals are granted into the scene. Apparently, Goan trance parties are made up not only of Western or Westernised hippies, but also of "wealthy Indian tourists, brought to the parties by taxi from posh hotels in Baga",[18] as well as of a "highly competitive 'mat economy' consisting of villagers selling chai, snacks, cigarettes and water" (Saldanha 1999b). Then, there are flocks of Indian men from the area watching the spectacle and, finally, "young Indian men from neighbouring villages and towns who want to join in the fun." Saldanha goes on to say that "these men pose a serious threat to club culture aesthetics […]: they can't afford drugs, can't dance, wear silly clothes and don't behave in Western heterosexual fashion" (Saldanha 1999b). The scene thus grants access only to two types of Indians – the very rich and the very poor. The rest are spectators.

The celebration of cosmopolitanism we have outlined so far is, it seems, highly exclusive. It is not a cosmopolitanism that embraces the world, but only a specific group of transnational partygoers engaged in similar practices that translate into similar values. The statement that Swiss Goa parties are about "having a little bit of India here" now appears in a new light: The India implied is the India of Goa freaks, an India at the margins and yet at the centre of traveller experiences.

The Goa scene we have outlined is a complex, hybrid phenomenon not easily grasped in conventional terms. It is made up of so many moving subjects and objects that one is tempted to regard it as a fleeting, insubstantial and superficial thing. We have shown that this is not necessarily the case, and that many Goa freaks frequenting the parties both in India and Switzerland have made this scene their home. It is a home that lies both in place (India and Switzerland), but also between places – in the ethos of travel that underpins the entire scene. Homeliness lies also in the collective, "tribal" reproduction of parties and rituals with people who share one's cosmopolitan philosophy, and who embody the spirit of travel. However, we pointed to the necessity of critically embedding this celebration of the cosmopolitan within larger global hierarchies and asymmetries, for the Goa scene in both India and Switzerland is made possible, first and foremost, by a massive global tourist industry from which many are excluded. Not all can be moving subjects, and move objects, to the same degree.

17 Anthony D'Andrea, personal communication.

18 An upmarket beach resort.

Mariele Neudecker

Another Day

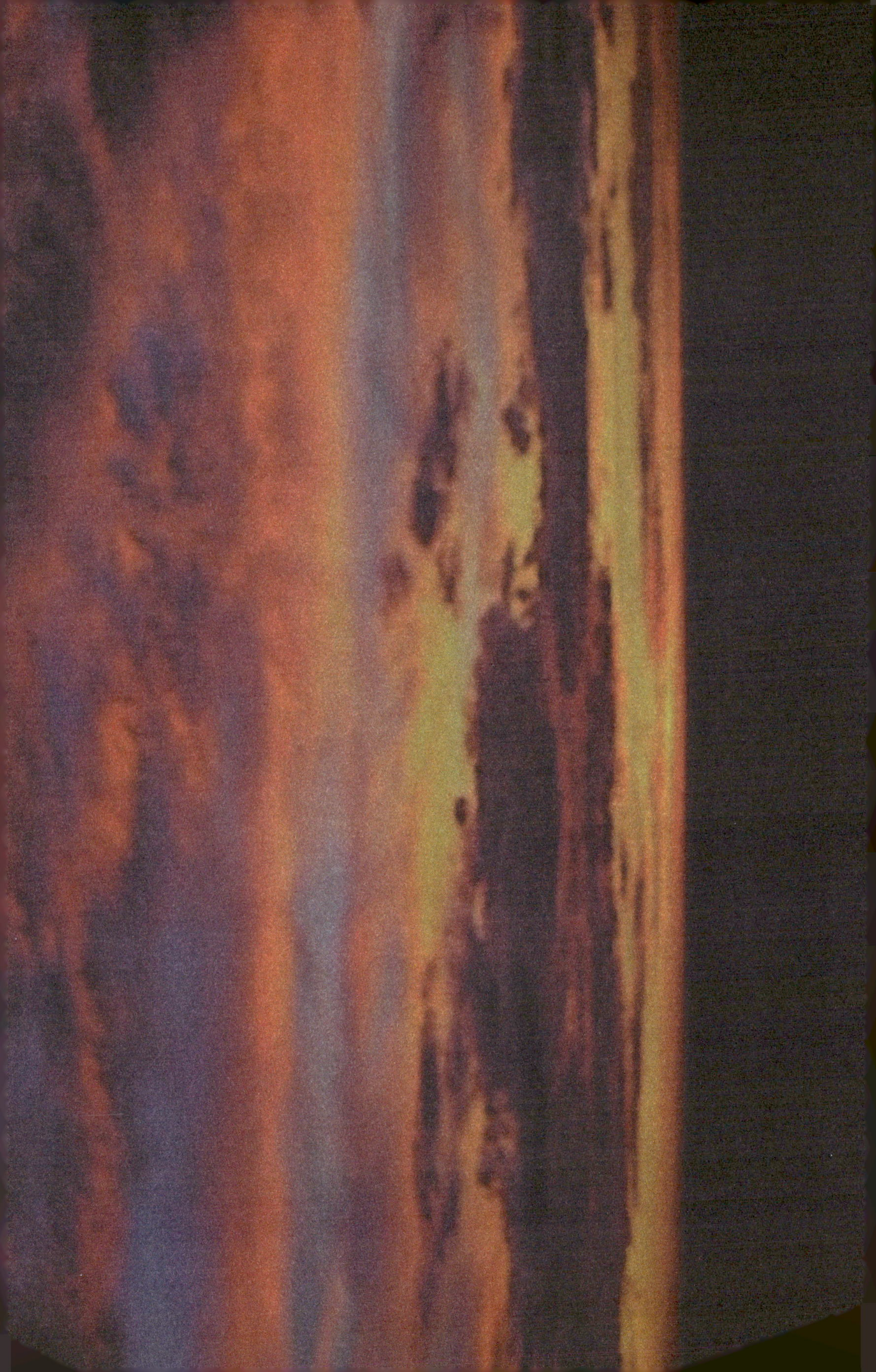

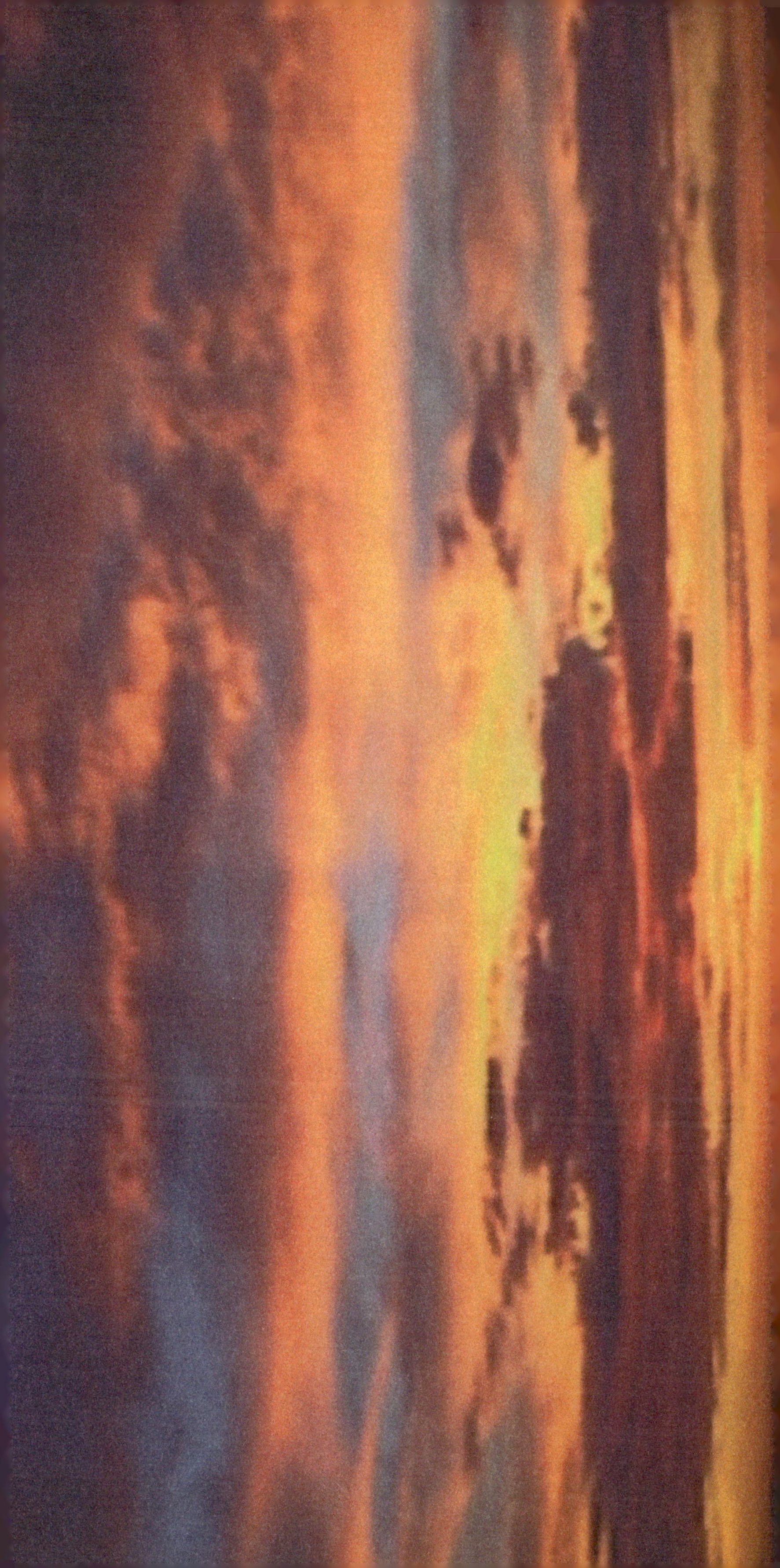

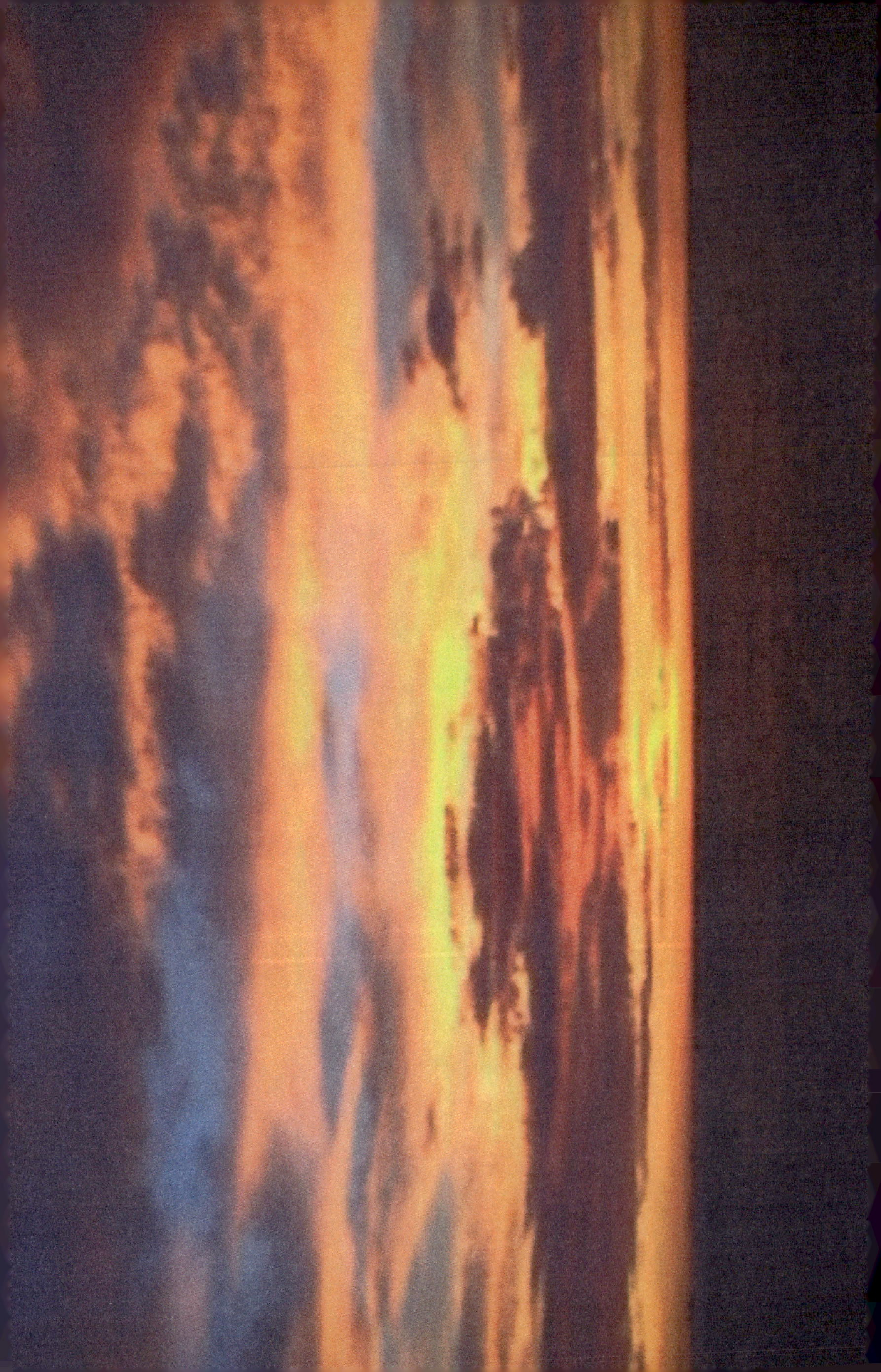

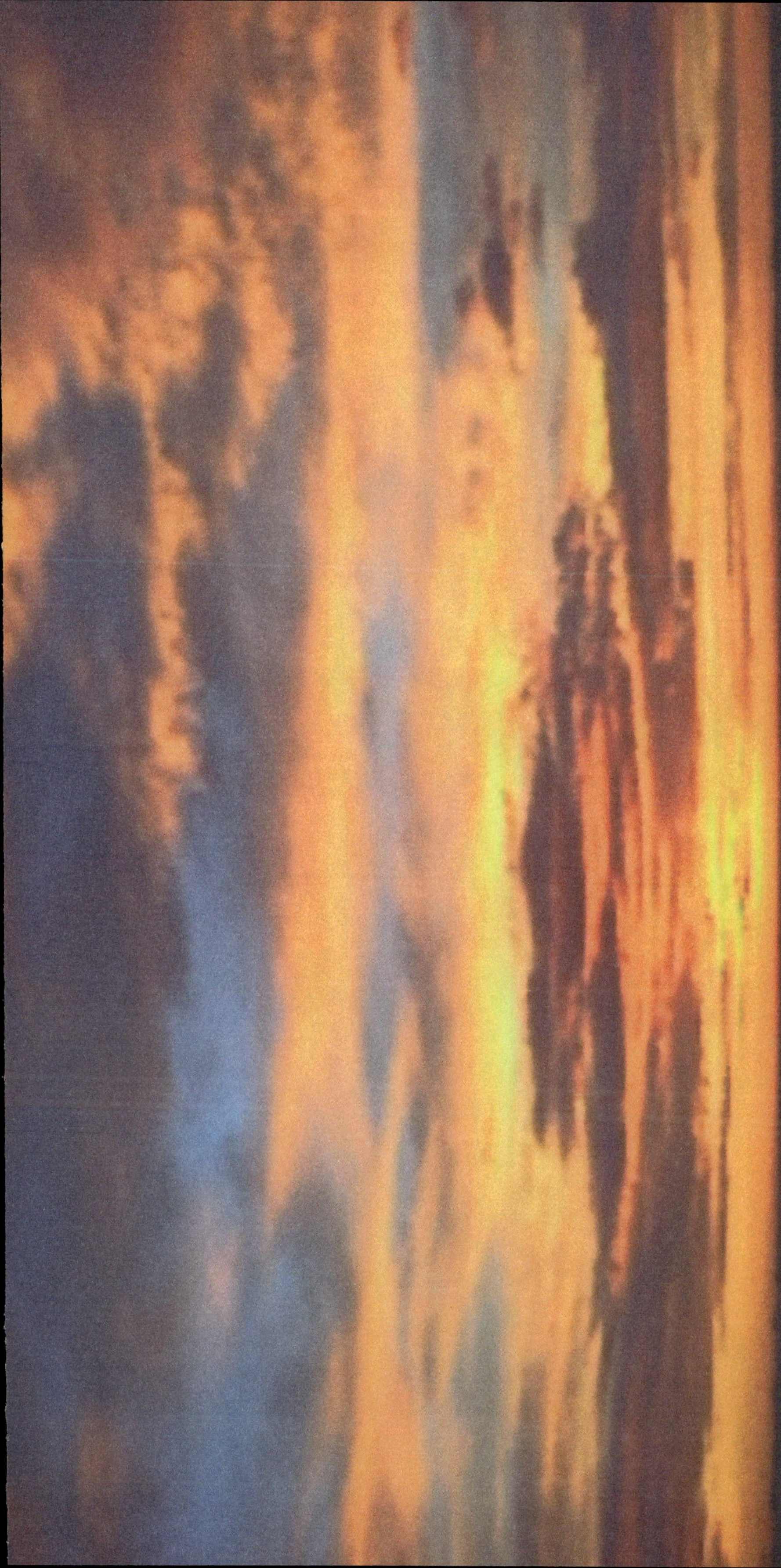

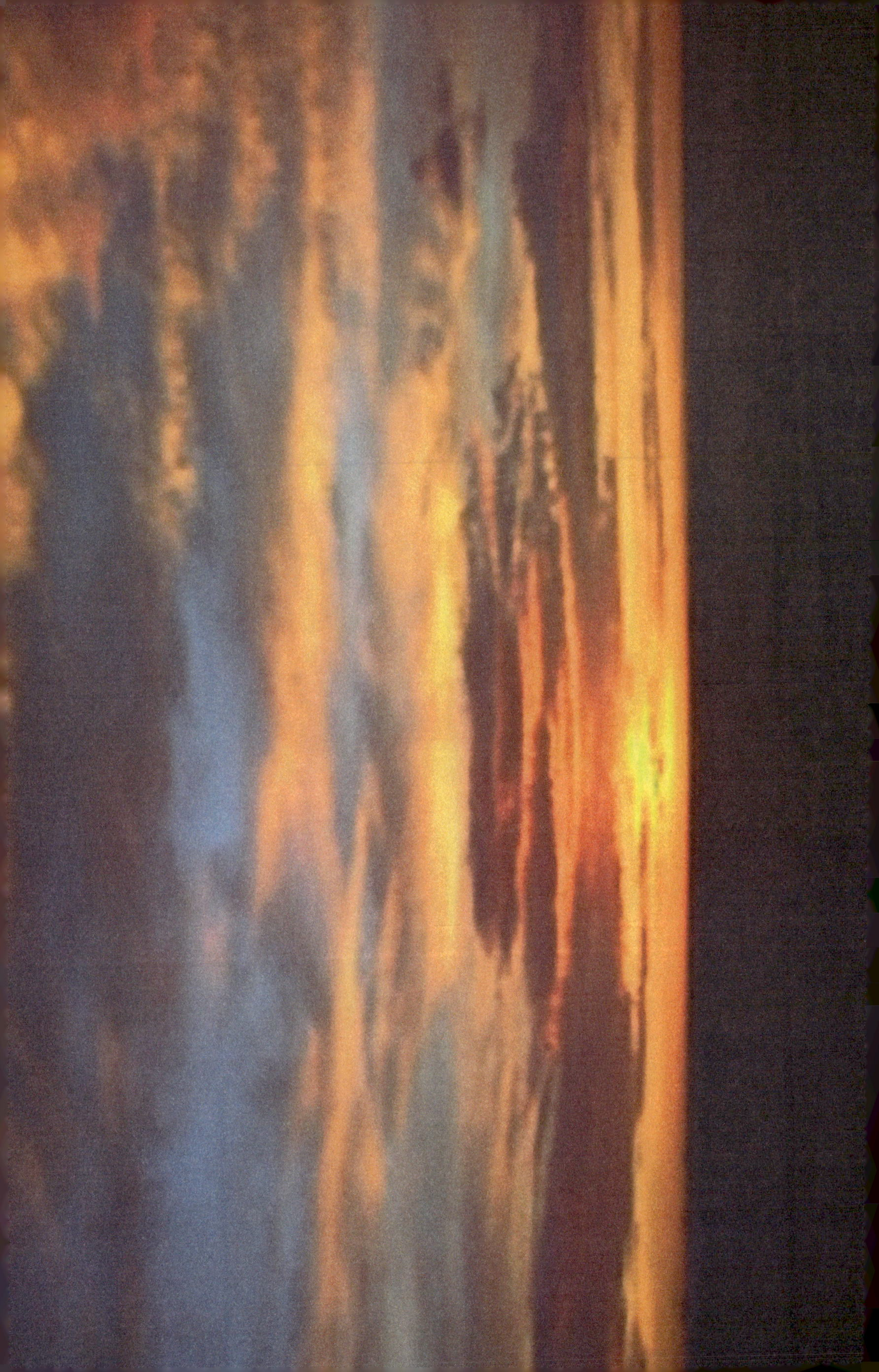

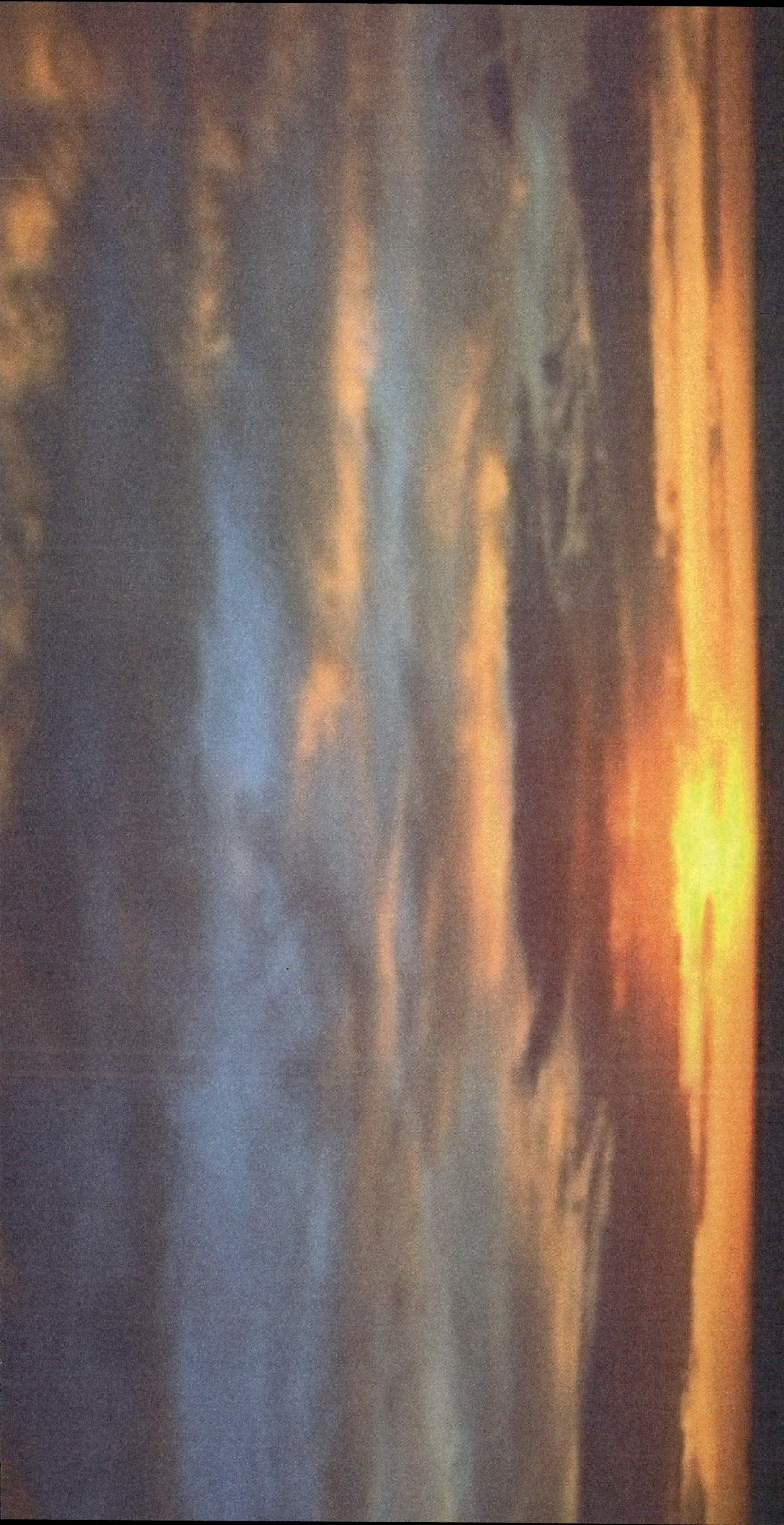

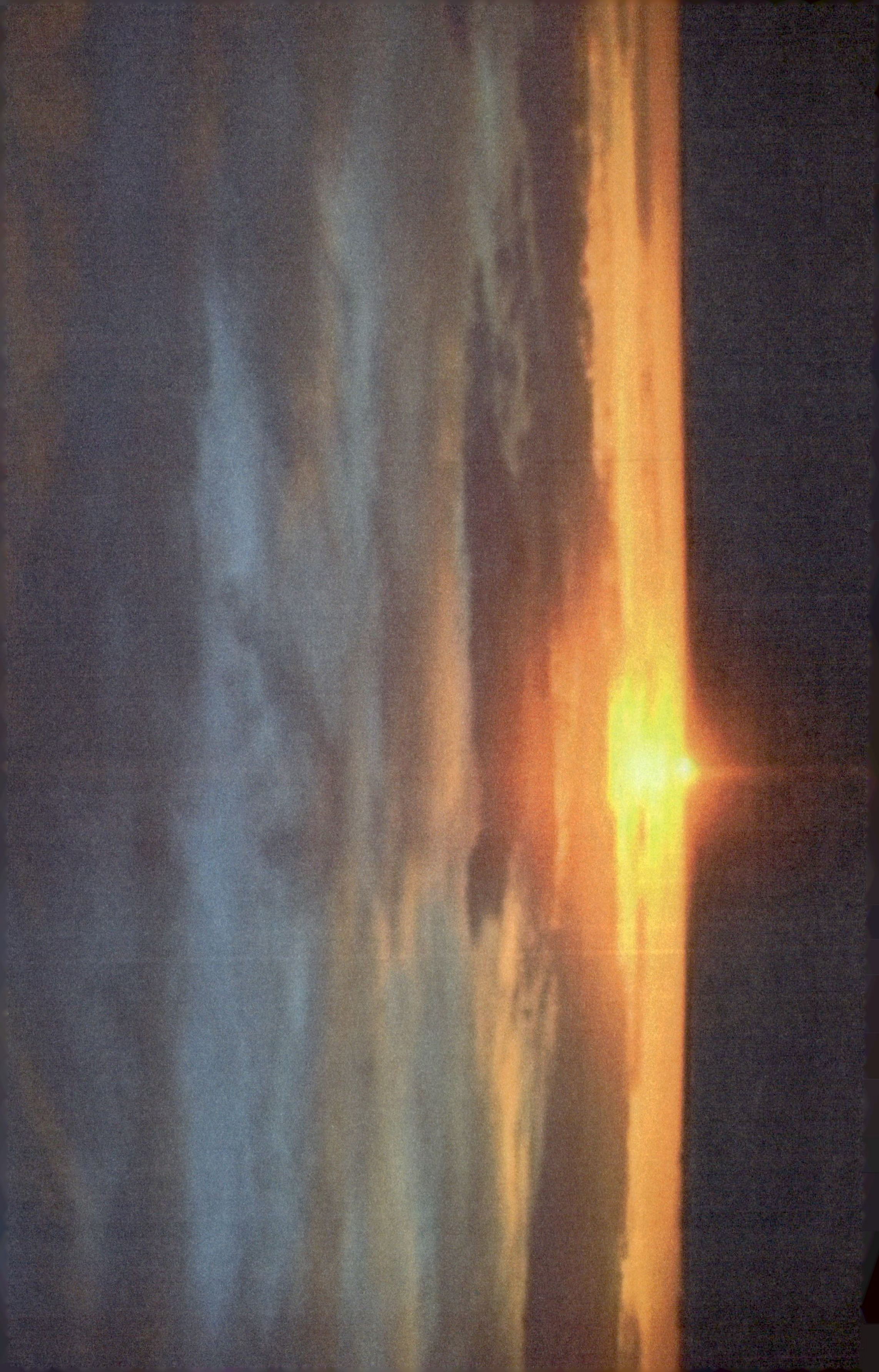

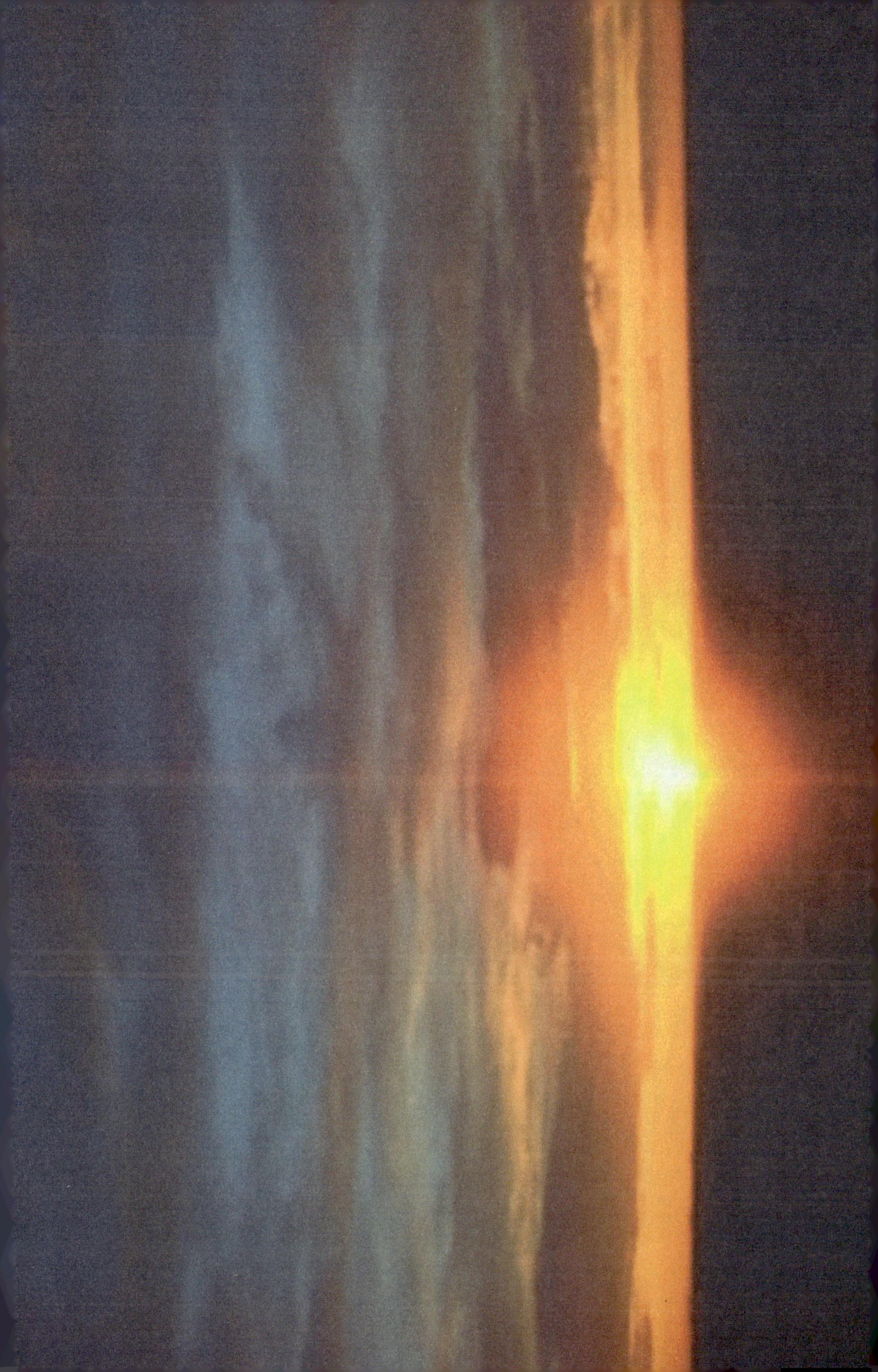

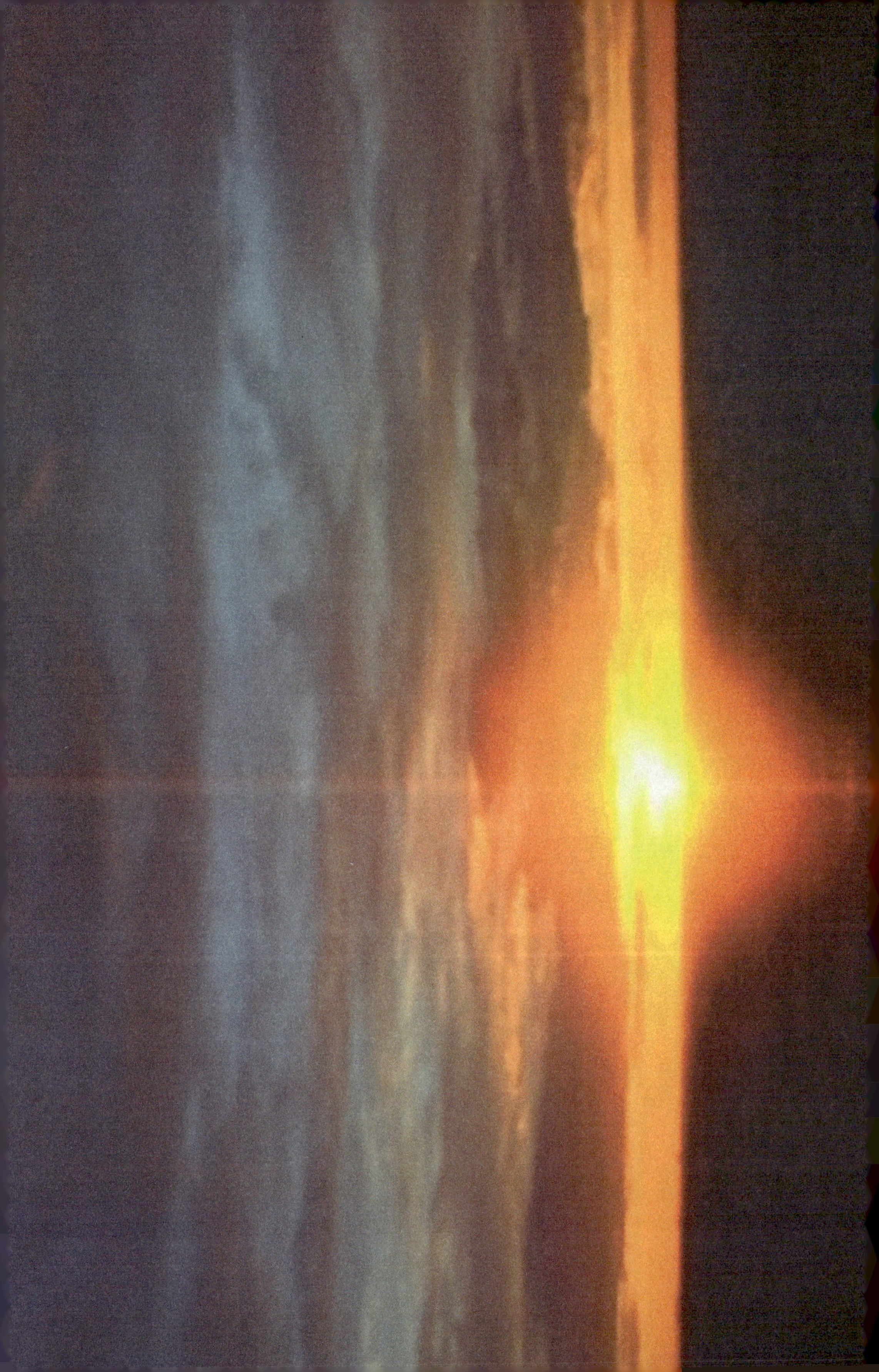

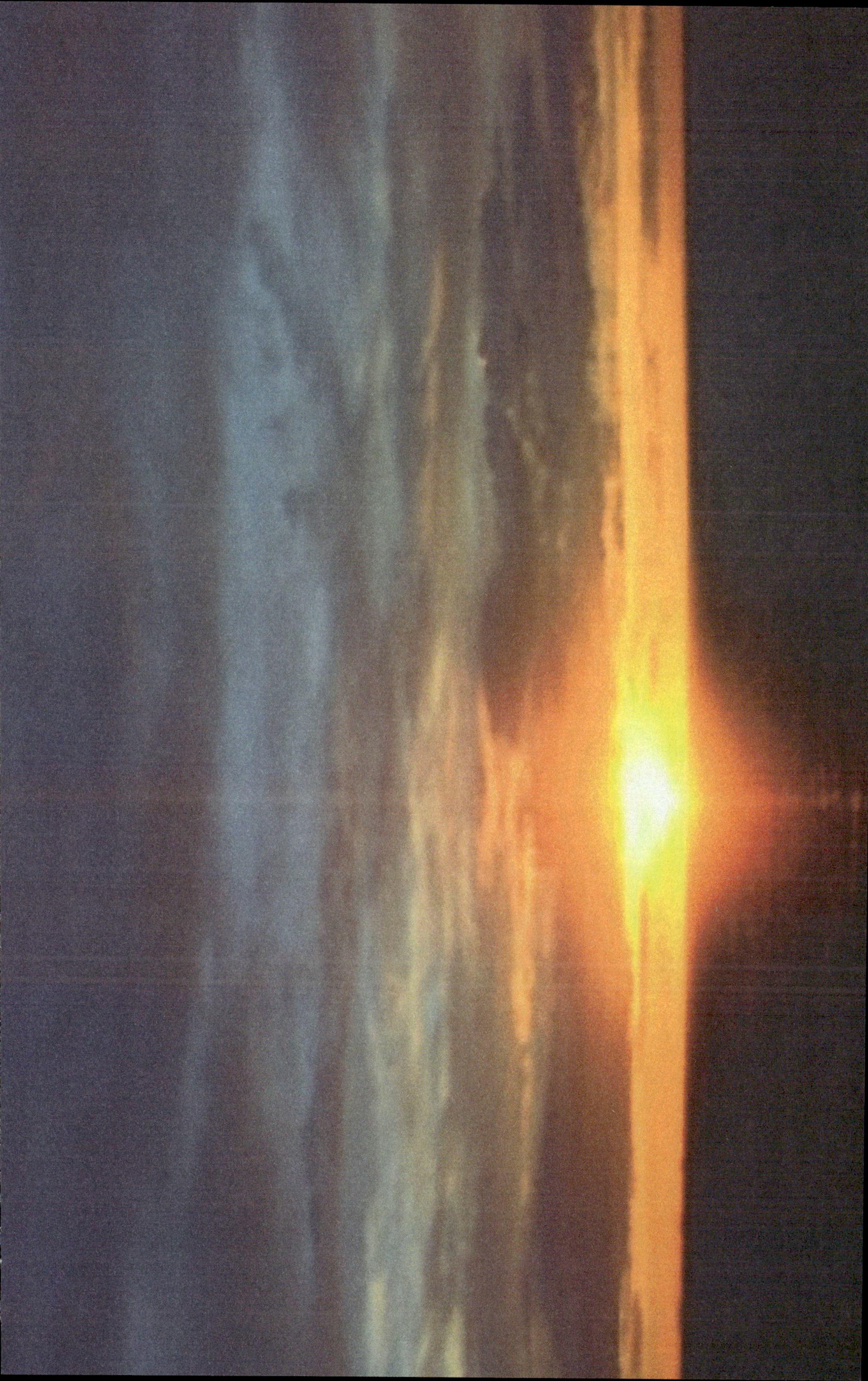

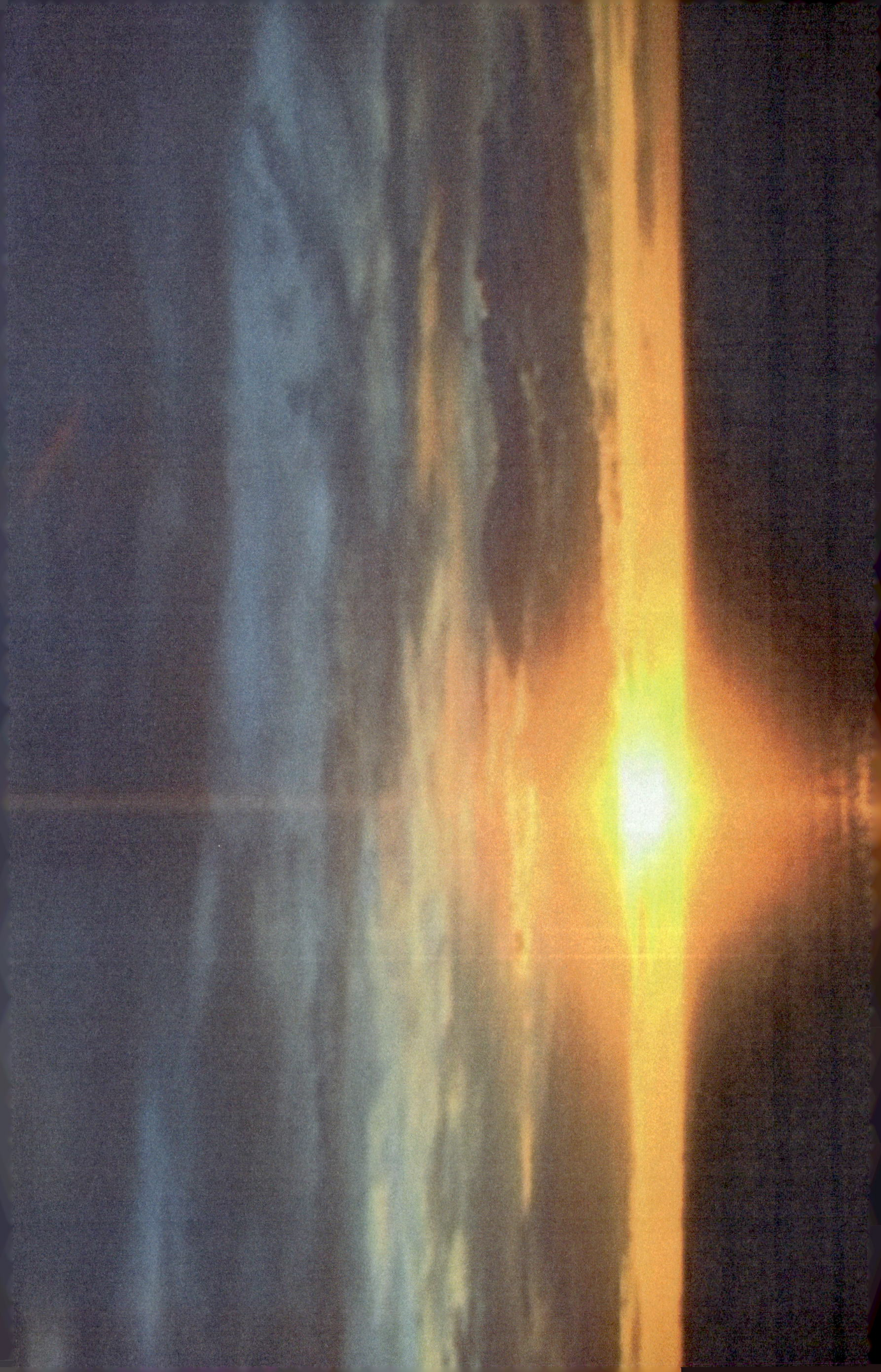

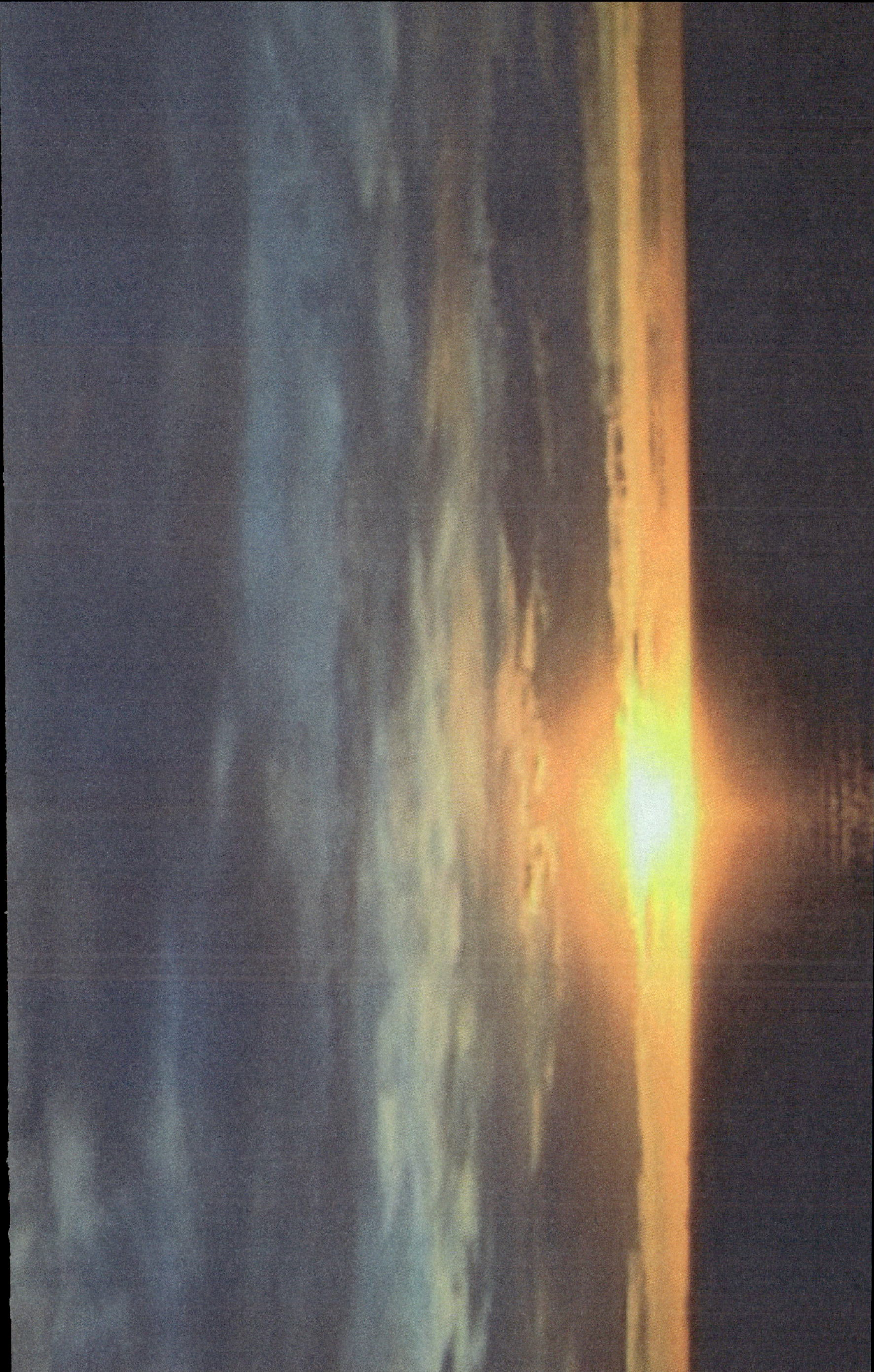

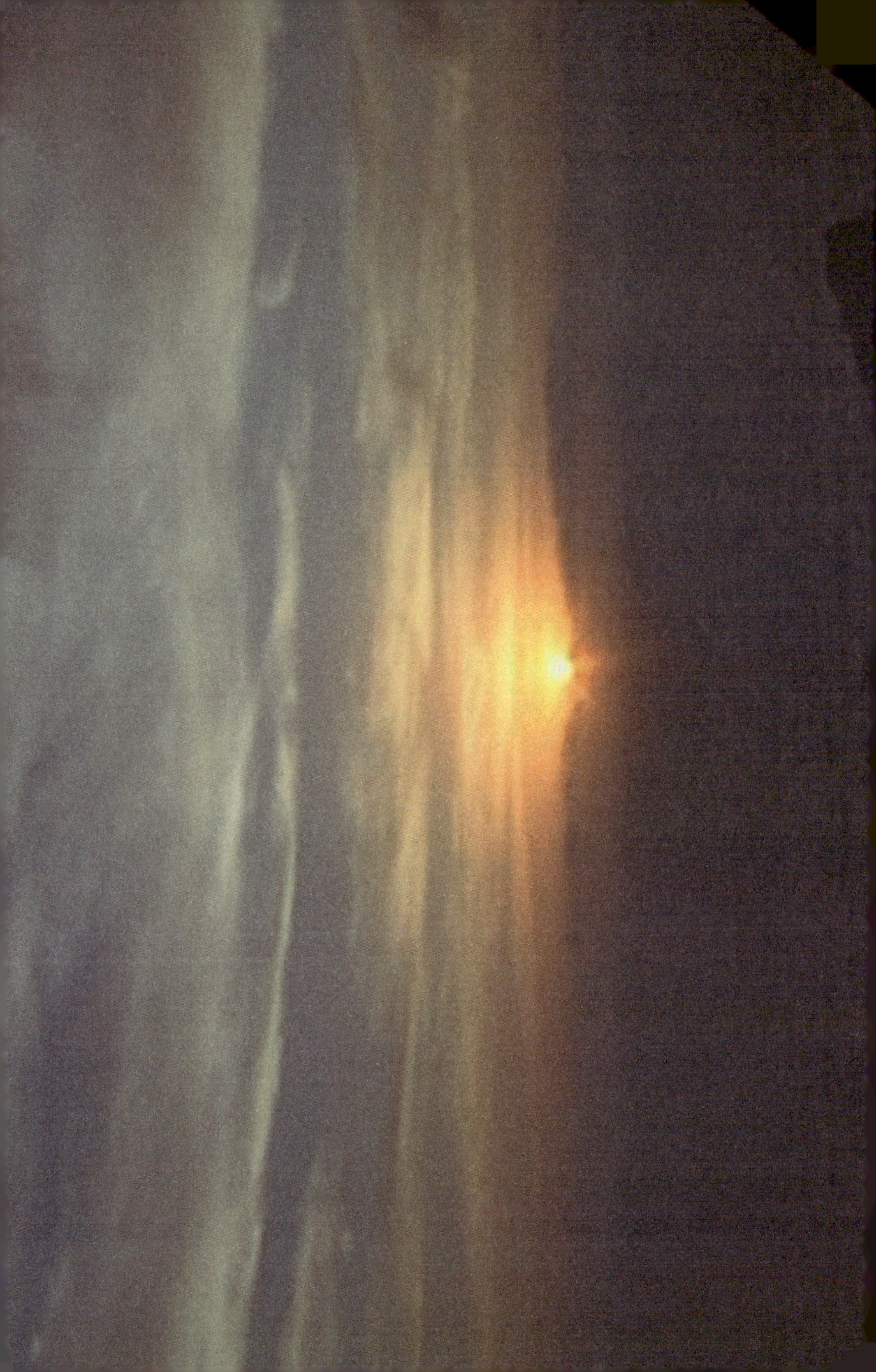

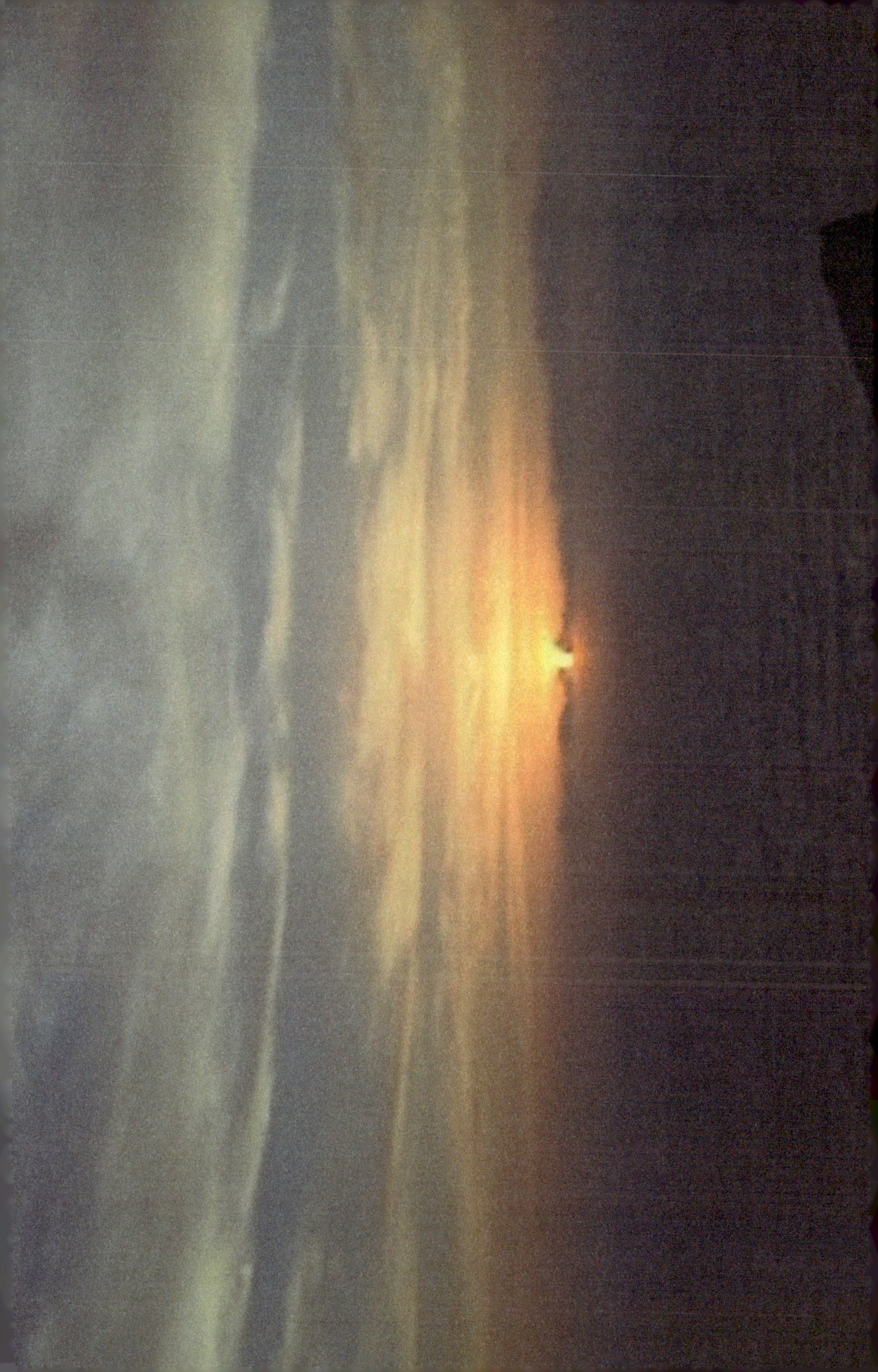

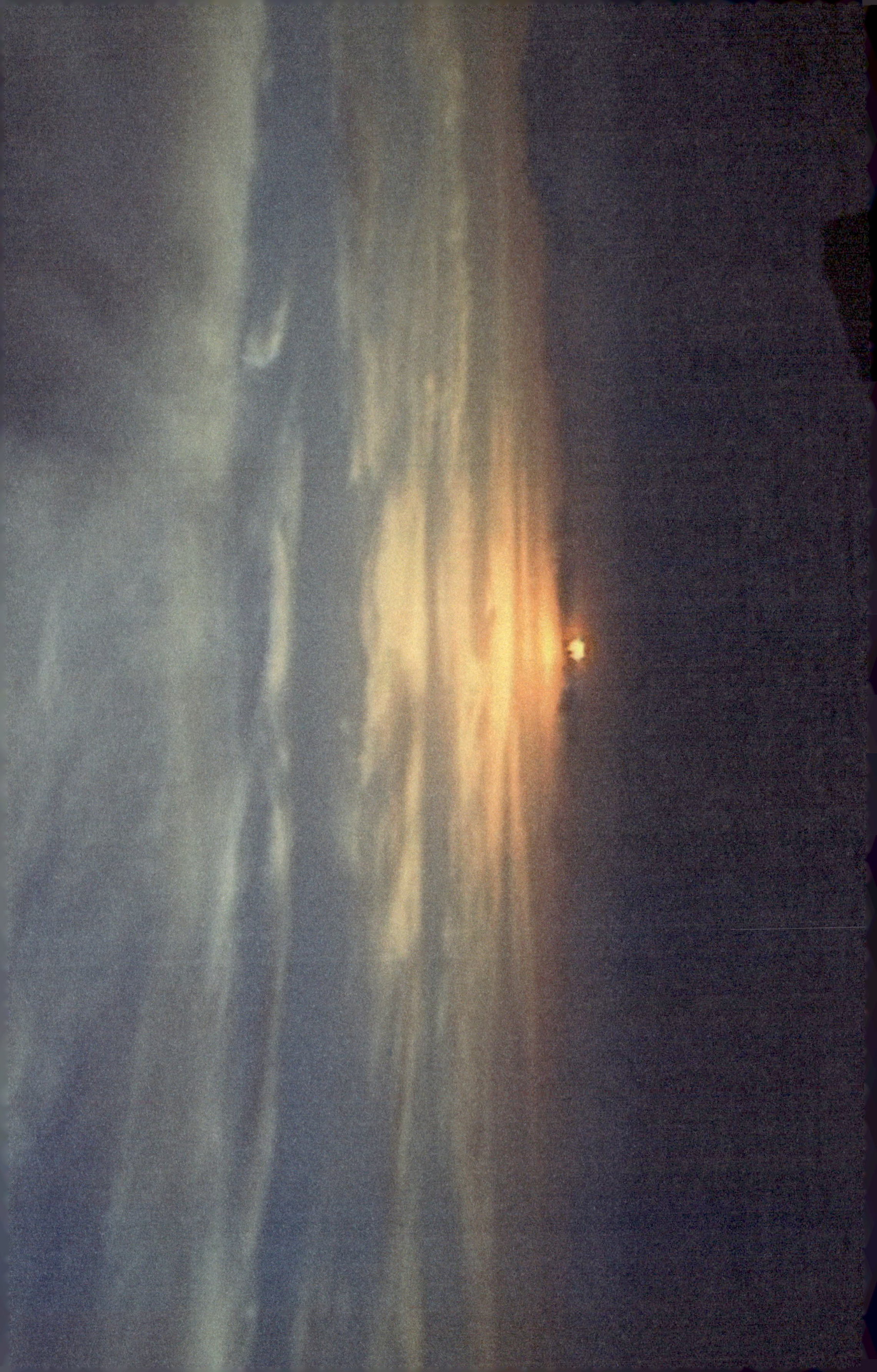

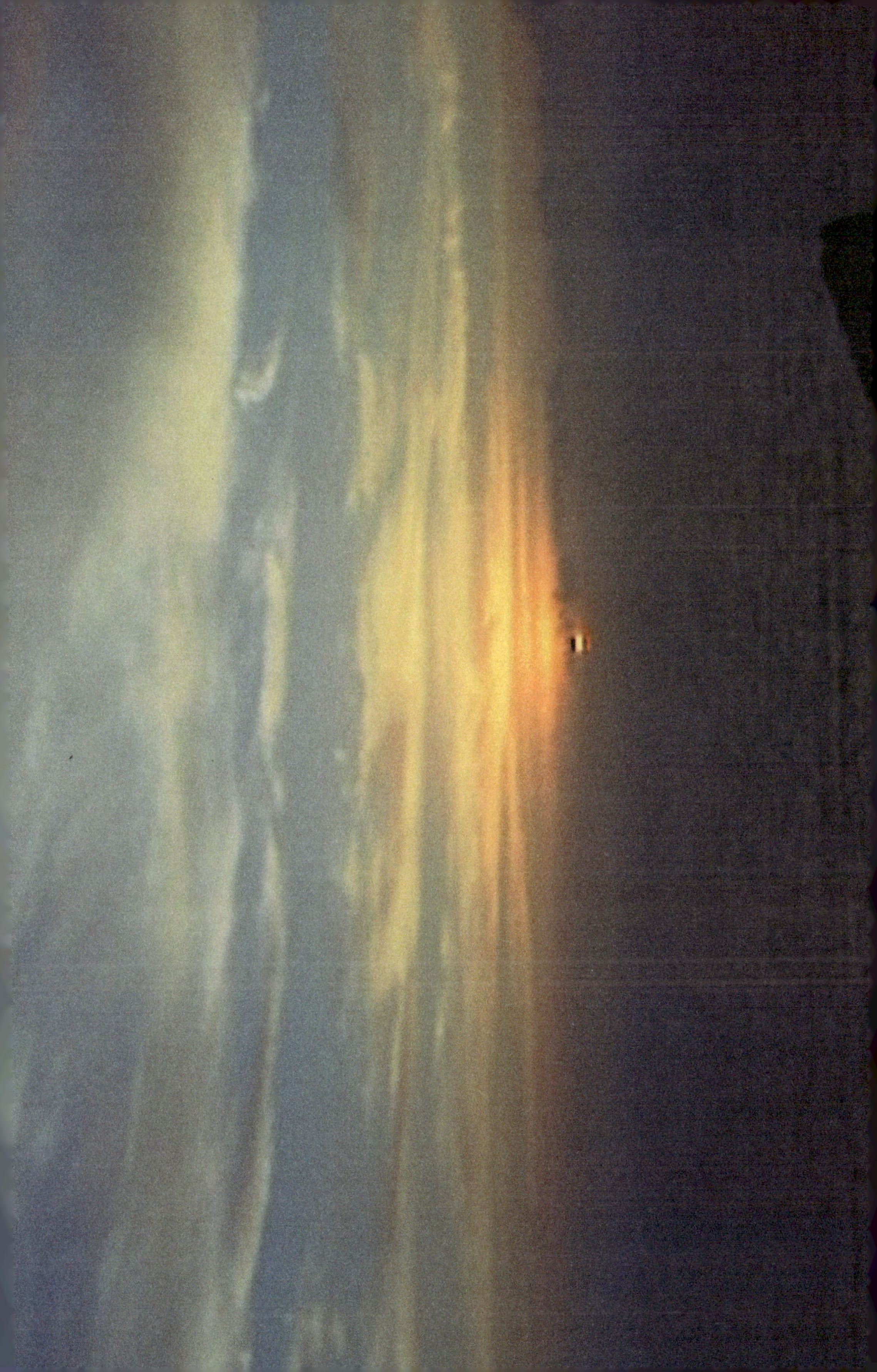

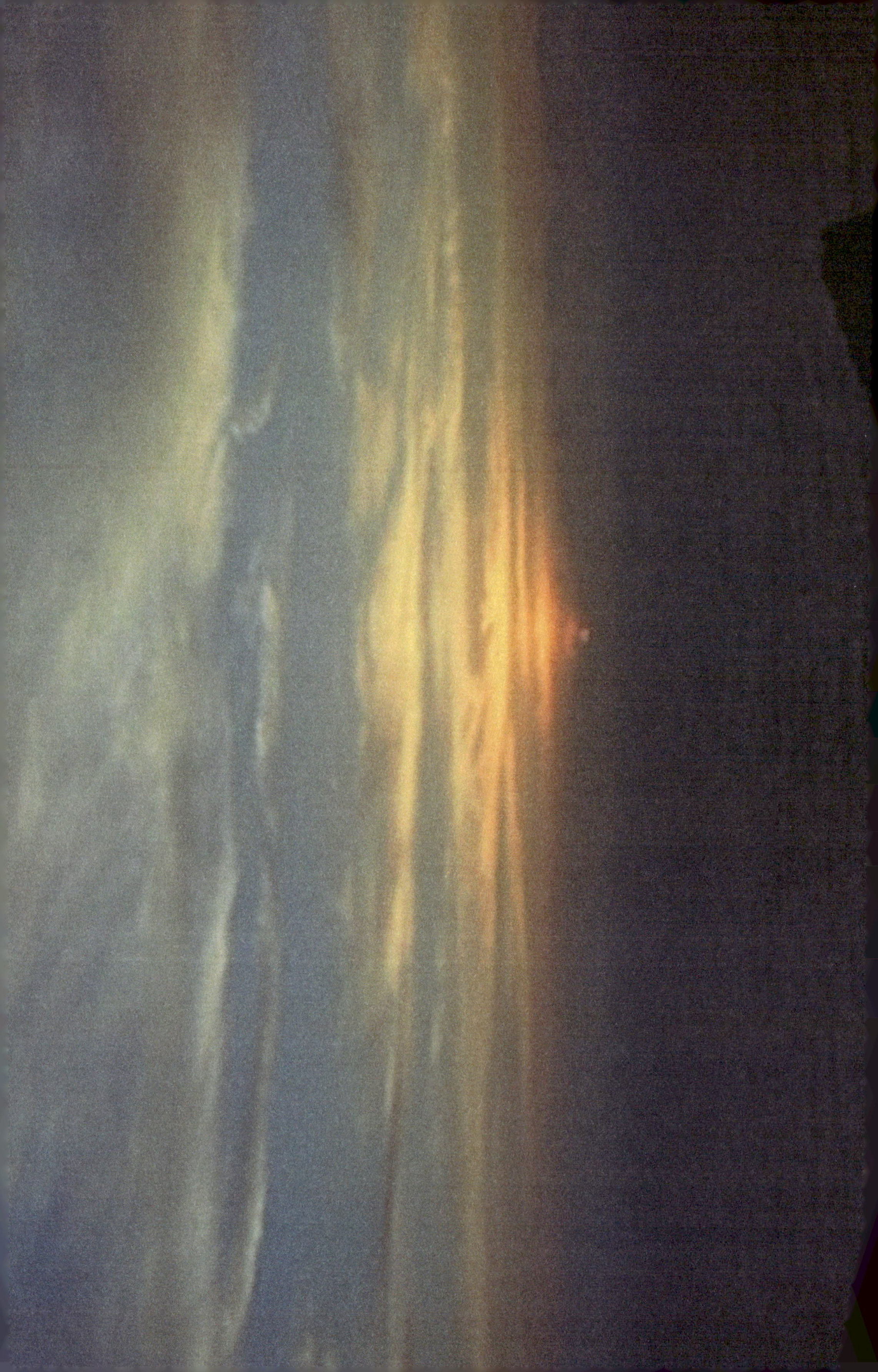

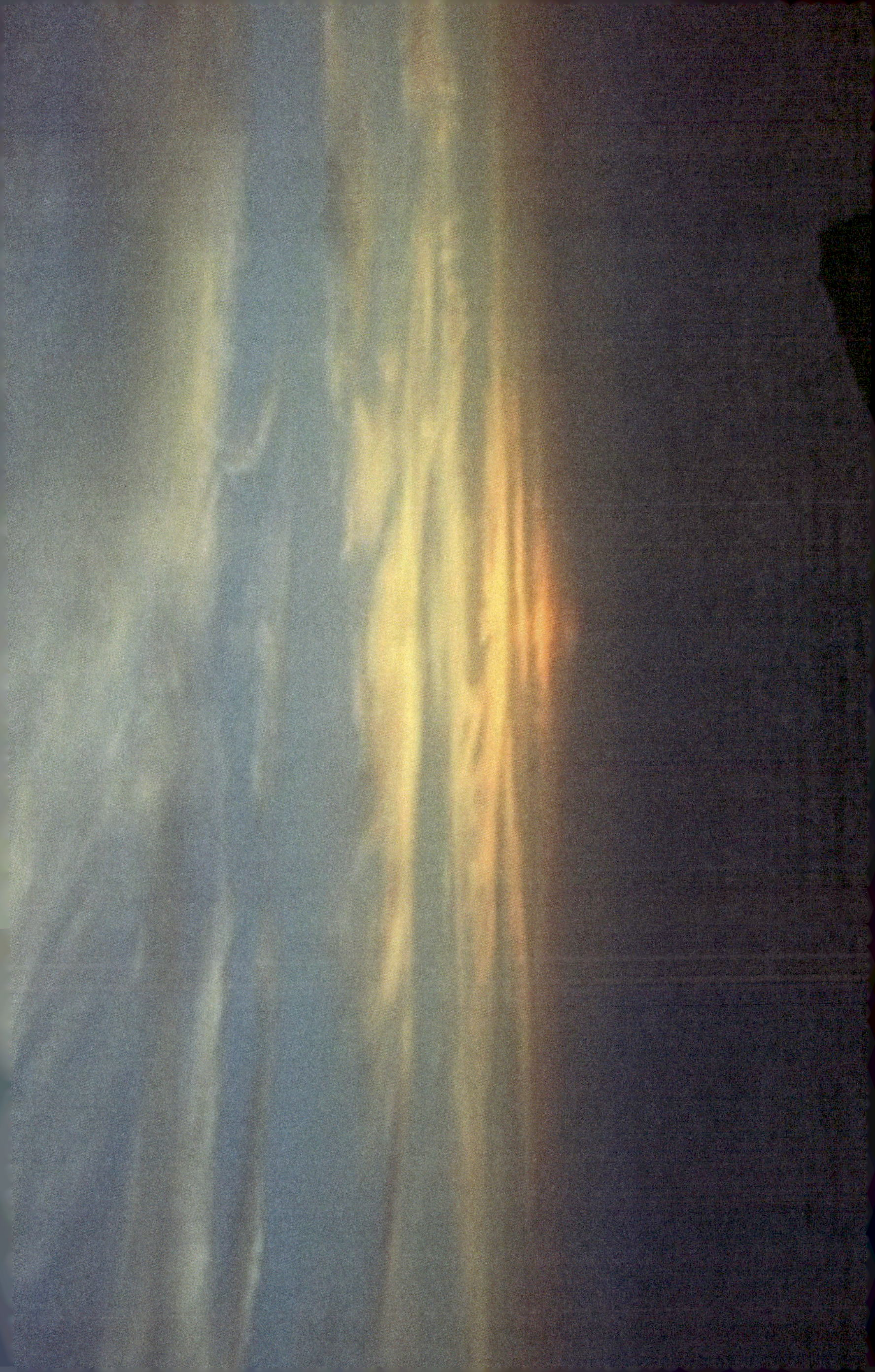

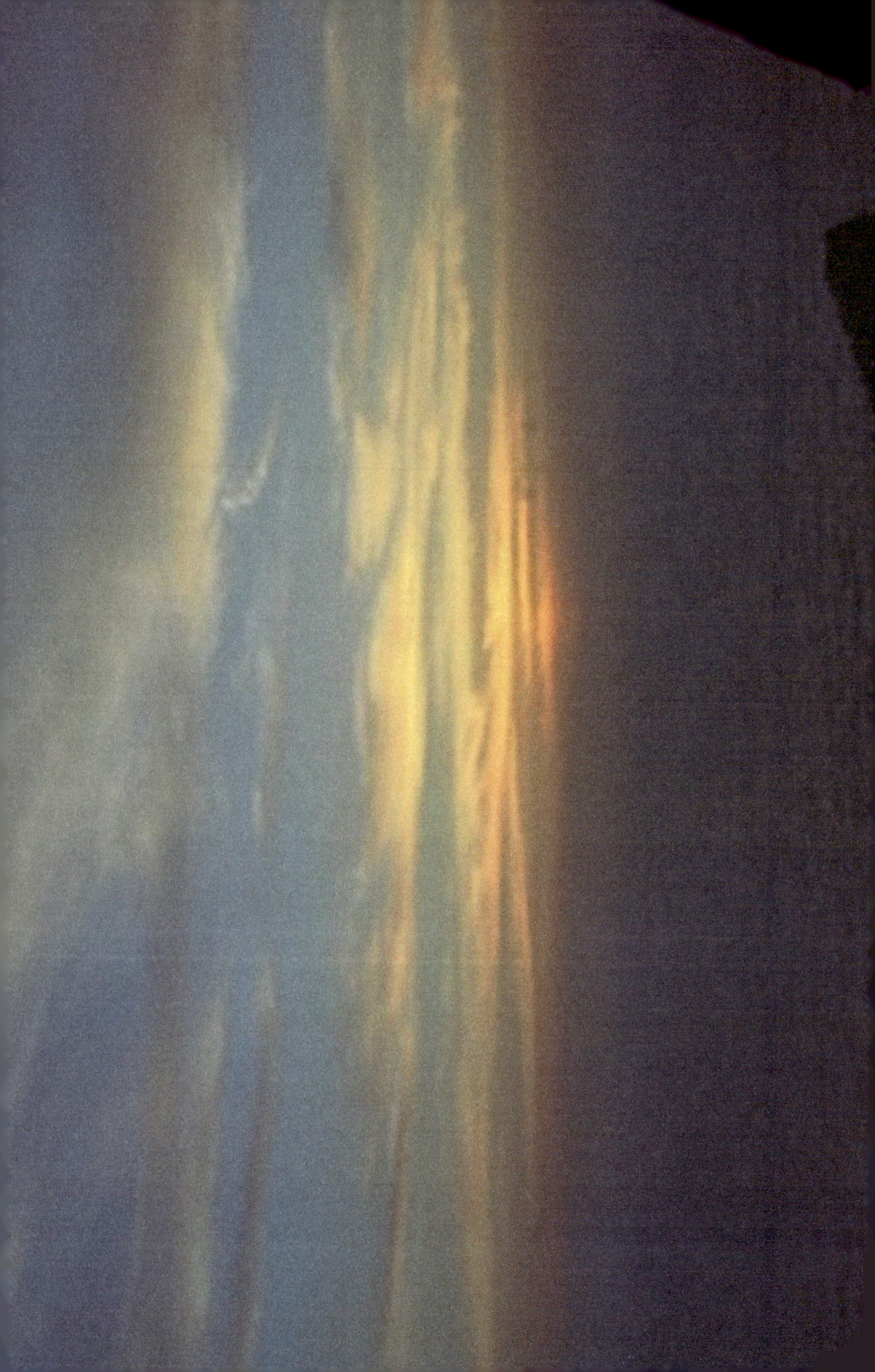

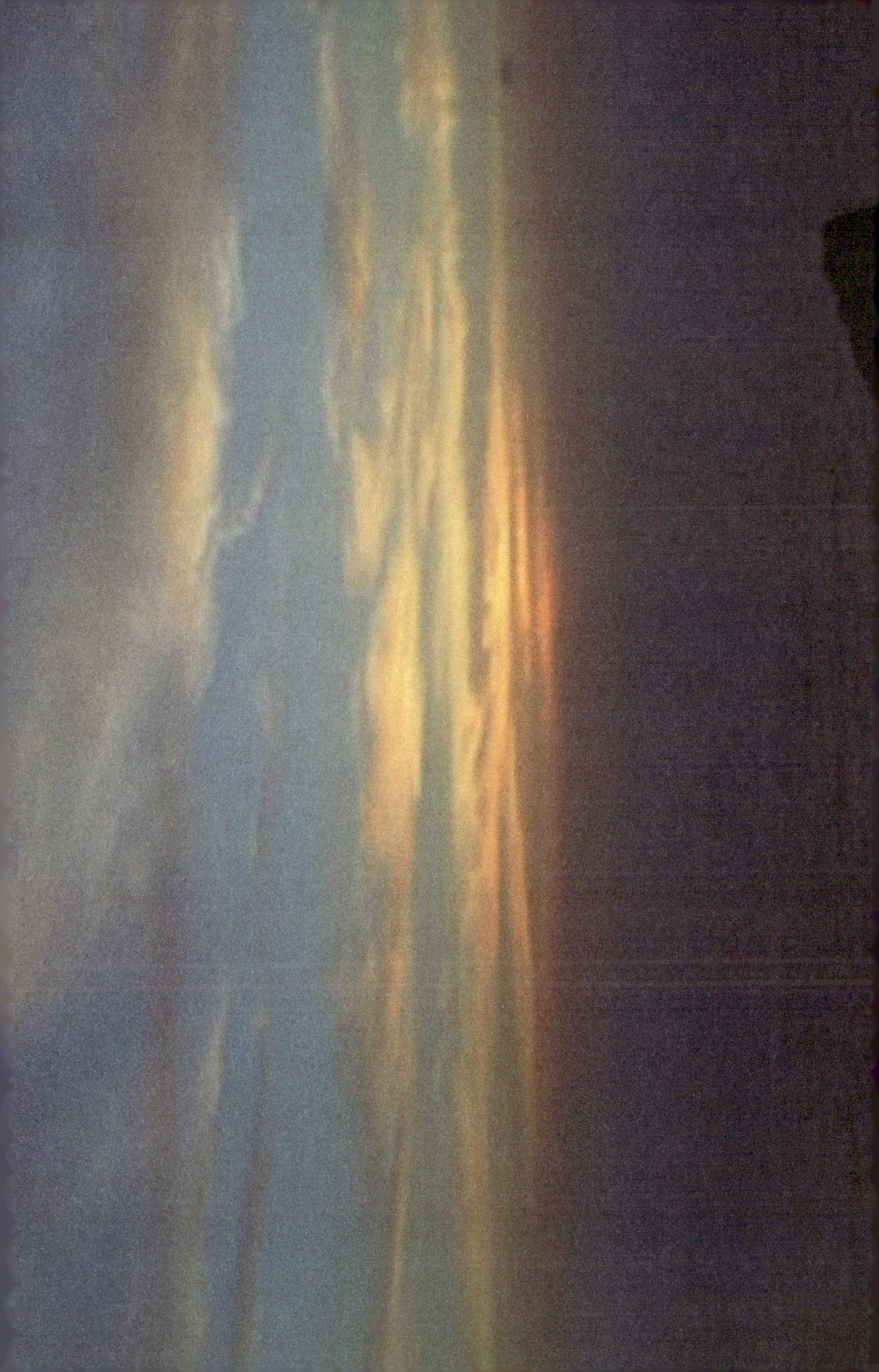

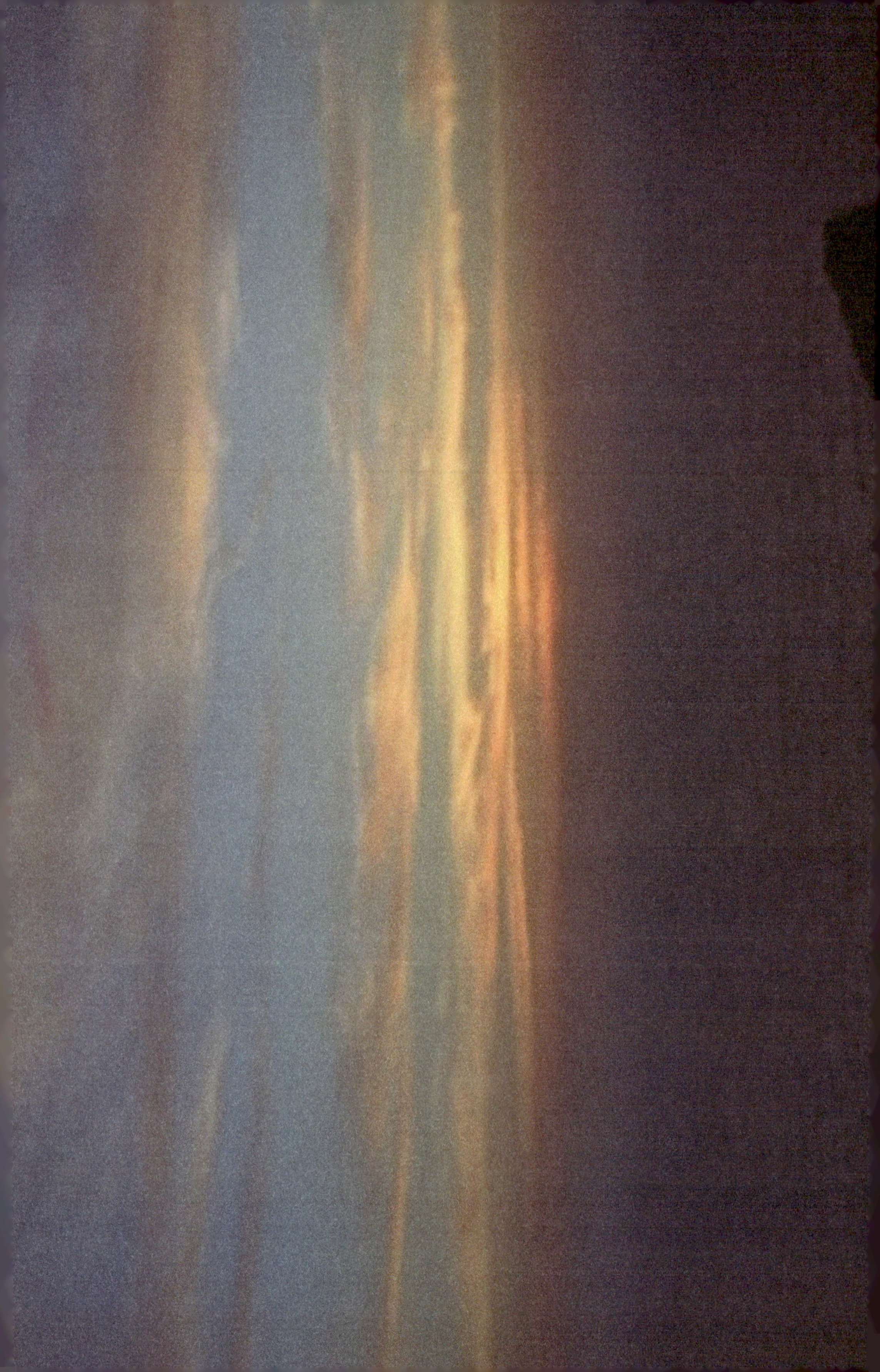

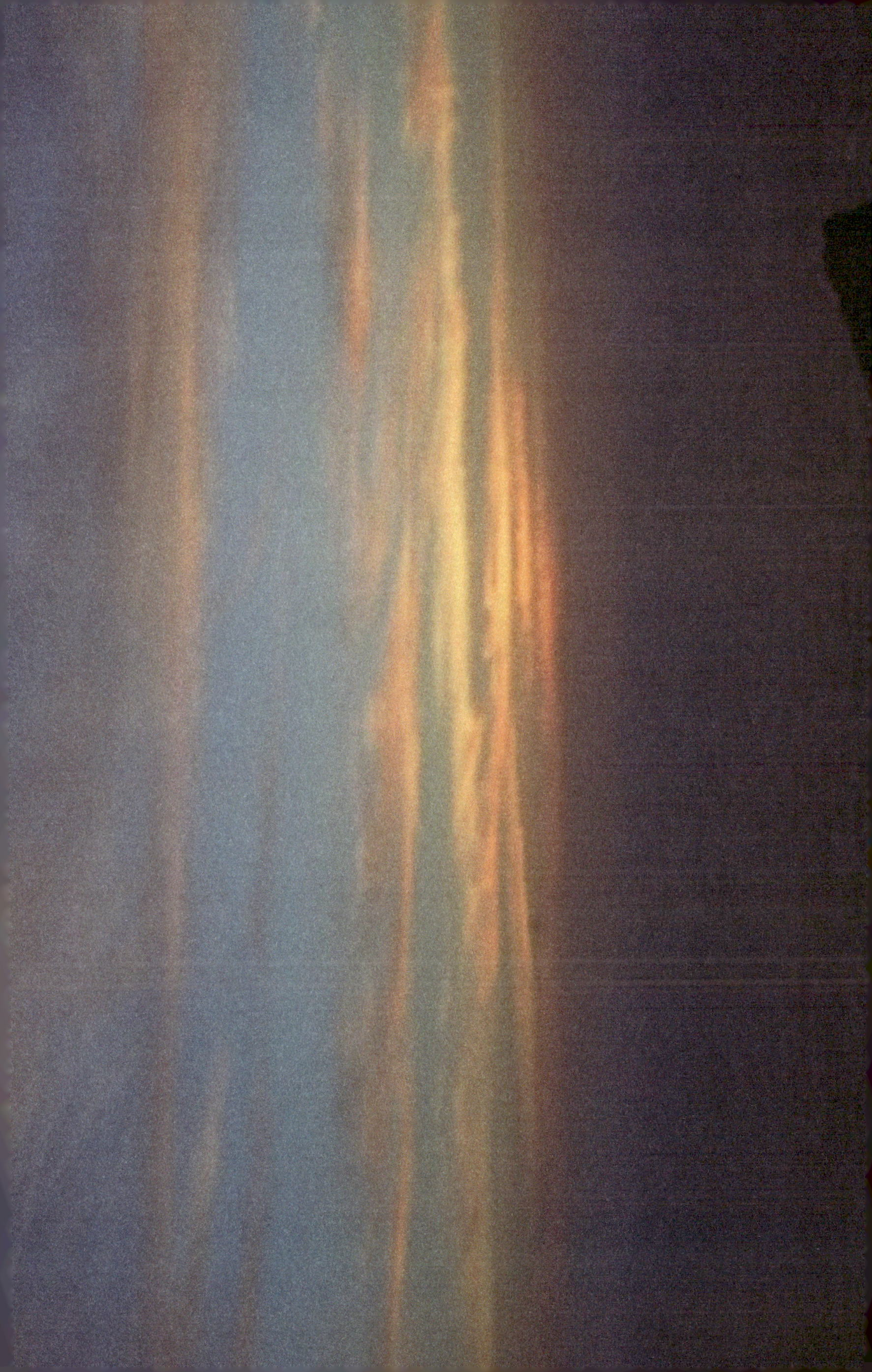

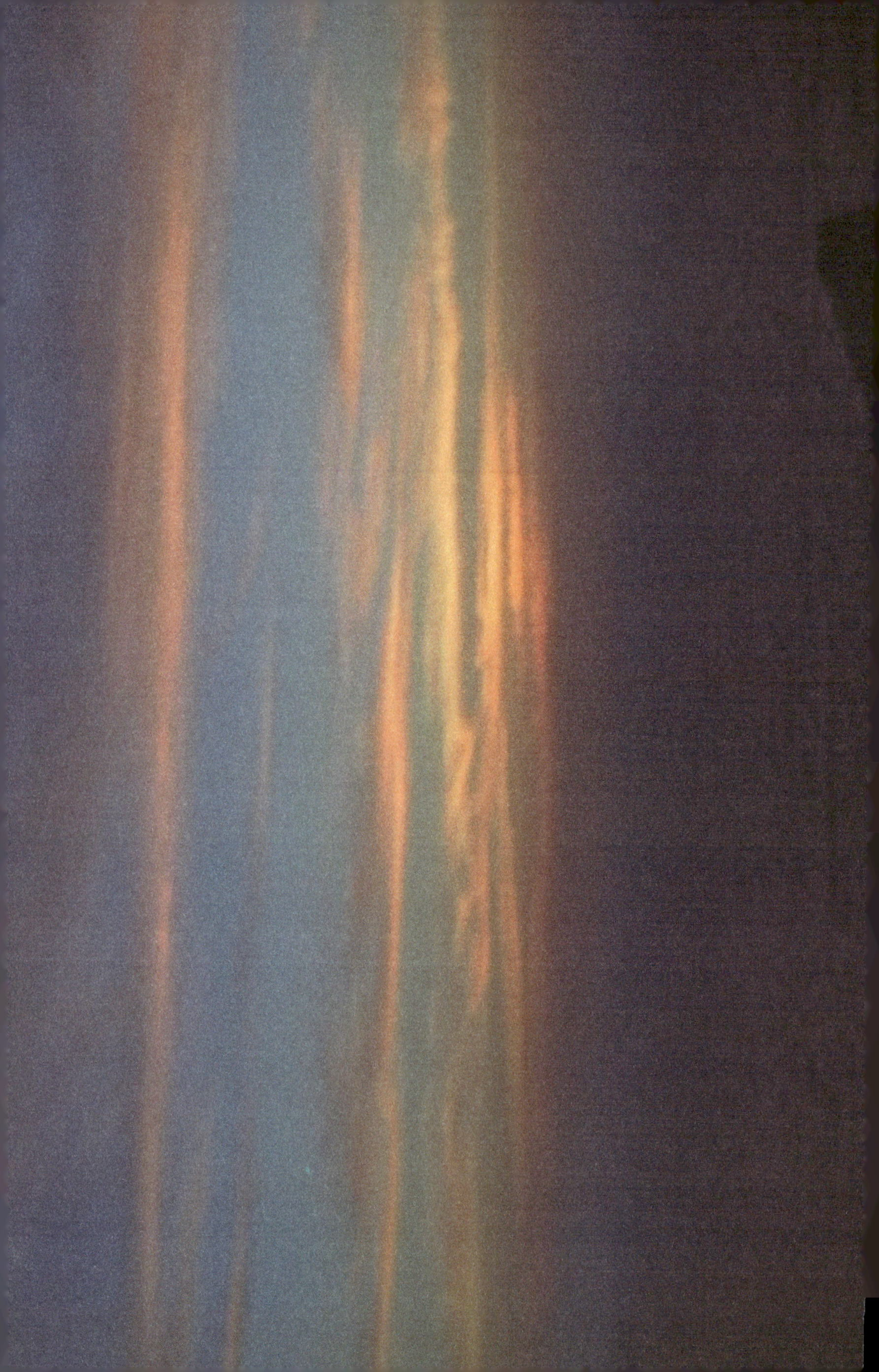

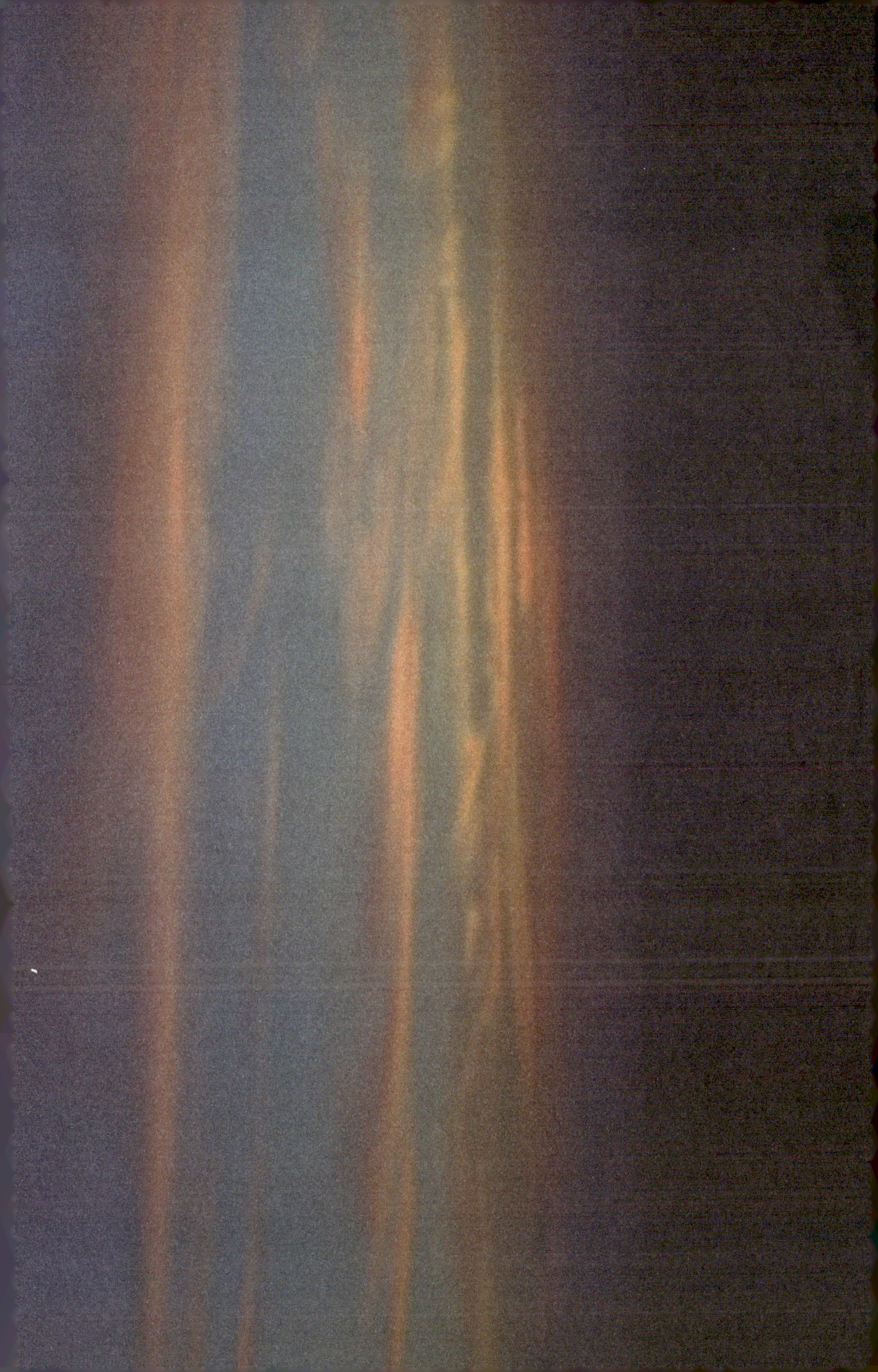

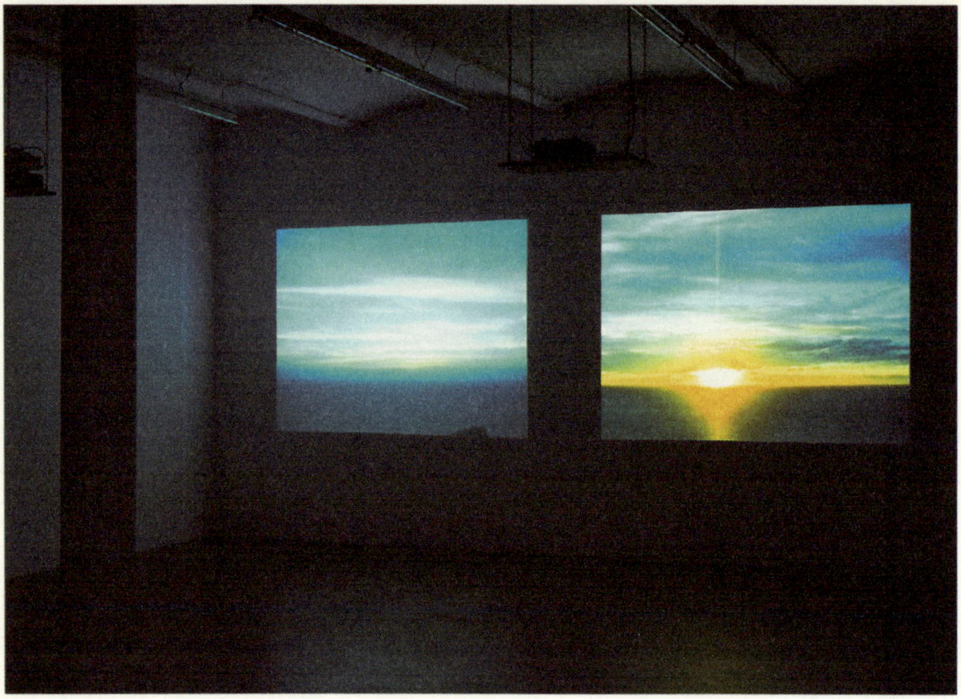

Another Day (2000), Installation view
Galerie Barbara Thumm, Berlin
Photograph: David Brandt

Prisoners of the Californian Dream: Panic Suburbs in Hong Kong

Laura Ruggeri

Saturday night and Sunday morning at Palm Springs

Waiting for the shuttle bus that will take me from Central to Palm Springs, where the Chans are having a barbecue party, I receive a phone call from a friend who invites me for a drink at the California Bar in Lan Kwai Fong, a mere five minutes walk from where I am standing. While I explain that I cannot join him because I am heading to a party in the New Territories, I catch a glimpse of a palm-shaped neon sign pointing to the California Fitness Club. Something is telling me this is going to be a 'Californian' night. This moment of uncanniness creates a creeping sense of déjà-vu... There she is again, Ah Faye dancing to the sound of *California Dreaming* in Wong Kar-Wai's *Chungking Express*, #633 waiting for her at the California Bar while she has decided to go to the real California instead. Unlike Ah Faye I am on my way to a parallel California, one I can reach by bus.

The bus journey lasts for approximately 45 minutes, during which we pass Kwai Chung freight container station (the largest in the world), Yuen Long public housing projects, Kam Tin walled village (a 12th century Hakka settlement), several car demolition sites, industrial estates, illegal dumping sites, and an endless row of 'massage' parlours. When we finally arrive at the gate of Palm Springs two men in uniform ask the passengers to produce proof of identity. As I don't carry any identification document, I am requested to wait inside the guard post while they inform the Chans of my arrival. When Sui-man finally comes to my help he greets me by saying, "Welcome to Palm Springs. Did you really think you could travel to California without a passport?" He then drives me through a maze of identical avenues and alleys, all named after Californian towns: we turn into Sacramento Avenue, Pasadena Avenue, Santa Monica Avenue... After covering most of California in less than five minutes, we finally reach Monterey Avenue, where the Chans live. Eva is waiting for us in front of their green and pink three-storey semi-detached home.

Saturday night barbecue is a collective ritual. Smoke fills the air as hundreds of Palm Springs residents proudly grill pork ribs, king prawns and cuttlefish in their back garden. Before the customary mahjong game Sui-man invites me to climb to the flat roof top, from where he says I could enjoy a "spectacular view". The roof is partly occupied by a small prefab shed, where their Filipino maid sleeps, with neither light nor air conditioning, a situation shared by thousands of foreign domestic workers in Hong Kong. What Sui-man intends to show me is the view that stretches across the Chinese border, which is only a few miles away from Palm Springs. We gaze upon the largest industrial concentration in the world, with more than 3 million workers employed in enterprises and joint ventures located in China but controlled from Hong Kong. The sky is incredibly bright, but the moon plays little part in it. Here the night is turned into day by the neon signs of Shenzhen, whose skyscrapers rival those of Hong Kong. The industrial base of Hong Kong has been shifted across the border into Shenzhen and beyond. What has emerged since the Deng reforms, implemented from 1979, is a vast mega-urban region spreading from Hong Kong around the Pearl River delta to incorporate not only the Special Administrative Region of Shenzhen, but also the southern Chinese provincial capital of Guangzhou (Canton) and its satellite towns and as far as Zhuhai and Macau. This is a functionally integrated economic system, as well as being a rapidly expanding urban region, with Hong Kong constituting the service and financial centre linking this region to the international economy and society.

Only ten years ago tourists would come here with binoculars to catch a glimpse of rice paddies and Red Guards.

When I decide to leave the mahjong table it is past ten o'clock, already too late to catch the last shuttle bus. Luckily the Chans invite me to spend the night in their daughter's room.

Sunday morning at Palm Springs holds some surprises. My suggestion to go for *yám cha* (dim sum) is received with stupor. Eva hastily explains that there are no dim sum restaurants at Palm Springs and that those outside are not worth the effort. We have breakfast in the garden: cereals, croissants and French baguettes served with butter and jam. It is my first continental breakfast since I moved to Hong Kong and I am not particularly pleased to trade shrimp dumplings for frozen baguettes. But one would be wrong to assume that the Chans are going out of their way to make me feel at home. The Chans' neighbours, despite the absence of a westerner at their table, are having the same type of breakfast in the adjacent garden. Only an elderly man, (the grandfather?) is served a bowl of rice and what looks like chicken liver. I suppose the American lifestyle has failed to capture the imagination of the elderly. Later, we watch Sui-man play tennis and we stroll through the theme park, where Disney comic strip characters are surrounded by miniaturised Greek columns and neo-classical pavilions. Everybody seems to be wearing Ralph Lauren polo necks, khaki shorts and immaculate white trainers. Smart casual, as they call it here.

The settlement is surveilled by heavily armed Gurkhas, recruited from the thousands laid off by the British Army in 1997. By a strange irony some of their present employers are likely to be the same 'illegal immigrants', now wealthy homeowners, they once tried to prevent entering the colony. On leaving Palm Springs I have to check out at the guard post. One of the security guards, looking at the roll of visitors realises that I have spent the night there and gives me and Sui-man, who is standing next to me, a complicitous look. Sui-man, to dispel my embarrassment, turns to the guard and adds, "She is my sister, by the way", to which everybody, including myself, laughs with relief.

An hour later I am walking in Wanchai and the contrast could not be more striking. Along the streets commercial signboards attached to the lower level of the buildings hang above my head. They form layers covering and obscuring one another; overhead, lattice-work cages, both glass-enclosed and open to the air, cling to each apartment. Leaking air-conditioners, clothes poles sticking out of windows, and weed springing from ruptured concrete verandahs all contribute to animate the sooty façades. Along the pavement huge cement urns for flowers contain rotting cigarette butts and styrofoam boxes: store managers put tables piled with goods on the sidewalk and arrange with vendors to sell goods in front of their stores, breaking down the boundary between private and public space. They bring the sidewalk into the building by using their vestibules as selling space or indenting the whole façade of their store to create a kind of super vestibule for open air sales. I jostle in the crowd, among the wavering fumes of diesel and cooking oil, a haptic geography wherein there is a continuous touching of others, weaving between and amongst bodies and brushing against different textures. "We rub shoulders with each other everyday, we may not know each other, but we could become good friends one day."[1] Electric and lurid city, whose 'smellscapes' and 'soundscapes' are as exciting, rich and varied as its skyline. I have become used to this symphonic chaos, it sounds as if the coordination of pulses and bounds is just two measures away and you want to linger in the streets for a little longer, in the hope of seizing that moment. Somebody walks home with a live chicken in her bag. I remember my friend May insisting that young housewives should learn how to kill, pluck, dissect and cook a chicken, for the sake of their marriage.

In Hong Kong you cannot be a distanced spectator of some urban spectacle, you are always part of a heterotopic diversity where the senses are excited by the most variegated set of stimuli. Coping with the city, its sultry heat, the jumbled mix of pungent aromas – a veritable olfactory geography – and the combination of noises generated by numerous human activities my body comes to life, is roused by the resistance which it experiences. All other places now seem insipid to me.

A gigantic billboard displays pictures of a busy street market, a Chinese junk, two rickshaws, and Pei's Bank of China. The caption reads, 'The city owes its liveliness to the movements of life that unfold in the streets. Hong Kong. City of Life'. This is the (fast disappearing) city promoted by the Tourist Board, an oriental cliché. Barthes once observed that it is the peculiar mixture of bells, rickshaws, and opium dens that constitute 'China' for a European. Myths die hard, especially when they are reappropriated for marketing purposes. The Chans have chosen to live the American dream. I am probably unable to awaken from an orientalist two-hundred-year-old dream.

1 From Wong Kar-Wai's film, *Chungking Express*. He Qi Wu's voiceover perfectly expresses the feeling of proximity without reciprocity that is experienced by millions of Hongkongese everyday, except that this state of affairs does not completely exclude the growth of intimacy.

Why do the Chans choose to live at Palm Springs?

The Chans moved to Palm Springs in 1991 when major construction works were still under way. They said they felt like pioneers. According to the pictures they showed me the development looked a far cry from the computer simulated images that had captured their imagination six months earlier. Construction rubble still surrounded their house, the newly planted palm trees looked unhealthy and unpromising, Monterey Avenue had not yet been paved. Both working as executives in the Trade Development Council, they had moved with their daughter and the Filipino maid from their small flat in North Point (on Hong Kong island) to what was still regarded by most Hongkongese as a borderland. The surroundings were neither picturesque nor healthy as local farmers had already realised that they could make a better living by renting their plots to car demolishers or by turning them into dumping sites and container parks. Besides, moving to a place that is just a stone's throw away from the People's Republic, surrounded by barracks and (then) British soldiers, could not possibly be regarded as a sound decision. Yet the Chans, whom a sociologist would describe as upwardly mobile middle class, had been lured to this new development near Wo Shang Wai.

But why would the Chans live at Palm Springs? A few weeks after my visit, the question still turning in my mind, I decide to call Eva in the hope that she could satisfy my curiosity. Keen to help, she suggests that I look at the promotional material she collected before buying the property and offers to meet me for *yám cha* a few days later. Armed with some glossy brochures, a video, a CD-ROM and relying on Eva's infinite patience and invaluable help I can finally try to understand the reasons that lie behind the Chan's decision to move to Palm Springs.

Unpacking the myth

Palm Springs and other similar developments appear to be underwritten by an explicit marketing text, a strategy of 'place advertisement' which is accentuated by the compelling products of postmodern architectural imagineering. In Palm Springs both the direct advertising message and the motifs of landscape form seem to be received and re-transmitted as cultural signals by those who live there. One brochure claims:

> We bring to Hong Kong the look, feel and beauty of southern California. You can hear gentle laughter as you walk along the streets and sense the warmth of your neighbourhood as it welcomes you with open arms. Palm Springs has been designed with quality of life in mind. That's why the atmosphere here will enchant you. There are palm-lined streets and picturesque scenery. You'll also marvel at the dancing fountains, colourful flowers, nostalgic lampposts and street sculptures. All of it created to give you a sense of well being and happiness.

A dreamscape is conjured up by means of space compression – one can experience California, the ultimate place-myth for the cosmopolitan Hong Kong citizen, without leaving home. Palm Springs becomes the base camp for an adventure of the imagination, an imagination that clearly feeds on films and TV. A neighbourhood that 'welcomes you with open arms' suggests a friendliness that is supposedly missing outside, while 'gentle laughter', an oxymoron in Hong Kong, is obviously interpreted as an index of civility. The reference to 'nostalgic lampposts and street sculptures', ubiquitous in shopping malls, reinscribes the urban in a purely aesthetic form. The picture placed at the bottom of this text shows a red phone box. The British icon could either suggest that Palm Springs residents are British passport holders – a prestige symbol in certain social circles – or simply compress the colonial past into a decorative element, infused with nostalgia. Further on the brochure states:

> Unlike communities anywhere else in Hong Kong, Palm Springs presents a total concept in living. This includes community activities and celebrations that bring everyone together to share happy moments and events. We have brought back the real meaning of neighbourhood(...) Feel the burdens of the day melt away as you go from your work mood to play time. Enjoy yourself in the refreshing and relaxing atmosphere of the Clubhouse, your heart and soul are reborn. It is all a clear reflection of the true easygoing California lifestyle.

The language used is both lyrical and evocative. It aims to elicit an emotional rather than rational engagement. Ways of living are objectified as 'lifestyle'. The Californian lifestyle is made the subject of a myth. Palm Springs is not presented as 'merely a place to live – that is to reside – but also the stage upon which one may practice the 'art of living' whilst following the proposed script: 'Loosen your necktie, toss aside the suit and the Rolex, and see just how wonderful life is'. The gated community is described as a world apart, a place where one can 'get away from it all', a holiday resort to which one can retreat every day. The holiday is therefore not a break with home life, but an integral part of it. Palm Springs is presented as a sophisticated club where one can enjoy a 'total way of life'. As the rigidities of established social distinction become increasingly hard to sustain in eras of rapid social and physical mobility new forms of distinction are continually being elaborated. The Rolex is no longer an exclusive status symbol when one is a slave of time. In Hong Kong leisure activities are seen as ways of accumulating or losing distinction: being a member of a golf or tennis club immediately bespeaks one's socio-economic status. What emerges from the description is a constructed landscape of collective aspirations, which have been fuelled and mediated through the complex prism of modern media. New social constituencies articulate their identity with new cultural insignia and even features of the landscape become a means for fixing social position.

Another brochure is organised as a photo album, 'a collection of the most exciting, memorable moments of the Palm Springs community's happiness and harmony'. Its declared aim is to offer 'an unforgettable picture of the real California lifestyle'. Buying a house in Palm Springs would enable anyone to become a welcome member of what is portrayed as a happy extended family and escape the anonymity and isolation that supposedly characterise urban life. It is worth keeping in mind that many Hongkongese look back at the traditional extended family with a sense of nostalgia: due to migration and family planning, large families have become a thing of the past. The album features pictures of parents playing with their children in the swimming pool, engaging in healthy activities both in the clubhouse and in the park, taekwondo classes, handicraft and drawing classes in which children portray their dream home. Needless to say, the drawings that are reproduced in the album invariably feature a swimming pool surrounded by palm trees: your children's dream home is the place where they are already living. A section is devoted to traditional Chinese celebrations, such as the Mid-Autumn Festival, during which Palm Springs hosts a variety show and singing performances. Under the full moon, parents and their children carry lanterns and stroll along the enclave's avenues. The next page presents pictures of a Halloween party: a caption reads, 'Every child looks cute and creative in his special costume'. A juxtaposition that seems to suggest that Palm Springs residents are cosmopolitan yet respect and uphold their Chinese traditions. To convey the message that Palm Springs is a healthy and green environment, many pictures show community members involved in tree planting, natural food products sales and recycling activities. The photo album is sprinkled with words like 'village', 'community', and 'cosy' to suggest a friendliness and a manageable scale that is allegedly missing outside: 'Under the radiance of sunshine, swaying palms and lush greenery friends call out and greet you warmly. We have created a truly harmonious neighbourhood'.

The promotional material presents the image of an island to which one can return every day, an escape from the city and its deteriorating environment, where one can encounter an exclusive world of pleasure among peers. Both isolation and distance from the city are presented as offering the possibility of a better lifestyle. The latter is expressed, for example, in the use of phrases inspired by ecological discourses. Since gated communities are constructed by the same calculuses that produce advertising and shopping malls, those of 'pure imageability'; litter, dirt, a rapidly deteriorating environment, traffic, noise, and social inequality must all be erased in what is presented as a holiday resort.

Despite the 45 minutes drive to reach the city centre Palm Springs is advertised as, 'close to the city'. One of the brochures deals with the issue of transport in the usual evocative tone: 'Driving enthusiasts will love to take the car out for a spin. With the wind in your hair and the sun in your face, the trip to work will seem all too short'. What the brochure fails to mention is that residents have no choice but to rely on private transport as the shuttle bus service provided by the community can hardly cater for all their needs (buses run every 45 minutes, and stop at 10 pm). Palm Springs is not served by public buses or trains. In spite all the emphasis put on environmental issues Palm Springs can hardly be considered an environmentally-friendly development as it requires private car ownership. In Hong Kong, due to the vicinity of China's largest manufacturing region, air pollution levels are alarming and a constant matter of concern for local authorities who try very hard to discourage individual car ownership.

All brochures devote little space to the issue of security, only in the very last page do they mention the presence of a '24 hour surveillance service provided by trained, professional personnel' and display some very small pictures of a Gurkha guard, either standing next to his Alsatian dog or driving an American 4 wheel drive. An excessive stress on security would probably create a sense of anxiety in the reader and impair the success of a marketing campaign based on the enchantment of prospective buyers.

How the Chans found out about Palm Springs

Sun Hung Kai Properties promoted Palm Springs (a 286,740 m^2 development, whose 374 units are arranged as terraced and semi-detached three storey houses) the way most developers do in Hong Kong, by advertising on TV, newspapers, popular magazines and on large billboards placed in central Hong Kong. The Chans went to look at the models, computer simulations and videos that were being shown in an upmarket shopping mall. There they were treated to a variety show hosted by a well known TV personality – who repeatedly hinted at the fact that some Canto Pop stars were planning to move to Palm Springs – enjoyed some complimentary refreshments and took part in a draw for a holiday in Europe. According to Eva, it was an 'exciting experience, a bit like being in a TV show'. From the beginning they were made feel part of a dreamworld. They were welcomed with large smiles, shook hands with celebrities and were dazed by the glitz and glitter.

The return of the walled city

In Hong Kong, social inequality is obvious and the process of spatial segregation is not new. When British colonisers moved to Hong Kong they chose to live on the Peak, distancing themselves from the Chinese population and from the diseases that supposedly plagued the lower, less salubrious areas. Their imposing residences were patrolled by armed soldiers, and access to Peak Road was granted only to coolies and Chinese notables. Walled villages, on the other hand, were a common feature of pre-colonial Hong Kong, and to a minor extent of colonial Hong Kong too. Some of these villages can still be seen in the New Territories, now converted into museums and tourist attractions. But whereas the residents of those villages belonged to a clan and shared common ancestors, the residents of the new gated communities share only the dream of living in a safe and socially homogeneous environment.

In Hong Kong, socio-economic differentiation, either imagined or real, is likely to be represented through spatial categories and images. But the model that once informed the strategies and the imaginations of social groups is changing. Traditionally, the closer one moved to the top and the centre, the greater one's social power – power and prestige diminished as one moved toward the peripheries. This obsession with the 'centre' lead to a very high concentration of tall residential buildings in what is improperly described as the 'business district'. This vertical and stratified arrangement of space, where top floors are the most prestigious and desirable, is now challenged by the proliferation of upmarket gated communities in the periphery.

Developers can maximise profit by acquiring unattractive lots, the market price for which is very low, and then building luxury homes and first class facilities similar to those found in more prestigious areas. It is only by virtue of their isolation from their dreary surroundings and the security systems that enable it, that these enclaves become suitable for the middle and upper classes. These communities can be situated almost anywhere, independent of their surroundings. In fact most of them have been placed in the periphery and have as their neighbours squatters' settlements, impoverished rural surroundings, dumping sites and landfills. Moreover, the planning regime which instituted zoning regulations for medium density low-rise buildings in the New Territories required developers to think of a way of maximizing profit other than building 30-storey-high tower blocks. Developing elite communities provided the solution.

Gates not only protect leisure amenities such as golf courses, swimming pools, and tennis courts, but they also protect economic and social status. They provide points of coherence around which the residents can organise social experience into meaningful patterns. The domestic environment becomes, then, the theatre for the re-enactment of forms and scripts introduced from the outside. Property developers are able to construct new landscapes of power, dreamscapes for visual consumption constituted of designer-reconstructions of spatially remote objects and lifestyles. Myth is more important than reality in selling places like Palm Springs.

The use of American or European elements in order to sell all types of commodity is a very common practice in China; they are codified as something conferring high status. Gated communities, fashioned after their American counterparts, have become a standardised product, like cars or television sets, offered in a finite range of models. The same developer, Sun Hung Kai Properties, has developed an almost identical enclave just a mile away from Palm Springs, and called it Royal Palms. Sun Hung Kai is also involved in similar projects across the Chinese border and in the Philippines. Repetition has defeated uniqueness. Repetitious spaces are the outcome of repetitive gestures associated with instruments which are both duplicable and designed to duplicate: machines, bulldozers, concrete mixers, cranes, pneumatic drills, and so on. Are these places interchangeable because they are homologous? Or are they homogeneous so that they can be exchanged, bought and sold with the only differences between them being those assessable in money – i.e. quantifiable terms (as volumes, distances, etc)? Can a space of this kind really still be described as a 'place'?

A further important aspect of spaces of this kind is their ever increasing pronounced visual character. They are built and bought on the basis of images. The concept of community has also been commodified, marketed piecemeal and in standardised units, like any other consumer product. However, these are not communities in the sociological sense because, rather than constructing rich networks of relationships, residents tend to isolate themselves in their homes.

The developers of gated communities go to great lengths to ensure that the purity of the community-as-commodity they have packaged will not be tampered with by the home buyers. This is the purpose of the detailed regulations and restrictions that they impose upon the home owners who were unable to purchase property in the development without first becoming a member of the residents' association and thereafter without agreeing to abide by its rules. The covenants and restrictions enforced by residents' associations may dictate hours and frequency of visitors, colour of paint on a house, style and colour of the front door, size and number of pets, parking rules etc. Not only the developers but also the customers are interested in exchange value. Sui-man expects the value of their property to appreciate substantially because, he says, an increasing number of people want to live in a safe and healthy environment. In his opinion, buying a house in Palm Springs is a very good investment indeed.

The Californian Lifestyle

The 'texture' of Palm Springs is accessible by means of a variety of 'texts', presented in advertising, expressed in interviews and made concrete in the landscape itself. Upon several occasions the Chans have mentioned the Californian lifestyle as their main reason for moving to Palm Springs. Security was perceived as part and parcel of what they had bought and was not regarded as an important issue.[2] Yet living behind gates is seen as a prestige element, what separates the merely well-off from the truly rich. As Mike Davies has observed, 'The trend of living in a walled-off community has assumed the frenzied dimension of a residential arms race as ordinary suburbanites demand the kind of social insulation once enjoyed only by the rich'.[3] If Americans flock to gated enclaves because they are terrified by crime and worried about property values, the Hongkongese seem more interested in the promise of a socially homogeneous, friendly, and glamourous neighbourhood – a place where you might have a chance to run into a celebrity – and experience the lifestyle others can only dream of when they see it on television.

My 'informants' claim that security was not their primary concern when they moved to Palm Springs, and actually thought that the cost of maintaining a 24 hour surveillance was too high and unjustified[4] since the New Territories were already heavily militarised due to their vicinity to the Chinese border. Nevertheless they feel that 'times have changed', and that 'Hong Kong has become a far less safe place than it used to be'. In spite of the fact that the crime rate has not substantially increased,[5] they perceive a potential danger outside their protected environment. 'Fear proves itself: the social perception of threat becomes a function of the security mobilisation itself, not crime rates'.[6] It should also be noticed that the media contribute to magnify potential dangers as they beat a daily drum of hysteria about violent crime, illegal immigrants, drug use, litter and health hazards. Living behind walls, in an encapsulated environment, becomes a powerful symbol for being protected, buttressed, and coddled. Whilst being on the 'outside' evokes exposure, isolation, and vulnerability.

Palm Springs ushers in the new (cosmetic) style of 'real imitation life', the Californian lifestyle, which can be imported, like any other commodity. After all, in Hong Kong it is no longer possible to distinguish what is local and what is not. The transnational is the local. Therefore, if

2 The crime rate in Hong Kong is very low compared to other world cities. In 1991, the year when Palm Springs was built, the crime rate was: 1,550 reported crimes per 100,000 population. (Hong Kong Government statistics.)

3 Mike Davis, *City of Quartz: Excavating the Future in Los Angeles* (London: Verso, 1990) p 246.

4 The huge cost of employing guards 24 hours a day means that behind the superficially impressive uniforms and security badges there is a near minimum wage employee.

5 The crime rate has actually decreased. In 1995 reported crimes dropped to 1,490 per 100,000 population and has not varied substantially during the last five years. (Hong Kong Government statistics.)

6 Mike Davis, 1990: p 224.

people, in particular the middle and upper class, are fully conversant in transnational idioms – which include language, music, sports, clothing, satellite television, cybercommunications, global travel and cuisine – nothing can stop them from choosing what is perceived as a fashionable lifestyle. As the Hong Kong based anthropologist, Gordon Mathews, observed: 'The Hongkongese had to invent their identity, neither Chinese nor British, they had no choice but going lifestyle shopping in the global cultural supermarket '.[7]

Yám cha with Eva

The following Friday I meet Eva for *yám cha*. We end up in the restaurant where I had my wedding reception. I mention this to Eva and the conversation immediately veers towards wedding dresses, banquets, menus and table manners. I cannot fail to see the irony of questioning her Californian life-style while describing my Chinese wedding dress; she is slightly disappointed, "You are Italian, I thought you would go for onc of those fabulous wedding dresses they make in Italy". She does not share my fascination with China, she has not been back to her native Guangdong village since the rest of her family emigrated to Canada ten years ago. She describes it as dirty, poor, grim and polluted. While she embarks on a tirade against the People's Republic, I am suddenly reminded of what lies beyond the high walls of Palm Springs: the shanty towns, dumping sites, brothels, and sweatshops that the residents refuse to see, in what could be described as a case of reverse hallucination. Like the walls of a Takunyan – that feudal compound of Chinese literature acting as a defence against evil spirits and human enemies – the walls of Palm Springs protect the Chans from the ghost of poverty.

The Other Side of the World

Terris Nguyen Temple

I was born on 5 May, 1944 in Bakersfield, California, which was a good place to grow up in those first few years. Plenty of space, with canyons, a beautiful river, lots of farms and orchards and vast open spaces. Play was my prime objective and life was easy. When I got to ten years of age we moved to Glendale, just outside Los Angeles. Now I had a big city to explore as well as access to the Pacific Coast and the wilderness around our house. 1950s America was an amazing experience, you could actually drink the water straight from the tap and breathe the air in most places other than in LA. Antibiotics were still a wonder cure and it felt like a time of innocence and prosperity. The American Dream was a reality and materialism was the force that shaped most people's lives. The environmental horrors of today weren't even a thing of fiction in those days. Everyone was imagining life for our future generations to be golden.

I left school young, at fifteen, having chosen freedom (which was how I regarded expulsion) over corporal punishment for some minor act of non-conformism. I now had a great deal of time on my hands. I remember taking part in late night discussions with my cronies about inequality and the meaning of life, the cold war, segregation and issues like the Bomb. Reading occupied much of my time, when I wasn't sleeping or eating. My lifestyle changed since all my friends were studying during the day; I began to hang out with older guys who considered themselves as members of the beat generation and, rather than get a job and develop a mature sense of responsibility, I went to San Francisco to write poetry instead.

I found myself on the streets of San Francisco towards the end of the beat era and began meeting some of the characters who were hanging out there: artists, writers and members of the mystic community. I was friendly with Alan Watts (the Zen poet and writer) who gave great houseboat parties across the bridge in Sausalito and I remember the activity around the Zen Centre in San Francisco headed by a serene Roshi from Japan. Poets like Alan Ginsberg, Ferlangetti Whelan, and Kaufman added extra color to the scene. Coffee houses with music, readings and cool conversations were a contrast to the 'rat race', which was how many of us regarded the mainstream way of the world. We were not interested in the automobiles, the next TV programmes or the next war. We craved an alternative way of life, something with more sanity and a lasting harmony. It was a time full of wonder to me and each day became more interesting than the last. More and more people with similar attitudes were showing up. The world looked to have a good chance to change for the good. And it was during this period that Buddhism first entered my life, not only as philosophy but also as a practice. Today there is so much literature available on the subject, but those days it was a new frontier.

I travelled to Mexico. The country was a treasure trove: a new culture to delight my senses, unspoilt natural landscapes, endless beaches, strange foods and spices, diverse peoples with different points of view. I became a tireless traveller, walking as well as hitchhiking, riding rickety buses and visiting remote mountains and strolling on deserted beaches. On the way I met Indians living as they had for centuries and, being completely free, I could take my time and learn what I could. I made several six-month journeys to Mexico until the end of 1965 and each time felt very blessed to have been there.

When I returned to California I met someone who influenced my decision to go to India. He had been in New Delhi in the late 1940s as a Marine Corps Guard at the US Embassy. His story was the stuff of fantasy. Tom was a yogi, a seer and a mystic with a small following and he lived in Venice, California. He had been initiated into the mystic arts of Yoga high in the Himalayas by a band of itinerant yogis while he was AWOL from the Marines. He attained, through the practice of exercise and meditation, a high degree of control of his body and mind as well as a quantum view of the Universe. One of several pieces of advice that he gave me was that I should arrive in India without any money so that I could really experience the place. I understood what he meant and made that one of the goals of my journey. I was twenty years old then.

Back in San Francisco I moved into a shared 'Victorian' house with my friend Frank Melton. Frank attracted all the forerunners of what was to become the hippy movement. The place was always full of artists, musicians, dreamers and wanderers. My last night in SF was spent with Neil Cassidy who was renown for his marathon dialogues. There was never a dull moment. I had more money than I needed for my passage to India. How was I to get rid of it? I had the idea of a pilgrimage so I invited six of my friends to join me as far as Bombay.

April Fools Day 1966, the next port of call was New York City. One of my last days before leaving the US was spent viewing a Tibetan thang-ka, an ancient scroll painting used to illustrate the Buddhist canon, at Allen Ginsberg's flat on the Lower East Village. His thang-ka (the first I remember seeing) was made with vivid bright colours and extremely fine attention to detail. It contained many fierce creatures performing magical feats which related, as I learned later, to *The Tibetan Book of the Dead*, a text that explains the stages between life and death in Tibetan culture.

Before I knew it I was in Istanbul at the doorway to Asia. Iran, Afghanistan and Pakistan turned out to be wild places, to say the least. In Pakistan I learned how to deal with the process of immigration the hard way. My fellow pilgrims and I had entered the country without visas since we had been told by the embassy that we did not need them. Iran and Pakistan were separated by a desert, a no-man's-land. After walking many kilometres we arrived in a place called Nakundi, where we were promptly arrested. We were treated very kindly, however, and our week-long arrest was spent wandering around the town, waiting for the magistrate to arrive to try our case: we were in the far south of the country.

Nakundi town consisted mainly of a few tea shops serving a limited range of cuisine, some nomadic looking folks, some mangy dogs, a government hash dealer, a train stop, a cluster of mud brick dwellings, a cinder block court house and several goats. Eventually we were tried and found guilty, fined 10 rupees each and ordered to report to Karachi to obtain our visas. I asked the magistrate to be more lenient with us and he dropped the fine to 5 rupees each. As we were awaiting judgment in the scorching heat I recall watching one of the goats eat a nine yard sand-encrusted dhoti (a local cotton garment) off the street in one continuous go.

On the way to Karachi we treated ourselves to accommodation in a modest hotel at a place called Queta. Soon after arriving we set about exploring the area and looked for some *chai*, one of the most delicious drinks I have ever tasted. We were directed to a place which was indicated by a small black sign bearing the words, 'Out of Bounds Area'. The notice also advised that we would enter at our own risk and that no law enforcement existed beyond this point. We stepped into a tea house and were shown to the back room. In one corner was a man with green tinged skin sitting cross-legged on the floor kneading patties from a large pile of green powder. The dust was cannabis pollen and patties were made by mixing the pollen with cannabis resin. About a dozen men – some in turbans or native attire, others in uniforms or casual western style clothes – were sitting around a large stand-up hookah in the middle of the room. Three of them I remember well, the Chief of Police, a general in the army and the governor of the provence. Each of them was taking turn at the hookah, which had an enormous clay bowl filled with pounds of hashish patties topped off with blazing hot coals. These men were inhaling so deeply that huge flames were sent shooting from the top of the bowl several feet into the air. The room was full of smoke. I tried to imagine their American counterparts in the same situation, relaxing over a good pipe after a long day. Paradoxically, alcohol was illegal here yet opium and cannabis were readily available in government shops. I was later to find that the same situation existed in India, where smoking cannabis was an accepted ritual of the Hindu religion. Nowadays alcohol, Prozac and other mood suppressing pharmaceuticals are the drugs that western society finds acceptable. I guess that TV also falls in to this category too.

After spending a week in Karachi to obtain our visas we were finally on our way to Bombay. This was where I would separate from my fellow pilgrims. I clearly remember disembarking and approaching the friendly immigration officer at the port. He was a tall, dark, portly man of about thirty years who asked for my papers, the purpose of my visit and my financial status. He was not at all fazed by my reply that I was a pilgrim and had just 50 Indian paisa. He folded his hands in the *namaste* position and welcomed me to India saying, “Mother India welcomes all”.

My lasting impression of India was defined within the next hour. It was a land of wonders. I would say the mirror opposite of America. Everyone was so friendly and most people spoke English. I saw two policemen walking hand in hand in pleasant conversation followed by politicians daintily holding the ends of their gossamer dhotis aloft with two fingers and looking very important, their heads crowned by what I thought of as Coca-Cola hats without the logo. I met so many friendly people everywhere, of all castes and occupations. I was dazzled by the color and culture. Everyone delighted in conversing about spiritual matters, the interconnectedness of all religions and gods. There were families with all the generations intact together, again something that was vanishing from my culture. Suddenly, my own society and upbringing began to look dull and primitive. It was a good time to examine my values; many of the things that I had been taught seemed now to be untrue. I felt as if I'd finally come home. My pilgrimage was to have lasted about six months but, in the event, I just whipped out my straw and sucked up the new experiences over the next nine years.

I headed north to the Himalayas. Initially I spent time in Rishikesh, the famous pilgrim spot, in the Summer of 1966, staying in the Shri Shivananda Ashram, learning some yoga asanas and taking early morning dips in the icy waters of the holy Ganges River. There I made many friends, one of whom was a dreadlocked sadhu with leprosy and another a recognised Hindu saint. The sadhu, who was missing several body parts, lived on a bridge over the Ganges. He observed his religious practices, was very intelligent and kind and behaved very generously towards me. He lived near other holy men and, although he possessed nothing, he seemed to have something more than the majority of the people I had met anywhere before. He made me realize that suffering was an attitude. We laughed together about the absurdity of the universe, or at least of our attachment to it. The saint, with whom I spent about a month, was from Gita Bahwan in Gorakhpur and from what I understood was the Baba of the Congress Party in India; I only knew him as ‘Baba’. When I first met him tears streamed out of my eyes, and this was not from sorrow. I knew immediately that I was in the presence of someone special. This was confirmation to me that life was about much more than was presented to me in the classroom.

Baba was also on a pilgrimage with a retinue of attendants and dressed in the robes of a Hindu ascetic. He was a rather gaunt and unassuming figure and looked about seventy years old. His face was like many that you see on the streets of India but, unlike them, he radiated love and compassion from every pore of his body. I was finally faced with a living example of a human who had transformed himself to achieve an exalted state of mind. I felt extremely blessed. If I had taken money with me when I visited India I would have missed out on so many lessons that were only there to be learned without the safety net of financial security. Baba told me he would leave his body soon, it was in pain and ready to be retired. The departure date he gave me was April the following year. Every evening, wherever he was, he would take a slow stroll in a circular path. For thirty years Baba, if he ate at all, ate only one chapati a day. I had fasted, but not like that. This was the invisible world made solid. My journey to India gave me the strength to realise that my life choices were valid and that the goals of the society of my birth were very different from my own.

I met so many people during this period, including Ravi Shankar with whom I toured to Benares as he was being filmed for a USA TV documentary. And Baba Ram Dass came to my hotel room one night when I was in Delhi with his slate board, writing that after an entire year's vow of silence he was ready to speak. We spent the night in animated conversation. There was a a good sized group of western students at the Sanskrit University in Benares with whom I spent many long hours, and still meet today in various places around the world. I became good friends with lots of Neem Koreli Baba's disciples. Life was one big spiritual adventure, and I meant to keep it that way.

After many adventures in India I hitchhiked to Nepal. At this time Nepal was the most wonderful place I had ever seen. It is hard to believe how much it has changed now, from pristine beauty to a polluted nightmare. We no longer take care of our planet.

My first sight of the Kathmandu Valley will remain etched on my mind forever. The temple complex in Durbar Square was silhouetted against the Himalayas just before sunset. In those days there were no roads other than the one leading from India to the Nepalese Royal Palace and the New Road which ends at the temple complex. If you walked ten feet from that main road you would step back hundreds of years in time. There was beautiful traditional architecture and stunning green rice fields that made for a peaceful mind. The colorful peoples of various ethnic groups were living in harmony together while still observing their ancient traditions. There was a feeling of enchantment in this place that has stayed with me all my life.

My landlord, a Newari who had spent most of his life in Lhasa in Tibet as a wool merchant, took me to his shrine room and showed me a thang-ka scroll painting of the Glorious Copper Mountain, the paradise of Guru Rinpoche, the 8th century Indian tantric master and founder of Tibetan Buddhism. This painting consisted of a many tiered pagoda with intricate gilt roofs. Flying fairies filled the sky alongside goddesses offering auspicious essences to the assembled multitudes. The palace was surrounded by what I later learned were Guru Rinpoche's eight manifestations, each of which created special blessings venerated to this day. Fierce protectors guarded the entrance way keeping the mandala pure, and the background landscape included some heavy beings sitting in castles made of skulls and human bones surrounded by foliage. The brilliant stone colors and the incredibly detailed fine line work were simply stunning. Strangely, I could not stop thinking about this image; if I closed my eyes I could see it in full detail. Even today, that thang-ka image is still crystal clear in my mind.

The next morning I visited a Tibetan friend, Gyaltsen, who together with Tobgyal owned a restaurant called The Blue Tibetan. This was the meeting place for all the travellers visiting Kathmandu in the 1960s. Mentioning this image of the Buddhist scroll I speculated that maybe I should be learning to paint thang-kas. He asked whether I was serious and I replied that I was. I was duly introduced to his friend, the State Artist of Tibet, Kapa Jampa Sedan, who had just arrived as a refugee with his family. He had a very distinctive face with high cheek bones and two long braids. On the occasion of our first meeting he was sitting on the floor of a mud house mincing meat with a cleaver for what I now know to be the traditional dish known as *momo*. His wife, who was wearing a Tibetan dress with the rainbow apron called a *chuba*, poured delicious butter tea while their young children played. It felt as if I had become part of a documentary.

This was how I started my apprenticeship in traditional thang-ka painting. I began that very day, drawing the Buddha's head. Initially language was a problem between us but my teacher was very patient although having a westerner as a student must have been strange for him. I was mindful that he himself was also living in an alien world now, out of his homeland. I also remember seeing a painting which he had made in Lhasa of the thousand-armed deity, Avalokitesvara, who is the bodhisattva of compassion and the main protector of Tibet. This painting had been completed in Tibet for His Holiness the Dalai Lama: it was so perfect and beautiful. Counting each of the thousand arms it was hard to believe that anyone could have possibly accomplished such a thing by hand.

My study continued until 1975 with various master painters in the Nyingmapa, Kargyudpa and Gelugpa schools of Tibetan Buddhism. During this period I married and had two lovely children, my daughter Tenle Pema Chodon and my son Tashe Dorje. The Tibetan reincarnated Lamas, His Holiness the 16th Gyalwa Karmapa, the Venerable Lamas Sabchu Rinpoche, Daptsang Rinpoche, Urgyan Tulku, Dilgo Khyentse Rinpoche and Tsulshig Rinpoche became my points of reference in the universe. I began to learn that our own nature is the most difficult for us to see, others close to us have an easier view. Those times of doing things we don't like can give us a glimpse of our true self. I had found my life work and had met many acknowledged spiritual masters in my first year away from America. Daily I knew how blessed I was, by being in Nepal and painting thang-kas there.

During my training period I learned the sacred geometry and how to mix the preparation of mineral and botanical pigments. I also translated the text of three ancient Tibetan sacred painting manuals into English as well as some other commentaries on Tibetan art. In 1969, with my then teacher, Pargyaltsan the Sherpa artist, I painted the Buddhist Temple at Tharkyegang, Helambu in the Himalayas of northern Nepal. This Temple was inaugurated by King Mahendra of Nepal in 1970.

In 1974 after a period of time in Kyoto, Japan where I was studying ancient painting techniques, I went back to Bakersfield to introduce my new family to my older family, especially my beloved grandmother Hazel. After a great reunion we then returned north to San Francisco. Through my friend Glen Eddy, another American thang-ka painter, I learned that I had been invited to teach at America's first Buddhist university, the new Naropa Institute in Boulder, Colorado (by the Venerable Chogyam Trungpa Rinpoche). Consequently I became a teacher, putting my student days firmly behind me (though of course learning never stops). I met many old and new friends and had many meaningful sessions with Rinpoche, but my connection with the West did not feel strong any longer and so we returned to Nepal. Sadly the place seemed changed almost beyond recognition since 1966 when we first got there, so where to go instead? In the end we found ourselves trading locations and contacts with a friend – ours in Nepal for his on Maui, Hawaii. Our arrival in Maui coincided with the arrival of the Venerable Nechung Rinpoche from

India. At the time, being the only other person to speak some Tibetan in Hawaii, I had the good fortune to spend a great deal of quality time with him. He was an extraordinary Lama.

Hawaii was, and is, a beautiful place full of wonderful people with similar interests and lifestyles. At this time many masters of various traditions passed through Hawaii on their way to the USA from the East as teachers to the new school of interest in Asian culture. During this period many counter cultural refugees from the 1960s found their way to this magical tropical paradise. There was a desire to escape from the mainland cities to live a more laid-back lifestyle. During the time I had lived in Asia the hippie movement had come and gone but the Eastern spiritual interest in the West was a lasting legacy of those times. In my new home I made my first contact with the Western Dharma Centers through the Venerable Kalu Rinpoche's Temple, Karma Remay O'd Sal Ling, located in the jungle, and at the home of the artists Carmen and Mathew Westcott. Carmen told me years later that she had prayed for a thang-ka painter to come to Maui so that she could learn the tradition too. Every day was wonderfully full between taking teachings from the Lamas, doing my artwork and experiencing the natural beauty of Maui. For eight of the fourteen years that I lived on the islands I taught Tibetan thang-ka painting, first at the temple in Honolulu, Kargyu Thek Chen Ling, and then at the temple on the Big Island, Nechung Dorje Drayang Ling.

In 1976 His Holiness the 16th Gyalwa Karmapa spent fourteen days at the jungle Dharma Centre with eleven of his Lamas. There he gave the famous Black Crown Ceremony, dedicated the first Tibetan stupa in North America (if Hawaii counts) at a place called Huelo, where I still live. It was here that he introduced me, as His Holiness was a great lover of birds, to the idea of flower and bird painting. Many great Lamas have visited Hawaii, but His Holiness the Karmapa is my root Lama and this has a special meaning for me. When I had first met His Holiness in Nepal in 1969 I had given him my first completed painting of the Mahasiddha Naropa, a founder of his Kargyudpa lineage. One of my regrets is that when he invited me to accompany him back to his monastery of Rumtek in Sikkim, I declined. Not realising how precious an offer it was, I felt I would rather remain in Nepal at the time.

In 1985, the year my daughter Chodon graduated from high school, the family visited Holland, Denmark, Sweden, Finland, Russia, China, Nepal, Tibet, India, Thailand, Malaysia and Indonesia before returning home to Hawaii. Having previously lived so many years in Asia I missed being in that rhythm of life. What a fantastic reintroduction that trip was. In Europe, having heard that Tibet was open to foreigners again after the 1959 Chinese invasion, we bought tickets in Copenhagen to Beijing on the Trans-Siberian Railroad and from Chengdu to Lhasa by Southwest China Air. We were elated by the prospect of finally going to Tibet.

My first impressions of Tibet were of the smells, the wind, the air, the light and the sight of so much destruction. We made the ride from the airport to Lhasa in an ancient Chinese bus and the road, if you can call it that, was extremely bumpy. Our ears were ringing from the high altitude. We saw the Potala and the Jo Khang and on the streets there were elderly people just released after 20 years of imprisonment as well as their families, lots of children, pilgrims, beggars, yaks, donkeys and stray dogs. Being able to speak Tibetan was a bonus and I spent two months there. I found it particularly moving to meet the Panchen Rinpoche. Our first meeting was in the Jo Khang, Lhasa's main temple built in the 8th century. We met again at the Dorje Jigs Che initiation and Lama dances in Shigatse, Southern Tibet. This was the first initiation since the Chinese occupation. I didn't want to leave.

The return to Hawaii was so peaceful and quiet after our world tour. Unfortunately, our idyllic existence did not last and I found myself in the throes of a painful divorce. I managed during this time to do some nice painting though; to explore beauty through pain is a healing experience. After the dust settled, two friends and I decided to take a holiday in Thailand with a stopover in Japan where we attended the funeral of the Emperor Hirohito. Mike left after a few months while Mat and I retired to Kho Samet and I set up a simple atelier there at Naga, a small resort on the Gulf of Thailand. Little did I know that another decade would pass before I would live in Hawaii again.

During this perfect year, on another April Fools Day, I met and fell in love with Leslie Nguyen, a Buddhist art therapist from a Franco-Vietnamese family, a woman of beauty and vision. She was on R&R from Hong Kong where she was working organizing social services in the Vietnamese refugee camps. Leslie asked me to teach her traditional thangka painting. Together we set up our art studio on Pra Nang Bay, South Thailand's most beautiful scenic spot, with its wonderful karst formations surrounded by an emerald Andaman Sea.

We worked hard from our bungalow. Sunrise and sunset were our only times of leisure. Leslie spent the first year drawing the Vajrayana sacred geometry and practised fine-line brush work before she began to paint on cotton with stone colour. Apart from an exciting few months on an artistic field trip to Ammo in Eastern Tibet and the Dunghuang Magao Caves in North Western China we continued to draw and paint in the Pra Nang area. This was a very productive time for me, teaching and painting a series of Thai birds and flora on Japanese silk. At one point we learned the art of scroll mounting on a visa run to Malaysia. Several years passed and I felt it was time to become colleagues rather than teacher and student. To celebrate this hard-won achievement, we decided to initiate a joint art project that would end Leslie's apprenticeship on the highest possible note. This project became a thank-you to the people of Thailand in appreciation of our stay in that lovely, peaceful country.

We began to create a life-size Theravada Buddha in silk, with mineral and botanical pigments in the Tibetan tradition, to be presented to His Majesty the King of Thailand. This work took four months to complete. Two months into our painting we awoke in the middle of the night feeling very ill. It was not until the next morning that we heard of the pro-democracy massacre in Bangkok on the BBC World Service. This strange illness, which vanished when morning came, made us realise how deeply connected with the country we were through our painting. When we had completed our gift, we gave it to His Highness's secretary and left Bangkok for China and Tibet.

Chengdu, which we knew well from previous trips, was to be the doorway to a new life. Tibet had recently opened its borders again to foreign visitors following its 1987 closure. We signed on for the one-way trip with about a dozen other foreign travellers. During the days preceding our departure, we were offered the job of making a giant thang-ka for Tsurphu monastery, the original seat of all the Gyalwa Karmapas in Tibet where, only recently, the 17th incarnation had been found and was soon to be enthroned. We heard this news from an old friend who was raising funds for Tsurphu's restoration.

Lhasa had not changed much in the past seven years. The huge matted dogs were still there, sleeping in overflowing dumpsters. It was the Fall, smells were muted, Summer all but gone and there were giant clouds of sacred incense everywhere. As usual, people were showing their ardent devotion in the many holy places. Energetic pilgrims were arriving from all over Tibet.

The coronation of the new incarnation of my root Lama at Tsurphu and the exciting possibilities of working for the Temple enhanced our happiness at being in Tibet. We had our first viewing of the thang-ka wall that was cut into the mountain where the first giant thang-ka was displayed for hundreds of years. It is the only original structure to survive intact after the Cultural Revolution. Thousands had arrived for this ceremony. Seating in the inner sanctum was very limited and thousands of devotees were rushing for the entrance. If you have never been to a Tibetan dharma ceremony it is hard to imagine the energy – it's something like a fire in a movie house with people joyously running for the exits.

At one point we found ourselves pushed up against the Temple's massive front doors. The crowd was making waves like a turbulent sea at our backs when a tourist from our group collapsed at my feet. I pulled her up and pounded on the doors shouting in Tibetan, "Open the door, someone is sick!" Miraculously we were pulled inside the Temple and into complete tranquility, as if we had plunged into a still lake. The ceremony was just starting and we seated ourselves about eight feet to the left of the six-year-old Karmapa and, ironically, at the very feet of the Abbot, Drupon Dechen Rinpoche with whom we were to work closely over the next few years. At the conclusion of the ceremony we received hands-on blessings from the 17th Karmapa, Urgyen Trinley Dorje.

Drupon Dechen Rinpoche had been told in India by his teacher, the 16th incarnation of Karmapa, shortly before he passed away in 1981, that he should go to Tsurphu and restore the monastery. Our first meeting with the Abbot established that we were the artists predestined to assist His Holiness in this task, so we became the first ever foreigners allowed to work in Tibet on a religious project.

The restoration of the monastery required a silk brocade appliqué thang-ka measuring 108 feet by 75 feet. This was to replace the destroyed piece and consisted of nine figures. As there was no photographic record of the previous image, we had to redesign the thang-ka using the Karma Kadri principles. The central figure of the Buddha with his throne was to be 60 feet tall. These images had to be very accurate: the better the sacred geometry, the better the image's ability to bless the viewer, which is the main object of the elaborate displaying ceremony.

First we proposed to make a replica of the thang-ka to find a patron to fund the main project. As it turned out a devout German woman, Katya Oberwellander, came forward. Since then she has generously donated the replica to the Pullahari temple in Nepal, the Temple of the five year old Jargon Khamtrul the 4th, who was recognised by the then ten year old Karmapa at Tsurphu.

We bought the silk in Hong Kong with the help of the Karmapa Center there, had it dyed the appropriate colours and took more than 1,000 metres back to Lhasa. Later we made a second trip to Souchou, China, to the factories that manufactured what we needed. Virtually nothing was available in the local market. We then located a factory in Lhasa to do the all important sewing, a monumental undertaking. Obtaining work visas was not simple, but by the end of our work in Tibet we had been given six annual residency visas. We purchased 1,000 metres of paper, which we needed for all the drawing that would be used for the sewing patterns. We took a room at the Snowlands Guesthouse, near the Jo Khang, for the cold night's rest before another day's work began. Our usual Thai attire changed from shorts, T-shirts and flip-flops to long underwear, layers of down, fleece and boots.

In two years, Leslie and I completed 700 square metres of drawings, supervised all the sewing work, collected, prepared and physically carried all the materials needed back to Lhasa. Six months into the work we were told we needed to make the many ceremonial objects for the showing, so fund-raising continued.

The White Conch Factory, our work place in Tibet, was made up of a very special group of people. This was their first experience of working with foreigners as well as of using silk and creating such a huge important religious image. The administrators, Tashi Dopgyal, Tseden Lundru and Tenpa Rabgay, gave us much invaluable help. Six women – Nagchu La, Tsering Drolkar, Tsering Yangdzom, Dikyi Ongmo, Udru Drolma, and Yangdzom Drolkar – worked all day and the hours were filled with smiles, laughter, joking, gossiping, singing and listening to Sino-Tibetan music on the radio. Often, when work was finished, they would stay late and have a small tea party and sometimes drink *chang* – Tibetan rice or barley beer – to celebrate our team effort. Most workers in other countries I visited would have been more anxious to head back to their homes than to spend extra hours at their place of work.

Giant thang-kas are an ancient tradition in Tibet, dating back to the 14th century. Tsurphu's first, the one we helped to replace, was completed in 1590 during the life of the 10th Karmapa, who was a very accomplished painter. Part-way through the project we were given the Buddha's head from that ancient work and we placed this behind the present image's heart. We also had permission to update the new thang-ka with the 16th Karmapa in the lower left-hand corner of the Buddha's throne and, in the right-hand corner, to place the 3rd Jargon Khamtrul Rinpoche, a disciple of the 16th, both of whom were responsible for introducing Tibetan Buddhism to much of the world. These figures replaced the 9th Karmapa and one of his disciples.

The first showing at Tsurphu after a thirty-six year absence was nothing short of a miracle. Heavy snowfall throughout the week before the day of the pageant made us nervous since snow could destroy all our hard work. However, the Karmapas are renowned for their ability to control the weather and the morning of the event was crystal clear for the three hours of the first showing. Afterwards the Thang-ka in its huge yak-skin bag was returned to the temple's main shrine room for safe storage. The ceremony was immediately followed by a violent hailstorm.

Upon completion of the Thang-ka ceremony the Abbot and His Holiness congratulated us and asked us to make a second appliqué for the

Temple, the Thang-ka of the Protectors. We were told that the original Protector Thang-ka had been presented to the 15th Karmapa by the King of Mongolia. It had been burned rather than ripped-up like the original Buddha Thang-ka. When we agreed, Rinpoche informed us that this second work would not be easy like the first thang-ka, but would encounter many obstacles. An important task of the Dharma Protectors is to remove obstacles, so it followed that we would experience these as part of this magic work.

The first thing we did upon finishing the first work was to make the replica for the patron. This image was created by Leslie and I over a four month period using an Eastern Tibetan appliqué technique which combines silk brocades and painting. Our next major concern was to find funding for the new job. A Belgian couple working in Lhasa for MSF (the Belgian group, Doctors Without Borders), had lent us a video camera. We had used this to document our first work, the giant Buddha. Therefore we were able to produce a low-budget documentary, a 27 minute film on the making, displaying and hanging of the thang-ka, which we began in Nepal and completed in Hong Kong at the end of 1994. We successfully showed this film, mainly in Hong Kong, Taiwan and Malaysia. In each of those countries we met wonderful hospitable followers of His Holiness and presented copies of our video to each centre we visited. Three quarters of the funds for the Mahakala thang-ka were raised from these visits.

During this busy period Leslie became pregnant with our son and was advised by His Holiness and Drupon Rinpoche to give birth in the UK rather than Lhasa. The Karmapa named him Sonam Dorje. Sonam was born in London and we did not return to Tibet until he was six months old. Work progressed well for about six months until our son became ill. Eventually Leslie had to take him to Nepal for treatment, which was a very stressful time. For a period it looked difficult for them to return to Tibet, but they did and the work continued, but not without additional trauma. Tenpa Rabgay, our good friend and colleague, became very ill and died after the project was completed.

Despite these obstacles there were many good times. This image is also shown annually to purify the New Year. This religious festival with its lively, beautifully-costumed lama dances attracts many pilgrims and, at sunset, the thang-ka unfolds in a colourful ritual ceremony. We had now spent five years making two thang-kas for Tsurphu and it seemed time to take a break from Tibet and return to the cruel world and figure out how to make a living with our art. Before we left, His Holiness and Drupon Rinpoche requested us to make the next necessary appliqués for the Temple. Again we agreed, but said we would need to take a break first. When we did return to Tibet at the end of 1999 to set up this new project we learned that His Holiness the Karmapa had left for India. Our work there is now on hold.

In Hawaii we live in beautifully lush benevolent jungle surroundings, with a stream, but no electricity or phone. We are busy even without thinking of our work. After living in Asia for years, America has became our third world. Asia always provided us with basic utilities; our present environment requires us to carry drinking water and propane to survive. Our house is a tetrahedron built in the 1970s by the artist and architect, Steve Wilmoth. This provides us with a particularly large studio on the second floor which overlooks a garden full of tropical flowers. Asian songbirds serenade us with their lovely melodies and when the stream runs strong it reminds us of the Himalayas.

Thinking about the world now in comparison to 1950s America, it is as if we have entered a classic science fiction novel. We benefit from technological advancements but socially and environmentally we have lost more than I could ever have imagined back then. The hippy movement was America's last wake-up call and hardly anyone listened; we have continued to destroy our nest – no water, no animals, no trees, no ozone, no clean air, no fish, no end to our greed. All our empty space is being filled. Children are being subtly trained for future wars with video games. Calculators have replaced the mind for simple math. Cable TV holds nothing to watch except commercials for useless services and products that have been cynically conceived to eat-up hard earned wages. These programs seem to be followed by shows of mindless violence or comedy written around sexual innuendo. School children are starting to slaughter their classmates instead of being thankful for education. America, the international watchdog for other people's elections, recently ushered its new president under very shady circumstances indeed. We are told that the destruction of our precious environment is not the issue that counts. No, it's fossil fuel, the motor car and nuclear power that are the basic needs that require our protection. Greed has become a feather in our caps rather than the great shame that it is. I dislike complaining about our material advances – technology has lead us into a new way of life – but wouldn't it be smart to get our social and environmental situation into a more harmonious balance?

The building boom has begun in our neighbourhood now. There are more people here now than at any time since the fall of the Hawaiian Kingdom. It is interesting to see how 'spirituality' has gained in popularity in the West, and how 'materialism' has become the new spirituality in the East. If our possessions didn't make us slaves, think what a different world it would be. The 1960s movement is still very much with us. Change is slow, but it is constant. Of the basic building blocks of the universe, we are simply the same as everything else around us. We must work on our own nature, and remember to help others around us. We have two basic choices: to be happy or miserable. Of the two, misery comes without doing anything at all, happiness requires effort. I'm told that molecules form habits – well then we must make more positive molecules so that our children are left with a better world than the one that we have inherited. We are riding on this dirt ball hurtling through infinite space at unbelievable speed dodging debris in some backwater of the universe and yet thinking we are so important. In all this chaos we still find it necessary to take more than we need and inflict pain and suffering on our fellow beings. Isn't that a lot of bullshit? After all, how many bowls of rice can you eat and still not be sick?

Opposite:
Giant Tsurphu appliqué thang-kha ceremony, Tibet

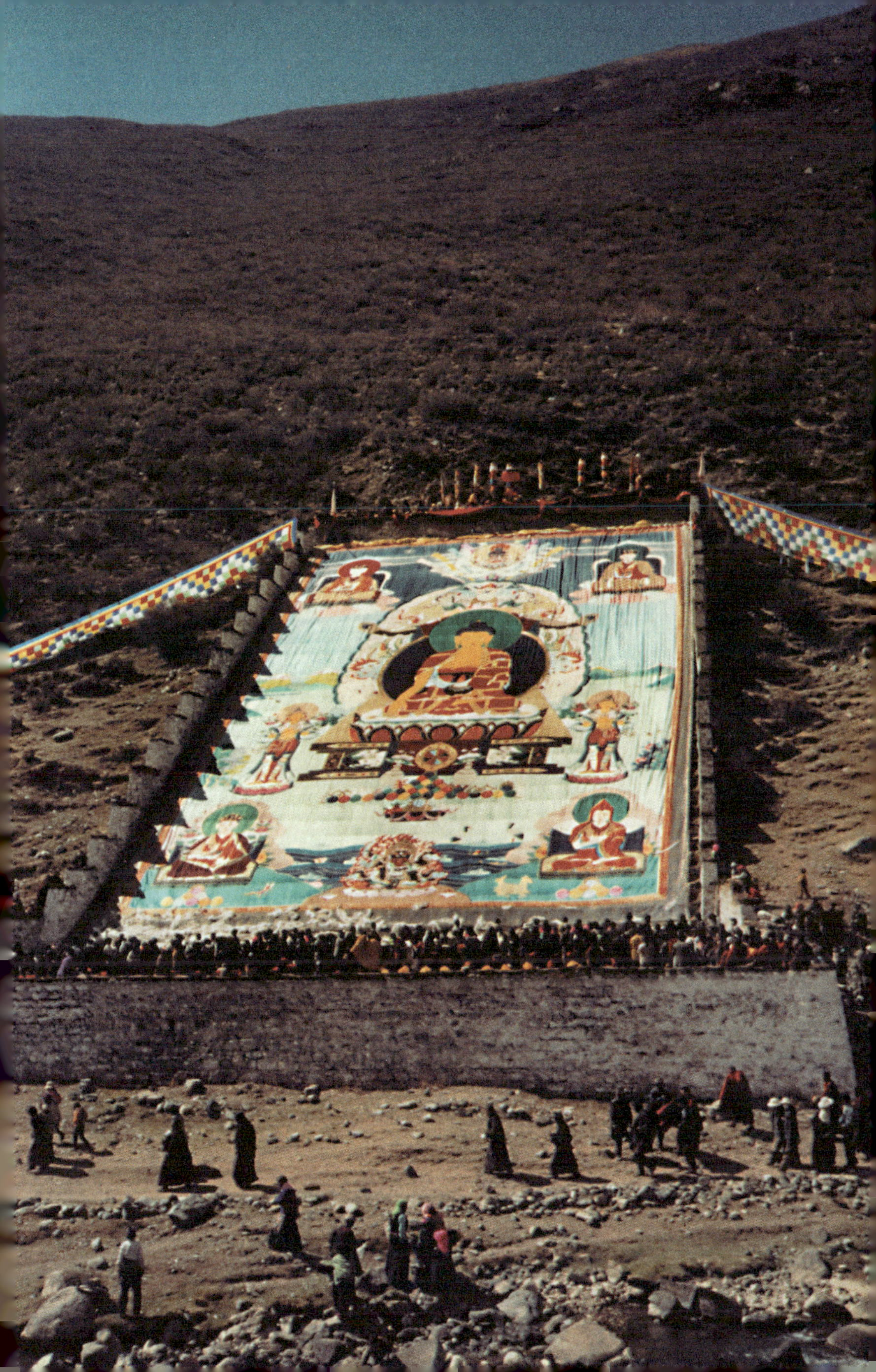

Safe Way

David Blamey

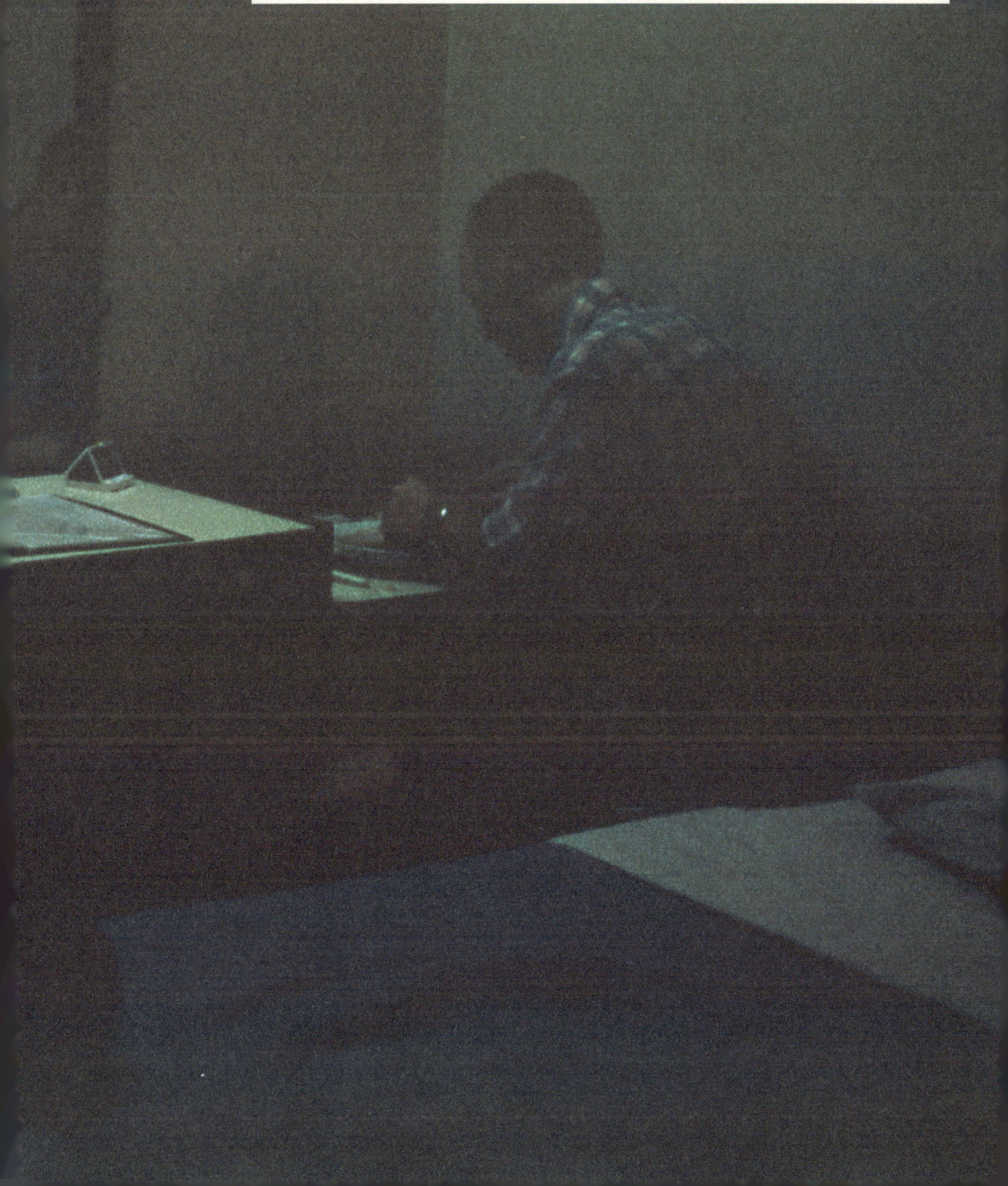

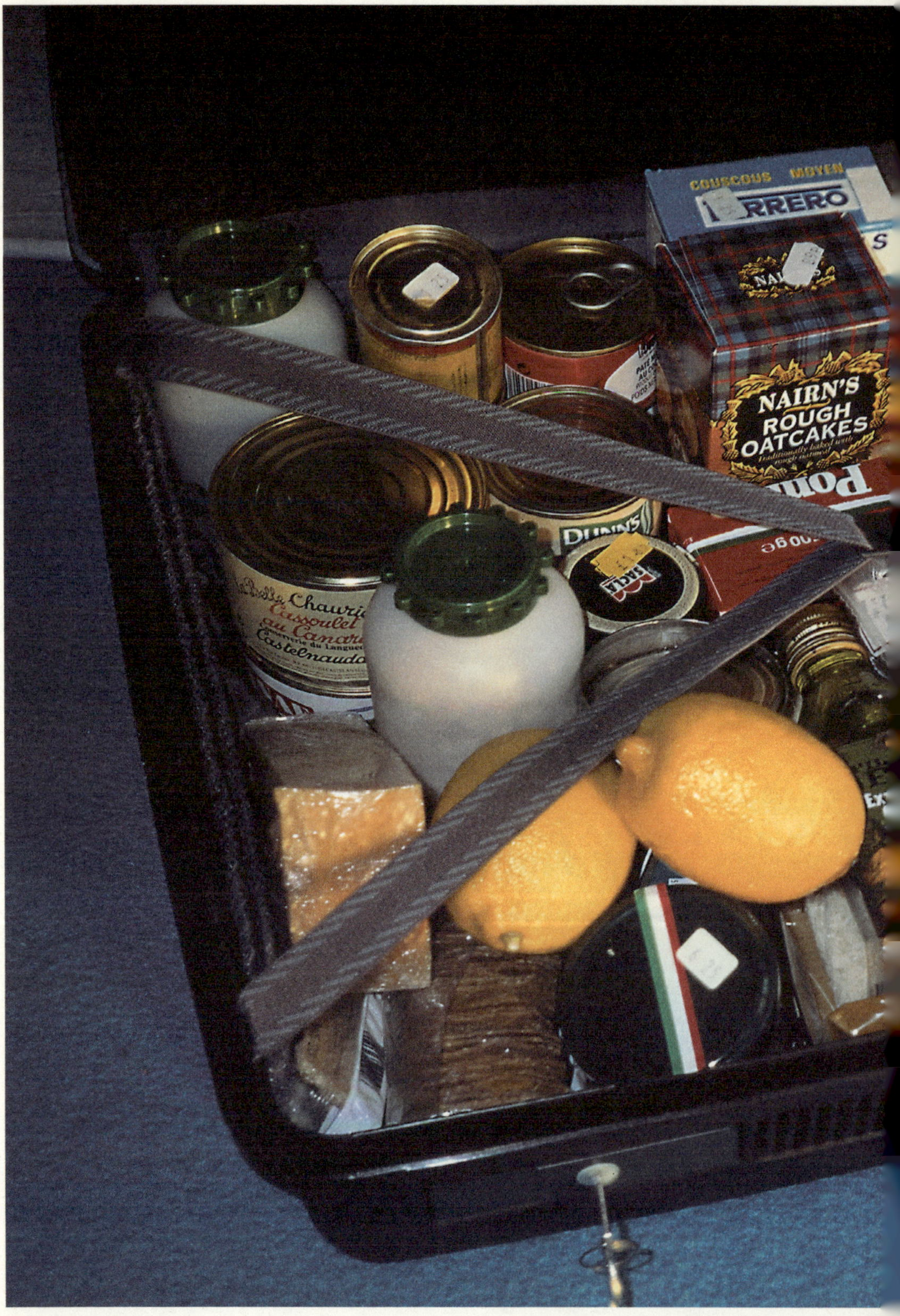
COUSCOUS MOYEN
NAIRN'S
ROUGH
OATCAKES

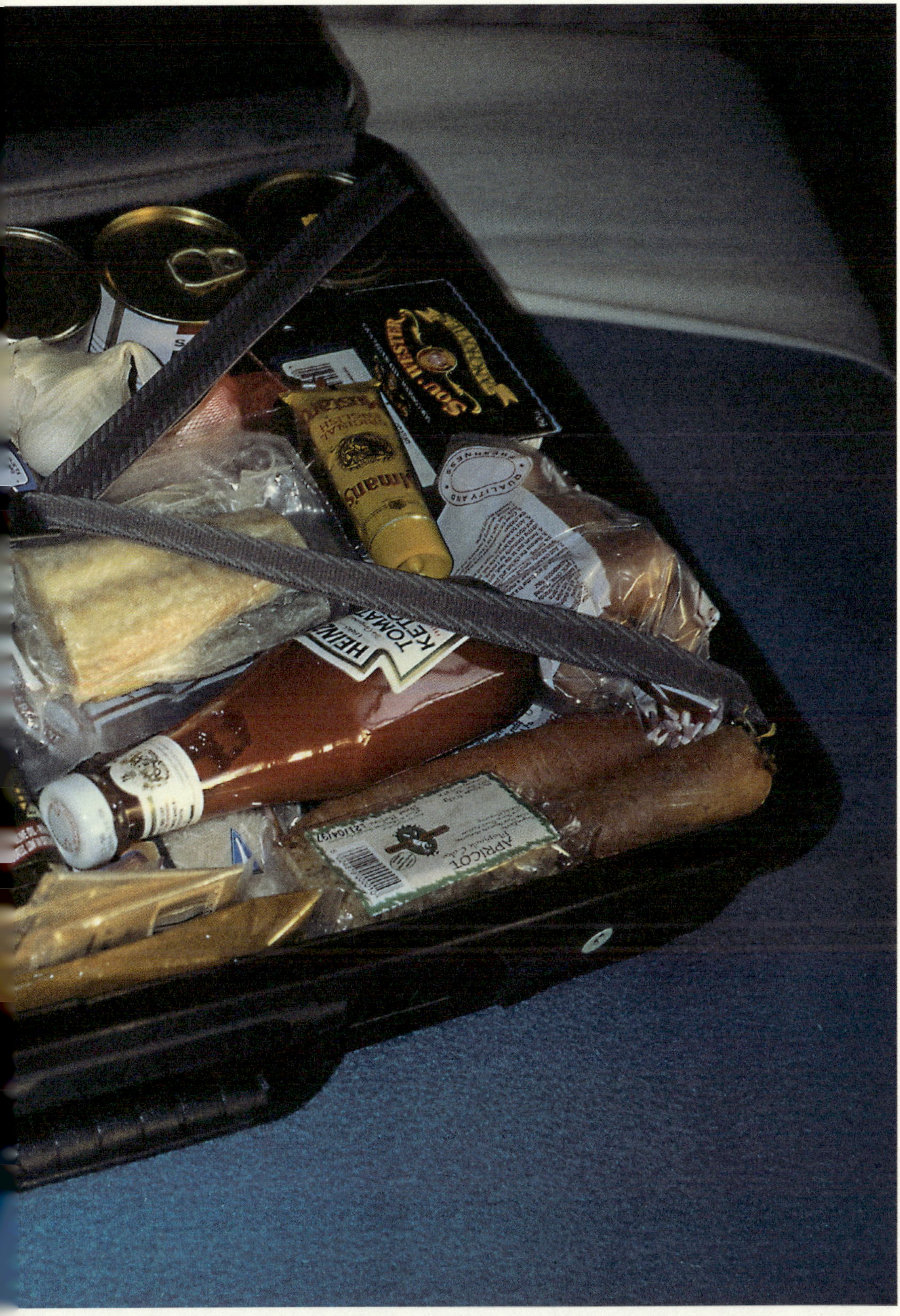

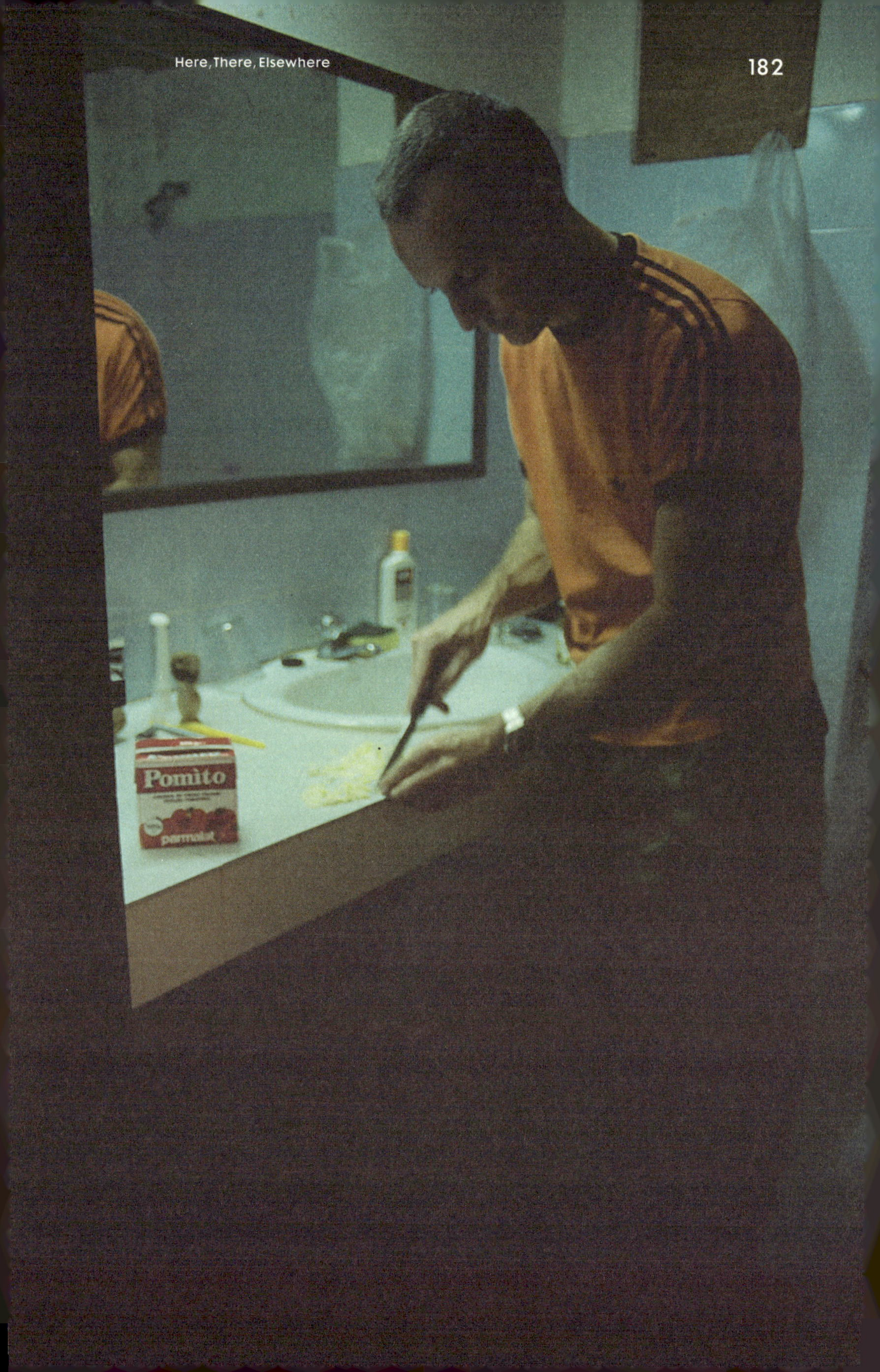
Pomito
parmalat

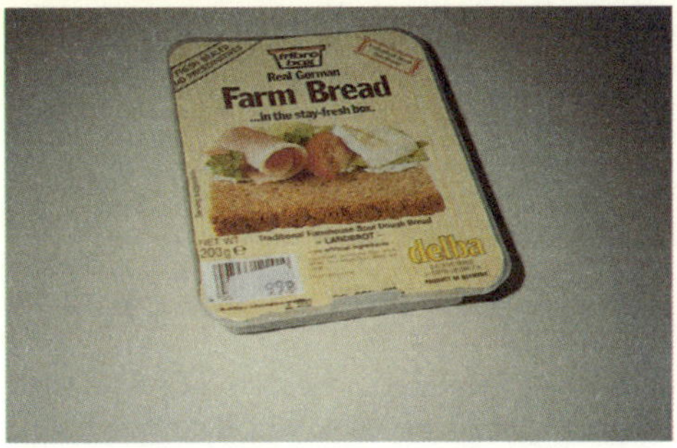
Real German
Farm Bread
...in the stay-fresh box.
delba

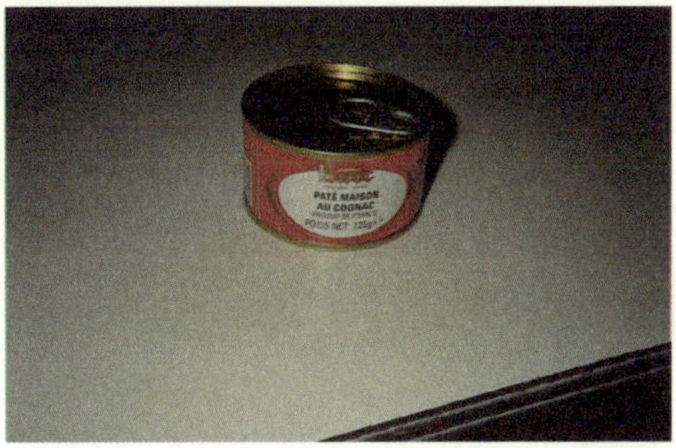
PATÉ MAISON
AU COGNAC

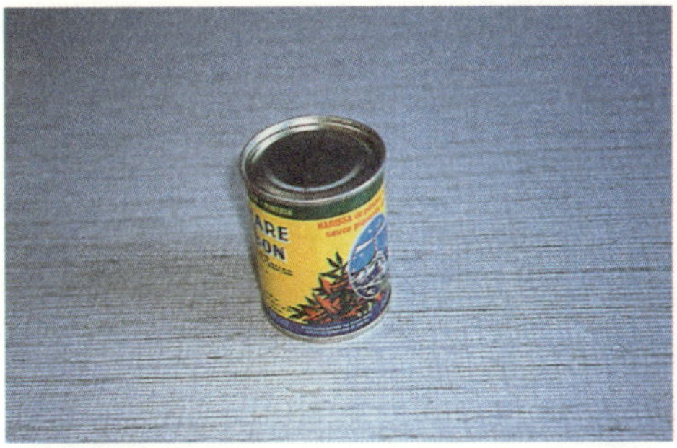

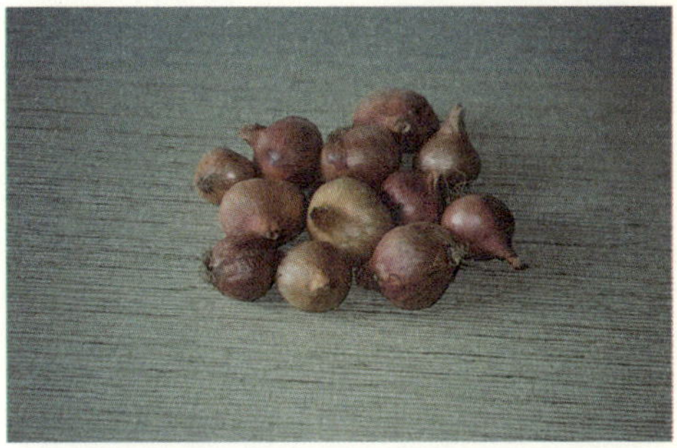

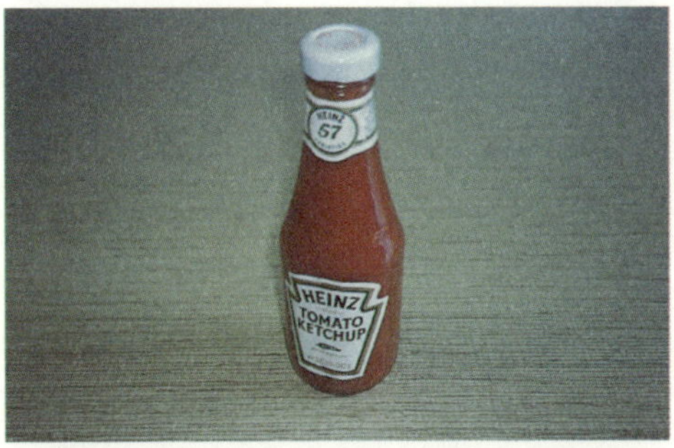
HEINZ
57
HEINZ
TOMATO
KETCHUP

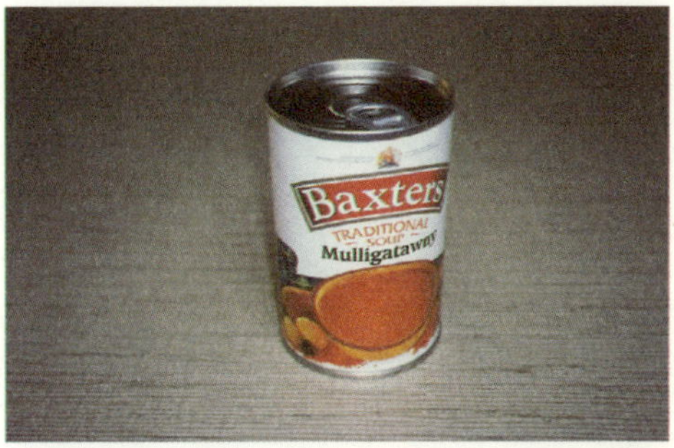
Baxters
TRADITIONAL
SOUP
Mulligatawny

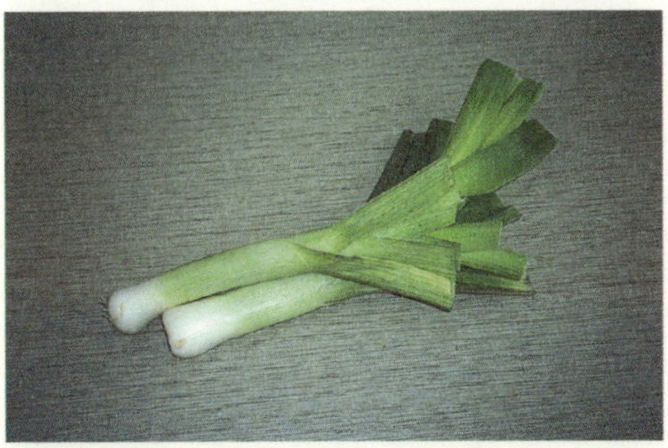

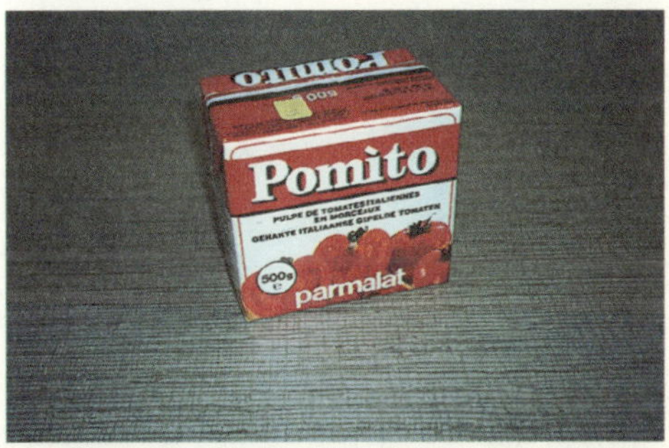
Pomito
500g
parmalat

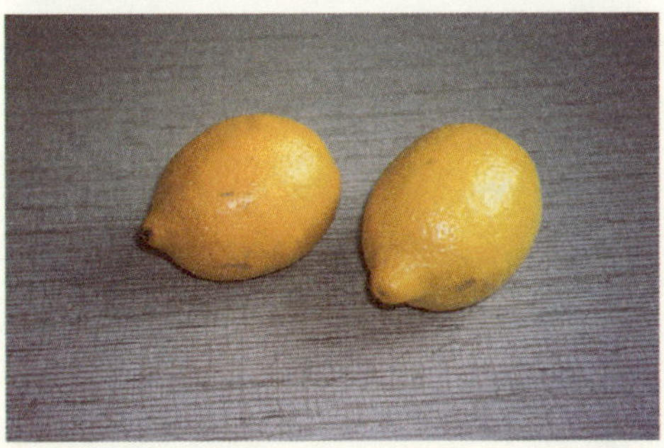

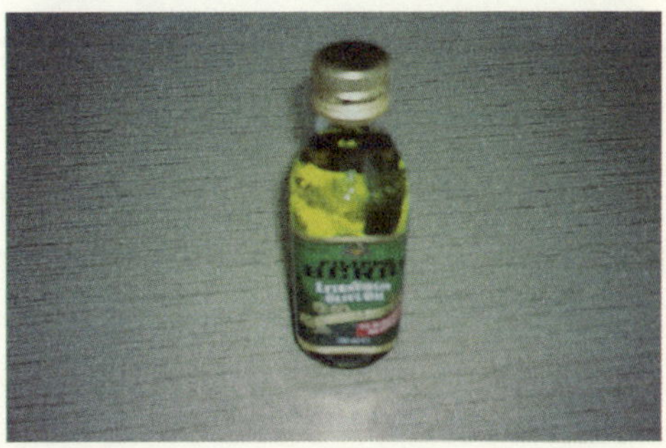

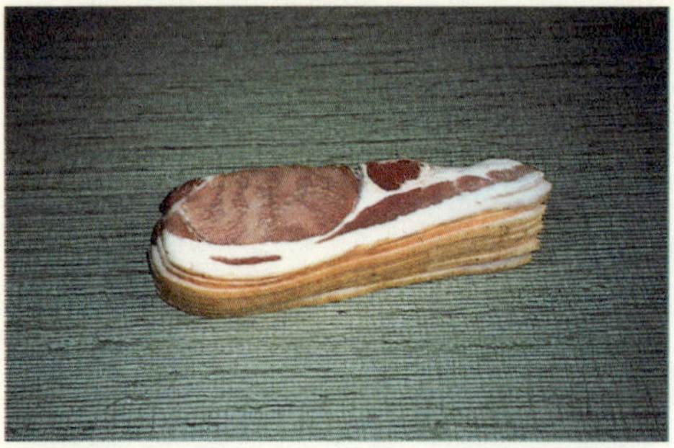

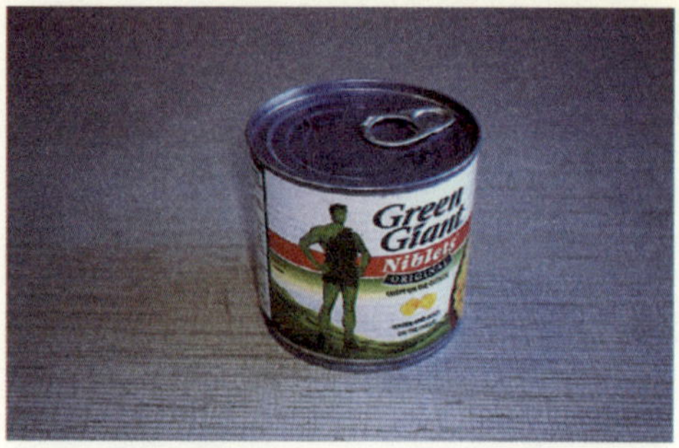
Green Giant
Niblets

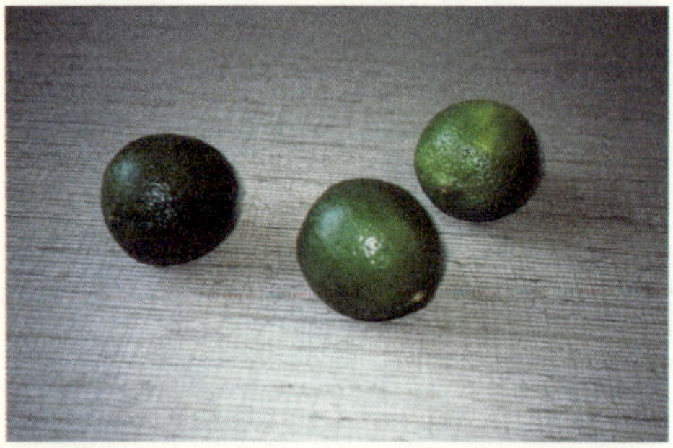

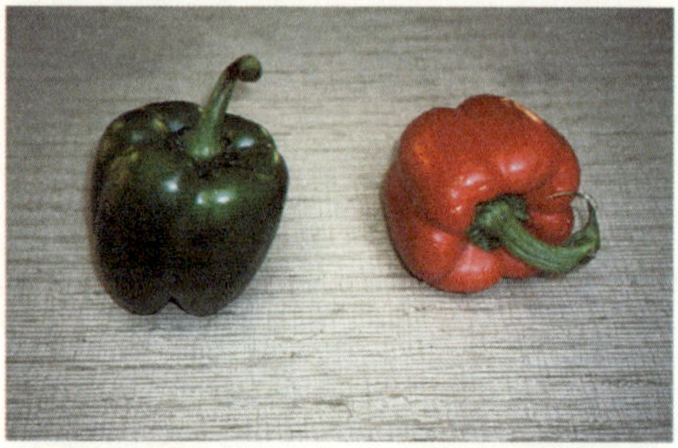

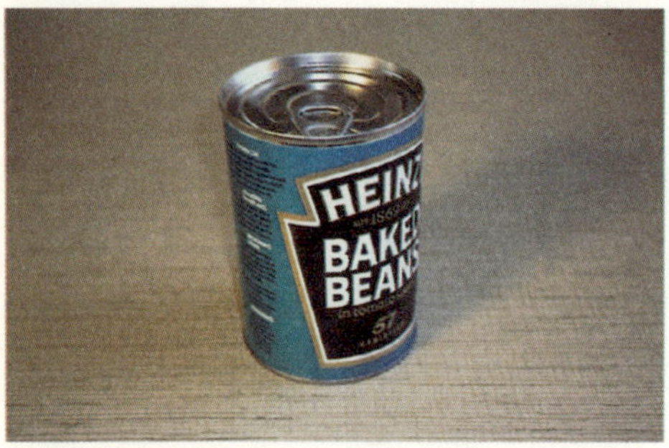
HEINZ
BAKED BEANS

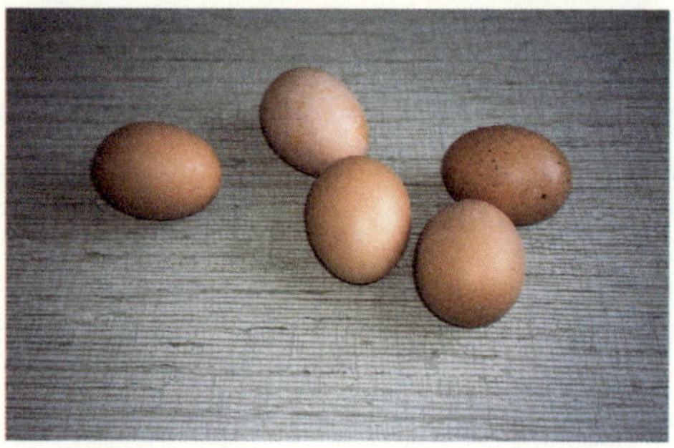

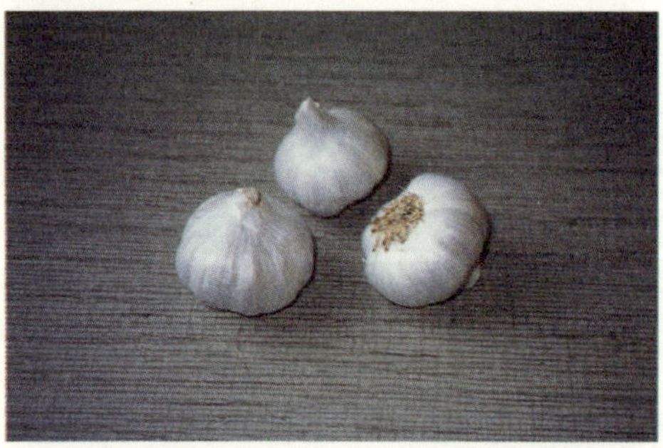

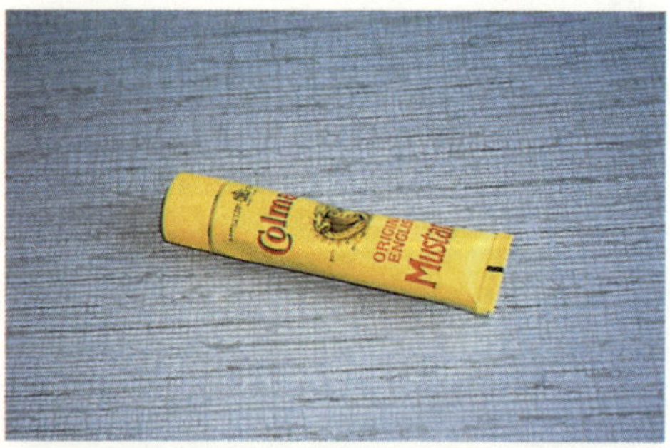

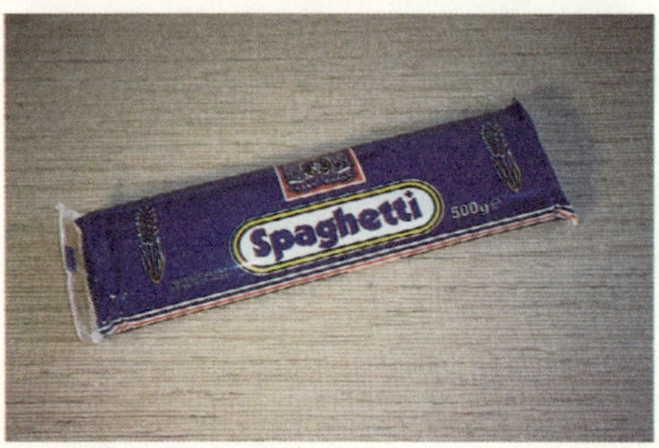
Spaghetti
500g

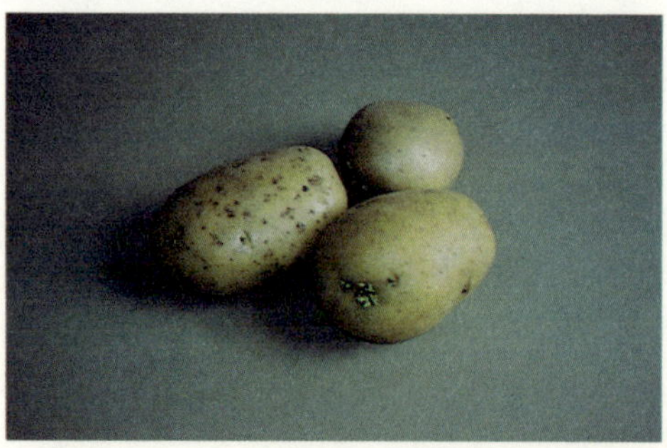

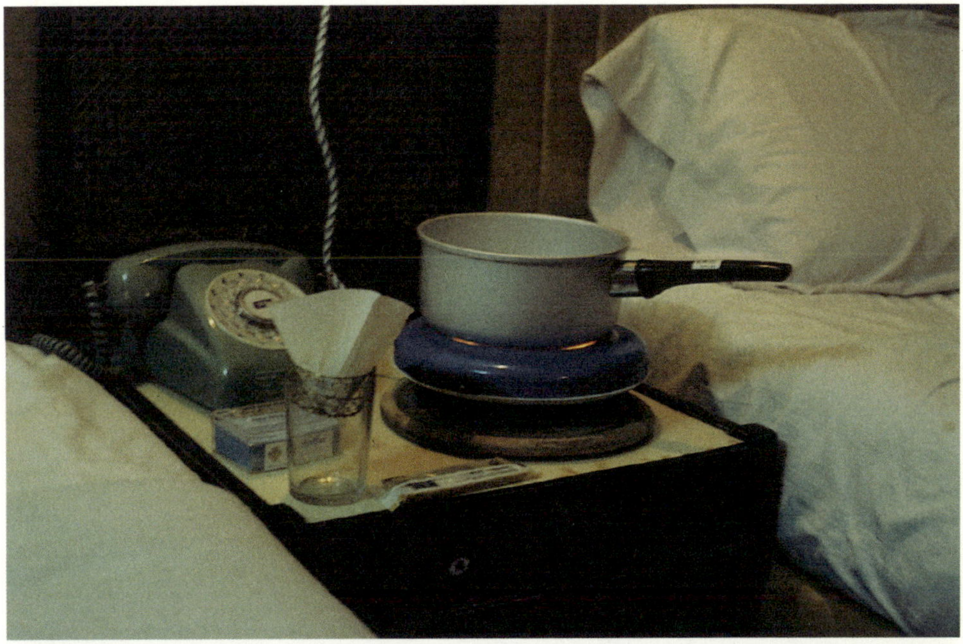

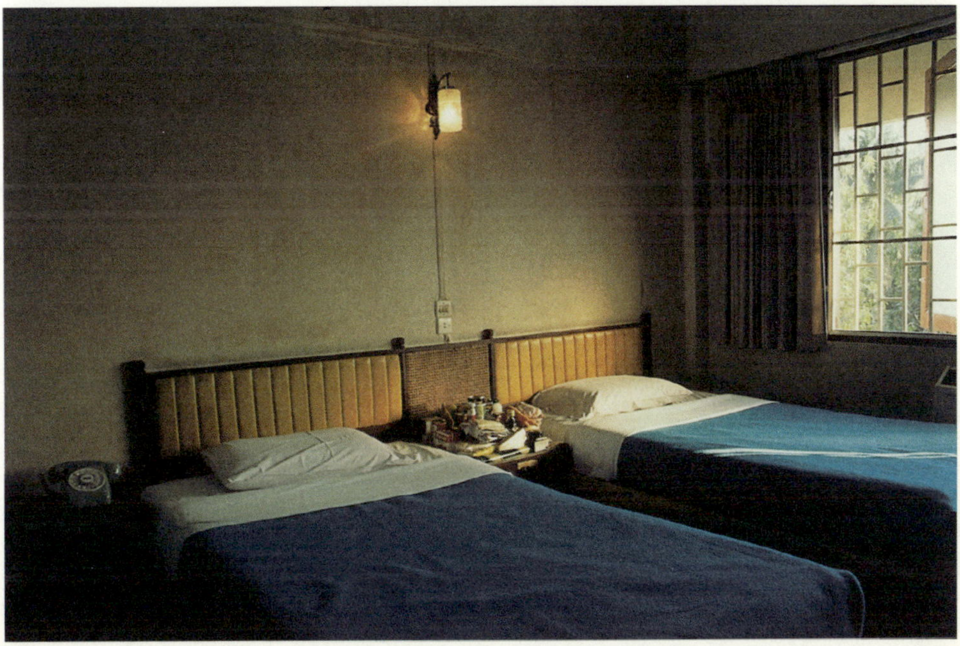

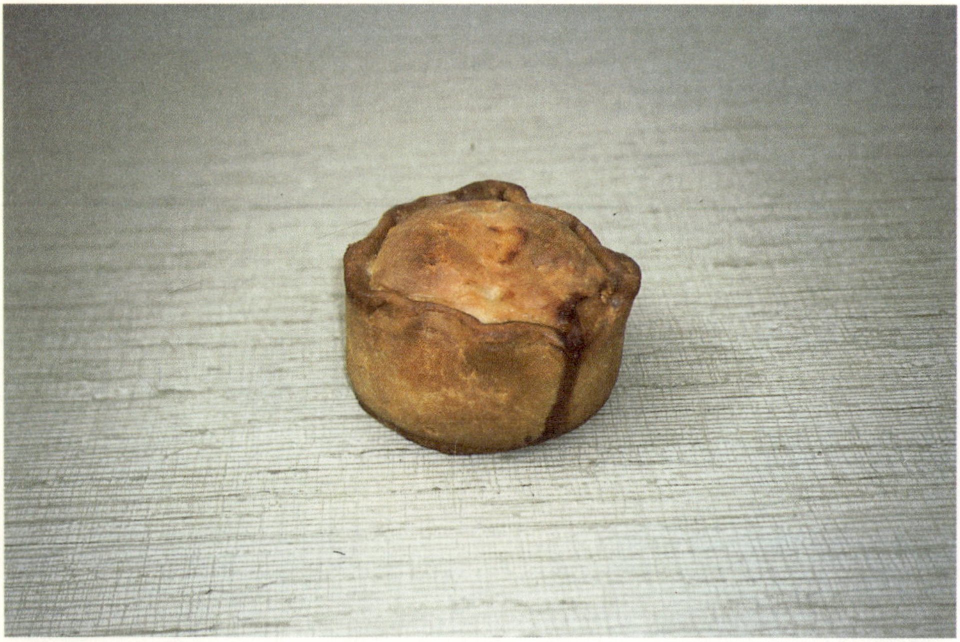

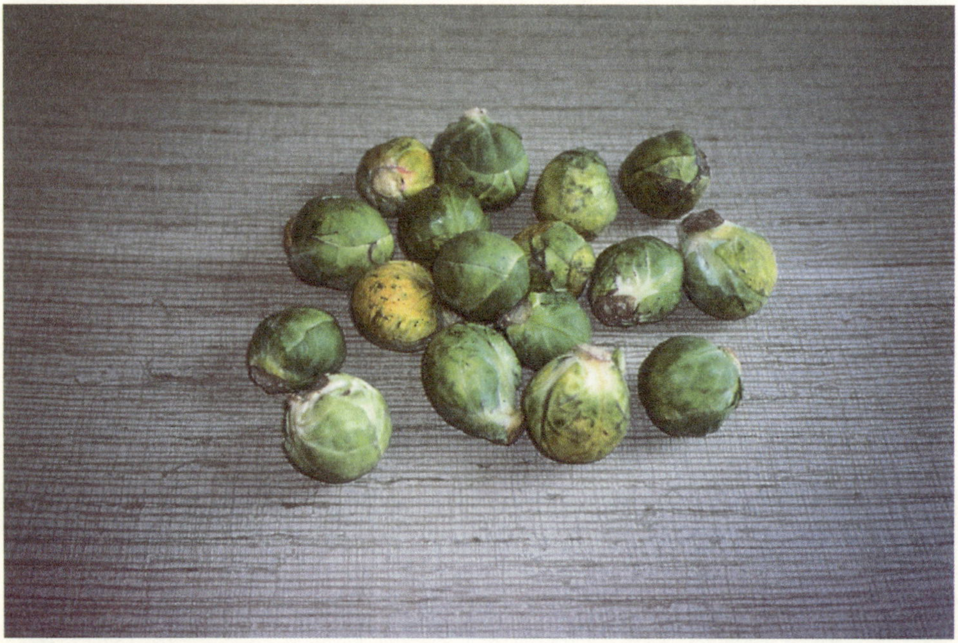

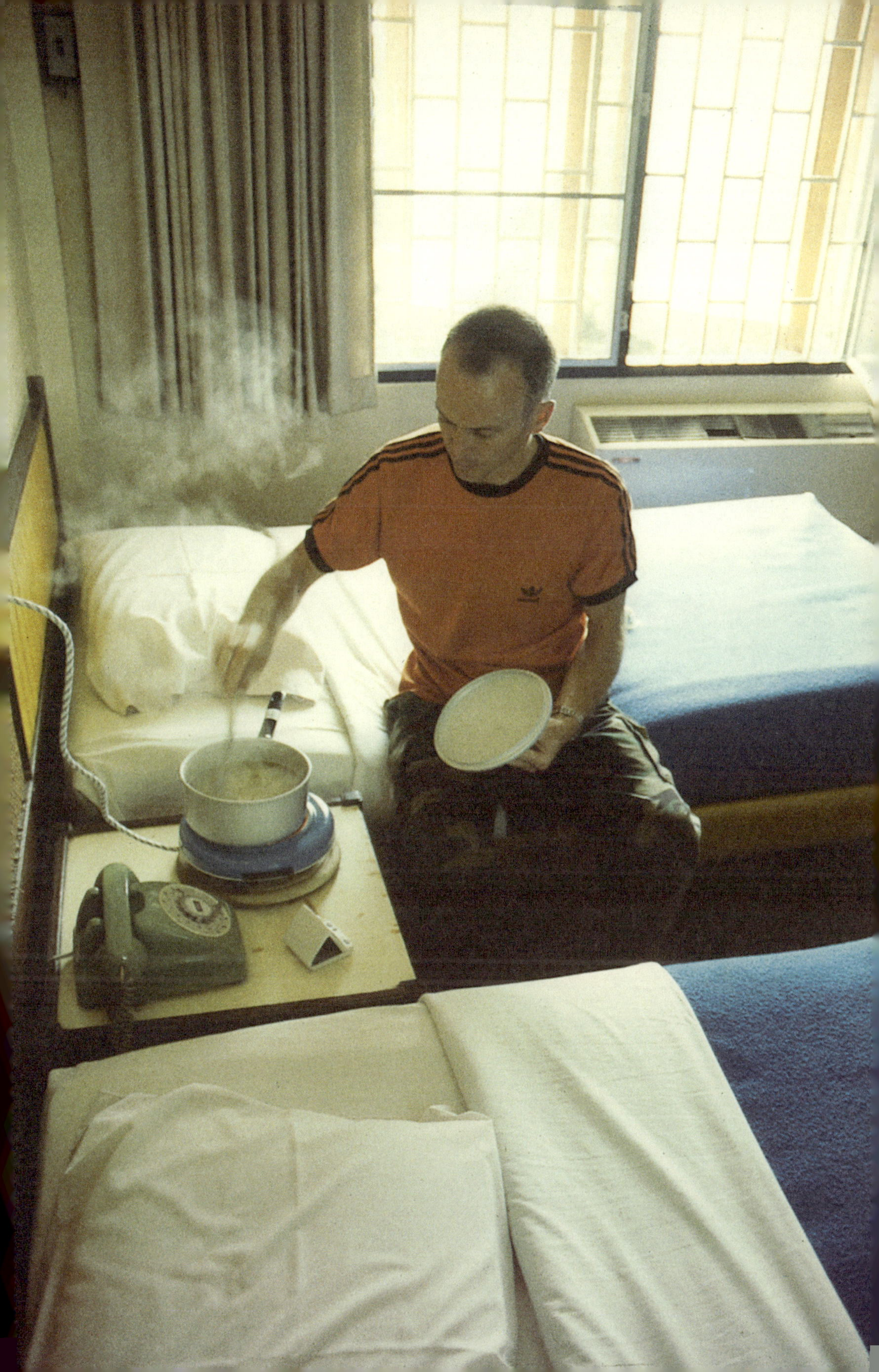

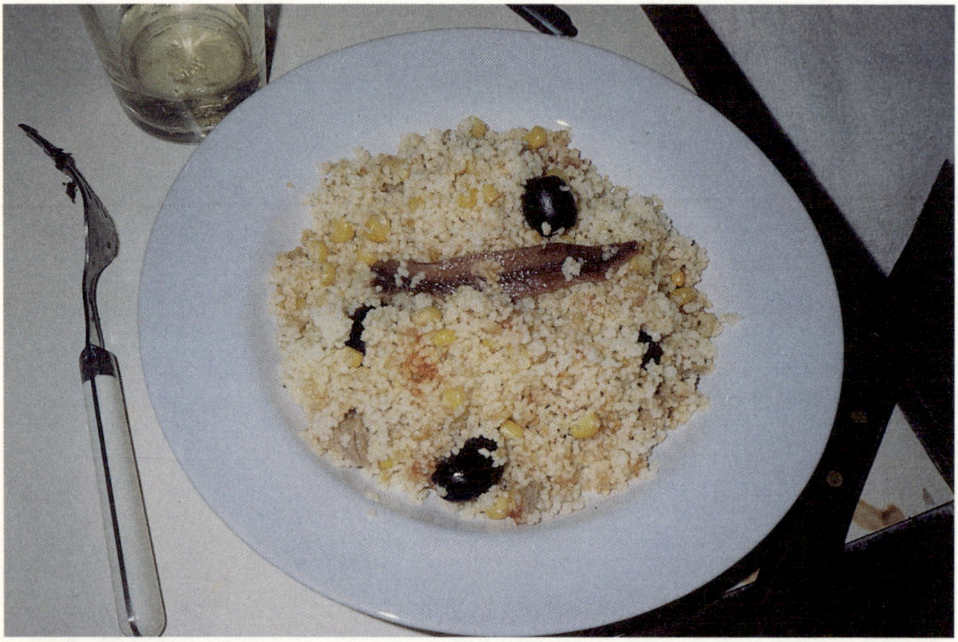

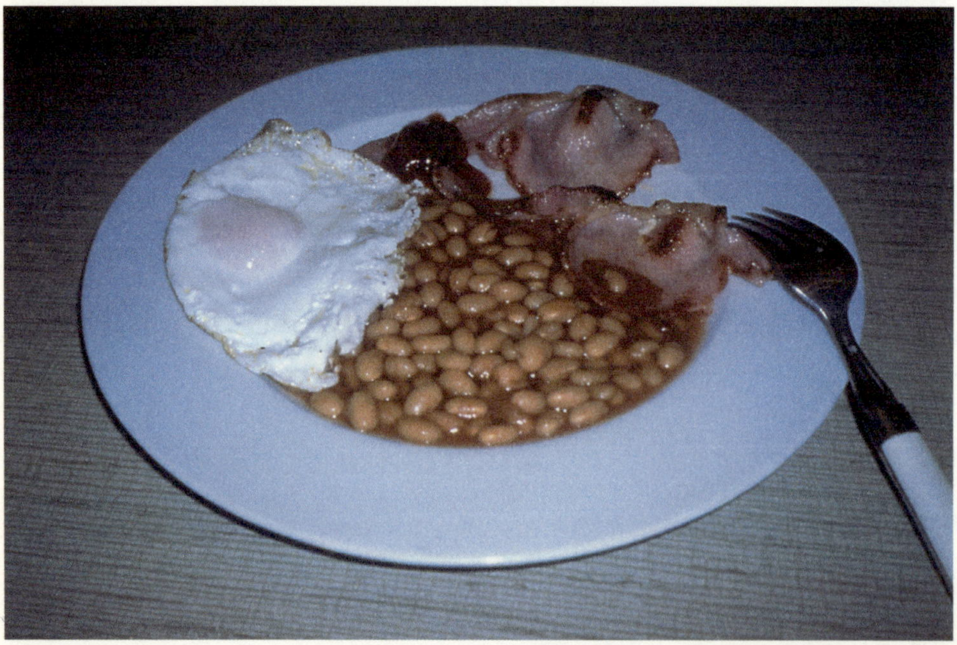

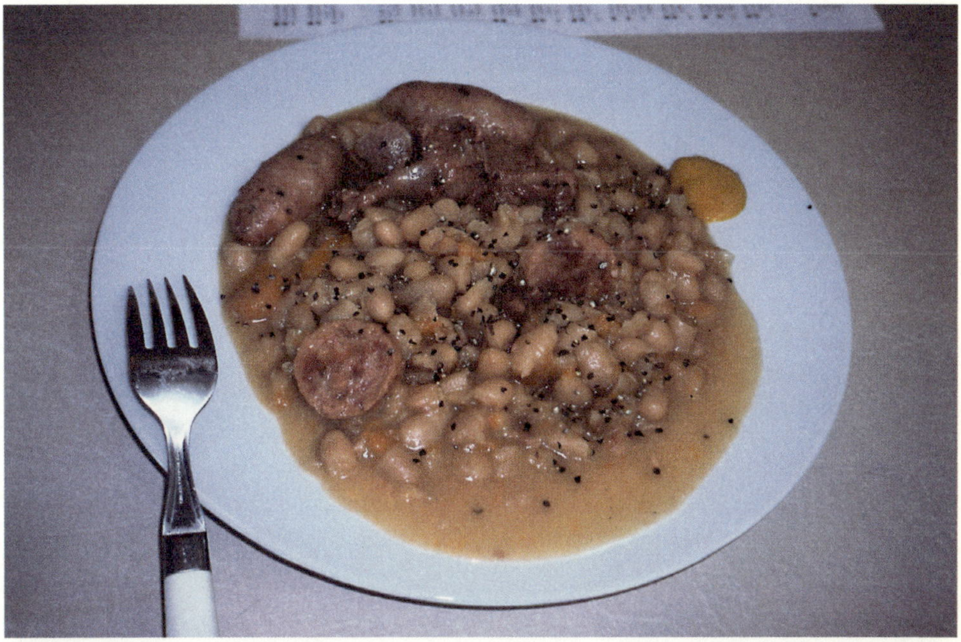

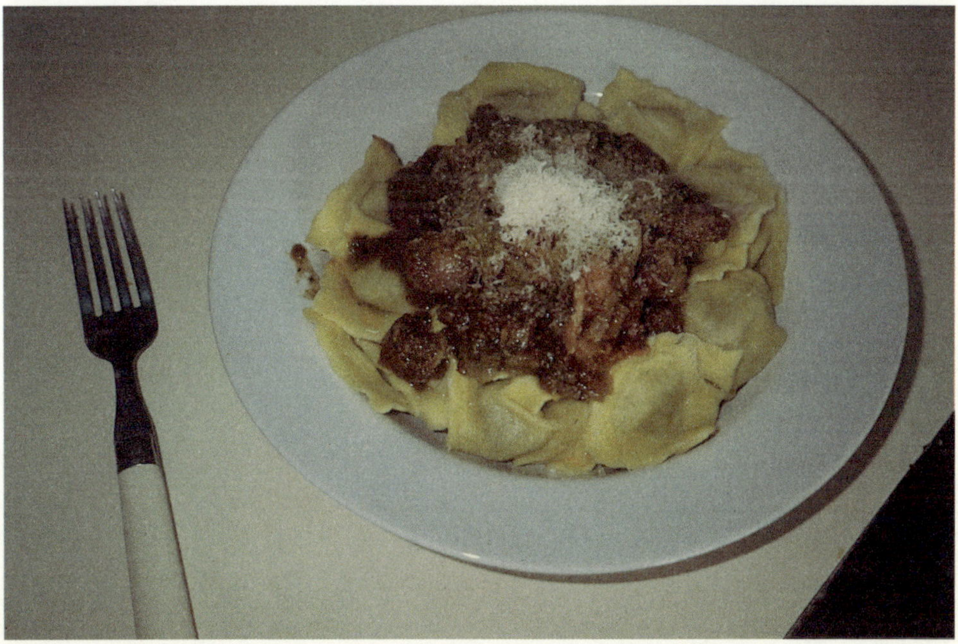

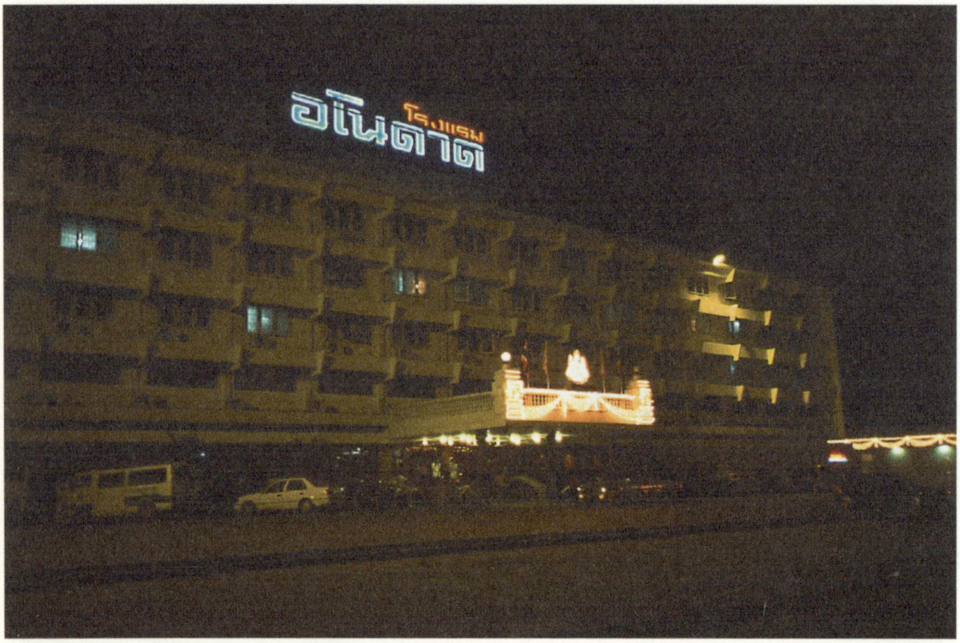
โรงแรม
อโนดาต

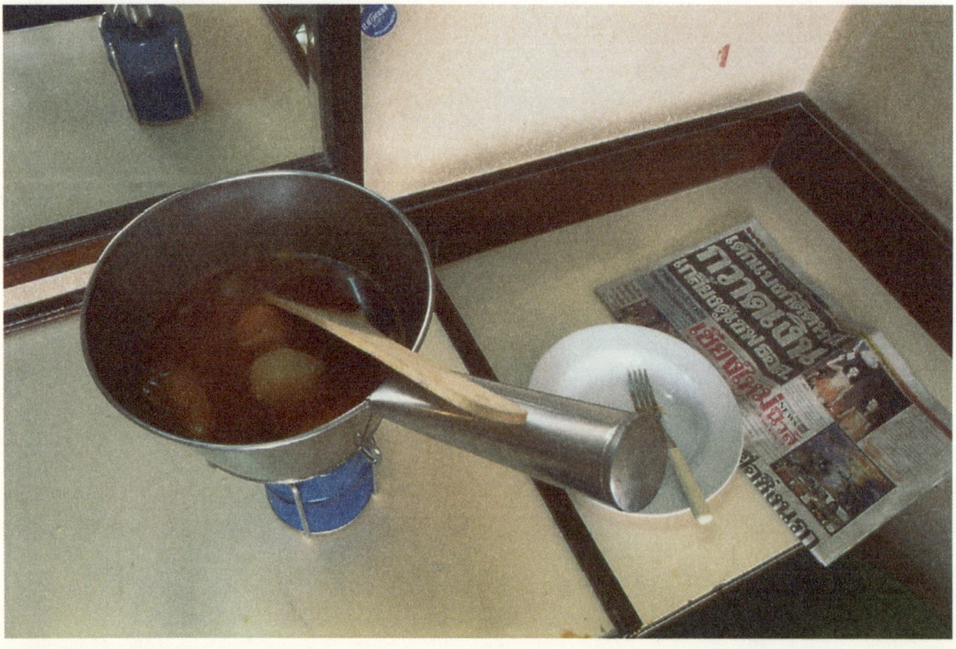

Fiona Banner

As the Crow Doesn't Fly

==

london: too far already

vilnius: a million miles away

liverpool street - leaving rushour, surrounded by skirts and suits - harwich, feeling like everything's further away already. what a shitty place. why aren't ports great, should make it inviting - i mean coming the other way this is the first place you are, cant wait to get away - it's a dispersal tactic. i hate the smell of ferries and oil and vomit - those huge chains and python ropes.

this is fiona banner in shitty HARWICH waiting for the boat
27.5.97

==

london: somewhere

vilnius: somewhere

its been hard getting started, but i'm up and RUNNING now - get this to you later sorry make contact for last night - not through lack of trying.

banner in the night for beaconsfield
27.5.97

==

london: 447

vilnius: 1743

across holland. kind of warped, like drunk - it's the heat. the haze, sea, the lo rez skyline. maybe it's just all stretched. don't think it's straight. the clouds look blown in from a gentle puff. turn it over see what's on the other side - wish you were here. the flat plains retching in on each side. the empty sky totally bloody flat with tulips. would be different if you could have the front and the back the same time, wish I were here. you like waiting as well. waiting for something to happen. waiting for something to come carve up this blue. It looks still because everything else's so fast. still because its screaming through the sky and then the roar turns to a deafening screech, and it takes off. gone. maybe nothing happens atall. Tthe jet stream blurs and fades into the sky like sea, but the rails keep on and on, never touching.

fiona banner for beaconsfield in holland
28.5.95

==

london:487

vilnius:1703

a small country with a big reputation for bikes, blazing flower fields, dykes, mills and not very many hills. the landscapes endlessly flat, just a few church steeples. all's so the same it's like not even moving. sky's lo and wide - it goes fast. gone stoned.

this is fiona banner in the nethernetherlands, nederland, or holland as it is commonly but incorrectly known, for beaconsfield.
28.5.95

==

london: 537

vilnius: 1653

today it's the same only its raining, this journeys funny, because I haven't got anywhere. only getting off to change trains, and platforms. but the rain - hard to send from the mobile in the rain, connections sodden. rain without the pleasure of getting wet, running through the dust, sticking to it slowly, horizontal rain. now i've got these veins on the window like another map, and its fucking up my sense of time. the rains got the G's., boiling, frying on the window.

banner in krautland for beaconsfield
29.5.95

==

==

london: ?

vilnius: ?

when your not lying down, just squished in a chair up by the window, everything still moving, its not really like sleeping - night's a long tunnel, then it's over - sudden like switching on a light. looking around at people you never saw before. do you know you can travel something like just under a million miles in one day? you can cram time, travelling at supersonic speed, chasing the dawn for seven and a half days - weaving the time zones so over a weeks worth of time can be crammed into one day?

this is fiona banner in, on, through, krautland
29.5.97

==

london: 447

vilnius: 1740

could be rotterdam or anywhere. mirrored skyscrapers gone before i even saw them.

in holland for beaconsfield.
29.5.95

==

london: 759 miles

vilnius: 1431 miles

micz i have been advised to change "fiona banner in krautland..." to "fiona banner in germany..." think it's the second report on the list apparently krautland is racist
hope you were not personally offended!
ta
fi

this is fiona banner in GERMANY for beaconsfield

==

london: 1039

vilnius: 1151

nuremberg is an odd place because it was entirely rebuilt after shelling in 1945 they reconstructed the castle and three old churches stone by stone, like a ruin in reverse. makes you realise that history's going to be really confusing in the future. toilets on the german trains are fantastic. whatever foreign country I'm in i only ever seem to have foreign coinage. currency is always foreign.

this is fiona banner in bavaria for beaconsfield
30.5.97

===

london: <-

vilnius: ->

I'm getting insecure, still no word from no one, is this getting through. hello. can you e me back, just a quick waive - tell me if you have my last three e's if not give me first words of the ones you do have.

this is fiona banner in bavaria still
30.5.97

===

london:1448

vilnius:1301

not my idea to head south instead of east, got on the wrong train, and was too scared to get off at night in the middle of nowhere. i think i'm going to slovakia, which is a place i've barely heard of - but am going any way. i think slovakia's a very very new country. maybe i'm there. it doesn't look new. hardly any tourists on this train. train's different here. always playing cards, loosing korun ceskych by the polystyrene cup load.

it's fiona banner only just in czech republic for beaconsfield.
31.5.97

==

london:1121 miles

vilnius: 1069 miles

the buildings the people even the colour of the sky are already asiatic, in the extent to which the word means wars plagues and barbarian invasions. the first suburbs the next, and on. on the train to kracow the czech countryside is green and fast. when I leave the compartment (leave the compartment?) to go to the w.c., dining car, or merely to stretch the legs, have to leave some object on the seat - newspaper, hat, something to deter unreserved seat grabbers from settling into my space when I'm gone. no amount of beer will help you pronounce czech-budejovice (chess-kay-bood-yay-yov-ee-tzeh) we're calling it budweiser, I like time tables - they got the rhythm of this whole thing, the loads of connections destined and missed. ages thumbing thorough holding all journeys - the parallel atlas. and the names, the irrelevant names, the way the n's become z's the further east you get, makes you never want to get off...., dot dot dot, which means 'no stop here, through train', it all gets so condensed comes at you quicker. it all slips past the window one long stroke, there aren't any pieces or blades of grass or anything, time smeared.

this is fiona banner
drinking in the czech republic for beaconsfield
31.5.1997

==

london: 1448 miles

vilnius: 742 miles

the transiberian is the only continuous land route from western europe to the pacific coast of the ussr - the train crosses a hundred degrees of longitudinal europe and asia and traverses seven time zones by the time it reaches the pacific it's seven hours ahead of moscow time, but it's observed moscow time throughout, as have all the clocks in all the stations on route. for a native ruskie it takes seven twenty-four hour days, or put another way 170 hours

and five mins. there is no railway journey of comparable length anywhere in the world, the trans siberian is the big one all the rest are peanuts, train's the only transport that lets you to turn your back on your destination, watching the track disappear, all the yellow flowers burning behind.
31.5.97

this is fiona banner in moravia for beaconsfield

==

london: 1323 miles

vilnius: 861 miles

this journey is long enough
expect to arrive in vilnius on tuesday
31.5.97

this is fiona banner in south bohemia for beaconsfield

==

london: 1456

vilnius: 725

praha holesovice	12:07
praha hlavina	..:..
brno hlavina	15:56
breclav	16:26
bratislava	07:33
bratsliva nove mesto	17:56
rajka	18.30
rajka	18:58
hegyeshalon	19:10
gyor	19:40
nove zamky	..:..
sturovo	..:..
szob	..:..
komarno	..:..
komarom	..:..
budapest nyugaty	20:17
budapest keleti	21:38

slovakia is very flat apart from this one ginormous mountain range in the middle which is misty up top, but then you realise its snow. echoey mountains - the train shudders heavy and regular over the sleepers, someone's forcing the window and the blazing cold air fills up the carriage. for once everyone in the carriage has shut up, breathing out these big empty clouds. the trains really brown, reassuringly brown - i don't know what it looks like on the outside - frosted over i suppose, ice brown. i haven't made any decisions about where to go - one connection leads to another. the Slovakian train atmosphere is cool- you don't have to think about where you're going someone else's doing that. it's really noisy as well with the wind gushing in. if i didn't have to think about the idea of the train going somewhere it'd be a perfect atmosphere. stations and trains have the best colours and views and symmetry of anything, the - the best voyeuristic distance, the best tannoys and the best horizons, rhythm etc.

fiona banner in slovakia for beconsfield
1.6.97

===

london: 1496

vilnius: 795

i'm on my way to hungary - it's looking more like the end of the week for my arrival in vilnius. will for sure let you know.

lots love fi
1.6.97

===

london: 1564

vilnius: 870
the rich wildlife includes wolves, lynxes, marmots, otters, wild geese, eagles and bears. for atmosphere see the movies, 'death calls itself engelchen' - jan kadar (1963) and 'the shop on the main street' - elmar klos (1963)

fiona banner in central slovakia for beaconsfield
2.6.97

===

===

london: 1770

vilnius: 920

a law making slovakian the only official language (the hungarian minority cannot use their mother tongue in public places) means than you have to use sign language to communicate in public.

this is fiona banner in west slovakia for beaconsfield
2.6.97

===

london: 2198

vilnius: 1320

best thing is walking across the danube to get from slovakia to hungary (avoiding the cost of an INTERNATIONAL train ticket) - all the signs are in a different language on the other side - but I cant speak either... so what. the hungarians are really into their language. there are more writers in hungary per capita that any other country in the world. fact is the president's a well known writer of contemporary fiction.

this is fiona banner on the slovakia hungary border

2.6.97

===

london: 1780

vilnius: 1020

the danube is famous because of a song the something something danube. any way this is it, the great grey green greasy danube river. never liked castles (ruined ones i mean) like mountain top turrets on the top of the mountain their disappointing, always piss and fag butts and old rusting cans - the castle in, near, brastilava is ok though - devin castle. i always have thought that castles are ruins because their so ancient, but they're just war blown. the danube is a colossal river, it starts in the black forest in germany and ends in the black sea, romania.

this is fiona banner in western slovakia for beaconsfield
3.6.97

===

london:1110 miles

vilnius: 1000 miles

it's so historic full of fairy tail castles, chateaux, manors, it's so fantastic not having to stop, look at them, just flicking by like a book, sometimes all you see is a pointed roof jabbing up out of the forest, and the forest when it comes goes on forever. it's almost total. then at night it's misty and everything is like the same tone, the green is blacker than the night. the night train saves staying the night anywhere, it's hypnotic. we're sharing the cabin, it's become a total dump - it's just really nice getting things out of the ruck sack and not bothering to put them back. i brought nothing with me - but it's still a lot to cart about, you can make hideous disorder out of nothing. i just took a photo - you'll see what i mean. someone just came in which a huge aluminium jug of beer, which were now knocking back, tastes like metal. the czechs serve their beer with a high head of foam, which makes a flat brew beneath. pivo is beer.

this is fiona banner getting parallel-litic towards plzen for beaconsfield.
3.6.97

===

london: 2079

vilnius: 2001

hungary has one of the highest rates of suicide in the world. someone told me this, but i can't remember who - someone i don't know, i don't know anyone here - someone i just met I suppose. it's surprising because it looks a beautiful country.

fiona banner slovakia hungary border for beaconsfield.
3.1.97

===

london: 1965

vilnius: 1900

everything works and the food is great - it's just like any european city but things are cheaper.

fantastic baroque buildings with communist concrete, cakes, thermal pools and massage, harry houdini, receipts in triplicate, great bridges, shops with no names, close weather, impossible language- nem ertem. the double fry, halaszle soup with fried egg, fried fried cheese and refried mushrooms- egy pohar sor korzonom.

this is fiona banner in budapest for beaconsfield.
4.6.97

===

> Hi Fiona
> Hope all is well...
UHUHH

> When will you be arriving in Vilnius??
DUNNO
> Time and Day then we can meet you and treat you
> for motion sickness.
FANTASTIC

SEE YOU SOONISH

===

>> london: 1564
>> vilnius: 870
>>

vilnius sometime - not this week maybe w.e. will just turn up may miss the others tho, reunion in london later, make it just like vilnius.
>>> fiona banner in central slovakia for beaconsfield

===

london: 2788

vilnius: 3210

XYZAB CDEFG HIJKH LMBNO PHQZG XYZRS TUVHW

fiona banner in hungary for beaconsfield

===

london: 2290

vilnius:1876

lake battalon is right in the middle of transdanubia. its about 100 km long and is the biggest bit of freshwater in europe. so even though it's in the middle of the country, it's like the sea. it's got sandy beaches, it's nice and shallow, there's a sort of sea side atmosphere. it's all lined with seasidey towns. i'm on the train which goes all the way along. so it's like the coast only joined up. though there appear to be a lot of people about, the place has the air of being empty. apparently a lot of people with bad hearts etc come here for medicinal bathing. the train is calm and serious. the trees strobe by on one side and it all falls into the water on the other. the southern part of the lake is lined with beach resorts and the northern side is more historical, but i can't tell the difference. it takes ages to do a full circle, it's a long way. things look different but the same, maybe it's just that i've seen it already. i've started going round again.

this is fiona banner in hungary for beaconsfield
5.6.97

===

london: 2371

vilnius:1966

the train's pulling out of the station into a dim industrial wasteland. the mountains gradually are falling away, everything is factories. but the mountains never seem real. then theirs just the shadow of clouds drifting across 'the great plain'. mostly nothing just pulverising heat coming up off the ground making everything wavy and it isn't even summer. the windows are really scummy, lots of dust, which is good because it makes it less hot in. the suns not yellow it's a chicken.

banner on the great plain for beaconsfield
6.6.97

===

vilnius: somewhere

london: somewhere

post the lot - including replies hey how about some replies anyway!! cant check website as no net access.

7.6.97

===

vilnius: 1999

london: 2391

i've forgotten where I am.

this is fiona banner hungary in hungary for beaconsfield
7.6.97

===

> Hi Fiona,
HI
>
> I received your messages from Central Europe. It
> sounds really interesting. I am very curious what
> kind of messages you would send from this country
> Lithuania is... I've been there once. Everything
> was fine except one little incident: the locals
> offered me for breakfast something made out of...
> worms and beetles... Can you imagine that? In
> "the >centre of Europe" (that's how they define
> the position of their country...). I tried to eat
> that stuff and it was quite OK. But I was ashamed
> to tell about that when I came back home. This
> astonishing dish was called "Vagnorius". Please
> ask them to show you the way they prepare it.

MMM - I"LL LOOK OUT FOR IT
>
> Looking forward to hearing from you soon.
>
FI
7.6.97

===

london: 2382

vilnius:1977

oseltwisel.

this is fiona banner in hungary for beaconsfield
7.6.97

===

london: 1965

vilnius: 1900

the standard c.s.d. heavy freight engine in the last quarter century of steam was the skoda 556.0 decapod, 510 of which were built from 1952 to 1957... traversing the now electrified mainline up the danube valley from budapest toward home rails.

this is fiona banner traversing for beaconsfield
8.6.97

===

london: <-

vilnius: ->

im taking my time and am in hungary just hanging a bit if stuff comes in out of sequence, as the crow flies (doesn't) whatever. no word back from anyone. polish food is really stuffing - the weather is... doesn't matter becos i'm on the train all the time, but it all looks bright and sparky. don't know when i'll arrive with you lot in vilnius. depends.

fb hungary
8.6.97

==

london: <-

vilnius: ->

I will let you know time and day then you can meet me and treat me for motion sickness.
>

fb
9.6.97

==

vilnius: not sure

london:not sure

the high tatra mountains on the polish border.

its weird imagining this landscape all covered over with snow, but you know it should be, all the poles sticking out marking the depths. all the buildings are wood, everything's brown or green. spangley and cold.

this is fiona banner in east slovakia for beaconsfield
11.6.97

==

london:2198 miles

vilnius:868 miles

in my studio where i hear trains a lot, but they're always steaming in from the distance, getting loud and disappearing at the same time. then the underground ones which are like the sound of engine rooms, they do the same only more slowly. this train seems as loud as if it's passing but it's like that all the time.

this is fiona banner in poland for beaconsfield
12.06.97

==

vilnius: 711 miles

london: 1268 miles

today i made the incredible discovery that my laptop talks. theirs a range of voices all of which are moronic - then again it may be the script. the voices are fred, bahh, albert, badnews, whisper, hysterical etc. and there not too good at punctuation. they're not too expressive. but it's something.

this is fiona banner in poland for beaconsfield
12.6.97

===

vilnius:close

london:far

this is fiona banner in poland
13.6.97

===

Bird Island

Janice Kerbel

Mile after mile of white sandy beach. The sound of the waves and the heat of the sun. Night-blooming cereus, white straw lilies, orange-spotted filefish and ruby-throated hummingbirds.

Just above the Tropic of Cancer, deep in the Great Bahama Bank, lies an island virtually untouched by human life. Located at 24°36′N and 76°8′W, this secluded, uninhabited treasure measures almost two miles from sea to sea and boasts sixty-four lush acres of pristine tropical landscape. A place of indescribable intoxication removed from all the world, this remote island remains one of the last shares of paradise. It is known as Bird Island.

From above Bird Island looks like a boomerang lost in the Tongue of the Ocean. Eleven miles from nowhere, it is a stray gem off the glorious Exuma Cays, a glittering necklace of 365 islands. In its isolation, the island flourishes as a unique ecosystem of unmatched diversity. It is covered in dense palm grove and flowering vines; coconut, banana and bougainvillaea grow as if from the same tree, their canopy of green forming a natural aviary. Generally flat, the land rises to just over two metres above sea level but for a single bluff, the island's highest and most dramatic feature. Here a small yet brilliant waterfall embraced by lush flora falls to a glistening pool. White sand beaches and calm, crystal clear waters skirt the perimeter of the island, offering more than six-and-a-half miles of magnificent coastline. Bare coral rock, the island's natural defense against rising sea levels, is exposed at the northern end of the island, where a sandbar appears 200 metres from shore at low tide. A coral reef lies 300 meters from the windward shore and a little-known blue hole is found just two miles north of the island.

The island's habitat is a combination of Coastal Beach and Tropical Deciduous Forest, exemplified by the nutrient-rich soil characteristic of oceanic islands and the wet-and-dry tropical maritime climate. Moderated by the Gulf Stream, the average winter temperature rarely falls below 25°C/77°F, while summer temperatures rise to a beautiful average of 30°C/86°F. The island is blessed with an average of 330 days of sunshine per year and approximately 43 inches of rainfall, most of which fall as short yet heavy cloudbursts providing a welcomed cooling effect.

Most oceanic islands are volcanic in origin, believed to have erupted directly from the ocean floor. Bird Island, unlike the majority of its sister islands, is unique in its formation. It is part of an underwater mountainous plateau formed of oolitic limestone, a reef-shelf of solid sea fossil 20,000 feet thick and rising sheer-sided from the Atlantic seabed. Technically an atoll, Bird Island began to take its present form more than 500,000 years ago, as tiny marine organisms grew atop the solid stone, continually adding their skeletal remains causing the mass to slowly grow. During the late Pleistocene period, a reddish mineral-rich soil formed atop the lime and skeletal remains laying fertile ground and making Bird Island a most obliging host. Today green and plentiful, surrounded by coral reefs, sandbanks and the glorious blue sea, Bird Island is home to many strange and wonderful species.

The tradewinds have and continue to play a major role in the evolutionary development and biodiversity of Bird Island, bringing life from farther afield and spawning migrant flora and fauna across the island. The organisms which colonise Bird Island arrived by crossing open ocean, at times from great distances, with the sea acting as a natural barrier to dispersal. As a result, relatively few continental organisms reach Bird Island, and the distinct ecological niche found here further determines the establishing species development. Bird Island, rich in both flora and fauna typical of the Greater Antillean region, remains vast and incomparable in its uniqueness.

Dense palm grove covers most of the island, the majority of which is coconut palm offering succulent white meat and sweet pearly milk. Less frequent yet still plentiful is the banana palm, found predominantly to the south-west end of the island, the fruits of which grow in abundance. Flowering vines grow up and through the palm while exotic seagrape, with its brilliantly sour fruit, sweet mango and tropical guava dangle through the heavy growth. Red, white and black mangrove canopy the water's edge, their tangled roots diving straight into the saltwater thereby preventing the island's erosion and providing ideal cover for small marine life. The island is a riot of colour and fragrance twelve months of the year, with a variety of flowers always in bloom. The aphrodisiac scent of frangipani mingles with sea-side almond and mimosa; hibiscus, ixora and passionflower grace the island alongside tall razor grass, bamboo and lobster claw heliconia. Closer to the ground still, tiny ernodea can be found poking out from beneath the soil. Bougainvillaea are widespread, blooming brilliantly in papery shades of purple, pink and orange, as is the scent of honeysuckle and jasmine, their heady aromas attracting the likes of the yellow sulphur, the zebra longwing, and the brilliant blue morpho.

While the interior of Bird island is dense with palms and blossoms, its outer edge is ringed with blinding white beaches, their silky sands fringed by the gentle lapping of turquoise waves. The boomerang shape of the island forms a natural harbour and small lagoon on the east side, known as Ajaia Lagoon. At the northern end of the lagoon, where the

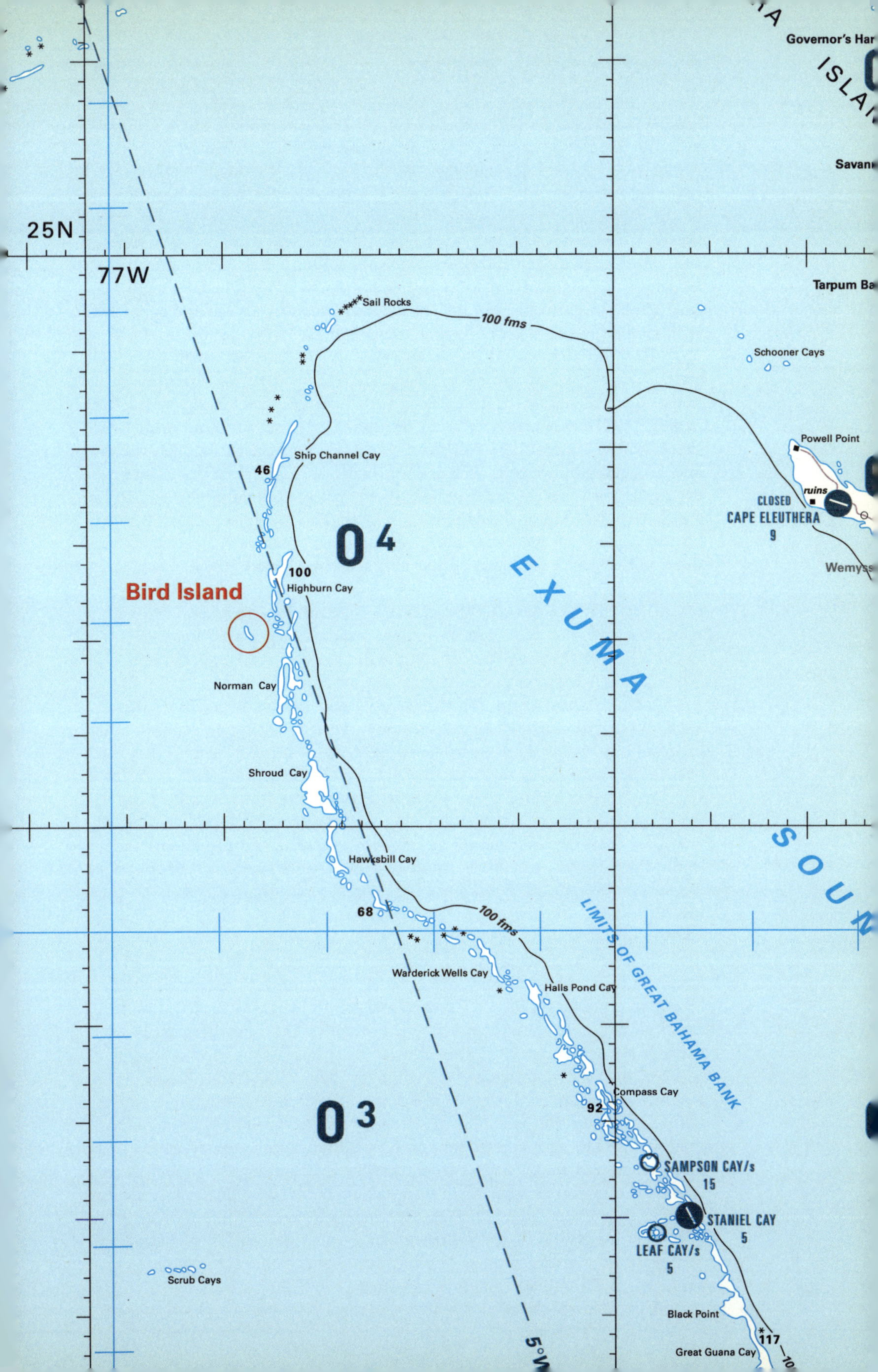

Governor's Har
ISLA
Savan
25N
77W
Tarpum Ba
Sail Rocks
100 fms
Schooner Cays
Powell Point
ruins
CLOSED
CAPE ELEUTHERA
9
Wemyss
Ship Channel Cay
46
04
EXUMA
100
Highburn Cay
Bird Island
Norman Cay
Shroud Cay
SOUN
Hawksbill Cay
68
100 fms
LIMITS OF GREAT BAHAMA BANK
Warderick Wells Cay
Halls Pond Cay
Compass Cay
92
03
SAMPSON CAY/s
15
STANIEL CAY
5
LEAF CAY/s
5
Scrub Cays
Black Point
117
Great Guana Cay
5°W

beach widens again, lies perhaps the most tranquil spot on the island; here the Roseate Spoonbill, *Ajaja Ajaia,* after which the lagoon is named, gather to feed from the shallow waters. This beach extends well beyond the palm grove to where Pelican Cove is nestled on the northern-most end of the island, facing a sandbar which shows itself daily at low tide. Straight from Pelican Cove, on the west side of the island, lies the serene and continuous Solitaire Bay, its beach stretching unbroken for the entire length of the island, narrowing and widening as it goes. Ibis Point marks Bird Island's southern-most tip and is surrounded by a wide and beautiful beach which basks in the sun from dawn to dusk.

Beneath the crystalline waters lies an enchanting world all to its own. Thousands of varieties of coral, fish, mollusks, sponges and anemones make their home in the miles of reefs which surround the island. Jewelfish, parrotfish and the Atlantic spade, to name but a few, swim amidst the intricate and delicate coral, their swift iridescent bodies and unforgettable colours shimmering brilliantly as light refracts against the surface of the clear sea. Not only is the water a diver's paradise, rich in opulent species found nowhere else in such density of colour and variety, but further out to sea swim snapper, marlin, sailfish and tuna, tempting those with a taste for sportfishing and succulent meals. Bottom feeders, including lobster, crab, giant prawn and oysters are plentiful – as ubiquitous in the sea as they are at a Bahamian fisherman's market. Humpback whales can often be spotted windward of Bird Island's shores in the Great Bahama Bank en route to mating grounds, along with the ever-playful Atlantic blue-nosed and spotted dolphins.

Most islands of the Exumas boast their own sub-species of lizard, each having developed entirely independent of their neighbours. The blue-backed curly-tailed lizard is indigenous to Bird Island, and is but one of the wealth of reptiles found here. Iguanas, shy and harmless vegetarians that spend most of their days on the hot rocks by Pelican Cove, are a throwback to the dinosaur age. Sea-turtles, large four-legged creatures carrying their homes as protective wear, have been known to lay their eggs on the beaches of Ajaia Lagoon. The Bahamian Dragon, the infamous and much-loved gecko, 200-year-old tortoises, and the tri-banded skink are but a few familiar reptiles which grace the island, silently relishing all it has to offer.

As its name suggests, birdlife on the island is rich. An abundant world of avian variety, vast numbers of year-round, breeding and non-breeding residents, along with rare and exotic migrants and wanderers make Bird Island their home for part or all of the year. Elegant, snow-white terns and long-tailed tropicbirds soar protectively above the island while pelicans dive gracefully for their dinner. *Fregata magnificens* – the magnificent frigatebird – courts the opposite sex with his inflatable scarlet throat, a colourful and blatant display of wooing from deep in the mangroves. The rare scarlet ibis roosts on Ibis Point; the bananquit and honeycreeper share their nest in the palms; and the secretive great-lizard cuckoo is more often heard than seen, believed to call on the hour. Further in from the water's edge, birdlife explodes once again where hundreds of tiny hummingbirds hover amidst ground and tree-nesting macaws and parrots of impossible colours. And just beneath the undergrowth hides the small and fleeting fly-catching yellowthroat.

Bird Island's most marvelled treasure, however, is the illustrious and elusive Exuma Emerald. Endemic to Bird Island, this brilliantly iridescent bird found nowhere else in the world is perfectly adapted to her environment. With her ruby-red beak, feisty, pugnacious character and scalloped streamers extending from her long forked tail, the Exuma Emerald lives off the nectar of the flowering hibiscus, beats her wings more than 68 times per second, and camouflages her tiny four-inch body for defense.

There are no land-dwelling mammals on Bird Island and its human population is, to date, zero.

The Lucayans, deriving their name from *'lukka-caire'* meaning island people, are believed to have been the first to settle in the Exumas, early in the 9th century AD. They set up egalitarian communities in the coves along the islands' fringes, built thatched-roof shelters, and lived off the land and from the sea. Though there is no trace of past life on Bird Island itself, it is unlikely that the Lucayans would have missed the opportunity to inhabit such a glorious location, perfectly situated and abundant in natural resources. Thousands of years passed before Columbus, perhaps the first tourist to Bird Island, arrived in the Bahamas in 1492, thinking he had found India. Spanish explorers soon followed in Colombus's trail and, within 25 years, the entire Lucayan population was virtually gone. The Spanish bestowed on the islands the name *'Baja Mar'* – meaning shallow seas – and ever since the islands have been coined the Bahamas.

Pirates and buccaneers adopted the string of islands, as the shallow rim of the Tongue of the Ocean was a known shipping lane for Spanish boats heavy with spoils from their plunderings in South and Central America. Attracted by the hundreds of islets and cays, pirate ships could hide from and pounce on their unwitting prey while the numerous sandbars and banks put the treasure-laden ships at even greater disadvantage. The likes of famous pirates dominated the Bahamas for the next hundred years, and to this day the waters are rich with treasure from ships lured into the shallow waters. Tales of fortune from this 'Golden Age of Piracy' are still told – the illustrious swashbuckler Henry Morgan, whose treasure has yet to be found, wrote of a 'glittering island teeming with birds of unthinkable origin ... alone and promising, surrounded by reef and coral ... perhaps ideal ...' shortly before his final disappearance from the sea.

Following Britain's defeat in the American Revolution, southern loyalists brought slaves to the larger islands of the Exumas, where cotton was grown under the crown's protection. A few brave young men and women, strong enough to weather the unpredictable sea and escape from the clutches of evil masters, took refuge on the smaller islands. Remains of a small woven vessel made from palm frond and bamboo was found hidden in the palm grove on Bird Island just beyond Solitaire Bay. The only evidence of human life ever found on the island, this vessel is thought to have belonged to fugitive slaves seeking safety and refuge.

In 1964 Great Britain granted the islands self-government and the status of the Bahamas was changed in 1969 from colony to Commonwealth. In 1973 the Commonwealth of the Bahamas was returned to its independent state and today this rich and vast archipelago, of which Bird Island is a part, proudly thrives as a stable, democratic, tropical nation.

Bird Island is located eleven nautical miles north of Norman Cay and nine nautical miles west of Highburn Cay. The nearest amenities to Bird Island are found on Highburn Cay where there is a small marina and provisions store. The nearest town, and in fact the main settlement of the Exumas, is on Staniel Cay, located 45 miles to the south of the island with a post office, medical clinic, church, library, grocery store and weekly market. The nearest airport is also found on Staniel Cay, and accepts only private planes. But to date, aside from the vast avian, reptilian and marine life, the only regular to pass within sight of Bird Island is Sam – a kindly gentleman who travels down through the Cays weekly on Thursdays, delivering mail and necessities to the few dwellers on neighbouring islands.

Sweet bird song in air heavy with jasmine. Gentle swaying palms canopying boundless privacy. Remote yet accessible, tropical but temperate, brimming with life, colour and fragrance. Bird Island is, perhaps, paradise.

Flight Times: London to...

Ian Whittlesea

AARHUS, DENMARK

1 HOUR 40 MINUTES

ABU DHABI, ARAB EMIRATES

7 HOURS 5 MINUTES

ABUJA, NIGERIA

6 HOURS 25 MINUTES

ACCRA, GHANA

6 HOURS 35 MINUTES

ADEN, REPUBLIC OF YEMEN

8 HOURS

ALEPPO, SYRIA

4 HOURS 45 MINUTES

ALEXANDRIA, EGYPT

4 HOURS 50 MINUTES

ALGHERO, ITALY

2 HOURS 25 MINUTES

ALGIERS, ALGERIA

2 HOURS 45 MINUTES

ALICANTE, SPAIN

2 HOURS 40 MINUTES

ALMATY, KAZAKSTAN

7 HOURS 20 MINUTES

AMMAN, JORDAN

5 HOURS 5 MINUTES

AMSTERDAM, NETHERLANDS

1 HOUR 10 MINUTES

ANCONA, ITALY

2 HOURS 20 MINUTES

ANTALYA, TURKEY

4 HOURS 15 MINUTES

ANTIGUA, LEEWARD ISLANDS

8 HOURS 25 MINUTES

ASHGABAT, TURKMENISTAN

6 HOURS 25 MINUTES

ASTURIAS, SPAIN

1 HOUR 55 MINUTES

ATHENS, GREECE

3 HOURS 40 MINUTES

ATLANTA, USA

9 HOURS 5 MINUTES

BAHRAIN, BAHRAIN

6 HOURS 40 MINUTES

BAKU, AZERBAIJAN

5 HOURS 25 MINUTES

BALTIMORE, USA

8 HOURS 25 MINUTES

BANGKOK, THAILAND

11 HOURS 35 MINUTES

BARBADOS, BARBADOS

8 HOURS 45 MINUTES

BARCELONA, SPAIN

2 HOURS 5 MINUTES

BEIJING, CHINA

10 HOURS 10 MINUTES

BEIRUT, LEBANON

4 HOURS 30 MINUTES

BELGRADE, YUGOSLAVIA

2 HOURS 40 MINUTES

BENGHAZI, LIBIYA

4 HOURS

BERGEN, NORWAY

2 HOURS 5 MINUTES

BERLIN, GERMANY

1 HOUR 50 MINUTES

BERMUDA, BERMUDA

7 HOURS 45 MINUTES

BIARRITZ, FRANCE

1 HOUR 55 MINUTES

BILBAO, SPAIN

1 HOUR 45 MINUTES

BILLUND, DENMARK

1 HOUR 40 MINUTES

BOGOTA, COLUMBIA

11 HOURS 20 MINUTES

BOLOGNA, ITALY

2 HOURS 5 MINUTES

BORDEAUX, FRANCE

1 HOUR 45 MINUTES

BOSTON, USA

7 HOURS 10 MINUTES

BREMEN, GERMANY

1 HOUR 55 MINUTES

BRUSSELS, BELGIUM

1 HOUR

BUCHAREST, ROMANIA

3 HOURS 10 MINUTES

BUDAPEST, HUNGARY

2 HOURS 30 MINUTES

BUENOS AIRES, ARGENTINA

13 HOURS 30 MINUTES

CAGLIARI, ITALY

2 HOURS 30 MINUTES

CAIRO, EGYPT

4 HOURS 45 MINUTES

CALCUTTA, INDIA

9 HOURS 40 MINUTES

CALGARY, CANADA

9 HOURS 20 MINUTES

CANCUN, MEXICO

10 HOURS 30 MINUTES

CAPE TOWN, SOUTH AFRICA

11 HOURS 30 MINUTES

CARACAS, VENEZUELA

9 HOURS 25 MINUTES

CARCASSONNE, FRANCE

2 HOURS

CASABLANCA, MOROCCO

3 HOURS 25 MINUTES

CHAMBERY, FRANCE

1 HOUR 40 MINUTES

CHARLOTTE, USA

9 HOURS 5 MINUTES

CHENNAI, INDIA

9 HOURS 55 MINUTES

CHICAGO, USA

8 HOURS 20 MINUTES

CINCINNATI, USA

9 HOURS

CLEVELAND, USA

8 HOURS 45 MINUTES

COLOGNE, GERMANY

1 HOUR 15 MINUTES

COLOMBO, SRI LANKA

11 HOURS 10 MINUTES

COPENHAGEN, DENMARK

1 HOUR 50 MINUTES

CORK, REPUBLIC OF IRELAND

1 HOUR 20 MINUTES

DALAMAN, TURKEY

3 HOURS 45 MINUTES

DALLAS/FORT WORTH, USA

10 HOURS

DAMASCUS, SYRIA
4 HOURS 20 MINUTES

DAMMAM, SAUDI ARABIA
6 HOURS 50 MINUTES

DELHI, INDIA
8 HOURS 20 MINUTES

DENVER, USA
9 HOURS 55 MINUTES

DETROIT, USA
8 HOURS 15 MINUTES

DINARD, FRANCE
1 HOUR 5 MINUTES

DOHA, QUATAR
6 HOURS 55 MINUTES

DORTMUND, GERMANY
1 HOUR 30 MINUTES

DOUALA, CAMEROON
8 HOURS

DUBAI, ARAB EMIRATES
6 HOURS 55 MINUTES

DUBLIN, REPUBLIC OF IRELAND
1 HOUR 10 MINUTES

DUBROVNIK, CROATIA
2 HOURS 40 MINUTES

DUSSELDORF, GERMANY
1 HOUR 30 MINUTES

EDMONTON, CANADA
9 HOURS 5 MINUTES

EINDHOVEN, NETHERLANDS
1 HOUR 5 MINUTES

ENTEBBE/KAMPALA, UGANDA
8 HOURS 35 MINUTES

ESBJERG, DENMARK
1 HOUR 30 MINUTES

FARO, PORTUGAL
2 HOURS 40 MINUTES

FLORENCE, ITALY
2 HOURS 15 MINUTES

FRANKFURT, GERMANY
1 HOUR 30 MINUTES

FUNCHAL, MADEIRA ISLANDS
3 HOURS 30 MINUTES

GDANSK, POLAND
2 HOURS 20 MINUTES

GENEVA, SWITZERLAND

1 HOUR 35 MINUTES

GENOA, ITALY

2 HOURS 10 MINUTES

GERONA, SPAIN

2 HOURS 5 MINUTES

GIBRALTAR, GIBRALTAR

2 HOURS 55 MINUTES

GOTHENBURG, SWEDEN

1 HOUR 55 MINUTES

HALIFAX, CANADA

6 HOURS 25 MINUTES

HAMBURG, GERMANY

1 HOUR 20 MINUTES

HANOVER, GERMANY

1 HOUR 30 MINUTES

HARARE, ZIMBABWE

10 HOURS 30 MINUTES

HAVANA, CUBA

10 HOURS 10 MINUTES

HELSINKI, FINLAND

2 HOURS 55 MINUTES

HONG KONG, HONG KONG

11 HOURS 55 MINUTES

HOUSTON, USA

10 HOURS 5 MINUTES

ISLAMABAD, PAKISTAN

7 HOURS 45 MINUTES

ISTANBUL, TURKEY

3 HOURS 45 MINUTES

IZMIR, TURKEY

4 HOURS

JEDDAH, SAUDI ARABIA

6 HOURS 5 MINUTES

JEREZ DE LA FRONTERA, SPAIN

2 HOURS 50 MINUTES

JOHANNESBURG, SOUTH AFRICA

10 HOURS 55 MINUTES

KERRY, REPUBLIC OF IRELAND

1 HOUR 20 MINUTES

KIEV, UKRAINE

3 HOURS 20 MINUTES

KINGSTON, JAMAICA

9 HOURS 45 MINUTES

KNOCK, REPUBLIC OF IRELAND

1 HOUR 25 MINUTES

KRAKOW, POLAND

2 HOURS 30 MINUTES

KUALA LUMPUR, MALAYSIA

12 HOURS 10 MINUTES

KUWAIT, KUWAIT

6 HOURS 30 MINUTES

LA ROCHELLE, FRANCE

1 HOUR 30 MINUTES

LAGOS, NIGERIA

6 HOURS 25 MINUTES

LAHORE, PAKISTAN

7 HOURS 50 MINUTES

LANZAROTE, CANARY ISLANDS

4 HOURS

LARNACA, CYPRUS

4 HOURS 30 MINUTES

LAS VEGAS, USA

10 HOURS 45 MINUTES

LIBREVILLE, GABON

7 HOURS

LISBON, PORTUGAL

2 HOURS 35 MINUTES

LJUBLJANA, SLOVENIA

2 HOURS 5 MINUTES

LOS ANGELES, USA

11 HOURS 10 MINUTES

LUXEMBOURG, LUXEMBOURG

1 HOUR 5 MINUTES

LUXOR, EGYPT

5 HOURS

LYON, FRANCE

1 HOUR 45 MINUTES

MAASTRICHT, NETHERLANDS

1 HOUR 10 MINUTES

MADRID, SPAIN

2 HOURS 15 MINUTES

MALAGA, SPAIN

2 HOURS 50 MINUTES

MALMO, SWEDEN

1 HOUR 55 MINUTES

MALTA, MALTA

3 HOURS 15 MINUTES

MARRAKECH, MOROCCO
3 HOURS 40 MINUTES

MARSEILLE, FRANCE
2 HOURS 15 MINUTES

MAURITIUS, MAURITIUS
11 HOURS 55 MINUTES

MEXICO CITY, MEXICO
11 HOURS 25 MINUTES

MIAMI, USA
9 HOURS 25 MINUTES

MILAN, ITALY
2 HOURS 5 MINUTES

MINNEAPOLIS, USA
8 HOURS 50 MINUTES

MINSK, BELARUS
3 HOURS 5 MINUTES

MONTEGO BAY, JAMAICA
9 HOURS 45 MINUTES

MONTPELLIER, FRANCE
1 HOUR 55 MINUTES

MONTREAL, CANADA
7 HOURS 15 MINUTES

MOSCOW, RUSSIA
3 HOURS 45 MINUTES

MUMBAI, INDIA
8 HOURS 40 MINUTES

MUNICH, GERMANY
1 HOUR 45 MINUTES

MURCIA, SPAIN
2 HOURS 35 MINUTES

NAGOYA, JAPAN
11 HOURS 50 MINUTES

NAIROBI, KENYA
8 HOURS 20 MINUTES

NANTES, FRANCE
1 HOUR 10 MINUTES

NAPLES, ITALY
2 HOURS 45 MINUTES

NASSAU, BAHAMAS
10 HOURS 5 MINUTES

NEW YORK, USA
7 HOURS 40 MINUTES

NICE, FRANCE
2 HOURS

NIMES, FRANCE

2 HOURS

NUREMBERG, GERMANY

1 HOUR 55 MINUTES

OLBIA, ITALY

2 HOURS 10 MINUTES

ORAN, ALGERIA

3 HOURS 5 MINUTES

ORLANDO, USA

9 HOURS 10 MINUTES

OSAKA, JAPAN

12 HOURS

OSLO, NORWAY

2 HOURS 5 MINUTES

OTTAWA, CANADA

7 HOURS 20 MINUTES

PALMA DE MALLORCA, SPAIN

2 HOURS 20 MINUTES

PAPHOS, CYPRUS

4 HOURS 15 MINUTES

PARIS, FRANCE

1 HOUR 5 MINUTES

PERPIGNAN, FRANCE

2 HOURS

PESCARA, ITALY

2 HOURS 30 MINUTES

PHILADELPHIA, USA

7 HOURS 55 MINUTES

PHOENIX, USA

10 HOURS 50 MINUTES

PITTSBURGH, USA

8 HOURS 30 MINUTES

POITIERS, FRANCE

1 HOUR 25 MINUTES

PORTO, PORTUGAL

2 HOURS 5 MINUTES

PRAGUE, CZECH REPUBLIC

1 HOUR 50 MINUTES

PULA, CROATIA

2 HOURS 15 MINUTES

RALEIGH, USA

8 HOURS 50 MINUTES

REYKJAVIK, ICELAND

3 HOURS

RIGA, LATVIA

2 HOURS 50 MINUTES

RIJEKA, CROATIA

2 HOURS 15 MINUTES

RIMINI, ITALY

2 HOURS 10 MINUTES

RIYADH, SAUDI ARABIA

6 HOURS 15 MINUTES

ROME, ITALY

2 HOURS 30 MINUTES

ROTTERDAM, NETHERLANDS

1 HOUR 15 MINUTES

SALZBURG, AUSTRIA

1 HOUR 55 MINUTES

SAN DIEGO, USA

11 HOURS 5 MINUTES

SAN FRANCISCO, USA

10 HOURS 55 MINUTES

SANTIAGO, SPAIN

2 HOURS

SAO PAULO, BRAZIL

11 HOURS 40 MINUTES

SEATTLE, USA

9 HOURS 40 MINUTES

SEOUL, REPUBLIC OF KOREA

10 HOURS 50 MINUTES

SEVILLE, SPAIN

2 HOURS 40 MINUTES

SHANGHAI, CHINA

11 HOURS 15 MINUTES

SHANNON, REPUBLIC OF IRELAND

1 HOUR 20 MINUTES

SINGAPORE, SINGAPORE

12 HOURS 45 MINUTES

SKOPJE, MACEDONIA

3 HOURS 30 MINUTES

SOFIA, BULGARIA

3 HOURS 15 MINUTES

SPLIT, CROATIA

2 HOURS 20 MINUTES

ST ETIENNE, FRANCE

1 HOUR 30 MINUTES

ST JOHNS, CANADA

5 HOURS 25 MINUTES

ST KITTS, ST KITTS

9 HOURS

ST LOUIS, USA

9 HOURS 25 MINUTES

ST LUCIA, ST LUCIA

8 HOURS 45 MINUTES

ST PETERSBURG, RUSSIA

3 HOURS

STAVANGER, NORWAY

1 HOUR 35 MINUTES

STOCKHOLM, SWEDEN

2 HOURS 25 MINUTES

STRASBOURG, FRANCE

1 HOUR 20 MINUTES

STUTTGART, GERMANY

1 HOUR 35 MINUTES

TALLINN, ESTONIA

2 HOURS 55 MINUTES

TAMPA, USA

9 HOURS 25 MINUTES

TANGIER, MOROCCO

2 HOURS 50 MINUTES

TASHKENT, UZBEKISTAN

6 HOURS 35 MINUTES

TBILISI, GEORGIA

4 HOURS 55 MINUTES

TEHRAN, IRAN

5 HOURS 40 MINUTES

TEL AVIV, ISRAEL

4 HOURS 45 MINUTES

TENERIFE, CANARY ISLANDS

4 HOURS 10 MINUTES

THESSALONIKI, GREECE

3 HOURS 10 MINUTES

TOBAGO, TRINIDAD & TOBAGO

8 HOURS 55 MINUTES

TOKYO, JAPAN

11 HOURS 30 MINUTES

TORONTO, CANADA

7 HOURS 50 MINUTES

TOULOUSE, FRANCE

1 HOUR 50 MINUTES

TRIESTE, ITALY

2 HOURS 10 MINUTES

TRIPOLI, LIBYA

3 HOURS 40 MINUTES

TUNIS, TUNISIA

2 HOURS 50 MINUTES

TURIN, ITALY

1 HOUR 45 MINUTES

VALENCIA, SPAIN

2 HOURS 25 MINUTES

VANCOUVER, CANADA

9 HOURS 50 MINUTES

VÄSTERÅS, SWEDEN

2 HOURS 10 MINUTES

VENICE, ITALY

2 HOURS

VERONA, ITALY

2 HOURS

VICTORIA FALLS, ZIMBABWE

10 HOURS 30 MINUTES

VIENNA, AUSTRIA

2 HOURS 10 MINUTES

VILNIUS, LITHUANIA

2 HOURS 50 MINUTES

WARSAW, POLAND

2 HOURS 25 MINUTES

WASHINGTON, USA

8 HOURS 5 MINUTES

ZAGREB, CROATIA

2 HOURS 10 MINUTES

ZURICH, SWITZERLAND

1 HOUR 50 MINUTES

Elsewhere, Perhaps [1]

Lesley Naa Norle Lokko

Positions

'Where you live is who you are.' [2]

'[1959] What is apartheid? It depends who's answering. If you ask a member of the South African government, he will tell you that it is separate and parallel development of white and black. If you ask an ordinary white man who supports the policy, he will tell you that it is the means of keeping South Africa white. If you ask a black man…well, he may give you any of a dozen answers arising out of whatever aspect of apartheid he has been brought up short against that day, for to him it is neither an ideological concept, nor a policy, but a context in which his whole life, learning, working, loving, is rigidly enclosed. He could give you a list of the laws that restrict him from aspiring to most of the aims of any civilised person, or enjoying the pleasures that everyone else takes for granted. But it is unlikely that he will.' [3]

In *S/Z*, Barthes' seminal work on the relationship between reading and writing, he states that his goal is, 'to make the reader no longer a consumer,

1 With apologies to Amos Oz. 'Elsewhere, Perhaps' is the translated title of his 1981 novel. Oz, A. *Elsewhere, Perhaps* (London: Picador, 1981.)

2 For a much more substantial reading of the phrase, see 'Geo-demographics: where you live is who you are', by David Morley in which he aligns consumer market research, identity and census segmentation. In the UK, the ACORN (A Classification of Residential Neighbourhoods) system divides the population into 150,000 districts for census purposes using the 1.3million postcodes in current use, which are then converted into 54 residential types for marketing purposes. In the US, a similar system operates known as the PRIZM (Potential Rating Index by Zip Market). In their most basic forms, both systems (and doubtless similar other systems in other countries) argue that the single best predictor of lifestyle and consumer patterns (and, disturbingly as the last general election showed, political affiliation) is place of residence.
See Morley, D. 'The Media, the City and the Suburbs', in Morley, D. *Home Territories: Media, Mobility, Identity* (London: Routledge, 2000) p 140–141.

3 Gordimer, N. 'References: Codes of Culture' *Living in Hope and History: Notes from Our Century* (London: Bloomsbury, 1999) p 105.

but a producer of the text', to make the reader aware of 'what can be read but not written'.[4] Beneath, or perhaps between, the words 'here', 'there' and 'elsewhere' lies something – another story, perhaps – that, over the past few weeks as I have worked on this piece, has been surprisingly hard to grasp. Here-There-Elsewhere. Three words signifying… what?

In this instance, as writer and reader, and mindful of Morrison's sharp observation that crucially, writers are readers before they are writers, I am interested in constructing and describing my own text out of the narrative that is suggested by the words: Here-There-Elsewhere. 'Here' and 'there' align neatly, linguistically as well as epistemologically. Mutually interdependent. 'Elsewhere', on the other hand, is problematic, the third spoke in the wheel. By its own definition, 'elsewhere' is both somewhere and nowhere, a place that is known but not fixed. It implies movement, deferral, a continuous process of arrival. It implies an edge. The edge of Empire. It comes to me slowly that 'elsewhere', by virtue of history and genealogy, is the place (literal, metaphorical) in which I have mostly lived. Here? There? Where? It depends on who's doing the talking. This chapter is an attempt to look at positions – geographical, biological, ideological. Some things may be written, and not read.

Position I – Here: Right Little, Tight Little Island [5]

> [Westminster, 1999] A House of Commons standing committee is discussing the government's proposal to replace welfare benefits (of around £46 per week) with a system of food vouchers worth £35 a week. "Many asylum seekers come from communities where wealth may be stored in jewellery", explains the Home Office minister, Mike O'Brien, "and it is right for us to take account of that wealth."
>
> "Is the minister suggesting", asks Dianne Abbott, MP, "that asylum seekers should sell their jewellery, perhaps their wedding rings, as an alternative to the government meeting its moral and international responsibilities to provide a reasonable level of support?" When O'Brien replies, "I certainly am suggesting that," a Tory backbencher is heard to mutter: "You'll be wanting the gold fillings out of their teeth next."[6]

Here-There. A rhizomatic jumble springs to mind: home/away; now/then; belonging/otherness; native/foreign; immigrant/migrant; race/place… you get my drift. The semi-colon (;) and the slash (/) are a neat cartography that separates and contains the signifiers, moulding them into convenient, if slightly dubious, pairs. A shift left or right results in a slightly different reading, different connotations, particularly in time and space. Between 'tourist' and 'then', for example, or between 'native' and 'foreign' and 'race' and 'place'. Depending on who and where you are, depending on how attuned you may be to 'the layer of common culture spread thin over the Worlds, First, Second and Third',[7] the assumptions generated either by the pairing of opposites or by the list itself will be substantially different. I have a hunch that the differences are significant.

Most of the literature focusing on issues of travel, tourism and even migration/displacement assumes a West–North orientation, even if the identity of the speaker/writer has at times been more expansive. Although

I will return to this point later, these associations invariably place the West as the point of departure from which most trips begin. (Speaking from bitter experience, it is easier and cheaper to get from one African country to another via a European capital). Major world airline routes [see Fig.1], serve a largely white or at least pale-skinned market on the North America>Europe>Far East axis. Even in our supposedly global era it must be obvious to anyone looking around airport lounges that the majority of travellers and tourists are white. Yet every year between 2.5 and 3 million people emigrate in the world. More than half of those go to the US, Germany, Canada and Australia. At the beginning of the 21st century 130 million people live outside the country of their birth. Not all of these travellers are white. Not all of these people are travellers. As Curtis & Pajaczkowska have noted, 'the opposite of tourism is not staying at home' but 'the involuntary travel associated with the predicament of the immigrant'.[8] Who is the immigrant? Well, it depends who's answering.

Contrary to popular belief, immigration is itself a complex and highly destabilising experience. The processes of immigration may bond previously disconnected peoples together in the same time and place, but the reasons and means by which people emigrate or move from one place to another are often very different. Ziauddin Sardar argues that, 'the dominant epistemology of the West lumps together the vast diversity of peoples all over the world into one gigantic category of Otherness, so that the distinctiveness of a particular Other…[is] lost in the generality shared with all Others, that of being different…from the West'.[9] From romantic notions of exiled American and British writers exchanging Dublin for Paris or Manhattan for Madrid, to the desperate discovery of 58 bodies in a freight truck bound for Dover, it is simply not possible to simplify the myriad experiences of movement, exile and estrangement as being in any way alike. At the very least, where one emigrates to significantly impacts the experience.

The idea (if not the actual body) of immigration in British history is equally complex. Unlike the US and most countries in the Americas, Britain (particularly England) does not include immigration as part of its national myth. To take a very basic example: in 1883, Emma Lazarus wrote the words which are inscribed as a welcome on the Statue of Liberty,

4 Barthes, R. *S/Z* (Paris: Farrar, Straus and Giroux, 1974) trans. Richard Miller.

5 Taken from the *Guardian* article, 'Right Little, Tight Little Island', by DD Gutenplan, Saturday, 22 July, 2000.

6 Ibid.

7 Gordimer, N. 'References: Codes of Culture' *Living in Hope and History: Notes from Our Century* (London: Bloomsbury) 1999, p 44.

8 Curtis, B., and Pajaczkowska, C., in 'Getting There: travel, time and narrative' in Robertson, G. et al (eds) *Traveller's Tales: Narratives of Home and Displacement* (London: Routledge, 1994) p 202.

9 Sardar, Z., quoted in 'Cosmopolitics', in Morley, D. *Home Territories: Media, Mobility, Identity* (London: Routledge, 2000) p 232.

'Give me your tired, your poor, your huddled masses, yearning to breathe free'.[10] Whilst US policy towards immigrants has departed radically from the arms-outstretched generosity described by Lazarus (at a time, incidentally, when the majority of immigrants to the US were white/European) there are striking and fundamental differences in the way in which outsider populations are absorbed and conceived of in relation to the construction of national identity in both countries.

Historically, in an island monarchy such as Britain, nationality was defined by case law and was principally concerned with allegiance to the king, defined by a combination of land, loyalty and birth,[11] exchangeable commodities between the monarch and his subjects. Astonishingly for an island-empire, it was not until 1948 that Britain's first citizenship law was passed (and perhaps not coincidentally, a year after India's independence and the beginnings of the end of imperial rule). In terms of the unease and ambiguity surrounding the identity of the immigrant, it is probably empire and the two basic conflicting languages of 'belonging' that empire produced – loyalty and race – that have been most instrumental in shaping and directing public opinion and understanding regarding what it means to be British. At that time (1948), loyalty, the historical principle on which nationality had hitherto rested, remained essentially intact, allowing colonial settlers to claim entitlement to national status as a reward for their loyalty to the king's dominion territories (Australia, New Zealand, South Africa and Canada). Race, the other category of 'belonging' resulting from Britain's imperial history, has remained far more problematic.

In the postcolonial periods of the 60s and 70s, the immigration debates in Britain revolved around labour shortages and the settlement of blacks from the Commonwealth Caribbean countries to fill in the gaps. (Ironically, much the same debate revolves around current labour shortages in the NHS and in British schools, with Filipino nurses and Australian and South African replacement teachers being drafted in to fill in the gaps.) In the 80s and 90s, coterminous with the rising numbers of immigrants from the former colonial powers (almost exclusively non-white), legislation against such settlement became increasingly restrictive, culminating in Thatcher's 1981 Nationality Act which dissolved the long-standing right-of-birth principle. From 1983 children born in the UK did not receive the automatic right to citizenship: one's parents also had to have entitlement. In the same time period Australians and South Africans (whites) born in independent countries 6–10,000 miles away, for example, only had to claim one grandparent (the 'Grandfather Clause') to achieve the same status. Partly because of this uncertainty surrounding 'Britishness', and partly because the concept of the colonial was similarly ambiguous (colonial, ruler, settler, ex-pat, neo-colonial, etc.), 'race' has become the dominant factor in contemporary public discussion about immigration and British identity.

In March of this year John Townend, the Conservative MP for Yorkshire East said in a speech to his local association 'our homogenous Anglo Saxon society has been seriously undermined by the massive immigration, particularly coloured immigration, that has taken place since the war. We should certainly have acted sooner and I believe Enoch Powell was right in his pessimistic forecast'.[12] He went on. 'Illegal immigrants now have a new ploy. They call themselves asylum seekers. In my view, the only way to deal with the problem is to send them back quickly. Many come from violent societies and, inevitably, crime is already beginning to rise'.[13] The associations created by the linking of 'race' with 'immigrants' and, subsequently, 'aliens' are directly responsible for the feelings of alienation experienced by so many 'people of colour' (terrible phrase) in Britain today. 'It is this identification of people of colour with 'immigrants' and the systematic assimilation of 'immigrant' to 'alien' in law, in public discussion and in thought that [has] create[d] a context in which black Britons can perceive themselves as strangers in the land of their birth or choice'.[14]

At present, there are six categories of 'national', with varying degrees of rights, identities and obligations. British Citizen (the only category to confer the full set of human rights); British Dependent Territories Citizen; British Overseas Citizen; British Subject; British Protected Person and British National (Overseas). It is in these distinctions that the full scale of empire, territory and the complex notion of 'belonging' can be read. I was born in the UK. I am a British Citizen. My siblings, who were born in Ghana, are 'subjects'. I do not know yet what the difference actually *means*.

Position II – There: Out of Place [15]

> "Dirty nigger!" Or simply, "Look, a Negro!"
>
> 'I came into the world imbued with the will to find a meaning in things, my spirit filled with the desire to attain to the source of the world, and then I found I was an object in the midst of other objects'[16]

In retrospect, yes, we moved around a lot. Although I was born in the UK, I like to think I grew up in Ghana, West Africa. I like to think of myself as

10 From the *Guardian* article, 'High Fliers Get First Class Welcome But Unskilled Stay Grounded', in Monday, 30 October 2000 issue by Duncan Campbell in Los Angeles.

11 For a much more accomplished and insightful account of how immigration policy and law in the UK has been shaped (and continues to be shaped) by ideas about belonging, English-ness and 'otherness', see Christopher Davis' excellent essay, 'Exchanging the African: Meetings at a Crossroads of the Diaspora' in Mudimbe, Y., and Engel, S., (ed) *Diaspora and Immigration, The South Atlantic Quarterly*, 98: 1/2 Winter/Spring 1999, Duke University Press, Durham, NC, 1999, p 59–82.

12 From the *Guardian* article, 'Tory Leaflets Inflame Race Issue after MP's Attack', in Thursday, March 29 issue by Nicholas Watt and Patrick Wintour.

13 Ibid.

14 op cit., Davis, C., p 67.

15 From the title of his 1999 memoirs, Said, E. *Out of Place* (New York: Alfred Knopf, 1999).

16 Fanon, F., 'The Fact of Blackness', in Donald, J., and Rattansi, A., (eds.) *Race, Culture & Difference* (The Open University, 1992; reprinted by Sage Publications, 1994) p 220.

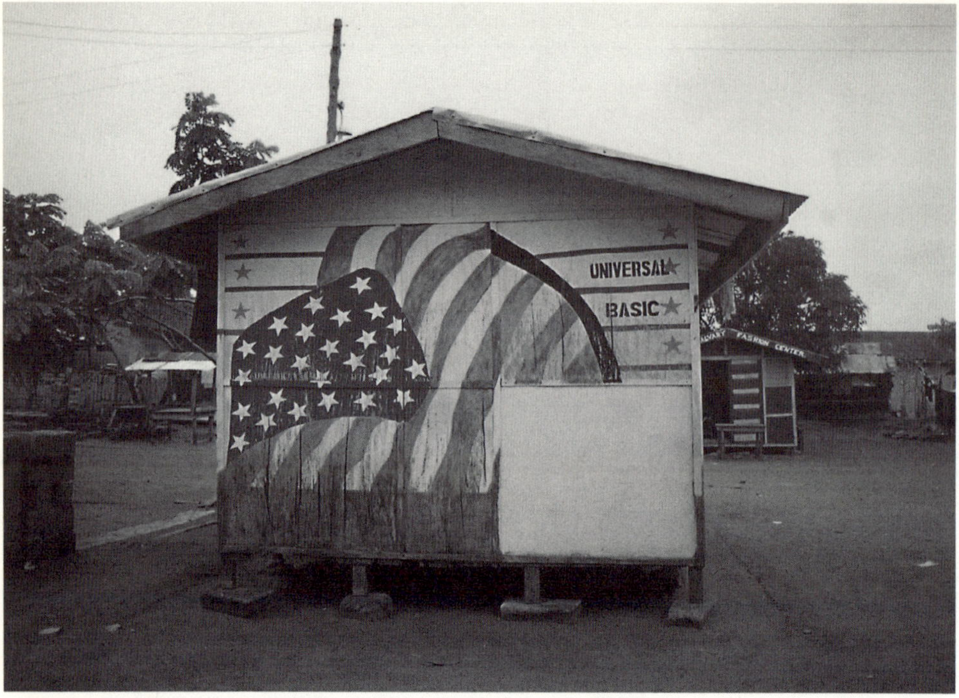

Rights of Man Hairdressers
Mamprobi, Ghana, 2001.
Photograph: L Lokko.

'coming from' there, having roots, a sense of oneself as belonging 'somewhere'. In reality, however, there was far too much to-ing and fro-ing. Some time in Scotland, some time in Ghana; some time in Scotland, more time in Ghana. Back and forth, like ping-pong. Nowadays there are many terms to describe what seemed to us to be unusual (in the sense that we always seemed to be leaving people 'behind' – airports, for my family, were sites of extreme trauma or extreme joy) and quite normal (in the sense that we knew many other people for whom this was equally true). Nowadays, almost forty years later, the talk is of movement: distance, displacement, diaspora. Metaphors of travel and displacement abound. The world is 'getting smaller' (they say) as time and space compress. Boundaries shift and fragment, identities dissolve. Back then, things were different, we were different. Scotland: 'and where are you from?'

Like so many men of his generation, my father left Ghana in his twenties, just after independence, and came to Britain (or Germany, or Russia or France… Nkrumah[17] was not fussy). When he returned some ten years later, as a qualified surgeon, he brought with him a wife and children. In that period many men (and perhaps even a few women, although I personally don't remember any) returned home with new families. These families were both literally and culturally new. For many of the men who journeyed overseas marrying 'outside' was the last step in a series of rapid breaks with tradition and the abrupt acquisition of a 'new' way of life – formal education, a profession, a bungalow in Accra (the capital city of Africa's first independent nation) and perhaps small car.

In the neighbourhoods in which we lived there were many, many 'half-castes'. English-Ghanaian; Scots-Ghanaian (a popular combo); German-Ghanaian; Dutch-Ghanaian… Russian-Ghanaian, even Chinese-

Ghanaian. Somewhere along the way we were asked to stop referring to ourselves as 'half-castes'. It wasn't nice. Mulatto... now, there was a better term, sophisticated, more cultured. Someone later pointed out that that term referred to the union between a donkey and a mule and it was hurriedly withdrawn. No one used the term 'mixed-race'. Race? I doubt we would have known what it meant. I knew my father was Ghanaian and my mother Scots. As a result of this I knew my father was 'dark' and my mother 'light'. I knew too that what I was (half one, half the other) had been 'constructed', quite literally, through them. I loved the symmetry of what I perceived the equation to be: 'dark-brown' and 'light-brown' = 'medium-brown' (me). In every case I saw, and there were many, the outcome was exactly the same. Mixing paints one day I announced, to their amusement, that 'you can't be black and you can't be white, 'cos if you were, I'd be grey!'. A childish observation: probably accurate.

In ways that I still do not fully understand, our identities were intertwined with those of our parents: without them 'we', as a tiny, minority sub-culture, could not exist. We depended on them, not only as children depend on adults (parents) but in a raw, biological sense. This dependency was an uneasy one: within it subtle power struggles existed, mirrored by or perhaps resulting from the fragile state of many of the marriages. Back then in the early 60s few white mothers worked: for many of them marrying a professional meant an escape from depressed, post-war Europe and an upwards move in class. (This confrontation between race and class brought about its own peculiar vocabulary – and often vicious resentment.) The majority stayed at home, spending proportionately more time with the children and constructing (perhaps purposefully?) a strange, hybrid 'home' condition in which many of the women struggled to assert their own cultures. Possibilities arose to 'lean' one way or the other: through language, dress, food, especially. We begged for 'beans-on-toast', ketchup and Coke. Few of us learned a local language. We spoke English, or German or French, our mothers anxious to 'protect' our accents. They talked of us going 'home' to study, like our fathers had done and what an advantage *we* would have, compared to *them*... knowing the language, culture, food and so on. In their small coffee–and–cake circles (run by the German mothers; all welcome), they gossiped (and despaired) about 'them'. How 'they do things here'; how 'clumsy–stupid– backward–lazy the maids/garden boys/drivers... are. Ach, *they* are just *so* different'. I would feel my cheeks redden, aware that listening in or giving even the *tiniest* gesture of understanding was a betrayal of sorts. In 1978 the government declared that all Ghanaian children would begin the day at school by singing the national pledge, like Americans. At the international school which I and my siblings attended there were few half-castes and even fewer Ghanaians, especially in the early years. Anxious not to appear different, we would stare at the ground and mumble the pledge as the rest of the school watched, patronisingly amused. It was excruciating. Torn between wanting to be British, or, even better, American, and *having* to be Ghanaian... from

17 **Dr Kwame Nkrumah, first Ghanaian head of state and the founding father of the Organization of African Unity. Nkrumah sent many young Ghanaians overseas on national scholarships; he himself had studied in the US between 1935 and 1945.**

where did this awareness come? I read Enid Blyton and longed to be Daryl Rivers.[18]

We were vaguely aware that it was 'better' to have a European mother than say, an Indian mother or (and there were probably only two or three) a Russian or Yugoslav mother. We were not able to articulate the instincts which divided the world (East/West; European/non-European; First World/Second World) but we knew what they meant. Kids who spoke German at home ate waffles and potatoes, baked stollen at Christmas (in the heat) and wore Adidas to school. Their mothers were great cooks. Scottish mothers became (by and large) teachers of different sorts. Many of the English went home. Many of the marriages failed, brought about by one 'cultural' catastrophe or another.

Ghana: 'Obroni! Obroni! Obroni molasses!' When we walked/rode/hung out together, children would run past shouting and laughing at us, 'Obroni! Obroni! Obroni molasses!' 'Obroni' meant 'white person'. 'Obroni molasses' meant 'white-person-the-colour-of-molasses'. There was curiosity. I don't recall animosity per se. When Flight Lieutenant Jerry John Rawlings, himself half Scots, became President of Ghana, there were those among us who were secretly pleased, relieved. It proved we belonged. We knew that 'Obroni!', the signifier of difference, was not the same as the one encountered on the yearly (or every two, four or perhaps even ten-yearly trip to Europe). Nigger. Sambo. Wog. Over there, (here?) the difference was hostile. Now, when I 'return' to Ghana, I see it becoming so.

Position III – Elsewhere: Best of Both?

> 'She went on holiday to Lourenço Marques and she fell in love, yes – but it was with what she suddenly imagined real life to be. She fell in love with that wailing fado, she wanted passion and tragedy. Passion and tragedy were not where she would have looked for them, here – they were around her, but in the lives of blacks. I know Ruthie. Poor thing, she was all our colonial bourgeois illusions rolled into one; she thought that [Mozambique] was Europe. Latin. She thought it was European culture. And she hated South Africa – but she thought what was wrong with this country was that it didn't have that.'[19]

> 'Who would have thought that "travel" could come to mean so many things?'[20]

'Did you travel?'

The colonial tradition of 'leave' – going 'home' once a year to Europe – has somehow found its way to Ghana, to the 'mixed-race' (in hindsight) households, the upper middle-class Ghanaian households and to the schools the children of such households attend. Every September, at the start of the new year, every year, the same question: did you travel? No need to ask where. Those children whose parents can afford it look forward to September, to showing off new clothes, shoes, hairstyles and, most importantly, 'new' vocabulary, acquired at breakneck speed through movies, TV and holiday acquaintances. Those whose parents cannot, are quiet.

Ironically, in much the same way as tourists consume the 'other', we (foreign exchange rates permitting) attempted to consume the West.

Curtis & Pajaczkowska describe the 'three paradigmatic moments of tourism: eating, shopping and sightseeing.' Eating and sightseeing were almost irrelevant: being able to order a Big Mac had almost nothing to do with the taste of the burger but everything to do with the ability to casually drop the words, 'yeah, and when we went into the McDonald's...' into conversations 'back home'. We travelled not to see or eat the West, but to bring it back. Trips to Europe, contrary to Freudian analyses of vacation time being 'child-time', were trips into the *future*,[21] into an artificially adult setting where, once a year, usually without our parents, we (mis)handled 'real'[22] money, often spending the entire holiday's allowance in two or three days. Why are these observations significant?

I want to move now towards the most difficult and knotty set of issues in this piece, to the Third Position. (Ouch!) Looking back through time and history, as I am whilst I write this piece, and trying to locate the culture(s) I inhabited as a child (and to some extent, still continue to inhabit) in a broader, more critical context, I sense that something is missing. Europe was neither the place in which we 'symbolically stopped growing old',[23] nor was it the place in which we encountered the 'other'. We were neither immigrants in the classical sense, nor were we tourists. At home in Scotland we were 'other'. At home in Ghana, we were 'other' too. With the peculiar mistrust that accompanies miscegenation, we were both – but more often and for me, at least, more interestingly, we were neither.

To return to an earlier point, so much has already been written about the meaning and associations of travelling, of being 'on holiday' or taking a trip. From the search for the 'place in which happiness may be found'[24] to the ways in which travel fuses 'two fundamental axes of

18 Daryl Rivers is the 'heroine' of the *Mallory Towers* series of children's books by Enid Blyton. Whilst I read everything Blyton ever wrote, from the *Famous Five* to the *Secret Seven*, it was the English boarding school 'experience' that I most craved. It appeared then to be utterly out of reach.

19 Gordimer, N. *A Sport of Nature* (New York: A Knopf, Inc., 1987) p 47–48.

20 Arshi, S., et al, in 'Why Travel? Tropics, Entropics and Apotropaics', in 'Getting There: Travel, Time and Narrative'; in Robertson, G. et al (eds) *Traveller's Tales: Narratives of Home and Displacement* (London: Routledge, 1994) p 225.

21 In another sense, the Western vision presented to us was also the vision towards which Africa (or whichever 'Third World' nation one departed from) was supposedly travelling. Europe (or the US) represented the future to which we felt we ought to belong. Those kids whose mothers were Russian, or Indian, or Malaysian, for example, were not so 'lucky' for obvious reasons. At that time, McDonald's had not reached Red Square.

22 When we (as a family) first returned to Ghana in 1966, the exchange rate was roughly 2:1 (Cedis 2 to £1.00). When I left in 1981, it was roughly Cedis 2,000 to £1.00. Today, it is approximately Cedis 10,000 to £1.00). One's sense of the 'worth' of money was unstable, partly because the yardsticks by which value could be calculated were constantly shifting.

23 Ibid., p 202.

24 op cit., Curtis, B., and Pajaczkowska, C., p 199.

reality, time and space',[25] travel and movement have become the dominant metaphors in our attempts to understand and control what appears to be an increasingly unstable condition of modernity. Caren Kaplan suggests that 'the prevalence of metaphors of travel and displacement in [this body of] critical work suggests that the modern era is fascinated by the experience of distance and estrangement, reproducing these notions through articulations of subjectivity and poetics.'[26] Nomadicism and the romantic notion of the pilgrim, exile or nomad has long been a staple of Western art, literature and even theological tradition, as embodied in Christianity's story of man's expulsion from the Garden of Eden onwards. It is possible to trace a line through medieval and nineteenth century narratives of exile and sojourn, through the 'great' nineteenth and twentieth century anthropological texts and ending (or perhaps not yet) with contemporary travel writers, and even writers who are not of the 'travel' genre whose work examines space, distance and territory.[27] We can detect throughout a fascination with the 'heroic' nomad or noble savage, living beyond Western modernity and in possession of qualities that have somehow escaped contamination by the demands of modern life. (Forget hunger, poverty, fear, oppression, etc.) In contemporary terms, this fascination has often been translated as cosmopolitanism, a desire for diversity and a 'multicultural' society. However, as Morley remarks, 'once one inserts the question of power into the equation, one might equally say that, a cosmopolitan is simply one empowered to decide who is provincial.' The oppositions between home and abroad, staying and moving, have often 'been naturalised along lines of gender (female, domestic space vs. male travel), class (the active alienated bourgeoisie vs. the stagnant, soulful poor) and race/culture (modern, rootless Westerners vs. traditional, rooted natives)'.[28]

The logical move out of the impasse brought on between here/there; male/female; black/white (and any number of related oppositions you care to think of) is, of course, the hybrid. Conceptually and structurally, the 'both/and' position relieves some of the pressure exerted by 'either/or' and certainly, in terms of the globalising trends of postmodernity, has become a necessary and much valued construct, particularly within the fields of cultural studies and postcolonial theory. Stuart Hall's description of hybrids as 'people who belong to more than one world, speak more than one language (literally and metaphorically) inhabit more than one identity and have more than one home; who have learned to negotiate and translate between cultures and who, because they are irrevocably the product of several interlocking histories and cultures, have learned to live with, and indeed speak from, *difference*[29] is persuasive, and probably largely true. However, to repeat the point made a few paragraphs ago, in terms of our relationship to place, we were not hybrids, we were...what? Can the hybrid be thought of differently? What is the position of one who is not 'both/and' but 'neither/nor'? Not nomad, not migrant, not native. There are no real antonyms for 'hybrid', despite my best efforts to locate one. Perhaps that is not the point.

So, finally, having written myself into a little cul-de-sac all of my own, it is Gayatri Spivak's caution that is most immediately useful in constructing a possible way out. She cautions that too much [celebratory] hybridity 'leaves all the old problems of class exploitation and racial oppression unresolved.'[30] Despite the intense (and often seductive) temptation to assume that spatial and territorial displacements engender new forms of community and understanding (i.e., hybrid communities/persons/histories) I agree unreservedly with Vered Amit-Talai who warns us that it is important not to 'confuse the relationship between uncertainty, deterritorialisation and boundary. In celebrating interstitiality, [one can] end up being quite cavalier about the necessary and difficult work required to construct new forms of identity.'[31]

In many ways, the culture(s) I am attempting to explore emotionally as well as culturally is so small as to be historically insignificant. Half-castes (and I stress here that they – we? – are by no means the only form of hybrid identity) make up barely 1% of the population of Ghana. People of 'hybrid identity' probably make up far less than that in the UK. But each year, with 3 million people on the move globally, despite the 'hyperbole of global fluidity,'[32] identity is fast-becoming the most contested cultural issue of our times. Statistically, hybrid, mixed and co-dependent identities are on the rise. To return to the naivete of childhood for a moment: mixing paint was relatively straightforward, if linguistically inaccurate. Black + White = Brown. The mix is visually far more complex these days, even if the hidden power-positions remain the same. Yet those same power-positions have relied primarily on visual difference for so long. Black = Non-White. The terms are very clear. What now?

Just as this essay marks the beginning of a different type of work (I am an architect and trained to think in concrete oppositions: inside/outside; ground/sky; structure/skin; soft/hard, etc), it is almost impossible for me to construct an end. And all pieces require some type of closure. Perhaps I can leave this to Stuart Hall:

> 'It may be true that the self is always, in a sense, a fiction, just as the kind of "closures" which are required to create communities of identification – nation, ethnic group – are arbitrary closures...temporary, partial. [All] identity is constructed across difference...but doesn't the acceptance of the fictional or narrative status of identity...also require the

25 Ibid., p 199.

26 Kaplan, C., in *Questions of Travel: Postmodern Discourses of Displacement* (Duke University Press, 1996) p 1.

27 Rushdie, Okri, Ondaatje, Mahlouf, Roy, Smith... far too many to list here.

28 Clifford, J., quoted in 'Discrepant and Variable Cosmopolitanisms', in Morley, D. *Home Territories: Media, Mobility, Identity*, (London: Routledge, 2000), p 232.

29 Ibid., p 207.

30 Spivak, G., quoted in 'Cosmopolitics', in Morley, D. *Home Territories: Media, Mobility, Identity* (London: Routledge, 2000) p 233.

31 Ibid., p 227.

32 Amit-Talai, V., quoted in 'The Migrant in Limbo', in op cit., Morley, D., p 227.

moment of arbitrary closure? Is it possible for there to be an action or identity in the world without arbitrary closure…without what one might call the necessity [of] meaning of the end of the sentence? Potentially, discourse is endless, an infinite semiosis of meaning, but to say nothing at all, in particular, you have to stop talking. Of course, every full stop is provisional. The next sentence will take nearly all of it back. So what is this "ending"?…It is not forever…not underpinned by any infinite guarantees, but just now, this is what I mean; this is who I am.'[33]

33 Hall, S., 'Minimal Selves' in Appignanesi, L., (ed) *Identity: The Real Me* ICA Documents 6 (London: Institute of Contemporary Arts, 1988), p 45.

Notes

Markus Vater

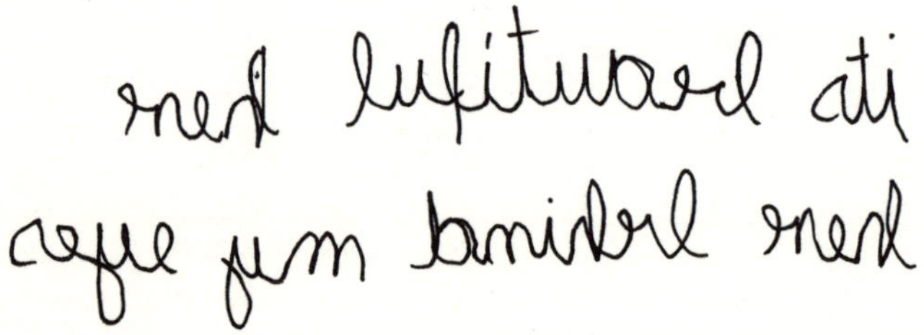

Realize!
you just been
to a place in
this universe
you will never
be again. But
don't be sad.

ti fi gninebrow m'I
taht ecnebrearnias a si
eer yaju nwaloar eht
nwaju esralr yaj fi
otni sdrtow tano cepue
emac eht si nua eht
celtalr eht no egnaro
?sdram ritulabbwre fo

A street is not
just a connection
between a place A
and a place B. It is
much more a third
place much bigger
than A and B.
But it's a very
alien place.

what do you
think? How does
the place look like
where all the words
are going to?

How on European
imagine a chinese
imagine how on
European imagine
a chinese.

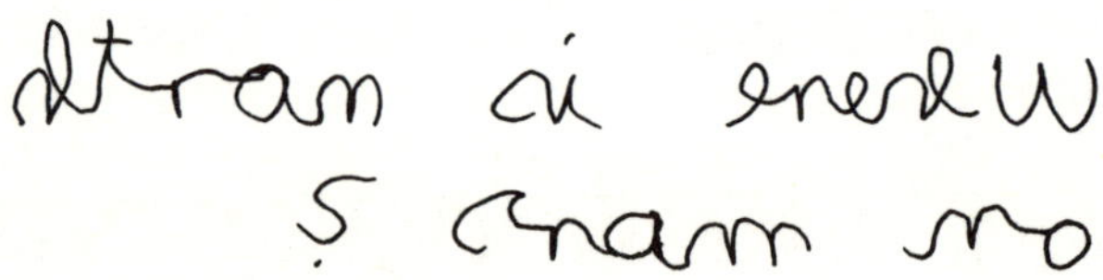

Reading Further

Paul O'Neill

A selection of *Lonely Planet Guides* of the country, city, place or continent of your choice.
Lonely Planet Publications

Abbas, Ackbar
Hong Kong: Culture and the Politics of Disappearance
Minneapolis: University of Minnesota Press, 1997

Angelou, Maya
I Know Why the Caged Bird Sings
London: Virago Press, 1993

Appleton, Jay
The Experience of Landscape
London: John Wiley & Son, 1996

Appleton, Jay
The Symbolism of Habitat: An Interpretation of Landscape in the Arts
Washington: University of Washington Press, 1991

Aragon, Louis
Paris Peasant
Boston: Exact Change, 1994

Ardener, Shirley (ed.)
Women and Space: Ground Rules and Social Maps
Oxford: Berg Publishers, 1993

Augé, Marc
Non-Places: Introduction to an Anthropology of Supermodernity
London & New York: Verso, 1995

Bachelard, Gaston
The Poetics of Space
Boston: Beacon Press Books, 1994

Bakhtin, M.M.
The Dialogical Imagination
Austin: University of Texas Press, 1981

Ballard, J.G.
Concrete Island
New York: Vintage, 1994

Ballard, J.G.
The Atrocity Exhibition
London: Flamingo, 2001

Baricco, Alessandro
Ocean Sea
London: Hamish Hamilton, 1999

Barnes, Julian
A History of The World in 10½ Chapters
London: Picador, 1990

Barthes, Roland
Image Music Text
London: Fontana Press, 1977

Barthes, Roland
Roland Barthes by Roland Barthes
London: Papermac, 1995

Barthes, Roland
Mythologies
London: Paladin Books, 1977

Baskas, Harriet
Stuck at the Airport: A Traveller's Survival Guide
New York: Fireside Books, 2001

Baudelaire, Charles
Paris Spleen
New York: W.W. Norton, 1970

Baudrillard, Jean
America
London: Verso, 1988

Baudrillard, Jean
The System of Objects
London & New York: Routledge, 2000

Baudrillard, Jean
Simulacra and Simulation
Ann Arbor: The University of Michigan Press, 1994

Baum, Frank L.
The Wizard of Oz
London: Penguin Books, 1995

Bauman, Zygmunt
Globalization: The Human Consequences
Cambridge: Polity Press, 1998

Bell, Michael & Sze Tsung Leong
Slow Space
New York: Monacelli Press, 1998

Benjamin, Walter
The Arcades Project
Cambridge, Massachusetts & London: Belknap Press of Harvard University Press, 1999

Benjamin, Walter
One-Way Street
London & New York: Verso Classics, 1997

Bergson, Henri
The Creative Evolution
New York: Zone Books, 1991

Bergson, Henri
Matter and Memory
New York: Zone Books, 1991

Berman, Marshall
All That Is Solid Melts Into Air
London & New York: Verso, 1983

Bhabha, Homi. K
The Location of Culture
London & New York: Routledge, 1994

Bhabba, Homi K. (ed.)
Nation and Narration
London & New York: Routledge, 1990

Bickley, Gillian
Hong Kong Invaded!
Hong Kong: Hong Kong University Press, 2001

Blanchot, Maurice
The Space of Literature (1955)
Lincoln: University of Nebraska, 1982

van Leeuw, Marianne & Anne Pontégnie (eds.)
Origin and Destination – Alighiero Boetti & Douglas Heubler
New York: Art Data, 1988

Bowles, Paul
The Sheltering Sky
London: Palladin, 1993

Blunt, Alison & Gillian Rose (eds.)
Writing Women and Space: Colonial and Postcolonial Geographies
New York: Guilford Press, 1994

Bourdieu, Pierre
Distinction: A Social Critique of the Judgement of Taste
London & New York: Routledge, 1990

Borden, Iain & Jane Rendell, et al.
The Unknown City
Cambridge, Massachusetts: The MIT Press, 2000

Borden, Iain & Jane Rendell (eds.)
Intersections
London & New York: Routledge, 2000

Borges, Jorge Luis
Labyrinths
London: Penguin Books, 1989

Borges, Jorge Luis
The Library of Babel
Boston: David R. Godine, 2000

Borges, Jorge Luis
Atlas
New York: EP Dutton, 1985

Breton, André
Mad Love (L'Amour Fou)
Lincoln: University of Nebraska, 1987

Brown, Mick
The Spiritual Tourist
London: Bloomsbury, 1998

Bulgarkov, Mikhail
The Master and Marguerite
London: Picador, 1996

Burroughs, William
The Naked Lunch
London: Picador, 1986

Butler, Judith
Gender Trouble: Feminism and the Subversion of Identity
London & New York: Routledge, 1990

Butler, Judith et al.
Contingency, Hegemony, Universality
London: Verso, 2000

Cage, John
Silence
New York: Marion Boyars Publishers, 1973

Calvino, Italo
The Castle of Crossed Destinies
New York: Vintage, 1997

Calvino, Italo
If On A Winter's Night A Traveller
London: Picador, 1982

Calvino, Italo
Invisible Cities
London: Minerva, 1997

Camus, Albert
The Plague
London: Penguin Books, 1989

Camus, Albert
The Exile and the Kingdom
London: Penguin Books, 1989

Carrington, Leonora
The Hearing Trumpet
Boston: Exact Change, 1995

Carroll, Lewis
Alice in Wonderland
New York: W.W. Norton, 1992

Carter, Paul
The Road to Botany Bay
London: Faber & Faber, 1988

Carter, Erica, James Donald & Judith Squires (eds.)
Space and Place: Theories of Identity and Location
London: Lawrence & Wishart, 1993

Casey, Edward S.
Getting Back into Place: Toward a Renewed Understanding of the Place World
Bloomington, Indiana: Indiana University Press, 1993

Certeau, Michel de
The Practice of Everyday Life
Berkeley, California: University of California Press, 1984

Certeau, Michel de, et al
The Practice of Everyday Life Volume 2: Living & Cooking
Minneapolis & London: University of Minnesota Press, 1998

Certeau, Michel de
Heterologies: Discourse on The Other
Minneapolis & London: University of Minnesota Press, 1997

Cervantes, Miguel de
Don Quixote
Ware: Wordsworth Edition, 1992

Chambers, Iain
Migrancy, Culture, Identity
London & New York: Routledge, 1994

Chambers, Iain
Border Dialogues: Journeys in Postmodernism
London & New York: Routledge, 1990

Chaney, David
Lifestyles
London & New York: Routledge, 1996

Chatwin, Bruce
The Songlines
New York: Vintage, 1998

Chatwin, Bruce
In Patagonia
New York: Vintage, 1998

Chomsky, Noam
World Order Old and New
New York: Columbia University Press, 1994

Chomsky, Noam & James Peck (eds.)
The Chomsky Reader
London: Serpent's Tail, 1988

Cheung, C.H. & David Y.H. Wu (eds.)
The Globalisation of Chinese Food
London: Curzon Press, 2001

Clarke, David
Hong Kong Art: Culture and Colonialism
London: Reaktion Books, 2001

Clifford, James
Routes: Travel and Translation
London: Harvard Press, 1997

Clifford, James
On Collecting Art & Culture
Cambridge, Massachusetts: Minnesota University Press, 1995

Colomina, Beatriz (ed.)
Sexuality and Space
New York: Princeton Architectural Press, 1992

Columbus, Christopher
The Diary of Christopher Columbus's First Voyage to America, 1492-1493
(Norman: University of Oklahoma Press, 1989)

Conrad, Joseph
Heart of Darkness
London: Penguin Books, 1994

Conrad, Joseph
The Mirror of the Sea
Oxford: Oxford Paperbacks, 1998

Cosgrove, Denis (ed.)
Symbolic Landscapes and Social Formation
London: Croom Helm, 1984

Cousineau, Phil
The Art of Pilgrimage: A Seeker's Guide to Making Travel Sacred
Berkley: canari Press, 1998

Crang, Mike & Nigel Thrift (eds.)
Thinking Space
London & New York: Routledge, 2000

Curtis, Barry et al (eds.)
Travellers' Tales: Narratives of Home and Displacement
London & New York: Routledge, 1994

Darwin, Charles
The Origin of the Species
London: Penguin Classics, 1985

Davies, Mike
City of Quartz: Excavating the Future in Los Angeles
London & New York: Verso, 1990

Debord, Guy
The Society of the Spectacle
New York: Zone Books, 1994

Defoe, Daniel
Robinson Crusoe
London: Penguin Books, 1965

De Landa, Manuel
A Thousand Years of Non-Linear History
New York: Zone Books, 1997

Deleuze, Gilles & Félix Guattari
Nomadology: The War Machine
New York: Semiotext(e), 1986

Deleuze, Gilles & Félix Guattari
A Thousand Plateaus
London: Athlone Press, 1988

Deleuze, Gilles & Felix Guattari
Anti-Oedipus: Capitalism and Schizophrenia
Minneapolis: University of Minnesota Press, 1983

De Lillo, Don
White Noise
London: Picador, 1988

Derrida, Jacques
Writing and Difference
Chicago: University of Chicago Press, 1978

Deutsche, Rosalyn
Evictions: Art and Spatial Politics
Cambridge, Massachusetts: MIT Press, 1996

Donalds, James & Stuart Hall (eds.)
Politics and Ideology
Milton Keynes: Open University Press, 1986

Drakulic, Slavenka
Café Europa
London: Abacus, 1996

Drakulic, Slavenka
How We Survived Communism and Even Laughed
London: Abacus, 1997

Duncan, Nancy (ed.)
Bodyspace: destabilizing geographies of Gender & Sexuality
London & New York: Routledge, 1996

Duncan, James & David Ley (eds.)
Place/Culture/Representation
London & New York: Routledge, 1993

Eco, Umberto
Travels in Hyperreality
London: Picador, 1987

Elliot, T.S.
The Wasteland
New York: Harcourt Publications, 1967

Ellwood, Wayne & John McMurty
The No Nosense Guide to Globalisation
London & New York: Verso Books, 2001

Emmorey, Karen & Judy S. Reilly
Language, Gesture and Space
Hillsdale, NJ: Lawrence Erlbaum Association, 1995

Evans-Wentz, W.Y. et al (eds.)
The Tibetan Book of The Dead
New York: Oxford University Press, 2000

Featherstone, Mike (ed.)
Global Culture: Nationalism, Globalization and Modernity
London: Sage, 1990

Felman, Shoshana & Dori Laub, M.D.
Testimony: Crises of Witnessing in Literature, Psychoanalysis and History
London & New York: Routledge, 1992

Fisher, Jean
Global Visions: Towards a New Internationalism
London: Kala Press, 1994

Fishman, Robert
Bourgeois Utopias: The Rise and Fall of Suburbia
New York: Basic Books, 1987

Foster, Hal (ed.)
The Anti-Aesthetic: Essays on Postmodernism
Washington: Bay Press, 1983

Foster, Hal
The Return of the Real
Cambridge, Massachusetts: MIT Press, 1996

Foucault, Michel
The Order of Things
New York: Vintage, 1970

Foucault, Michel
Discipline and Punish: The Birth of the Prison
London: Peregrine Books, 1979

Foucault, Michel
The Archeology of Knowledge
Harper & Row; New York, 1972

Frank, Robert
The Americans
New York: D.A.P., 1994

Freud, Sigmund
The Standard Edition of the Complete Phsychological Works of Sigmund Freud. Vol. XV
London: Hogarth Press, 1961

Friedberg, Anne
Window Shopping: Cinema and the Postmodern
Berkeley, Los Angeles: University of California Press, 1994

Garreau, Joel
Edge City: Life on the New Frontier
New York: Doubleday, 1991

Giddens, Anthony
Runaway Worlds: How Globalisation is Reshaping Our Lives
London: Profile Books, 1999

Ginsberg, Allen
Planet News 1961–1967
New York: City Lights Books, 1968

Gleber, Anke
The Art of Taking a Walk
New York: Princeton University Press, 1999

Goethe, Johann Wolfgang Von
Elective Affinities
London: Pengiun Books, 1971

Golding, William
Lord of the Flies
London: Faber & Faber, 1995

Gray, Spalding
Swimming to Cambodia
New York: Theatre Communications Group Inc., 1988

Gray, Spalding
Gray's Anatomy
London: Picador, 1994

Greene, Graham
Journey Without Maps
London: Penguin Books, 1991

Gregory, Derek
Geographical Imaginations
Oxford: Blackwell, 1994

Guevara, Ernesto
The Motorcycle Diaries
London: Fourth Estate, 1996

Guha, Ranajit
Subaltern Studies III: Writing on South Asian History and Society
New Dehli: Oxford University Press, 1984

Habermas, Jürgen
The Structural Transformation of the Public Sphere
Cambridge, Massachusetts: MIT Press, 1991

Hanks, William F
Referential Practice: Language and Lived Space Among the Maya
Chicago: University of Chicago Press, 1990

Harvey, David
The Urban Experience
Oxford: Basil Blackwell, 1989

Harvey, David
The Condition of Postmodernity
Oxford: Blackwell, 1990

Harvey, David
Justice, Nature & the Geography of Difference
Oxford: Blackwell, 1989

Hayles, N. Katherine
How We Became Posthuman: Virtual Bodies in Cybernetics & Literature
Chicago: University of Chicago Press, 1999

Hebdidge, Dick
Subculture: The Meaning of Style
London & New York: Routledge, 1997

Hegel, George
Wilhelm Friedrich, Lectures on the Philosophy of World History
Cambridge: Cambridge University Press, 1975

Heidegger, Martin
Poetry LanguageThought
New York: Harper & Row, 1971

Heim, Michael
The Metaphysics of Virtual Reality
New York: Oxford University Press, 1993

Hetherington, Kevin
The Badlands of Modernity
London & New York: Routledge,1997

Hetherington, Kevin
New Age Travellers: Van Loads of Uproarious Humanity
London: Cassell, 2000

Hirst, Eric & Michael O'Hanlon (eds.)
The Anthropology of Landscape: Perspectives on Place and Space
New York: Oxford University Press, 1995

Hitler, Adolf et al
Mein Kampf
Boston: Houghton Mifflin Co., 1998

Holmes, David
Virtual Globalisation
London & New York: Routledge, 2001

Homer et al
The Iliad
London: Penguin Books, 1987

Homer et al
The Odyssey
London: Penguin Books, 1991

Hooks, Bell
Yearning: Race, Gender and Cultural Politics
Boston: South End Press, 1990

Huxley, Aldous
Brave New World
London: Flamingo, 1994

Ishiguro, Kazuo
An Artist of The Floating World
London: Faber & Faber, 1999

Jabès, Edmond et al
From The Book To The Book: An Edmond Jabès Reader
Hanover & London: University of New England Press, 1992

Jackson, John Brinckerhoff
A Sense of Time, A Sense of Place
New York: Yale University Press, 1996

Jacobs, Jane M.
Edge of Empire; Postcolonialism and the City
London & New York: Routledge, 1996

Jameson, Frederic
Postmodernism, Or, The Cultural Logic of Late Capitalism
New York: Duke University Press, 1991

Jameson, Frederic
The Geopolitical Aesthetic: Cinema and Space in the World System
Bloomington & Indianapolis: Indiana University Press, 1992

Jay, Martin
Downcast Eyes: The Denigration of Vision in Twentieth-Century French Thought
Berkeley, Los Angeles & London: University of California Press, 1994

Joyce, James
Ulysses
London: Penguin Books, 1992

Kafka, Franz
The Complete Short Stories
New York: Vintage Books, 1992

Kafka, Franz
The Great Wall of China
London: Penguin Books, 2000

Kafka, Franz
'Metamorphosis' and Other Stories
London: Minerva, 1992

Kaplan, Caren
Questions of Travel: Postmodern Discourses of Displacement
Durham: Duke University Press, 1996

Karp, Ivan and Steven D. Lavine
Exhibiting Cultures: The Poetics and Politics of Museum Display
Washington: Smithsonian Institutional Press, 1991

Kay, Emma
Worldview
London: Book Works, 1999

Keiller, Patrick
Robinson in Space: and a Conversation with Patrick Keiller
London: Reaktion ,1998

Keith, Michael & Steve Pile
Place and the Politics of Identity
London & New York: Routledge, 1993

Kern, Stephen
The Culture of Time and Space, 1880–1918
Cambridge: Harvard University Press, 1986

Kerouac, Jack
Lonesome Traveller
London: Flamingo, 1990

Kerouac, Jack
On The Road
London: Penguin Books, 1999

King, Anthony D
Re-presenting the City: Ethnicity, Capital and Culture in the 21st Century Metropolis
New York: New York University Press, 1996

Knabb, Ken (ed.)
Situationist International Anthology
London & New York: Verso, 1988

Kofman, Eleonore & Lebas, Elizabeth (eds.)
Henri Lefebvre: Writings on Cities
Oxford: Blackwell, 1996

Kosof, Spiro
The City Shaped: Urban Patterns and Meanings through History
London: Thames & Hudson, 1991

Kureishi, Hanif
The Buddha of Suburbia
London: Faber & Faber, 1990

Landry, Donna & Gerald MacLean (eds.)
The Spivak Reader: Selected Works of Gayatri Chakravorty Spivak
London & New York: Routledge, 1995

Lang, Peter & Tam Miller (eds.)
Suburban Discipline
New York: Princeton Architectural Press, 1997

Lash, Scott & John Urry
Economies of Signs and Space
London: Sage, 1994

Leach, Neil (ed.)
Rethinking Architecture
London & New York: Routledge, 1997

Le Corbusier
The Modular
London: Faber & Faber, 1967

Lefebvre, Henri
The Production of Space
Cambridge, Massachusetts & Oxford, England: Blackwell Press, 1991

Lefebvre, Henri
Critique of Everyday Life Volume 1
London & New York: Verso, 1991

Legates, Richard T. & Frederic Stout (eds.)
The City Reader
London & New York: Routledge, 1996

Levi, Primo
The Periodic Table
London: Everyman Library, 1995

Liddy, Pat
Walking Dublin
London: New Holland Publishers, 1998

Lippard, Lucy R.
On The Beaten Track: Tourism, Art and Place
New York: New Press, 2000

Lippard, Lucy R.
The Lure of The Local: Senses of Place in a Multicentered Society
New York: New Press, 1997

Low, Seth M.
On the Plaza: The Politics of Public Space and Culture
Austin: University of Texas Press, 2000

Lunenfeld, P. (ed.)
The Digital Dialectic: New Essays on New Media
Cambridge, Massachusetts: MIT Press, 1999

McEwan, Ian
The Comfort of Strangers
London: Picador, 1982

McKenzie, E.
Privatopia
New Haven: Yale University Press, 1994

McLuhan, Marshall
Understanding Media: The Extensions of Man
London: Sphere, 1967

MacCannell, Dean
The Tourist: A New Theory of the Leisure Class
Berkeley & Los Angeles: London University of California Press, 1999

Massey, Doreen, John Allen & Steve Pile (eds.)
City Worlds
London & New York: Routledge, 2000

Massey, Doreen
Space, Place and Gender
Cambridge: Polity Press, 1994

Mann, Thomas
The Magic Mountain
London: Minerva, 1996

Marin, Louis
Utopics: Spatial Play
London: Macmillan Press, 1984

Marquez, Gabriel Garcia
One Hundred Years of Solitute
London: Penguin Books, 1993

Marx, Karl
'Transitional Writings' and 'Political Writings', in The Portable Karl Marx
London & New York: Viking Penguin, 1983

Marx, Karl
The Capital Vol.1
London: Penguin Books, 1976

Mathews, Gordon
Global Culture/Individual Identity
London & New York: Routledge, 2000

Matless, David
Landscape and Englishness
London: Reaktion, 1998

Melville, Herman
Moby Dick
London: Penguin Books, 1994

Merleau-Ponty, M.
Phenomenology of Perception
London & New york: Routledge and Kegan Paul, 1962

Millar, Jeremy & Michiel Schwarz (eds.)
Speed: Visions of an Accelerated Age
London: The Photographer's Gallery & Whitechapel Art Gallery, 1998

Millar, Jeremy & Stephan Bode (eds.)
Airport
London: The Photographer's Gallery, 1997

Miller, Daniel
A Theory of Shopping
Ithaca, New York: Cornell University Press, 1998

Mitchell, W.J.T. (ed.)
Landscape and Power
Chicago: University of Chicago Press, 1994

Mitchell, Timothy
Colonialism and Culture
Ann Arbor: University of Michigan Press, 1992

More, Thomas
Utopia
London: Penguin Books, 1965

Morley, David & Keith Robins
Spaces of Identity
London & New York: Routledge, 1995

Morley, D. Media
Mobility, Identity
London & New York: Routledge, 2000

Naipaul, V.S.
India
London: Minerva, 1991

Naipaul, V.S.
The Mimic Man
London: Vintage Books, 2001

Narayan, R.K.
The Guide
London: Penguin Books, 1992

Narayan, R.K.
The Mahabharata
London: Penguin Books, 2001

Nelson, Derek
Off the Map: The Curious Histories of Place-Names
New York: Kodansha America, 1999

Nietzsche, Frederick
On the Advantage and Disadvantage of History for Life
Indianapolis & Cambridge: Hackett Publishing Co, 1980

O'Casey, Sean
The Dublin Plays
London: Faber & Faber, 1998

Okri, Ben
The Famished Road
London: Vintage, 1992

Orwell, George
Nineteen Eighty-Four
London: Penguin Books, 1954

Orwell, George
The Road to Wigan Pier
London: Penguin Books, 1989

Osbourne, Peter
Travelling Light: Photography, Travel and Visual Culture
Manchester: Manchester University Press, 2000

Ovid
Metamorphosis
Oxford: Oxford Paperbacks, 1998

Oz, Amos
Elsewhere, Perhaps
London: Picador, 1981

Page, Michael & Robert Ingpen
Encyclopedia of Things That Never Were: Creatures, Places and People
London: Penguin Books, 1998

Paine, Thomas
The Rights of Man
London: Penguin Classics, 1999

Parker, Don & Nigel Thrift (eds.)
Time, Space and Places – A Chronogeographic Perspective
Oxford: John Wiley & Sons, 1980

Paxton, John
The Penguin Encyclopedia of Places
London: Penguin Books, 1999

Perec, George
Life: A User's Manual
London: Harvill Press, 1988

Perec, George
Species of Space and Other Pieces
London & New York: Penguin Books, 1997

Perec, George
Things
London: Harvill Press, 1991

Pile, Steve & N.J Nast (eds.)
Places Through the Body
London & New York: Routledge, 1998

Pile, Steve
The Body and the City: Psycho-analysis, Space and Subjectivity
London: Routledge, 1996

Pilger, John
A Secret Country
London: Vintage, 1992

Pilger, John
Distant Voices
London: Vintage, 1992

Pirsig, Robert M.
Zen and The Art of Motorcycle Maintainence
London: Vintage, 1999

Plato
The Republic
London: Penguin Classics, 1980

Pollock, Griselda
Vision and Difference; Femininity, Feminism and Histories of Art
London & New York: Routledge, 1988

Polo, Marco
The Travels
London: Penguin Books, 1957

Pratt, Mary Louise
Imperial Eyes: Travel Writing and Transculturation
London & New York: Routledge, 1992

Pugh, Simon
Reading Landscape: Country–City–Capital
Manchester: Manchester University Press, 1990

Quayson, Ato
Postcolonialism
Oxford: Polity Press, 1999

Raban, Jonathan
Soft City
London: The Harvill Press, 1998

Raban, Jonathan
Coasting
London: Picador, 1995

Regier, Terry
The Human Semantic Potential: Spatial Language and Constrained Connectionism (Neural Network Modeling and Connectionism)
Cambridge, Massachusetts: MIT Press, 1996

Ritzer, George
The McDonaldisation Thesis
London & New Dehli: Sage, 1992

Roberts, John
The Art of Interuption
Manchester & New York: University of Manchester Press, 1998

Rogoff, Irit
Terra Infirma: Geography's Visual Culture
London & New York: Routledge, 2000

Rojek, Chris & John Urry
Touring Cultures: Transformations of Travel and Theory
London & New York: Routledge, 1997

Rosenberg, Justin
The Follies of Globalisation Theory
London: Verso Books, 2001

Rosler, Martha
Positions in The Life World
Cambridge, Massachusetts: MIT Press, 1999

Ross, Kristin
Fast Cars, Clean Bodies: Decolonization and the Reordering of French Culture
Cambridge, Massachusetts & London: MIT Press, 1998

Ross, Andrew
The Celebration Chronicles: Life, and the Persuit of Property Value in Disney's New Town
London: Verso, 2000

Roussel, Raymond
Locus Solus
Paris: Editions Flamarion, 1998

Rushdie, Salman
Midnight's Children
London: Vintage, 1995

Rushdie, Salman
The Satanic Verses
New York: Consortium Inc., 1992

Said, Edward W.
Orientalism: Western Conceptions of the Orient
London & New York: Routledge, 1978

Said, Edward W.
'Travelling Theory', in The World, The Text, and The Critic
Cambridge, Massachusetts: Harvard Press, 1983

Saint-Exupéry, Antoine de
Le Petit Prince
London: Heineman, 1958

Sartre, John-Paul
The Outsider
London: Penguin Books, 1990

Schama, Simon
Landscape and Memory
London: Fontana Press, 1995

Schivelbusch, Wolfgang
The Railway Journey: The Industrialisation of Time and Space in the 19th Century
California: University of California Press, 1987

Schneider, Gertrude
Exile and Destruction
West Port: Praeger Publishers, 1995

Schorske, Carl E.
The Historian and the City
Cambridge, Massachusetts: MIT Press, 1963

Sennett, Richard
The Fall of Public Man
London: Faber & Faber, 1977

Sennett, Richard
Flesh and Stone
London: Faber & Faber, 1994

Sennett, Richard
The Uses of Disorder: Personal Identity and City Life
New York: W.W. Norton & Company, 1992

Sharpe, William & Leonard Wallock (eds.)
Visions of the Modern City
Baltimore: Johns Hopkins Press, 1987

Sheringham, Michael
Parisian Fields
London: Reaktion Books, 1996

Shields, Rob
Places on The Margin: Alternative Geographies of Modernity
London & New York: Routledge, 1991

Shields, Rob
Lifestyle Shopping: The Subject of Consumption
London & New York: Routledge, 1992

Sibley, David
Geographies of Exclusion
London, Routledge, 1995

Silverstone, Roger (ed.)
Visions of Suburbia
London & New York: Routledge, 1997

Simmel, Georg
On Individuality and Social Forms
Chicago: University of Chicago Press, 1971

Skeldon, Ronald
'Hong Kong: Colonial City to Global City to Provincial City?' in Unsettling Cities
London & New York: Routledge, 1999

Smithson, Robert & Jack Flam (ed.)
The Collected Writings
Berkeley: Los Angeles University of California Press, 1996

Soja, Edward W.
Postmetropolis: Critical Studies of Cities and Regions
Oxford: Blackwell, 2000

Sorkin, Michael (ed.)
Variations on a Theme Park
New York: Noonday Press, 1992

Spigel, Lynn
Make Room For TV: Television and the Familiy Ideal in Postwar America
Chicago & London: University of Chicago Press, 1992

Spivak, Gayatri Chakravorty
'Can the subaltern speak?', in Marxism and the Interpretation of Culture
Urbana: University of Illinois Press, 1988

Spivak, Gayatri Chakravorty
Outside The Teaching Machine
London & New York: Routledge, 1993

Stallybrass, Peter & Allon White
The Politics and Poetics of Transgression
London: Methuen, 1986

Stewart, Susan
On Longing: Narratives of the Miniature, the Gigantic, the Souvenir, the Collection
Durham & London: Duke University Press, 1993

Sturkin, Marita
'The Wall, The Screen and the Image: The Vietnam Memorial', in
Representations 35, Summer 1991

Swift, Jonathan
Gulliver's Travels
London: Penguin Books, 1994

Tanizaki, Junichiro
In Praise of Shadows
Stony Creek: Leete's Island Books, 1977

Taylor, Peter J.
The Way the Modern World Works – World Hegemony to World Impasse
Chichester: John Wiley & Sons, 1996

Thich Nhat Hanh
The Long Road Turns to Joy: A Guide to Walking Meditation
Berkeley: Parallax Press, 1996

Tester, Keith (ed.)
The Flâneur
London & New York: Routledge, 1994

Theroux, Paul
The Mosquito Coast
London: Penguin Books, 1995

Thrift, Nigel
Spatial Formations
London: Sage, 1996

Toibin, Colm
The Sign of the Cross
London: Vintage, 1995

Tolkien, J.R.R.
The Hobbit
London: HarperCollins, 1998

Trinh T. Minh-ha & C. West (eds.)
Out There, Marginalisation and Contemporary Cultures
Cambridge, Massachusetts: MIT Press, 1990

Trinh T. Minh-ha
Women, Native, Other
Bloomington: Indiana University Press, 1989

Twain, Mark
Following the Equator
New York: Dover Publications, 1990

Urry, John
The Tourist's Gaze: Leisure and Travel in Contemporary Society
London & New Dehli: Sage, 1990

Verne, Jules
Journey to the Centre of the Earth
London: Penguin Books, 1994

Verne, Jules
Around the World in Eighty Days
London: Penguin Books, 1994

Vidler, Anthony
The Architectural Uncanny
Cambridge, Massachusetts: MIT Press, 1992

Virilio, Paul
The Lost Dimension
New York: Semiotext(e), 1991

Virilio, Paul
War and Cinema: The Logistics of Perception
London: Verso, 1989

Virilio, Paul
Speed and Politics
New York: Semiotext(e), 1986

Virilio, Paul
Open Sky
London & New York: Verso, 1997

Virilio, Paul
The Vision Machine
Bloomington & Indianapolis: Indiana University Press, 1994

Virilio, Paul
The Aesthetics of Disappearance
New York: Semiotext(e), 1991

Weiss, Allen S.
Unnatural Horizons: Paradox and Contradiction in Landscape
New York: Princeton Architectural Press, 1998

Williams, Raymond
The Country and the City
London: Chatto & Windus Ltd., 1973

Wilson, Elizabeth
The Sphinx in the City: Urban Life, the Control of Disorder and Women
Berkeley: University of California Press, 1992

Wilson, Elizabeth
Cities, Culture and Women
London: Sage, 2000

Zukin, Sharon
Landscapes of Power
Berkeley: University of California Press, 1991

Wollen, Peter
Raiding The Icebox: Reflections on Twentieth- Century Culture
London & New York: Verso, 1993

Woolley, Benjamin
Virtual Worlds: A Journey in Hype and Hyperreality
London: Blackwell, 1992

Zizek, Slavoj
Did Someone Say Totalitarianism?
London: Verso, 2001

Zizek, Slavoj
Mapping Ideology
London: Verso, 1995

Fiona Banner

In 1998 Fiona Banner was asked to take part in an exchange exhibition with several Lithuanian artists. The Lithuanians came to the Beaconsfield gallery in London and the UK artists went to Vilnius. Banner proposed that she would travel on her own by train and post daily reports on the Internet; this diary would be her contribution to the show. She made her way across Europe, writing every day. These bulletins were downloaded by the galleries and posted on boards at the exhibition venues in Vilnius and London. As she travelled the project developed. Banner did not arrive in Vilnius at the agreed time. The others waited. A party hosted by the British Council in Lithuania was postponed twice, but still she did not show. The organisers of the exhibition do not know whether she actually made the trip to Vilnius or not.

David Blamey

...there is very little difference between the dark room at the top of the Desert Inn in Las Vegas and the retreat to the desert of the ancient hermits in search of the Eternal. Paul Virilio, 'The Aesthetics of Disappearance'

Kaja Silverman has talked about two modes of identification: 'heteropathic' where the subject aims to go outside the self, to identify with something/someone/somewhere different and 'cannibalistic' where the subject brings something other into the self to make it the same. These two modes of identification often operate through 'styles' or 'rhetorics' of consumption – through what we say, wear, eat, through where we've been and where we're going. This two-way street – with its parallel movements towards difference and sameness – is interesting to consider in relation to food and travel.

Critical debate around modes of movement, from flânerie to nomadology, has recently concerned the figures of the traveller and the tourist. I tend to see the traveller in the 'heteropathic' mode – desiring difference, and the tourist in the 'cannibalistic' mode – desiring the same. Our relationship with food could also be understood in the same way. On the one hand, eating is essential to self-maintenance, to staying alive, to producing more of the same, on the other hand, food is a transformative substance, it has the capacity to change us, physically and psychologically. So, when we move and when we eat, are we aiming for difference to transform ourselves, or the same – to incorporate external things and places?

These questions run through *Safe Way*, David Blamey's contribution to

Backpacker (January 1997), an international cultural festival held in Chiang Mai, Thailand where the brief was to engage in a dialogue between invited British artists and artists resident in the Pacific rim. Blamey likes new people, new food, new places. Travelling, conversing and eating are important ways for him to be 'elsewhere'. But for *Backpacker*, he spent a week alone in a hotel room in Chiang Mai preparing, cooking and eating food out of a suitcase he brought with him from England. By remaining apart from his setting he refused to do what we would normally expect of the tourist, to assimilate the other, but he also resisted the traveller in himself by not going out to experience a bit of the 'other'. By keeping himself separate he succeeded in keeping himself intact, but within the context of *Backpacker*, his absence strangely exhibited his difference. More heteropath than cannibal, one might say.

Concerns with eating-related issues such as genetic crops, corporate farming and the recent foot and mouth scare in the UK have focused our attention on the politics, economics and culture of food production and consumption on a local and global scale. There is a rising ethical concern about what we eat and where it comes from. Should we buy local and therefore cut down on global warming by reducing fuel consumption in the transportation of food stuffs. Or should we support resistance to the globalising forces of multi-national agriculture by buying food grown 'locally', but from the other side of the globe. Food makes tangible the most complex patterns of origin, migration, colonisation and cultural hybridity. With this in mind, what do we make of the list of food items contained in the artist's suitcase, bought in a London super-market and taken out to Thailand? What we choose to buy to eat is an attempt to tell others who we are – how we are alike and different from those around us, how much of the world we know and how much is alien to us. This selection of food is the choice of someone who knows about the world.

The location that was chosen to site this work was also of significance. Hotels occupy a borderland, somewhere between public and private space, a place where strangers are intimate behind closed doors. The hotel that Blamey stayed in was a furtive kind of place, where cooking was prohibited in the rooms. Low-key, low-brow international style from the outside; run-down, jaded elegance on the inside. Moist bed, damp walls, cigarette burns, sordid, but not so much as to be that interesting – until on the last night he found a crack pipe attached to the underside of the table on which he had been eating his meals every evening.

Hotel rooms offer the most extreme example of our ability to colonise space. As we place our soap tentatively between the taps, the yellow stain on the basin enamel is not so bad, it has become ours. In such strange destinations, transitory places where people move in and out overnight, our need to make a hotel room a home in a small space of time inspires our most cannibalistic instincts. As Blamey cooked and ate his meals, breakfast, lunch and dinner, day after day, night after night, he developed rituals adapted to the specific layout of the room. Mini bar became fridge, lockable suitcase acted as a storage cupboard, the table between the beds was used when boiling water, the dressing table designated a frying area, the tiled surfaces of the bathroom adapted as a preparation zone and the bathtub utilised for dish-washing. The strange juxtapositions, washing pans in the bath, olive oil next to shaving-cream on the bath ledge, also work to transform the room, to give it a new life. But the transformation is not complete, and not very comfortable. The objects do not quite get assimilated. It's something to do with the secretiveness of his cooking, the need to hide the evidence. It makes one feel sorry for him, feel the fear of not belonging, of alienation, of being found out. I'm reminded of the desperateness that being alone in the city can bring, when access is denied to a 'real' home. There is a pathos about this work; it serves as a potent reminder of those who do not choose to keep themselves apart, but who are forced to live in hotel accommodation and survive this way for months, years on end, living as outsiders, furtive, anxious, prisoners in their own home.

Blamey holds a particular fascination for the sort of mundane details and boring little tasks that pass us by. By focusing our attention on the 'everyday', often by acts of repetition, the small things that normally go unnoticed take centre stage and acquire all kinds of new meaning. This brings to mind, Henri Lefebvre's differentiation between the practices of everyday life that make us into docile creatures simply repeating tasks and reproducing the status quo, and those which serve as acts of resistance – tiny moves, moments that delight in creating a different order. And taking up Michel de Certeau's terminology, this approach is tactical rather than strategic. It is counter practice on a micro level, not just in terms of scale but in terms of visibility – and effort. Blamey's processes appear to fall into his lap, located, following Kaprow, on the territory between art and everyday life. His work focuses our attention on the significance of some of the quite ordinary things that happen all around us, all of the time. Jane Rendell (2001)